The Legacies of Two World Wars

The Legacies of Two World Wars
European Societies in the Twentieth Century

Edited by

Lothar Kettenacker & Torsten Riotte

Berghahn Books
NEW YORK • OXFORD

First published in 2011 by

Berghahn Books

www.berghahnbooks.com

©2011 Lothar Kettenacker and Torsten Riotte

Library of Congress Cataloging-in-Publication Data

The legacies of two world wars : European societies in the twentieth century / edited by
Lothar Kettenacker & Torsten Riotte.
      p. cm.
   Includes bibliographical references and index.
   ISBN 978-0-85745-180-4 (hbk. : acid-free paper)
   1. Europe—History, Military—20th century. 2. Europe—Social conditions—20th
century. 3. World War, 1914–1918—Influence. 4. World War, 1939–1945—Influence.
5. World War, 1914–1918—Social aspects—Europe. 6. World War, 1939–1945—Social
aspects—Europe. 7. War and society—Great Britain—History—20th century. 8. War and
society—France—History—20th century. 9. War and society—Germany—History—20th
century. 10. War and society—Italy—History—20th century. I. Kettenacker, Lothar.
II. Riotte, Torsten, 1972–
D396.L45 2011
940.3'1—dc23
                                                                       2011016794

British Library Cataloguing in Publication Data

A catalogue record for this book is available from the British Library

Printed in the United States on acid-free paper

ISBN 978-0-85745-180-4 (hardback)

Published in association with the German Historical Institute, London

Contents

Foreword

Since the turn of the twenty-first century the public attitude to war and peace has become a topic of acute importance. With the end of the Cold War, and in particular the return of war to Europe in the Balkans and the Iraq wars, European public opinion can no longer just be a reaction to 'imagined wars' of the Cold War era – it has to discuss and take on the concrete political and humanitarian responsibility for military actions carried out in the name of their respective nations. Still today debates on the legality and proportionality of these new military interventions divide European societies and their governments like no other public dispute.

Against the backdrop of these current issues, it seemed a worthwhile academic enterprise to revisit the established research area of the popular attitude to war and peace in various European societies before, during and after World Wars I and II. Such a comparative reappraisal of research was the aim of a conference organised by Professor Lothar Kettenacker for the German Historical Institute. The conference was entitled 'War and Peace in Europe's Collective Consciousness, 1900–1950' and was held at the Evangelische Akademie Meißen. As deputy director of the German Historical Institute London, Lothar Kettenacker shaped and influenced its research activities and general development over nearly thirty years. His own research focused very much on the questions that were at the centre of this conference. And it was particularly due to his research interests that the complex conundrum of public opinion and war at the outbreak of World War I as well as at the beginning and end of World War II were continuously part of the Institute's research interests. In Meißen leading historians of the world wars debated their research, which is mostly concentrated on one of the wars and also on one society, in a comparative approach. The result is this volume which provides us with a comparative conspectus of research which does not exist so far, and will provide a valuable tool for further research as well as for teaching.

As the new director of the German Historical Institute London I should like to take the opportunity provided by this preface to thank Lothar Kettenacker again for having organised the conference and for co-editing this volume. The Institute still profits from his contributions to its academic as well as organisational development. I should particularly like to thank Dr Torsten Riotte who agreed to act as co-editor and see this enterprise through even after he had left the Institute for a new position at Frankfurt University. Thanks also go to the translators Jonathan Uhlaner and Deborah Cohen in Berlin and to Jane Rafferty of the German Historical Institute staff who has also overseen the copyediting with her usual careful attention. Finally my thanks go to Berghahn Books and particularly to Dr Marion Berghahn, Ann Przyzycki and Melissa Spinelli who took great care of the book, to the publisher's anonymous external referees who added valuable suggestions for the revision of the manuscript, and, last but not least, to the contributors who were prepared to bear with us in the protracted processes of editing this volume.

—Andreas Gestrich, London, August 2010

1

'Old Europe' and the Legacy of Two World Wars

Lothar Kettenacker and Torsten Riotte

The aim of this book is to trace the moods and attitudes of the people of four Western countries before, during and after the First and Second World Wars. The contributions examine public opinion in Great Britain, France, Germany and Italy during the crucial moments of the two major conflicts of the twentieth century (in their differences and similarities).[1] The inspiration to look again at the attitudes of ordinary Europeans to the two wars came from the controversy surrounding the US invasion of Iraq in 2003. That decision, if one is to believe US policy at the time, was taken mainly to liberate the people of Iraq from the yoke of a dictator. In many ways, the language and arguments used to justify Operation Iraqi Freedom were in keeping with the Wilsonian tradition, according to which it is the responsibility of the USA to bring democracy and civilisation to suppressed and misgoverned people. However, the many protest marches – according to BBC reports, two million Britons marched against the war in London on a single day alone – imply that the policy of 'making the world safe for democracy' was, certainly in the UK context, essentially undemocratic. Government ministers ignored the people in the streets. Great Britain was, of course, only one of forty-eight governments who joined the 'coalition of the willing' despite massive global protest – not least from the populations of those countries.[2]

The question therefore arises as to whether governments can legitimately – or effectively – conduct a war without the backing of a majority of their people. It would certainly be far too simplistic to view the historic relationship between societies and war as one in which warmongering governments on the one hand are pitted against peaceful populations powerless to prevent conflict on the other. As Jost Dülffer, one of the most distinguished experts on de-escalation in the nineteenth and twentieth centuries argues, popular acceptance of a military solution is a necessary prerequisite, though not a sufficient explanation, for the outbreak of a war.[3] Similarly, historians have looked at peaceful periods in history to determine how war was avoided. While scholars have argued that on some occasions, wars are inevitable, the question remains why they occur at particular moments in time. A recent publication lists thirty-three incidents between the end of the Crimean War in 1856 and the outbreak of the First World War in 1914 in which a multi-lateral military conflict of global dimension seemed a possible option (or danger) and was discussed amongst contemporaries.[4] The number alone illustrates that the decision to go to war in 1914, after it had been avoided for so long, was a challenging one for the governments involved.

It is against this background that the present volume takes a closer look at how society responded to the outbreaks and the conclusions of the First and Second World Wars in order to examine the relationship between the conduct of wars and public opinion. Three hypotheses are implied. The first of these is that, in the case of the First World War, conflict did not come 'out of the blue'. The threat of military conflict had been almost palpable during the late nineteenth and early twentieth centuries and the final decision to engage in a war was predated by several occasions on which war was avoided.[5] Governments of the day decided to go to war on various grounds and the attitude of the people as expressed in the political press or in public demonstrations played into the decision to declare an active state of war.

Secondly, the population was aware of the danger that war might break out. It will be established that it was less the active wish for war than a perceived lack of alternatives that shaped the attitude of many. Enthusiasm for war was often accompanied by a degree of anxiety, fear, concern or uncertainty.[6] Hence, historians who argue that a great deal of support existed for military conflict are often challenged by evidence of more cautious or alarmed voices. The distinction between enthusiasm for war, and concern about its consequences, is therefore rarely clear cut, and more a question of shifting balances.[7]

Thirdly, war was experienced not only as an individual and personal encounter but also as a collective experience.[8] The present volume examines the latter with a particular focus on public demonstration, public debate and public discourse. Opinion polls are preferred to individual biographical narratives.[9] Writers have emphasised that people experienced the outbreak and the end of war in different circumstances at different times. As Richard Bessel demonstrates, many German privates were far from the frontline when fighting ceased in late 1918.[10] The experiences of people on the home front varied just as much. And yet, the book implies a moment of collective experience. Accounts of demonstration marches and public gatherings illustrate that a specific time and place existed when people voted with their feet. Such events often created their own particular dynamic, which was beyond government control and which shaped the way in which society later remembered war.[11]

This volume is not about the First and Second World Wars as such. Governmental politics, military strategy and the history of ideology are only subordinate reference points. The focus is less on politics and much more on how people experienced the pre- and post-war periods, the time immediately before the outbreak of war and the responses after fighting finally stopped. One chapter proves the exemption to the rule – Jost Dülffer discusses two international peace conferences as important political events. The First and Second World Wars changed public attitudes towards military conflict. Scholars have rightly stressed that the particular characteristics of total warfare and its impact not only on the military but also on other aspects of life gained a new quality after 1914.[12] However, the divide between traditional cabinet wars and total warfare should not imply that governments before the outbreak of the First World War were indifferent towards international efforts at peace-keeping. In 1899, fifteen years before the July Crisis, representatives of almost thirty nation states met at the peace conferences at The Hague seeking a multi-lateral agreement to resolve conflict peacefully. Most of today's accounts emphasise the shortcomings of the conference. In 1899, a text for the creation of a Permanent Court of Arbitration was adopted. However, the court did not receive coercive power over individual nation states and dealt only with minor political issues. The next conference in 1907 proved equally unsuccessful in establishing binding regulations to resolve international conflict. The leading powers refused to accept significant infringements of their national sovereignty. The two conferences at The Hague (a third was scheduled for 1915 but was never convened) were unsuccessful in securing peace internationally. So were their successors. The League of Nations, the Briand-Kellog pact and finally the United Nations seem, at first glance, to have done little to avoid war. However, as Dülffer stresses, both the former and the latter represented attempts to resolve political problems in a universal or global context. A total of forty-four states participated in the meeting of 1907. Although the more powerful nation states resisted the more restrictive or coercive obligations of the conference, they still recognized a need to participate and contribute.[13]

The peace conferences also proved influential in galvanizing pacifist movements, particularly in Germany and France. However, while pacifists criticised politicians for their lack of commitment to multilateralism, their own movement proved equally divided when it came to organisational matters. Pacifism did not produce a united political movement or party, either nationally or internationally, before 1914 or during the inter-war period. This made it difficult for pacifism to reach a wide public audience, or to substantially influence public opinion in the inter-war period.[14]

Today we know a good deal more about what people think of certain movements or events. Political surveys and opinion polling have been a vital part of political and public debate since the mid twentieth century. This was not the case in the period around the First World War. Instead, historians have had to create different tools to trace the public mood during the years 1914 to 1918. Writing the history of mentalities is still one of the most challenging tasks for any historical scholar. Just how difficult this can be is demonstrated by the recent debate around the outbreak of war in 1914. The general assumption that people living in Germany and France welcomed the war as an opportunity for their countries to establish their position as leaders in the struggle for power has been challenged for some time now.[15] The theory of 'war enthusiasm' was based on snapshots (to a certain extent quite literally) of bourgeois urban life and artistic representation. However, a more recent focus on rural communities has shown that there were large groups of people who found it difficult to deal with the uncertainties that were to come. As Gerhard Hirschfeld shows in his contribution, it is almost impossible to paint a coherent picture of German society in 1914. Despite the euphoria and excitement about the outbreak of the war by some Germans, there were many who feared the atrocities of war and articulated their unease. Hirschfeld's research follows the tradition of the French historian Becker whose work has proved crucial to a re-interpretation of war enthusiasm in his country. Many of the observations Hirschfeld makes for Germany are therefore equally true of the French situation in 1914.

On a more individual level, personal responses to the events can be traced in diaries, memoirs or private correspondence. However it is extremely difficult to generalise from such accounts. Similarly, press coverage, artistic representations and contemporary literature can help determine the public mood only to a certain extent. Historians today agree that there was a divide between more enthusiastic responses to war among the urban middle classes and greater anxiety in more rural regions.[16] Such a generalisation, however, is not without its problems. Stefan Geinitz's work on Freiburg has illustrated that it cannot explain the events in a medium-sized town on the Franco-German border inhabited by a Catholic majority.[17] A typology and juxtaposition of urban/bourgeois on the one hand and rural / working class on the other does not resolve the problem of the diversity in responses to the outbreak of war.

Although the situation presented itself somewhat differently in Great Britain, the variety of opinions that made up the public opinion was equally colourful. In Hartmut Pogge von Strandmann's interpretation, the confusing mix of Germanophobia on the one hand and a desire for political neutrality on the other created a situation which made it almost impossible to reduce public opinion to a single mood. Many voices spoke out in support of neutrality. Large groups within society, however, eagerly consumed the gutter press with its vitriolic attacks on Germany and the Kaiser. Anti-German spy novels were printed in their thousands if not millions to support the idea of the threat of a German invasion. Governments also played a significant role in shaping public opinion, or to borrow Pogge von Strandmann's terminology: 'Politicians like to react to and occasionally hide behind or even invent popular attitudes regardless of whether they had really been swayed by the public or not.' As in the German and French cases, the society in pre-war Britain showed differing attitudes towards war that coexisted and coincided.

It seems almost impossible to come to a conclusion as to whether European societies embraced or opposed war in 1914. Gerhard Hirschfeld, Hartmut Pogge von Strandmann and Nicolas Beaupré show convincingly how difficult it is to decipher the public mood of 1914. One crucial aspect in the interpretation is to look not only at separate groups of society and different places within a country but also to include several divisions in the chronology of events. Although the societies of Great Britain, France and Germany experienced the summer of 1914 very differently, there were still comparable moments of excitement and uncertainty within each of the countries. It is essential for the historian to differentiate between an acceptance of war as a means of politics, and responses after the actual outbreak, as well as responses to specific events and conflicts. While visual representations and the media mirror primarily the underlying current of opinions as part of a political discourse, success or failure in strategic movements, military confrontations, personal experiences of encountering war or domestic and foreign political changes also influence people's attitudes and can lead to sudden changes of opinion within weeks or sometimes even days. As Beaupré explains, France's take on the war not only changed continuously, but was characterised by several competing views.

Beaupré's interpretation of French society is particularly interesting as it follows the public debate beyond the armistice of 1918 and demonstrates how the mix of opinions was moulded into just one way of remembering the Great War during the post-war period.[18] Thus the chapter also provides a link to the time immediately after the First World War. The images left by the catastrophe of 1914–18 formed an important part of the political and historical narrative of the inter-war years. Despite encounters on the battlefields, remembering the Great War took on very different forms in Germany, Britain and France. As Jay Winter shows in his contribution on Britain, the national narrative proved very powerful in creating collective images of the Great War.[19] This was partly influenced by differing post-war economic and political challenges but what arguably played a far greater role were cultural differences between the three countries. In the British case, the 'cultivated detachment and distance' that shaped the national character is evident in literary expressions such as war poems but also in soldiers' letters home and in trench journals. This, to use Winter's term, 'national deflection' of remembrance also affected historical accounts. The British perception of the war as having been futile did not correspond with French views.

Winter's contribution also addresses the transformation of competing interpretations of war into a collective way of remembering. The public debate surrounding the British victory ceremony in London in July 1919 and the internment of the Unknown Soldier in Westminster Abbey a year and a half later show that these official occasions did not turn out as the authorities had originally planned. The people attending the ceremonies in London transformed the choreography into a mournful ceremony free from elitist distinctions. The staging of both rites developed its own dynamic which is an indication that more profound social and political changes were about to happen.[20] Against the background of labour unrest, colonial violence and civil war in Ireland the ruling class lost much of its credibility and power to shape public attitudes. This also shows that British people were less preoccupied than others with the idea of their victory in 1918.

Many historians have questioned whether the Versailles Treaty inevitably led to the Second World War.[21] However, Gerhard Krumeich insists that in the German case 'the lost peace of 1919 represents the beginning of the final decline of the old Europe of Nation states and Nationalisms into the barbarity of the Second World War.'[22] Krumeich's revisionist interpretation uses the leitmotif of the traumatic experience of war to explain the aggression of political thinking and political acts in the 1920s. The humiliating aspects of German defeat led to what can be termed the 'nationalism of frustration', an aggressive response by young men and women who had lost confidence in the state and now referred to categories of war. The presence of the terminology of war throughout the public and political discourse in Weimar Germany is a good indication that the defeat of 1918 remained part of the public consciousness. Heterogeneous groups were united under the categories of war and defeat combining old militarism and new militancy which entered into a symbiosis of new political brutality. To assume a 'conservative revolution' after 1918 does not necessarily lead to the inevitability of Nazi-dictatorship in 1933 but it illustrates that the burden of Versailles was too heavy for Weimar politics to bear.[23]

France as a victor state found itself in a different situation. Despite the many British and German losses, it was French and Belgian territory that had seen most of the fighting at the Western front. The peculiar situation of a victorious European power suffering in terms of fatal casualties, wounded, invalids, damage to buildings and agriculture, as well as the war debt created a much more ambivalent situation than that found in Great Britain or Germany. The presence of the 'gueules cassées' at the signing of the Versailles treaty illustrated the ambivalence of winning and mourning the war.[24] The French public responded to the traumatic experience by negotiating between concern to emphasise human tragedy and material destruction on the one hand and the wish to forget or ignore the war by expressing 'joie de vivre' on the other.

As Jean Claude Allain's article points out, the developments that originated in the French experience oscillated between extremes. The anti-German narratives found in French schoolbooks undermined the notion of a victorious nation succeeding over a barbarous enemy. Memoirs, biographies and eye-witness accounts published in the early years after the war, but also memora-bilia from the war such as postcards and tour guides of the battlefield, implied a much more ambivalent form of patriotism and attitude towards war. Hu-man suffering and the destruction of monuments or landscape as described or depicted in such evidence questioned a glorification of war. This led to a specific form of pacifism with different political notions, as is evident in the French terms *pacifique* and *pacifiste*. It was the collective fear that a renewed war might bring similar suffering rather than a political struggle for peace that characterised French society in the period from Versailles to the outbreak of the Second World War.

French historians have been tempted to link the prominent anti-war men-tality in France to the defeat by Hitler's army in 1940.[25] Barbara Lambauer illustrates in her chapter that the political polarisation of society, as well as a general desire for peace, played into French misapprehensions of German aggression in the 1930s. The traditional anti-German policies of the conserva-tives and right-wing associations were transformed by the dominance of anti-Bolshevist ideology, as vividly expressed by Emmanuel Monier in 1938: 'rather Hitler than Blum'. Antagonism to the left-wing government in France made German policies appear less threatening to a majority of the French people. Arguably, this could be seen as a crucial reason why French society entered the war reluctantly. As an opinion poll by the newly founded *Institut français d'opinon* established, the majority of the French population (57 per cent) were satisfied with the outcome of the Munich conference of September 1938.

France's reluctance to go to war and domestic uncertainties, however, were only part of the picture. The poll also claimed that more than two thirds (70 per cent) of the French expected that France and Great Britain would eventu-ally face direct confrontation with Germany. The French were not unaware of the danger of war. According to a poll of 1939, almost half the population ex-pected war to start within the year and more than two-thirds were convinced that Germany would not be pacified by peaceful means. The Russo-German treaty of 1939 gained particular importance in this context as it linked fears of a coming war with anti-communist feelings. These figures illustrate the gen-eral concerns that existed in France immediately before the outbreak of war and beyond.

Language is an unreliable tool with which to trace public opinion – accord-ing to the eighteenth century French diplomat Maurice de Talleyrand, it is more a weapon of disguise.[26] Maybe it was in this tradition that Hitler continu-ously spoke of preserving peace in Europe, even during the early stages of the Second World War. While a recent study on the first seven years of Nazi Ger-many concludes that the period 1933–1939 showed the 'overriding imperative of preparing Germany and its people for a major war',[27] Hans Mommsen argues the opposite in his chapter here. According to Mommsen's interpretation an important characteristic of the *Führer*-cult was its presentation of Hitler as the only statesman able to guarantee a peaceful future.[28] This helps to explain why – despite the aggressive terminology of Nazi propaganda – the majority of Germans lacked enthusiasm at the actual outbreak of the Second World War in 1939. The massive armament programme and Hitler's (and the Nazi leadership's) constant threat to go to war in the period of 1935 to 1939 did not prevent a large number of Germans from believing that Hitler had done every-thing possible to avoid it. Large sections of German society still remembered the events of 1914 to 1918 from first-hand experience. What the German ex-ample shows is that the experience of the previous war shaped views in 1939 and of subsequent events. Concerns and war weariness cannot provide a full answer to the question of why German society followed Hitler into the war. But they do illustrate that the memories of atrocities and suffering during the First World War, as well as the collective trauma of Versailles, survived into the Nazi era. However, after the German victories over Poland and France, or-dinary Germans began to view Hitler's decisions in a different light. To a large extent (although not exclusively) early military success bribed German society into accepting and, from 1941, supporting the war, which made it extremely difficult to return to a more distanced attitude after the experiences in Russia and the approaching defeat.[29]

Ambivalent experiences were equally true in the Italian case. Here, Mus-solini's success during the 1920s can be understood as a response to the trau-matic effects of the First World War, but also as a result of society's uncertainty about the sudden and wide-ranging changes during the first decades of the twentieth century. Angelo Ventrone's contribution to this book specifically looks at the Italian case and illustrates the impact of the fascist ideology of a 'culture of hierarchical brotherhood' as an alternative model to what had been understood as the development of modernity. Many strands of Italian fas-cism like the myth of rural life and simplicity or the role of the individual as such and as part of a group responded to the specific political experiences and expectations of Italian society. The tension between the old and the new developed its own dynamics which Mussolini tried to capitalize on. However, Mussolini's mission to remake the 'Italians through combat' did not meet with unrestricted support in Italy. The anti-war policy of the Vatican combined with a growing suspicion of Italian ruling elites demonstrated to the Duce that his expansionist goals did not enjoy unanimous support.[30]

The rise of modernity and the experiences of the Great War shaped society during the final period before the outbreak of the Second World War. While the years immediately after 1918 were characterised by continuing crisis and violence, the final year before the outbreak of the war showed a different face. Now, the societies of Europe seem to have reverted to a more normal routine of looking to great statesmen to avoid war. In Britain, people looked to Neville Chamberlain, the apparent personification of political common sense, to reign in a rogue like Hitler. But when he failed the self-respect of the nation was at stake. Lothar Kattenacker sees the 'appeaser' Chamberlain as being driven by public opinion to accept the inevitable. The British declaration of war can be described as 'a question of honour', much more 'the people's war' than the politicians'. The eventual rejection of appeasing Hitler was forced upon the government, the declaration of war a necessity. The latter meant honoring a pledge given to the Poles rather than the resolution to fight. This, to some extent, explains why the British declaration of war in September 1939 was not followed by immediate consequences and led to what is known as the phoney war. It was only after the handover from Chamberlain to Churchill, the tribune of the people, that decisive military action followed. So while the public elevation of the Second World War to a mythical conflict had not become apparent before the resignation of Chamberlain, the people of Britain had already taken ownership of it, and enforced their will.

The end of the Second World War changed many of the familiar patterns of society. Just like the earlier debate around 1918, it is not helpful to look at public attitudes in the simple terms of victory and defeat in 1945. The four great Western states had all suffered materially. For the Germans, 1945 has been described as 'zero hour' (*Stunde Null*), an end and a beginning at the same time. As Clemens Vollnhals shows, the 'German Catastrophe' was followed not by remorse and regret but by disillusionment and pragmatism. Shocked by the ruthlessness of the Nazi leadership and the latter's criminal and catastrophic conduct during the final months of the war, German society escaped the role of perpetrator by declaring itself victims of the Third Reich. Self-pity seems to have become a main characteristic of post-war Germans while the much-acclaimed community of the people (*Volksgemeinschaft*) dissolved into Germans individually struggling for survival and thus avoiding the question of collective responsibility.[31] As Vollnhals convincingly demonstrates, the democratic 'new beginning' of German society was reduced to a small minority, and to borrow Vollnhals's expression, the 'pragmatic retreat into the private world' which included an extremely generous policy of integrating all those with Nazi connections. Vollnhals is more critical than many recent historians who identify a German learning process after 1945. Despite the withdrawal into privacy and personal remembering Konrad Jarausch stresses the importance of the war experiences for Germans in distancing themselves from extreme nationalism and militarism.[32] It was in the light of the economic success of the Federal Republic in the decades after the war that the following generation of Germans engaged in a discussion about its past and established democracy on a critical level. This gained particular importance during the 1960s and here Jarausch and Vollnhals agree in their interpretations.

Although victorious, Great Britain struggled hard to come to terms with the war. As Toby Haggith shows, the first five years in Britain after 1945 were historically far more complicated and ambivalent than might appear at first glance. Despite the comparatively small effects of the war in material terms and human suffering compared with the other European nations and despite the heroic representation of war in popular culture and patriotic literature, the majority of the people did not engage in activities such as collecting military memorabilia or memorialising the Second World War as had been the case in 1918–19. As Haggith demonstrates, the majority of the British people were too tired and malnourished to celebrate the defeat of Hitler. The British government was expected to agree not only to international but also to a domestic peace. Would a 'just war' be followed by a 'just peace' in the sense that wartime sacrifices would be rewarded? Based on the sources available at the Imperial War Museum, ranging from eye-witness accounts to satirical magazines, Haggith paints a lively picture and demonstrates that despite the fact that Britain had won the war, many people felt the country had lost the peace.[33]

Similar to Haggith's approach Fabrice Grenard looks at the social dimension of post-war life. While popular remembering has termed the period from 1945 to 1975 the 'glorious thirty years' (*Trente glorieuses*) the late forties proved to be much more difficult for a majority of French society than is generally assumed. Food rationing, scarcity of other commodities and the presence of war in the form of destruction and potential danger to life (Michelin published a map indicating areas polluted by mines in 1945) make the end of the war less visible to a large proportion of the French. It was not until 1950 that the French economy recovered from the consequences of the Second World War. Hence Grenard prefers the term '*sortie de guerre*' to transcribe the five years from 1944 to 1949 to a clear-cut distinction between war and post-war societies.

On an ideological level we find French shame over the defeat in 1940 and the responsibility gained during the Vichy years blurred into a narrative of France as a 'grande nation' betrayed by a minority of German sympathisers. This divide into a majority of patriotic French and a small number of 'guilty collaborators' showed its expression in many variations ranging from legal prosecution by the new authorities to social exclusion by local communities. The examples of French women who were shaved bald due to their 'collaboration' with the Germans illustrates that the anger and aggression accumulated during the occupation years did not only hit political opponents. Next to women who had had affairs with German officials or soldiers, prostitutes and social outsiders were also recorded as victims.

The need to keep the idea of France as a great power alive is at the core of the post-war ideological discourse. In this respect the years after the Second World War differ essentially from the period 1918–20. Damage to national self-esteem were compensated by a particularly patriotic way of remembering the war. Despite the difficult economic situation the majority of monuments and public displays commemorating the war were erected or created during the years 1944 to 1950.

In this atmosphere of rehabilitating French claims for great power status there was little space left for remembering Jewish victims of the war or other minorities who had suffered under Nazi oppression. It was not until the end of the decade that French society had recovered enough to devote its attention to those groups that were less easily integrated into the picture of France's return to the '*beaux jours*' after 1945.

The Italian case is particularly suited to illustrate that a war-torn society did not necessarily come to a unanimous and morally justifiable verdict on the Second World War. As Gustavo Corni shows, Italian post-war ideology relied heavily on the Italian resistance movement for a moral justification of the events between 1939 and 1945. At the same time, Italian post-war society was not prepared to re-integrate resistance fighters and accept them as part of the political or governmental elite. Historicising the wartime events was used as an 'anaesthetic' to public criticism. As Corni puts it, ex-partisans grew more and more frustrated with 'the official celebrations of the Resistance and the Liberation' while their anger rose with regard to 'the political reality of the nation in which the left-wing parties were now completely side-lined'. At the same time the Italian case demonstrates how regional differences and individual experiences were key to later attitudes towards the war. The north-south divide in Italy is a case in point: the republican movement won the referendum on the Constitution of 2 June 1946 almost exclusively by votes from the northern region with two-thirds of the south voting for the restoration of the Savoy monarchy. The confrontations in domestic Italian politics led to a number of contested elections with political demonstrations bordering on civil war. It is partly due to the post-war violence that the partisan movement in Italy was unsuccessful in its attempts at gaining power. However, the tendency to de-politicise the memory of the war was overwhelmingly responsible for the absence of a historical debate. While personal suffering was mourned and moralised, collective responsibility was refuted. Corni concludes: 'An in-depth analysis by Italian society and culture of the war only took place during the 1990s when, initially, the war on Iraq (the "first war of 1991") ... refocused attention on the subject.'

The authors of this book emphasise the peculiarities of history in each of the individual nation states. The experience of the societies in France, Germany, Great Britain and Italy before and after the two world wars should be examined in their own right and without broad generalisation. However, the difficulties in coming to terms with the results of the First World War affected the way in which all four entered the Second. The collective experience of the atrocities of the events from 1939 to 1945 when all four were immediately affected left a further legacy. War may have remained the *ultima ratio* of politicians but for the populations of the four Western countries of Great Britain, France, Germany and Italy, previous experiences were too strongly embedded in the public memory to allow them to view wars as anything but disasters. Inevitably, such attitudes also influenced politicians, though to different degrees, in all four states. This could be the reason for the formation of the opposition to the war in Iraq in 2003 by what has been termed 'Old Europe'. Britain only proved to be an exception to the rule inasmuch as the government felt bound by its loyalty to the United States which had twice come to the rescue of the former mother country.[34] Generally history tends to tune down its verdict on horrendous events of the past. Not so in the case of the two World Wars: they appear more appalling, more incomprehensible with every decade gone by. The Hague conferences, the League of Nations, the Briand-Kellog pact, the charter of the United Nation – all those attempts at solving conflicts peacefully or at least to limit the fallout-out of wars – may not have proved an entire success. Nevertheless, combined with the suffering and death of so many people, they changed the mind-set of the European nations for good. After all, the efforts to create a European Union have been inspired by the resolution to make wars on the European continent a thing of the past.

Notes

1. The process of selecting the countries to be dealt with in this book proved one of the most difficult tasks. The countries discussed here represent the core of what has recently – in the context of the war on Iraq of 2003 – been termed 'old Europe'. The underlying hypothesis is that the experiences in all four countries (Italy is excluded in the debate about 1914–18 as it did not participate in the war in its early stages) shaped a common attitude to war. However, further research on different countries is important and has proved helpful to the discussion of war and society. In this context a study on Russian mentalities during and between both world wars deserves particular mention: Karl Eimermacher and Astrid Volpert (eds.), *Verführungen der Gewalt: Russen und Deutsche im Ersten und Zweiten Weltkrieg* (Munich 2005); and the second volume of the series: Karl Eimermacher and Astrid Volpert (eds.), *Stürmische Aufbrüche und enttäuschte Hoffnungen: Russen und Deutsche in der Zwischenkriegszeit* (Munich 2006). The two volumes focus on the mutual perceptions of Germans and Russians, but also say a great deal about how Russians perceived the events between 1914 and 1945.
2. BBC news coverage, for reference see the BBC webpage: 'Million March against the War in Iraq', Sunday, 16 February 2003, http://news.bbc.co.uk/1/hi/uk/2765041.stm, accessed on 24 August 2006.
3. Jost Dülffer, 'Dispositionen zum Krieg im wilhelminischen Deutschland', in Jost Dülffer and Karl Holl (eds.), *Bereit zum Krieg. Kriegsmentalität im wilhelminischen Deutschland 1890–1914* (Göttingen 1986), 9–19, at 10.
4. Jost Dülffer, Martin Kröger and Rolf-Harald Wippich (eds.), *Vermiedene Kriege. Deeskalation von Konflikten der Großmächte zwischen Krimkrieg und Erstem Weltkrieg, 1856–1914* (Munich 1997).

5. Dülffer, 'Dispositionen zum Krieg', 10.
6. Here we follow Christian Geinitz's interpretation of war enthusiasm in Freiburg, cf. Christian Geinitz, *Kriegsfurcht und Kampfbereitschaft. Das Augusterlebnis in Freiburg. Eine Studie zum Kriegsbeginn 1914* (Schriften der Bibliothek für Zeitgeschichte; N.F., Bd.7) (Essen 1998), 68.
7. See the discussion in Geinitz, *Kriegsfurcht und Kampfbereitschaft*, 20. For a very balanced view Wolfgang J. Mommsen, *Der Erste Weltkrieg. Anfang vom Ende des bürgerlichen Zeitalters* (Bonn 2004), 138. For a discussion of comparative aspects between the outbreak of war in 1914 and 1939 see: Bruno Thoß and Hans-Erich Volkmann (eds.), *Erster Weltkrieg – Zweiter Weltkrieg: Ein Vergleich. Krieg, Kriegeserlebnis, Kriegserfahrung in Deutschland* (Paderborn 2002).
8. Jay Winter, *Sites of Memory, Sites of Mourning. The Great War in European Cultural History* (Cambridge 2000).
9. The renewed tension during the 1920s coincided with the foundation of several institutes for research on public opinion.
10. Richard Bessel, 'Die Heimkehr der Soldaten. Das Bild der Frontsoldaten in der Öffentlichkeit der Weimarer Republik', in Gerhard Hirschfeld, Gerd Krumeich and Irina Renz (eds.): *"Keiner fühlt sich hier mehr als Mensch...". Erlebnis und Wirkung des Ersten Weltkrieges*, (= Schriften der Bibliothek für Zeitgeschichte; N.F.1) (Essen 1993), 221–241, at 224–9.
11. For a general discussion of collective remembering see: Winter, *Sites of Memory*, and the individual chapters for a more detailed discussion. For an interesting comparative approach see Thoß and Volkmann, *Erster Weltkrieg – Zweiter Weltkrieg*.
12. Stig Förster, *An der Schwelle zum totalen Krieg. Die militärische Debatte über den Krieg der Zukunft, 1919–1939* (Paderborn 2002). See also Roger Chickering, Stig Förster and Bernd Greiner (eds.), *A World at Total War: Global Conflict and the Politics of Destruction, 1937–1945* (Cambridge 2005).
13. Dülffer's contribution is based on his extensive study: Jost Dülffer, *Regeln gegen den Krieg? Die Haager Friedenskonferenzen von 1899 und 1907 in der internationalen Politik* (Berlin 1981).
14. For the German case: Karl Holl, *Pazifismus in Deutschland* (Frankfurt 1988); ibid. (ed.), *Pazifismus in der Weimarer Republik* (Paderborn 1981).
15. The central work is Jean Jacques Becker, *1914. Comment les Français sont entrés dans la Guerre* (Paris 1977). See also Gerhard Hirschfeld's review article 'Der Erste Weltkrieg in der deutschen und internationalen Geschichtsschreibung' published on the web platform: 'Themeportal Erster Weltkrieg', http://www.erster-weltkrieg.clio-online.de/_Rainbow/documents/poluzeit/apuz_hirschfeld.pdf, accessed 24 August 2006.
16. Mommsen, *Der Erste Weltkrieg*, 138.
17. Geinitz, *Kriegsfurcht und Kampfbereitschaft*.
18. For a comparative approach see also Nicolas Beaupré, *Écrire en guerre, écrire la guerre. France, Allemagne 1914–1920* (Paris 2006).
19. Also in Winter, *Sites of Memory*.
20. A more culturalist approach in: Wolfgang Hardtwig (ed.), *Ordnungen in der Krise. Zur politischen Kulturgeschichte Deutschlands 1900–1933* (Munich 2007) and ibid. (ed.). *Politische Kulturgeschichte der Zwischenkriegszeit* (Göttingen 2005).
21. Zara Steiner, *The Lights that Failed. European International History, 1919–1933* (Oxford 2005), 66–70.
22. See also Gerd Krumeich and Silke Fehlemann (eds.), *Versailles 1919. Ziele – Wirkungen – Wahrnehmungen* (Schriften der Bibliothek für Zeitgeschichte – Neue Folge; 14) (Essen 2001).

23. Ulrich Heinemann, *Die verdrängte Niederlage. Politische Öffentlichkeit und Kriegs-schuldfrage in der Weimarer Republik* (Göttingen 1983).

24. Stephane Audoin-Rozeau, 'Die Delegation der "gueules cassées" in Versailles am 28. Juni 1919', in Krumeich and Fehlemann (eds.), *Versailles 1919*, 280–287.

25. Anglo-American interpretations have been more reluctant in this respect: Julian Jackson, *The Fall of France. The Nazi Invasion of 1940* (Oxford 2003); Peter Jackson, *France and the Nazi Menace. Intelligence and Policy Making, 1933–1939* (Oxford 2000); Ernest R. May, *Strange Victory. Hitler's Conquest of France* (New York 2000).

26. Talleyrand to the Spanish envoy Izquierdo, see Bertrand Barère de Vieuzac, *Mémoires*, 4 volumes (Paris 1842–1844), iv, 447: 'La parole a été donnée à l'homme pour déguiser sa pensée.'

27. Richard Evans, *The Third Reich in Power* (London, 2005, pb. ed. 2006), xvii.

28. S. Marlis, G. Steinert, *Hitlers Krieg und die Deutschen. Stimmung und Haltung der deutschen Bevölkerung im Zweiten Weltkrieg* (Düsseldorf, 1970).

29. Ian Kershaw, *Der Hitler-Mythos. Volksmeinung und Propaganda im Dritten Reich* (Stuttgart 1980).

30. MacGregor Knox, 'Conquest, Foreign and Domestic, in Fascist Italy and Nazi-Germany', *The Journal of Modern History*, 56, 1 (1984), 1–57.

31. Steffen Bruendel, *Volksgemeinschaft oder Volksstaat. Die "Ideen von 1914" und die Neu-ordnung Deutschlands im Ersten Weltkrieg* (Berlin, 2003).

32. Konrad Jarausch, *Die Umkehr: deutsche Wandlungen 1915–1990* (Munich 2004).

33. In this sense: Correlli Barnett, *The Lost Victory: British Dreams and British Realities* (London 1995).

34. Britain's exceptional role in the first Gulf war is discussed in: Martin Shaw, 'Past Wars and Present Conflicts: From the Second World War to the Gulf', in: Martin Evans and Ken Lunn (eds.), *War and Memory in the Twentieth Century* (Leamington Spa 1997), 191–205.

Prevention or Regulation of War?

The Hague Peace Conferences as a Limited Tool for Reforming the International System before 1914

Jost Dülffer

One of the most remarkable episodes in nineteenth-century diplomacy was a reception given by the Russian Foreign Minister Mikhail N. Muravev in August 1898. As every week, diplomatic representatives in St. Petersburg received invitations to the event, but this time the minister presented them with an odd text. In this diplomatic note, clearly designed to uphold the interests of Czar Nicholas II, the system of state alliances was emphatically condemned and in its place a new goal proclaimed: 'to put an end to these incessant armaments and to seek the means of warding off the calamities which are threatening the whole world – such is the supreme duty which is to-day imposed on all states'. It continued:

> The intellectual and physical strength of the nations, labour and capital, are for the major part diverted from their natural application, and unproductively consumed. Hundreds of millions are devoted to acquiring terrible engines of destruction, which, though today regarded as the last word in science, are destined tomorrow to lose all value in consequence of some fresh discovery in this field. National culture, economic progress, and the production of wealth are either paralysed or checked in their development. Moreover, in proportion as the armaments of each Power increase, so do they less and less fulfil the object which the Governments have set before themselves.

Precisely because Nicholas II's manifesto addressed problems of the international system of the time, it was not taken seriously by many contemporaries. Yet the czar's statements should not be glibly dismissed as mere cant, a deliberate deception of the world public about the main elements of Russian imperial policy. Doubtless there were reasons that inclined Russian economic and military policy to favour a peace initiative. As a developing industrial nation, Russia, under its minister of finance, Sergey Yulyevich Witte, needed all the means it could lay its hands on for domestic development, so that savings in the military sector would have been an obvious option. However, since the Russian army was just then preparing to keep pace with an international surge in artillery development, an attempt would have to be made to solve the problem at the international level. Still, this could hardly have been the only reason for the czar's appeal.

Over and above this, there was a Russian tradition of peacemaking, a desire for a qualitatively new international order, based not only on material or financial difficulties, but also bound up with ideas of improving the world. Nicholas II could tie in with this tradition just as he could tie in with British liberal ideas which had found their way into international politics only a few years before. Even if the czar was not prepared to make similar concessions in his own country, as August Bebel straightaway noted in an SPD (Social Democratic Party of Germany) party rally resolution,[1] the challenge he had issued to the existing system of power, the appeal to convert its pathology into a new order, was more than a mere gambit.

The czar's unusual appeal resulted, in fact, in two general international conferences. In 1899 the European states formed the core of the twenty-six participants; in 1907 there were forty-four states, and so, with the participation of Latin American countries, the second conference comprised nearly all states then recognised as sovereign. Actually, the conferences paid only limited attention to the task formulated by the czar, namely to seek new paths in international politics, and therefore yielded only modest results.

Main Topics and Results of the Hague Conferences[2]

Broadly speaking, there were two strategies discussed at The Hague for reforming the international system: firstly, that of the peaceful settlement of disputes, and secondly, arms limitation or disarmament. A third strategy implicit in the czar's manifesto, namely social reform, played no part in the official discussions.

The czar's manifesto primarily addressed the limitation of arms, which in later phases could lead to discussing disarmament. The idea of arms limitation was a major consideration in the nineteenth century and periodically acquired international importance. In 1816, Czar Alexander I of Russia had already made a proposal for disarmament to the Concert of Europe's other important flanking power, Great Britain, and then to the other Great Powers. Confronted by the threat of civil wars after the July revolution of 1830, the European powers sought to scale down the danger of international war by limiting armaments competition. On the eve of the Franco-Prussian War, the British foreign secretary, Lord Clarendon, following insular tradition, sought to persuade the French and the Prussians to de-escalate tensions by reducing armaments. In the final decade of the nineteenth century, Clarendon's successor as foreign secretary, Lord Rosebery, attempted to gain the support of the Russian czar for a disarmament initiative among the militarised European states, but there was no response and this exercised no discernible influence on any of the czar's later initiatives.[3]

All these initiatives, which were in part the result of liberal free-trade ideas, were mainly inspired by the politics of national interest, which partly explains their failure. Detached from such incidental contexts, the idea of disarmament gained particular importance in the middle-class peace movement and was discussed extensively, especially at international meetings. A World Peace Congress of national pacifist associations was first held in 1889; in the same year Parliamentarians organised themselves internationally for the first time in the Interparliamentary Union. Both groups increasingly called for the creation of a new international order based on disarmament.[4] In the socialist part of the workers movement, the idea of arms limitation also became a topic of everyday political significance, even if the question of armaments in general was seen rather as systematically bound up with the social order and symptomatic of it.

Basically, the Russians' original goal in 1898 was to avoid a new round of armaments modernisation, that is, to suspend the improvement of heavy artillery through a multilateral agreement. This idea did not even enter the international debate. The negotiations at the first Hague Conference in 1899 showed that no sustained political will supporting general arms limitation existed or could be mobilised in another European Great Power (in contrast to 1907). The general point of avoiding the costs of armaments modernisation by means of disarmament was therefore not generally negotiated at The Hague in 1899. Instead, three groups of new proposals were introduced.

Firstly, at the qualitative level, a definition of certain characteristics of individual weapons systems was established. There were proposals about standardising land artillery, infantry rifles and naval artillery in connection with ships' armour. Once the technical capability of weapons could be couched in formulas, the upper limits of certain parameters could be set. Secondly, at the quantitative level, they set limitations of either state budgets or the strength of armies. Thirdly, they enacted the prohibition of weapons that were regarded as promising, but had not yet been tested or introduced.

The Russians presented all three categories of arms limitation with little expectation of success, and yet these proposals remained aspects of the international armaments discussion well into the time of the East-West conflict. The problem with all the proposals, but especially the second group, was lack of verifiability. Given enduring national sovereignty on the one hand, and continuing international mistrust on the other, only the age of satellite surveillance and electronics was able to provide a solution. The proposals for quantitative limitation were therefore quickly passed over as 'impracticable'.

The proposals for qualitative arms limitation failed because of the difficulty of defining the military features of only *one* weapon detached from its interaction with others (though to some extent this was only a pretext). In the third category, the promising new weapons of air war, poison gas and submarines were discussed, though of course their future significance was hardly fully grasped. Nonetheless, there were agreements in 1899 to ban the use of poison gas, the dropping of projectiles from balloons and the use of dum-dum bullets for five years. This was possible only because these weapons were still looked upon as ineffective and the military first wanted to test their applicability.

At the second Hague Conference in 1906–7, on the other hand, the connection between the naval armaments debate and concrete international political tensions between Great Britain and Germany was the major topic. In the long, wearying preliminary negotiations, Great Britain's main concern was a reduction of expenditure. However, the Liberal government in London did not propose budgetary arms limitation, but envisaged a limit on the number of big ships of the line and battleships. This was, assuming the political will of the relevant powers, a highly suitable proposal which could, from a military and technical point of view, constitute a realistic basis for agreement. The contemporary view was that the types of ships in question represented the core of peace-threatening and militarily decisive naval weapons which could, despite their interdependence with other armaments, form meaningful categories for seizing strategic naval fighting power. Moreover, as soon as they were built their size would make them subject to public surveillance, so to speak.

At the preliminary negotiations, however, the German Imperial Government, in accord with the Russians and Austrians, already succeeded in having the armaments question, which it viewed as harmful to Germany, removed from the official agenda. Dressed up as a friendly resolution on the subject of the Conference, the armaments question received 'a first class funeral'.

The chances of reaching agreement on arms limitation were generally regarded as slight. During the preliminary negotiations at both Hague Conferences hopes therefore shifted to a possible agreement on the peaceful settlement of disputes. The goal envisaged was not so much a conflict-free society of states as forms of resolving conflicts other than war. Courts of arbitration and other international arbitration authorities therefore become considerations of major importance. This idea gained its strongest support from the middle-class peace movement, and here too sustained efforts were made to develop a practicable, that is, gradual, process of resolution. The hope was that great results could come of small beginnings, that power relations could be increasingly recast as legal relations, and that a gradual acceptance of amicable resolution might find a place in international practice; in short, that a snowball effect could arise. The peace movement's greatest disappointment with both Hague Conferences was therefore on this point – for precisely such a snowball effect was feared by some governments and thus precluded, especially by the Germans.

The results can only be described as meagre. In 1899 a Permanent Court of Arbitration was founded in the Dutch capital, but the reality behind this was very much more modest than its name. In fact, only a bureau had been created, staffed with subordinate Dutch officials. The bureau kept a list of arbiters, for which individual states could nominate up to four members, mainly experts in constitutional law or politicians in favour of the idea of arbitrated settlements. In the case of a conflict, states could assemble a court of arbitration from this list with the assistance of the bureau, and this court could then give a non-binding verdict. A convention on arbitration laid down rules of procedure for such a court. These began with defining the matter in dispute and regulated the decision-making process of the court, which was to be formed from case to case. The Hague bureau was not allowed to take the initiative. Thus the Permanent Court of Arbitration really existed only on paper.

Procedures for arbitration, set up ad hoc by the participating governments, had already been common in international politics. It soon became apparent that these procedures would continue to be carried out in the traditional manner. Thus, for instance, the government of the United States paid its respects to both the national and international peace movement when it gave the Permanent Court of Arbitration its debut in 1901–2, by allowing it to decide a long and insignificant dispute with Mexico over church property.[5] There can be no question here of the government yielding to political pressure: from the list of arbiters, the United States chose a Russian and an Englishman, and Mexico two Dutchmen, who then jointly chose a Dane as a non-partisan member. After a month's negotiations at The Hague the court reached its verdict (in favour of the USA) in October 1902. By 1914, a total of fifteen conflicts, all essentially insignificant to peace-keeping, had been resolved using the instrument of the Hague court, the precursor of the International Court of Justice at The Hague.

These experiences showed that the procedure was time-consuming and costly. A fundamental improvement would have been possible only in the form of a court that was permanently in session. The attempt to set up just such a court failed in 1907 because the smaller states could not accept the loss of prestige involved in recognising a body in which they were not permanently represented. In 1899 declarations of intent were passed supporting the setting up of courts of arbitration for precisely defined legal cases and reliance on amicable mediation in the case of political conflicts. However, reservations were expressed about the restrictions on national sovereignty bound up with this, and these institutions consequently had little weight. Since no breakthrough could be achieved in institutionalising bodies for settling conflicts, in 1907 an attempt was made to place certain areas of conflict, even if trivial or narrowly defined, under the *obligation* to arbitration.

Such obligations already existed. The 1878 contract regulating the Universal Postal Union, for example, contained obligatory arbitration clauses. In 1907 in The Hague various parties sought agreement on making other areas, below the level of great conflicts, subject to obligatory arbitration. These areas ranged from the legal estates of seamen who died abroad to trade contracts. It was here, however, that questions of principle came into play, such as whether elements of national sovereignty would be surrendered by accepting this convention. The German Empire turned the argument in this direction, so that in the end no results were achieved in this sector. The most important lasting result of both Hague Conferences lay finally in codifying the laws of war – in *rules for a war that had already begun*. They had little to do with peace-keeping.

Reactions and Positions of the Great Powers

None of the Great Powers intended to surrender its unrestricted power of action in international politics, and all agreed that their capacity to decide autonomously matters of war and peace was an essential attribute of a Great Power. Nevertheless, it would be wrong to assume (as in Camus's *The Plague*) that the right starting-point is 'Everyone is guilty', that is, to condemn the pre-war international system and its main actors out of hand. The nations' willingness to engage in reforms of the international order was closely connected to the part played by an informed public in the formulation of foreign policy, to the influence that the peace movement, for example, could exert on national decision-making. It was expedient to accommodate strong political forces in the direction of peace, though presumably not necessary.

In terms of willingness to engage in reforms leading to peaceful agreement, Britain represented one end of the scale and the German Empire the other. However, this scale does not correspond to the nations' degree of democracy or dictatorship. In these terms, autocratic Russia would have come in last. If the initiative for both Hague Conferences originated in the Czarist regime, however, this was because, in addition to the motives already mentioned, it could afford to engage in pro-peace rhetoric, since it had no need to justify itself before a national public. Appeals for peace were aimed at world opinion; within Czarist Russia, they were neither necessary for legitimation nor opposed in any way.

Moreover, it is clear that responding to the population's longing for peace was also something of a domestic political tactic in liberal states. The French government, for instance, was represented at both Hague Conferences by a prominent radical socialist politician and former prime minister, Leon Bourgeois; his deputy was a senator who was a supporter of the peace movement (Paul d'Estournelles de Constant). With great sympathy on the part of the French public, these two men could celebrate the Hague plans for a stronger institutionalisation of arbitration, and in 1907 the obligatory arbitration in defined areas, as the dawn of a new golden age. French foreign policy gave these politicians a free rein since such matters had no impact on the pursuit of national interests in an imperialist context (for example, in the long Franco-German conflict over Alsace-Lorraine).

Characteristic of Great Britain both under the conservative government of Lord Salisbury (1898–99) and under the liberal-imperialist Foreign Secretary Sir Edward Grey (1905–7) was a pragmatic approach to the possibility of effective peace-keeping. The government deemed obligatory arbitration up to certain point to be a sensible measure and was prepared to go some way towards a limited trial of the new policy. In armaments limitation, the ruling liberals saw a good opportunity to set in motion a reallocation of state finances during the run-up to the second Hague Conference: less money for armaments (battleships) and more for civic reforms (especially old-age pensions). The government was under massive internal political pressure in these questions. Grey himself considered it highly unlikely that arms limitation would meet with success, but the Conference was a welcome opportunity: if disarmament were unattainable, at least another of the Great Powers, preferably the German Empire, could be left holding the baby. As the Germans refused even to discuss disarmament at the Conference, it was apparent to a great part of the British public that an acceleration of naval construction was necessary. Thus the screw of armaments was de facto turned by the British precisely *because* of the second Hague Conference. Failed disarmament negotiations justified a military build-up – in later years, too, a common principle.

The British military was responsible for this result only to a limited degree. Although their views had been considered in formulating the definition of national interests, they did not have the deciding word and loyally toed the government line in the relevant commissions at the Hague Conference. Nor can the decision to intensify the building of a fleet be traced to the basic approach of British politics at the turn of the century. For the British politicians at that time there were more important criteria than military security, and these finally prevailed when the foreign policy course was fixed. The British attitude at this time could be roughly summed up as 'Peace as a national interest'. This did not mean avoiding a protracted colonial war, as the Boer War (1899–1902) shows. The threat of violence against other Great Powers – for example, against France during the Faschoda crisis (1898–99) and in many other conflicts – was also part of Britain's foreign policy repertoire.[6] Clear priority, however, was given to peace in Europe. Even so, a willingness to consider and to wage a large-scale war under certain circumstances was a component of British politics, as 1914 shows.

The attitude of the German Empire was fundamentally different. In 1899 at The Hague, the German military delegate attempted to show that arms limitation did not come into question for his country in view of its material efficiency and especially its (supposedly) secure social order:

> I do not believe that even a single one of my honourable colleagues would be prepared to admit that his sovereign and his government is working for the unavoidable doom, the slow but certain annihilation, of his country. ... As far as Germany is concerned, I can fully calm its friends and dispel all well-meant fears. The German people is not being weighed down under the burden of taxes; it is not being pushed to the edge of an abyss; it is not hurrying towards exhaustion and ruin. Quite the contrary: public and private prosperity grows, the common wealth and standard of living improves from year to year. With respect to general conscription, which is closely connected to this question, the German does not look upon it as a heavy burden but rather as a holy and patriotic duty, to whose fulfilment he owes his existence, his prosperity and his future.[7]

By appealing to this militarily-centred politics of national interest, he succeeded in frustrating all further initiatives. The attitude of the civilian German leadership was no different. It allowed itself to be guided by categories of national strength, which were to be brought to bear precisely in the military sector:

> It is conceivable that small states, without interests in the issue, may be the subjects of arbitration, and small questions its object, but not great states and great questions. For the state (and the greater it is, the more it does so) considers itself an end in itself, not a means of achieving some higher, external goals. ... For the state, there is no higher goal than the safeguarding of *its* interests. This, however, is not necessarily identical in the case of a Great Power with keeping the peace, but rather with doing violence to the enemy and competitor by a truly cohesive and stronger group.[8]

This is the wording of the German chancellor's directive for the Hague negotiations. The state's absolute freedom of action forms its foundation. The sovereignty of a Great Power may not be curtailed by even the smallest obligation to arbitration or mediation. This was bound up with a defensive domestic political strategy: in the case of a stronger Parliament in future or the increased significance of the peace movement, the government meant to provide no basis in international law for restricting the state's freedom of action. Outwardly, it was a question of conceding smaller states no rights against the expansion of the Great Powers, but more important was preserving absolute autonomy in decisions to wage war against the other Great Powers.

Behind this German posture was not the intention of becoming a world power by means of a world war, a martial 'grab for world power' (as Fritz Fischer's book title was in German). On the contrary, it was a question of laying claim to the attribute of a supposedly not-yet-attained Great Power status or of the reputedly increasing importance of the World Powers in the twentieth century, to which Germany also wished to belong. The long-term goal of German politics was to revolutionise the system of power to German advantage – preferably by weakening the other powers through instigating wars between them rather than by means of a world war unleashed by German aggression.[9] A reform of the international system that would have enabled the stabilising of peace was therefore out of question from the outset. Thus between 1899 and 1907 in most cases Berlin did not pursue a fundamentally bellicose policy, but rather operated with relative caution.[10] Extrapolations of German economic growth increased the likelihood of a fundamental change in the international balance, and with a view to this expected improvement of Germany's position the imperial government rejected even the modest restrictions on sovereignty proposed at the Hague Conferences. Whether the improvement was then to come about by 'peaceful' or by military means remained open.

Great Britain, the German Empire, France and Russia were the most important actors on the international stage of the time. Although Austria-Hungary and Italy were also reckoned among the European Great Powers, they seldom developed their own initiatives. Like France and Great Britain, and with public opinion in mind, the political leadership of these countries showed a certain willingness to venture small steps in questions of arbitration and armaments. In the concrete politics of the Conferences, however, their conduct was dominated by deference towards the most powerful member of the Triple Alliance, the German Empire, so that both states neither introduced nor supported any far-reaching proposals.

The attitude of the United States was again different. It stood in an American tradition[11] in which courts of arbitration were given a high position, and such courts had developed independently of each other in both North and South America. In 1899, therefore, the American delegation was initially prepared to champion far-reaching arbitration proposals, even to transfer the principles of national dispute settlement by due course of law to the international order as a whole. In this a certain sense of mission, a desire to bring the blessings of the New World to the quarrelling Old World, was unmistakable. All the same, in the end the State Department was glad that no extensive and binding conventions were agreed to; even the Hague resolutions, such as they were, took the hurdle of ratification by the Senate only with difficulty, since the latter feared possible European interference on the American continent. This was one reason why the United States largely kept in the background in 1907.

The picture of an international system dominated by the Great Powers is completed by the smaller states, most of whom had great expectations of a world at peace. In part they feared giving the Great Powers new legal opportunities for interference, and in part they accepted the primacy of the Great Powers by abstaining from their own initiatives and more or less adapting themselves to the ideas of the Great Power that was most important for them. Public opinion played a role in individual smaller states to a greater or lesser extent, depending upon their domestic political commitments and the need to justify policy within their own societies.

Armaments Discussions and Contracts of Arbitration in Perspective

Theodor Mommsen's remark about the first Hague Conference, that it was a 'printer's error in world history',[12] is still one possible diagnosis. Or the verdict of Stanley Hoffmann, a political scientist, but also an outstanding historian, that it was a 'spectacular failure'.[13] A different question, however, which is raised about the Conference by liberal internationalists and radical pacifists, is whether it represented the beginnings of a new system for the whole of international politics, one which could be better developed only in the twenty-first century, as the great expert on international law, Walther Schücking, foretold in 1912.[14]

Recently, there have been clear attempts to re-evaluate precisely the legal internationalism to which the Hague Conferences testified. The remarks that Bertha von Suttner confided to her diary in 1899 – 'One hears nothing else but of "wounded, ill, belligerents". A pretty peace conference! St. George rides out to kill the dragon, not to polish his nails. … Imagine that a conference on the emancipation of slaves had taken place. Would not a convention be necessary pertaining to the treatment of blacks, on the number of lashes they should be given when they dawdle too much over their work at the sugar plantation?' – were obviously not in the spirit of the point-by-point intentions and goals actually implemented by the Conferences.

Madeleine Herren, among others, has argued[15] that the role played by an international public such as the circle of peace supporters, journalists and private sponsors who gravitated to The Hague, held salons there and published a daily newspaper, the *Courrier de la Conférence,* should not be underestimated. This circle, according to Herren, was not an alternative public to the state actors; government representatives and diplomats belonged to it, not only as guests but also as members of this new discursive community working for a peaceful world. This new kind of internationalism was an indication of future developments.

As regards the governments' decision-making process, I am more sceptical. Precisely because there were fears of public pressure on the purportedly 'rational', if culturally conditioned, activities of jurists and diplomats, competition for the public developed. One side wanted to exploit this for progressive purposes, the other emphatically rejected those purposes in the spirit of traditional international politics. The German stance in 1899, in particular, was determined by indignation at the new kind of negotiations. This points again to the diverse definitions of national interest. Since negotiations at The Hague required virtual unanimity in order for resolutions to be passed, this explains, to some extent, why the Conferences yielded such meagre results.

A different observation on the persistence of public law and the continuance of the Concert of Europe has been put forward by Matthias Schulz.[16] He sees a growing drive towards codification and thus a fencing-in of state relations through legal relations, so to speak. Especially experts in international law have constructed such systems since the days of the 'classical concert of Europe' (Edward Gulick) in the post-Napoleonic era. The variety of instruments used in the concert, ranging from ambassadorial conferences to multilateral military commissions, created new forms of international practice. It is not necessary to think of the international army under the command of Count Waldersee which put down the Boxer Rebellion (or what was left of it) in 1900; there was also the naval blockade of Crete in 1897 by (nearly) all the Great Powers, which prevented a regional Greek-Ottoman war. The admirals of the fleet sat together in a pub called 'Au concert de l'Europe' in the Cretan city of Chania and waited to see the fruits of their action.[17] But this system had its clear limits: the war of 1897 was fought as a land war in Thessalia and won by one side (the Greeks), so that the Great Powers could have their way only later in dictating the conditions of peace. Though Schulz argues it was especially the German withdrawal from the concert that destroyed it, I remain rather sceptical about the long-term results of the legal regulation of international relations.

A third tendency seeks to emphasise the opportunities for peace contained in the traditional co-operation between the Powers, their past experiences and expectations. One factor dominated the minds of leading politicians, military and monarchs between 1911 and 1914: the fear of a great war that would be a 'world conflagration', an 'Armageddon', a 'Muspili', a transvaluation of all values, and would bring with it a terrible cost in human life and material. Anxiety about such a long conflict aided forces that were working to prevent war[18] (Stig Förster, Jost Dülffer), yet preparations for war nevertheless continued. In this context, Holger Afflerbach and Friedrich Kießling[19] have pointed to the modes of co-operation in the years immediately before the First World War. Afflerbach has sought to reverse Wolfgang J. Mommsen's[20] phrase 'the inevitable war' into that of the 'improbable war', while Kießling has patiently and sensitively presented evidence for the efforts of the Great Powers to reduce tensions among themselves. Both studies point to something right – it is a matter of integrating their insights. It is not a question of describing the war as a catastrophe which suddenly erupted out of an era of détente. The merit of these studies lies rather in showing the openness of the situation then, the diverse and multi-stranded expectations of the many actors. The diagnosis of a one-way street to war, the ever more precipitous path, the idea of a boiler waiting to explode (Imanuel Geiss's image of German politics in the century after Napoleon[21]), has been put forward by the other side. More recent interpretations see events as having been less determined. A third Hague Conference was planned for 1915, for which many governments and chancelleries had already made preliminary plans. None went further than ideas about palliative methods and goals; international relations would not have been substantially changed by this continuation of the 'achievements at The Hague' (Walther Schücking).

There was also a curative strategy that was reflected in the diagnosis of the czar's manifesto; it was represented particularly by the socialist workers' movement, and here especially by its left wing: a change in the relations of production over the long-term, a phasing out of the military-industrial complex (also diagnosed by the czar). This strategy proved to be as ineffective as the emergency measure of the general strike, which the Second International Conference contemplated time and again and narrowly missed resolving upon in Stuttgart in 1907. It did not come about in the 'July Crisis' of 1914.

Were there alternatives in the July Crisis? Reflections on the long, the medium-sized and the quite short path to war have occupied and divided the historical disciplines for over ninety years now, more than virtually any another question. I should like to conclude with an anecdote. One of the last conferences of GDR historians on imperialism took place in Erfurt in spring 1989, under the direction of Willibald Gutsche. In addition to historians from the GDR and its 'brother countries', especially the Soviet Union, Gutsche had invited guests from the 'Federal Republic of Germany', Fritz Fischer and the author of this article.[22] After everything from financial imperialism to militarism had, as so often before, been turned this way and that and a general consensus of the participants seemed close, Fritz Fischer made the following passing remark: 'Well, you know, if during the July Crisis Bethmann Hollweg had succeeded in patching up the quarrel over the murder of the Archduke and Serbia – who knows, perhaps the whole thing would have taken another and peaceful turn'. I have seldom been so astonished by an observation; he did not, alas, elaborate further. But it can be stimulating for historians always to keep alternative possibilities in mind, the open situations, and not to content themselves over-hastily with necessities and irreversible developments. In this light, the Hague Conferences gain importance as unrealised alternatives to the First World War. Whether they could have averted that 'seminal catastrophe', to use George F. Kennan's phrase, and whether it could have taken another form, is not for the historian to say.

Notes

1. *Protokoll über die Verhandlungen des Parteitages der Sozialdemokratischen Partei Deutschlands* (Berlin, 1898), 65, cf. 220ff.
2. In the following, I rely heavily on material presented in Jost Dülffer, *Regeln gegen den Krieg? Die Haager Friedenskonferenzen von 1899 und 1907 in der internationalen Politik* (Frankfurt, 1981). Here, however, I assess the material differently and choose a different perspective. Parts of the summary are based on the article Jost Dülffer, 'Internationales System, Friedensgefährdung und Kriegsvermeidung: Das Beispiel der Haager Friedenskonferenzen 1899 und 1907', in Reiner Steinweg (ed.), *Friedensanalysen* 23 (Frankfurt, 1990), 95–116; but with respect to this, too, my perspective has changed.
3. Edward V. Gulick, *Europe's Classical Balance of Power* (Ithaca, 1955); Werner Näf, *Abrüstungsverhandlungen im Jahre 1831* (Bern/Leipzig, 1931); Klaus Hildebrand, 'Lord Clarendon, Bismarck und das Problem der europäischen Abrüstung 1870', in *Studien zur Geschichte Englands und der deutsch-britischen Beziehungen*, Festschrift Paul Kluke (Munich, 1981), 130–152; Klaus A. Lankheit, 'Preußen und die Frage der europäischen Abrüstung 1867–1870', *Einzelschriften zur Militärgeschichte* 37 (Freiburg/Br. 1993). Merze Tate. *The Disarmament Illusion: The Movement for a Limitation of Armaments to 1907* (New York, 1942), esp. 137–140; Merrill G. Berthrong, 'Disarmament in European Diplomacy, 1816–1870', unpublished doctoral thesis, University of Pennsylvania (1958).
4. For the IPU see Ralph Uhlig, *Die Interparlamentarische Union 1889–1914* (Wiesbaden, 1988). For the World Peace Congress, cf. Friedrich Karl Scheer, *Die Deutsche Friedensgesellschaft (1892–1932): Organisation, Ideologie, politische Ziele* (Frankfurt, 1981); Peter Broock, *Pacifism in Europe to 1914* (Princeton, 1972).
5. Francis J. Weber, 'The Pious Fund of the Californias', *Hispanic American Historical Review* 43 (1963), 78–94.
6. For a detailed discussion, cf. Jost Dülffer, Martin Kröger and Rolf Harald Wippich (eds.), *Vermiedene Kriege: Deeskalation von Konflikten der Großmächte zwischen Krim-Krieg und Erstem Weltkrieg 1856–1914* (Munich, 1997).
7. *Die Große Politik der Europäischen Kabinette*, xv (Berlin, 1923), No. 4259 (author's translation; earlier English translation in James Brown Scott (ed.), *The Proceedings of the Hague Conference of 1899,* New York 1920, not available)
8. Ibid., xv, No. 4245 (draft) and No. 4246 (final version).
9. Fritz Fischer has discussed the period up to 1911 in his two great works: *Griff nach der Weltmacht*, 3rd edition (Düsseldorf, 1964), translated into English in 1967 as *Germany's War Aims in the First World War,* and *Krieg der Illusionen. Die deutsche Politik von 1911–1914* (Düsseldorf, 1969); to this extent therefore the views presented here do not contradict his thesis. A more precise discussion of Fischer's arguments would exceed the scope of this article; with respect to the international system, cf. Klaus Hildebrand, 'Julikrise 1914: Das europäische Sicherheitsdilemma', *Geschichte in Wissenschaft und Unterricht* 36 (1985), 469–502.
10. For details, cf. Dülffer, *Regeln gegen den Krieg?*, 103–137.
11. Warren F. Kuehl, *Seeking World Order: The United States and World Order to 1920* (Nashville/Tennessee, 1969); Calvin D. Davis, *The United States and the First Hague Conference* (Ithaca, 1962); Davis, *The United States and the Second Hague Peace Conference* (Durham, NC, 1973).
12. *Der Bund* (Bern), 18 May 1899 (unverified).
13. Stanley Hoffmann, *Organisations internationales et pouvoirs politiques des etats* (Paris, 1953).

14. Walther Schücking, *Der Staatenverband der Haager Konferenzen, Das Werk vom Haag*, vol. 1 (Munich, 1912).

15. Madeleine Herren, *Hintertüren zur Macht. Internationalismus und modernisierungsorientierte Außenpolitik in Belgien, der Schweiz und den USA*, Studien zur Internationalen Geschichte, vx (Munich, 2000); Holger Afflerbach and David Stevenson (eds.), *An Improbable War? The Outbreak of World War I and European Political Culture before 1914* (New York/Oxford, 2007). A recent survey on the centenary of the Second Hague Conference: Jost Dülffer (ed.), *100 Jahre Zweite Haager Friedenskonferenz*. Special Issue of *Die Friedenswarte* 4 (2007) with contributions by historians Madeleine Herren, Matthias Schulz, Daniel Segesser, Alexander Rindfleisch et al.; some international law experts and a philosopher complete the issue.

16. Matthias Schulz, *Normen und Praxis: Das Europäische Konzert der Großmächte als Sicherheitsrat* (Munich, 2008).

17. Jost Dülffer, 'Die Kreta-Krise und der griechisch-türkische Krieg 1895–1898', in Jost Dülffer, Hans-Otto Mühleisen and Vera Torunsky (eds.), *Inseln als Brennpunkte internationaler Politik. Konfliktbewältigung im Wandel des internationalen Systems, 1890–1984* (Cologne, 1986), 13–60.

18. Manfred Boemeke, Roger Chickering and Stig Förster (eds.), *Anticipating Total War. The German Experiences 1871–1914* (Cambridge, 1999), (essay Förster). For a summary, cf. Stig Förster, 'Im Reich des Absurden: Die Ursachen des Ersten Weltkrieges', in Bernd Wegner (ed.), *Wie Kriege entstehen. Zum historischen Inhalt von Staatenkonflikten* (Paderborn, 2002), 211–252; Jost Dülffer, 'Kriegserwartung und Kriegsbild in Deutschland vor 1914' (1994); and Dülffer, 'Die zivile Reichsleitung und der Krieg. Erwartungen und Bilder 1890–1914' (1998), both printed in Dülffer, *Im Zeichen der Gewalt, Frieden und Krieg im 19. und 20. Jahrhundert* (Colgone, 2003), 107–123 and 124–140.

19. Afflerbach and Stevenson (eds.), *An improbable War?*; Friedrich Kießling, *Gegen den "großen Krieg"? Entspannung in den internationalen Beziehungen 1911–1914* (Studien zur Internationalen Geschichte, 12) (Munich, 2002); Kießling, 'Wege aus der Stringenzfalle. Die Vorgeschichte des Ersten Weltkriegs als "Ära der Entspannung"', *Geschichte in Wissenschaft und Unterricht* 55 (2004), 284–304.

20. Wolfgang J. Mommsen, 'Der Topos vom unvermeidlichen Krieg. Außenpolitik und öffentliche Meinung in Deutschland in den letzten Jahren vor 1914', in Jost Dülffer and Karl Holl (eds.), *Bereit zum Krieg. Kriegsmentalität im wilhelminischen Deutschland 1890–1914* (Göttingen, 1986), 194–224. Earlier and shorter English version in Volker R. Berghahn and Martin Kitchen (ed.), *Germany in the Age of Total War* (London, 1981), 23–45.

21. Imanuel Geiss, *Der lange Weg in die Katastrophe. Die Vorgeschichte des Ersten Weltkrieges 1815–1914* (Munich, 1990).

22. The proceedings of this conference remained unpublished in the midst of the transition; the style of conference corresponded to that of gala conferences under traditional socialism. The last conference of the Historical Society of the GDR in Wernigerode in May 1990 was different; its proceedings were, as it were, published posthumously: Jost Dülffer and Hans Hübner (in collaboration with Konrad Breitenborn and Jürgen Laubner) (eds.), *Bismarck. Person – Politik – Mythos* (Berlin, 1993).

3

'The Spirit of 1914'
A Critical Examination of
War Enthusiasm in German Society

Gerhard Hirschfeld

Anyone interested in the outbreak of the First World War will know those black and white photographs (now a few have also been found in colour) from the last weeks of July and the first two weeks of August 1914. They are pictures of cheerful masses gathered in the great squares and streets of European capitals, of more or less spontaneous-looking assemblies and demonstrations, mainly of middle-class young men waving their hats and caps and striking up patriotic songs; there are also young women handing the parading soldiers flowers and small presents, so-called *Liebesgaben;* and finally there are railway cars emblazoned with patriotic slogans or satirical caricatures. These are travelling to Paris (naturally to a boulevard), St. Petersburg or Belgrade and, along with their occupants, are expected to be back home no later than Christmas. The then eight year-old Klaus Mann described the patriotic mood of those days in his *Report of My Life* (first published in German in 1949): 'When I attempt to recapture the atmosphere of 1914, I see fluttering flags, grey helmets decorated with droll bouquets of flowers, knitting women, shrill posters and again flags – a sea, a cataract in black-white-red. The air is filled with general chattering and the noisy refrains of patriotic songs. "Deutschland, Deutschland über alles" and "There Roars a Call Like Thunder". … The roaring never stops.'[1]

There is hardly an idea that has had greater influence on the historical consciousness of both contemporaries and subsequent generations than the actual or supposed general war enthusiasm in the summer of 1914 conveyed by these images. On the other hand, the new generation of historians of the First World War, especially those who since the mid 1980s have studied the history of everyday life and mentalities, argue that these images are predominantly icons or 'cult images', and obfuscate rather than reveal the true mood at the beginning of the war. Jeffrey Verhey, the American historian of the First World War, argues that while contemporary photographs suggest that 'these people were without exception enthusiastic about the war', in August 1914 there was, on the contrary, 'no ecstatic war enthusiasm that seized all classes of the population, neither in Germany nor in France, Great Britain, Austria-Hungary nor Russia'. Instead the people of these countries evinced 'a broad spectrum of quite different reactions, ranging from rejection of the war, perplexity and shock, to patriotic ardour and even hysteria'.[2] With this appraisal Verhey aptly summarises the latest research on the 'spirit of August' or *Augusterlebnis* in Germany, while also noting similar reactions amongst the other major combatant countries. Although there are now studies on France and England as well as on Germany, comparable work on Austria-Hungary or Russia, is still to be done.[3]

The first study, as it were the pioneer work, on war mentalities in the German Empire at the beginning and in the course of the First World War was Volker Ulrich's book *Kriegsalltag*. Using the example of Hamburg, Ulrich noted that there had been no homogenous *Augusterlebnis* in the city and that the public mood, especially in the workers' suburbs, was subject to considerable ups and downs during the first days of the war, fluctuations which were again influenced by local circumstances and class-specific conditions. There was no question of rah-rah patriotism.[4] In the meantime we have a great number of studies dealing particularly with rural areas or border regions of Germany. All in all they confirm Ulrich's findings for Hamburg, and at the same time render them considerably more precise. Among these are Benjamin Ziemann's seminal account of the rural experience of the war in Bavaria, which was strongly coloured by anxieties about the survival of farming communities, and Christian Geinitz's extremely concise study of the beginning of the war in the university town of Freiburg im Breisgau.[5] Geinitz especially underscores again the strongly regional form of the *Augusterlebnis*, but points at the same time to a supra-regional, collective perception of the reality of the war and its absorption by the German population. Thus in Freiburg, near the French border, he not only notes the historical fear of invasion (on account of experiences in 1870–71), but also detects a 'synchrony of positive, war-affirming and negative, war-fearing states of mind', that is, a continuous ambivalence of feelings.[6] But in spite of the doubtless strongly regional character of the experience, the findings of Verhey, Ziemann, Geinitz, Chickering, Thomas Raitel, and Michael Stöcker, and the summary works by Thomas Rohrkrämer and Wolfgang Kruse, may be considered as representative and generally valid.[7]

How does the German *Augusterlebnis* look in light of this recent research? To begin with, an analysis of the experience of war in the summer of 1914 can be clearly divided into individual phases or chronological sequences. As to the actual or supposed war enthusiasm of the masses, it is important to distinguish above all between a 'July enthusiasm' and an 'August euphoria'. The strongly patriotic enthusiasm following the Serbian government's rejection of the Austro-

Hungarian ultimatum on 25 July expressed itself particularly in the big cities, the princely and royal residential cities (among others, Hamburg, Frankfurt, Leipzig, Nuremberg, Karlsruhe, Munich, Stuttgart, Königsberg) and in most of the university towns (for example, Freiburg and Jena). By contrast, there were no demonstrations, or only very few, the in the cities of the Ruhr region and the border provinces (Saarland, Alsace, East Prussia). Members of the conservative middle class, in particular, responded to the news of 'war between Austria and Serbia' with processions and public singing of so-called patriotic songs ('Wacht am Rhein', 'Gott erhalte Franz den Kaiser'). The figures for these demonstrations vary: in the centre of Berlin on the evening of 25 July about thirty thousand people are supposed to have assembled. In the following days there were large gatherings of people in front of several public buildings, national monuments and the embassies or consulates of the relevant countries. There are also reports of isolated excesses on the part of youthful participants in these often Carnival-like rallies against German opponents of the war or against Serbs and Russians or people thought to be such, mainly in the vicinity of restaurants and cafés. Three days later, the euphoria had clearly ebbed away and made way to a 'tension of curiosity', often noted in these days.[8]

There is not always hard evidence that the 'July enthusiasm' proceeded primarily from middle class youth, including numerous students, but it is suggested by the available information. By contrast, the much-reported reservations and cautious distance of older citizens, including the numerous veterans of the war of 1870–71, are striking. Thus the well-known historian Friedrich Meinecke described an evening walk through Freiburg (on 25 July 1914) that took him 'past the war monument for 1870, round which a band of students were gathered and jubilantly singing "Wacht am Rhein". We older people did not feel exultant. What now lay before us was far darker and unforeseeable than what had flared up in July 1870.'[9]

The number of participants in patriotic demonstrations during the last weeks of July was also comparatively moderate. By contrast, more than 100,000 people took part in the large SPD anti-war rally in greater Berlin on 28 July, in spite of a ban issued by the magistrate. Wolfgang Kruse, in 'a new interpretation of the Social Democrats' Burgfriedensschluß' (or truce with the other Parliamentary parties), cites a nationwide total of 288 anti-war demonstrations in 160 cities, in which altogether about three quarters of a million people participated.[10] Also on 28 July, the day of the Austrian declaration of war on Serbia, about seven thousand members of the SPD and its sympathisers are said to have attended a rally by its Freiburg local chapter. On the other hand, only about four thousand people took part in the patriotic, pro-Austrian demonstration on the evening of 25 July, according to the middle class and Catholic press – though they expressly mentioned that the crowd included 'residents of the outer districts' (Social Democrat strongholds).[11]

This brings us to the role of the press on the eve of the war. Historians of the *Augusterlebnis* agree unanimously that it was the deliberately focussed reporting of the patriotic processions and rallies in Berlin by the middle class press (some, for example Geinitz, call it even orchestrated 'propaganda') that laid the foundations for the myth of general war enthusiasm. It is argued that the regional reporting of the 'July enthusiasm', rather than offering a picture of reality merely reflected a reality that it had created itself. The 'July enthusiasm' was, it is maintained, a case (now well known to us) of a self-generated media reality. The Social Democrat *Vorwärts* had already made a similar observation on 28 July: 'Sensationalist middle class papers, which … lack all sense of the immense responsibility incumbent upon the press in this fateful hour, falsify these demonstrations into declarations of the people's will.'[12]

Nevertheless, it was not the case that the war enthusiasm of August 1914 was, as it were, already written up in July. Only a minority of the leading articles in the liberal and conservative middle class press openly advocated a general European war at this time. Instead most commentators hoped that the war, which was seen as inevitable, could be confined to the Balkans, as it were 'hedged in'. There can be no doubt, however, that most of them looked upon the situation as genuinely historical and earth-shattering.[13]

With news of the Russian mobilisation (31 July) the general tension became, as commentators of those days and other contemporaries unanimously report, 'simply unbearable'.[14] Again there were patriotic processions, spontaneous chanting of patriotic songs (especially in the many beer gardens and street cafés) and homage was paid to the respective monarchs – for instance on 1 August in Berlin, where between forty and fifty thousand people gathered in front of the imperial palace and Wilhelm II held the first of his famous 'I no longer see any political parties' speeches. There is evidence that such processions and demonstrations occurred in many of the larger cities of the German Empire on 31 July and 1 August. A similar gathering even took place in front of the Town Hall in the workers' city of Oberhausen. Yet reports of such 'jubilation' suggest that only a minority of the population took part in it, and that this minority was recruited predominantly from the middle classes.[15] This appraisal is supported by numerous reports from smaller cities and rural communities where the mood was described mainly as rather depressed and pensive. Thus, for instance, the western German city of Minden, where there were 'no rages of enthusiasm, no hay fire of overly loud cheering, only the expression of serious and self-confident seriousness'.[16] Even in the Berlin inner city the exultation was by no means ubiquitous, as an eye-witness noted in his diary: 'Earnestness and gloom. No jubilation, no enthusiasm. … Masses of people in front of the Schloßplatz. Cheers and singing groups in front of the Crown Prince's palace. Those standing off at a distance were passive.'[17] The 'general war enthusiasm' proves again to have been a big-city phenomenon, in which the rah-rah patriotism of young men, blended out in later stylisations, is particularly conspicuous.

This was strikingly different from the national 'July enthusiasm'. This is true even of middle-class Freiburg, where news of the German mobilisation changed the atmosphere considerably. The national-liberal *Freiburger Zeitung* of 1 August described the mood of the city as follows: 'Whereas on Saturday [i.e., 27 July] the citizens gave vent to a worthy enthusiasm in exultant hymns, a deeply serious silence now fell over the thousands that soon streamed together. A silence, however, under which a volcano of feelings brews and seethes. A dark earnestness of iron resolve is etched on the features of the men, and even the young are spellbound by the gigantic shadow of the threatening phantom World War. Women and girls weep and think with ardent concern of their husbands, their brothers, their fathers, who will perhaps soon follow the call of the commander-in-chief.'[18]

Very different perceptions of the beginning of the war came together in this 'volcano of feelings': fear at the coming uncertainty, concern for one's professional and familial future, but also the discharge of an immense mental tension. In the diary of a Freiburg housewife we can read the following in the entry for 2 August: 'Mobilisation. The tension of the past days was appalling.' (And she adds: 'I have saved the newspapers about the beginning of the war; they are in a box in the attic.')[19] The constantly described seesaw of feelings, the enormous nervousness and the extreme excitement of the last weeks before the war, now gave way, with the Kaiser's declaration of a state of war (or more precisely a 'state of the threatening danger of war') on 31 July at 1 o'clock PM, to a 'phase of order and clarity' (Geinitz). The 'mysterious chaos' of July, 'which had overshadowed events more and more' (according to the war diary of Heidelberg historian Hermann Oncken in Ernst Jäckh's contemporary kaleidoscope *Der große Krieg* of 1916)[20] appeared, thankfully, to be over: now order again reigned. The politicians relinquished concrete control to the military, which had, seemingly at least, very clear plans and schedules. Yet the hoped-for restoration of harmony was only temporary and ultimately proved to be an illusion.

The Bielefeld historian Joachim Radkau has described the Wilhelmine epoch as an 'age of nervousness'. Wilhelmine nervousness may be partly explained, he maintains, by the conflicting impulses, with different tempos, that confronted imperial foreign and armaments policy, the mutual interference of different velocities (especially in everyday experience). According to Radkau, a comparable 'discrepancy and problematisation of tempo' had hitherto never existed in German society.[21] If we follow this interpretation, then the Imperial government's decision to go to war meant that with the beginning of the First World War Germans, at least temporarily, again found a common denominator to their time. As the German pacifist Helmut von Gerlach observed afterwards, with the outbreak of the war Germans 'clung with almost superstitious tenaciousness to two dictums of the military authorities: "Time is on our side" and "Whoever keeps his nerve longest will win"'. Trust in time and trust in nerve – in August 1914 both seemed to be present to excess. For Radkau this phenomenon may be explained 'as a subsequent reflex of the "nervous age"'.[22]

Decisive for the perception of the war in August 1914, however, was not least the image of the imminent conflict that shaped people's expectations or fears in the time before. Here, too, Germans had harboured conflicting hopes and fears since the turn of the century. Some historians and cultural commentators (among them, Klaus Vondung and Bernd Hüppauf) have pointed out that the First World War was preceded by a 'veritable flood of war literature' which took the new weapons technology into account and projected pictures of the battles of the future that 'showed them as thousands of times more horrible than those of previous wars'.[23] While the German military writer Friedrich von Bernhardi was still explaining to the Wilhelmine middle class (and, thanks to numerous translations, also to interested foreigners) 'the duty to make war', according to which a 'war for the sake of our world significance' should 'under no circumstances be avoided', the Hamburg teacher and popular writer Wilhelm Lamszus described in his book *Menschenschlachthaus* (Human Slaughter House) the magnitude, brutality and horrors of a future war.[24] Both books appeared in the same year (1912) and their effect far exceeded their authors' expectations. Whereas Bernhardi looked upon the world war as virtually inevitable, and pleaded for every sector of society to be prepared for the coming conflict, Lamszus, for his part, demolished all the prevalent heroic clichés by creating an idealistic counter-figure who openly rebelled against war. Yet the 'enormous, monstrous curiosity about war'[25] was present even among those who rejected war in principle (for whatever reasons) or regarded it only as the *ultima ratio* in politics, that is, as purely defensive. How far this curiosity corroborated the 'topos of the inevitable war' (Wolfgang J. Mommsen) remains an open question.

Contemporary observers had already remarked on the pronounced German need to be in harmony with the spirit of the nation and the 'euphoria of unity in August',[26] exhibited and propagated everywhere. This of course was by no means only a German phenomenon, yet there was hardly another European society at the time in which the catchwords of a harmonious society united in feeling and action bore such a political stamp as in Wilhelmine Germany. As is known, at the beginning of the war the vast majority of German intellectuals, writers and artists showed themselves to be virtually addicted to national harmony.[27] Hardly any other social group had a more positive perception of the *Augusterlebnis*. Many artists volunteered for military service because they hoped that new artistic impulses could be drawn from the reality of war – for example, the painters August Macke, Franz Marc, Otto Dix and

Max Beckmann. The latter called the outbreak of the war, 'with characteristic ambivalence' (Wolfgang J. Mommsen), a 'grand catastrophe'.[28] The writer Ernst Toller, who had already longed for a war at the height of the second Morocco Crisis,[29] wrote of the troops marching to the front: 'Yes, we are living in an intoxication of feeling. The words "Germany", "Fatherland", "war" have a magic power when we utter them; they do not evaporate; they hover in the air, circle round each other, inflame each other and us'. Even in retrospect Otto Dix, whose blatant etchings and drawings of combat and his later great anti-war pictures probably made him the most important German painter of the First World War, testified to the hitherto unknown radical aesthetic quality of the front experience: 'The war was a horrible thing, but nevertheless something tremendous. It was something I could on no account miss. You have to have seen human beings in this unleashed state in order really to know something about man'.[30] Max Weber's frequently quoted remark about August 1914, 'All the same whether we succeed or not – this war is great and marvellous',[31] is, at least in this context, more representative than is commonly acknowledged.

The collective enthusiasm and national engagement ('war mission') of numerous German scholars, writers and artists has been the object of intense study in recent research on the war. Their enthusiasm, according to Steffen Bruendel (to whom we owe the most innovative account so far of the 'ideas of 1914'), had less do with the actual war than with the mobilisation of the entire people that only the war had made possible. This involved, above all, the subordination of the 'particular interests of parties, classes, religious communities and organisation to the welfare of the nation'.[32] The supreme guiding idea became the common good, to which everyone had to subordinate himself in order to create the new national community. At the same time, it seemed necessary to frame a 'binding self-image of the German nation in distinction to its enemies' (Bruendel). The result was the romantic construction of 'German culture' as an identity consisting in inwardness, mind and morality, which was defined as a brusque counter-image to 'western civilisation' and in particular as a rejection of the world view borne by externality, materialism and utilitarianism which was ascribed to the Anglo-Saxon peoples. Though the dichotomy of culture and civilisation already existed as a firm theorem in the German critique of civilisation at the end of the nineteenth century (which the Heidelberg Germanist Barbara Beßlich has referred to in her work), it was the demarcatory nationalistic discourse of the German 'culture warriors' of 1914 that gave it sharp contours.[33] The patent on the expression the 'ideas of 1914' belongs to the Münster economist Johann Plenge, who introduced it in his preface to his collected lectures *Der Krieg und die Volkswirtschaft* (The War and the National Economy) of January 1915 to explain his rejection of western capitalism in favour of a 'comradeship [*Volksgenossenschaft*] of national socialism'.[34] Notwithstanding the semantic proximity to later National Socialist expressions, all in all Plenge's ideological agreements with that movement were in fact quite few. I will not deal here with the flattening and abrasion already inflicted on these ideas during the world war at the hands of Rudolf Kjellén, Ernst Troeltsch and others.[35] '[I]n the end', said the Austrian writer Hermann Bahr in 1917, the 'ideas of 1914' degenerated into a catchword that 'everybody uses without really knowing what it means'.[36]

Later on, various German scholars made strenuous efforts to retain the 'spirit of August 1914' and exploit it for the purposes of the German war effort in domestic and foreign policy. The polemics already reached a peak at the beginning of October when 93 scientists, scholars, artists and writers (among them such highly respected figures as Adolf von Harnack, Gustav von Schmoller, Franz von Liszt, Engelbert Humperdinck and Max Liebermann) published an appeal 'To the World of Culture' which consisted of six sentences beginning with 'It is not true'. With this rhetorical trope, alluding to Martin Luther's Ninety-Five Theses in 1517, the authors (including the writer Ludwig Fulda) and the ninety-three signatories sought to counter foreign and in particular English charges against the brutal actions, sometimes in breach of international law, of German troops in Belgium and northern France (executions of actual or suspected franctireurs, the destruction of the University of Louvain, the bombardment of the Cathedral of Reims): 'against the lies and calumnies with which our enemies strive to besmirch the purity of the German cause in the hard struggle that they have imposed upon us'. The appeal culminates in the telling declaration that 'Without German militarism, German culture would long ago have been erased from the face of the earth. The former proceeded from the latter as its protector.'[37] Though several signatories such as the economist Lujo Brentano and the physicist Max Planck later distanced themselves from the content of the appeal, the damage it did was immense. The original text and about ten translations were read in many European countries. For most scholars in the countries of the entente, but also for many in neutral countries, this appeal by their German colleagues amounted to a declaration of intellectual bankruptcy. The corresponding reactions were massive, and they in turn were carefully registered on the German side. In vain did a few intellectuals such as Romain Rolland in France and Ernst Troeltsch in Germany speak up against the increasingly 'shallow polarisation of world views' (Wolfgang J. Mommsen). The upshot of this 'war of the mind' is well known: it contributed decisively to the permanent harm suffered by the community of scholars and scientists, which before the war had flourished in many fields.[38] It was not the least casualty of the war.

Let us turn again to August 1914. A phase of resolution amidst the crisis followed the psychological tension already described, especially in the last week of July. It was accompanied, particularly in the larger cities, by rejoicing in the streets and other eruptions of national feeling, which were everywhere, but above all in rural regions, mixed with fears about survival and anxiety for the future.[39] Wolfgang J. Mommsen is right to point out that the resolute 'enthusiasm' of these days 'would not have been possible without the political leadership's previous manipulation of public opinion'.[40] This included not only the management of diplomacy and the public, and the Kaiser's auto-suggestive defensive pleas. In particular the constant refrain of the need to defend Germany, the assumption that Germany was fighting a 'just war' and had to defend itself, proved to be a broadly accepted presupposition of the plangent 'sursum corda' that was now intoned, as Gerd Krumeich, using an analogy from the Mass, has described the 'high-minded' readiness of many volunteers and draftees to serve in the armed forces.[41] Even if the number of German volunteers, viewed altogether, was probably much smaller than propagandistic reports would have the population believe, the rhetorical figure of a 'voluntary military service, coupled with youth and sacrifice',[42] was an uncommonly effective element not only in the *Augusterlebnis* but also in the subsequent national war discourse.

However, the 'euphoria of collective mobilisation' (Steffen Bruendel) did not reach its height at the beginning of August but only in the second half of the month. Influenced by the successful German advance in the west and the swift victories in Belgium and northern France, there were public speeches proclaiming patriotic feelings and a considerable intensification of war enthusiasm. Even in many 'red' workers' districts of Hamburg and Berlin black-white-red flags sporadically appeared and in the clubs of working-class youths the popular patriotic song 'Heil Dir im Siegerkranz' (Hail the belaurelled victor!) resounded ever more frequently.[43] Even those scholars and artists whose initial reaction had been fairly restrained now no longer wanted to remain on the sidelines. The composer Richard Strauss, one of the few prominent figures who had refused to sign the 'Appeal to the World of Culture' in October 1914 ('Declarations on war and politics are unseemly in an artist, who ought to attend to his work and works'), dedicated the score of the first act of his opera *Frau ohne Schatten,* completed on 20 August, to the successful recapture by German troops of the town of Saarburg in the upper Alsace ('Completed on the day of the victory of Saarburg'). A few days later Strauss wrote to the Austrian poet Hugo von Hofmannsthal: 'It is a great and splendid time and both our peoples have conducted themselves really magnificently; one is ashamed in retrospect of every malicious word one may have uttered against this brave, strong German people. One has the uplifting awareness that this country stands just at the beginning of a great development and that it must and will obtain hegemony over Europe.'[44]

How euphorically and with what increasing lack of criticism even schooled observers responded to the initial series of German victories is illustrated by the following diary entries by the Heidelberg historian and medievalist Karl

Hampe.[45] The national-liberal Hampe had initially commented on the beginning of the war without enthusiasm, indeed with restraint and even with much concern, yet after only fourteen days his enthusiasm at the success of German arms knew no bounds: 'This morning again splendid news: victories and success all along the Western Front. It is an irresistible advance of the German millions. The Battle of Metz was the biggest in the history of the world' (*Kriegstagebuch*, entry of 24 August 1914, p. 11). At the same time the Heidelberg scholar had to admit that the war narrowed his historical judgement: 'Objectivity and humanity are rather frowned upon in war. Where history in the large is being made, the historian, who strives for objective truth, has no place' (entry of 8 August 1914, p. 111). Hampe remained, however, a resolute champion of the 'spirit and mood of 1914', which he thought he recognised again during the offensive in the spring of 1918: 'The mood of August 1914 returns' (entry of 3 March 1918, p. 671).

By this time, however, it was in vain that German propagandists and military invoked the topos of the *Augusterlebnis* ('God save for us the spirit of 1914'), which proved to be the most unsuitable possible call to mobilise the population for the final phase of a world war that was already lost, both militarily and politically. But the elevated war spirit of August 1914 became a myth and was revived only fifteen years later when Goebbels, Ley and other National Socialists turned the putative euphoria of unity at the beginning of the First World War into an ingredient of the idea of the national community, and thus of 'the concrete utopia of the National Socialist movement' (Joachim Radkau).[46]

In 1924 Kurt Tucholsky already foresaw, almost clairvoyantly, the return of that communal utopia when he remarked of the 'spirit of 1914': 'The wave of intoxication that went through the land ten years ago today left in its wake a swarm of crapulous drinkers who know no other remedy for their hangover than to get drunk again. They have learned nothing.'[47]

Notes

1. Klaus Mann, *Der Wendepunkt. Ein Lebensbericht* (Reinbek bei Hamburg, 1984), 50.
2. Jeffrey Verhey, 'Augusterlebnis', in Gerhard Hirschfeld, Gerd Krumeich and Irina Renz (eds.), *Enzyklopädie Erster Weltkrieg*, 2nd edition (Paderborn, 2004), 357f.; Verhey, *The Spirit of 1914. Militarism, Myth and Mobilization in Germany* (Cambridge, 2000).
3. Jean-Jacques Becker, *1914: Comment les Francais sont entrés dans la guerre. Contribution à l'étude de l'opinion publique, printemps – été 1914* (Paris, 1977). On Britain, see Jay M. Winter, *The Great War and the British People* (London, 1985); Trevor Wilson, *The Myriad Faces of War. Britain and the Great War, 1914–1918* (Cambridge, 1986).
4. Volker Ullrich, *Kriegsalltag. Hamburg im Ersten Weltkrieg* (Cologne, 1982).
5. Benjamin Ziemann, *War Experiences in Rural Germany, 1914–1923* (Oxford, 2007); Christian Geinitz, *Kriegsfurcht und Kampfbereitschaft. Das Augusterlebnis in Freiburg*.

Eine Studie zum Kriegsbeginn 1914 (Essen, 1998); see also Roger Chickering, *The Great War and Urban Life in Germany: Freiburg 1914–1918* (Cambridge, 2007).

6. Geinitz, *Kriegsfurcht*, 411.
7. Thomas Raitel, *Das,Wunder' der inneren Einheit. Studien zur französischen und deutschen Öffentlichkeit bei Beginn des Ersten Weltkrieges* (Bonn, 1996); Michael Stöcker, *Augusterlebnis 1914 in Darmstadt* (Darmstadt, 1994); Thomas Rohkrämer, 'August 1914 – Kriegsmentalität und ihre Voraussetzungen', in Wolfgang Michalka (ed.), *Der Erste Weltkrieg. Wirkung, Wahrnehmung, Analyse* (Munich, 1994), 759–777; Wolfgang Kruse, 'Die Kriegsbegeisterung im Deutschen Reich. Entstehungszusammenhänge, Grenzen und ideologische Strukturen', in Marcel van der Linden and Gottfried Mergner (eds.), *Kriegsbegeisterung und mentale Kriegsvorbereitung* (Berlin, 1991), 73–87; van der Linden and Mergner, 'Kriegsbegeisterung? Zur Massenstimmung bei Kriegsbeginn', in van der Linden and Mergner (eds.), *Eine Welt von Feinden. Der Große Krieg 1914–1918* (Frankfurt, 1997), 159–166.
8. Sönke Neitzel, *Blut und Eisen. Deutschland im Ersten Weltkrieg* (Zürich, 2003), 35–40.
9. Friedrich Meinecke, *Straßburg, Freiburg, Berlin 1901–1919* (Stuttgart, 1945), 136f.
10. Wolfgang Kruse, *Krieg und nationale Integration. Eine Neuinterpretation des sozialdemokratischen Burgfriedensschlusses, 1914/15* (Essen, 1993), 30–36.
11. Geinitz, *Kriegsfurcht*, 64, 81.
12. Ibid., 69–80.
13. Verhey, *Spirit of 1914*, 20. See also Elfi Bendikat, '"Krieg oder Frieden?" Liberale Presse und Kriegsfrage in Berlin und Paris (1911–1914)', *Historische Mitteilungen* 3 (1990), 268–292.
14. Michael Salewski, *Der Erste Weltkrieg* (Paderborn, 2003), 99.
15. Verhey, *Spirit of 1914*, 64–71.
16. Quoted ibid., 68.
17. Diary R. Franz, 1 August 1914, quoted in Kruse, 'Kriegsbegeisterung?', 163.
18. Geinitz, *Kriegsfurcht*, 131.
19. Ibid., 141.
20. Hermann Oncken, 'Die politischen Vorgänge im Juli 1914', in Ernst Jäckh (ed.), *Der Große Krieg als Erlebnis und Erfahrung*, vol. 1: *Das Erlebnis* (Gotha, 1916), 1–13, at 8.
21. Joachim Radkau, *Das Zeitalter der Nervosität. Deutschland zwischen Bismarck und Hitler* (Munich, 1998), 415f.
22. Ibid., 416. In his *Nervenschwäche und Krieg. Modernitätskritik und Krisenbewältigung in der österreichischen Psychiatrie (1880–1920)* (Vienna, 2004), Hans-Georg Hofer argues against Radkau's idea of a 'nervous Wilhelminian society' and in favour instead of an individual approach.
23. Klaus Vondung, 'Geschichte als Weltgericht. Genesis und Degradation einer Symbolik', in Vondung (ed.), *Kriegserlebnis. Der Erste Weltkrieg in der literarischen Gestaltung und symbolischen Deutung der Nationen* (Göttingen, 1980); Bernd Hüppauf, 'Kriegsliteratur', in Hirschfeld et al. (eds.), *Enzyklopädie*, 177–191, 182f.
24. Friedrich von Bernhardi, *Deutschland und der nächste Krieg* (Stuttgart, 1912); Wilhelm Lamszus, *Das Menschenschlachthaus. Bilder vom kommenden Krieg* (Hamburg/Berlin, 1912).
25. Michael Salewski, *Zeitgeist und Zeitmaschine. Science Fiction und Geschichte* (Munich, 1986), 171.
26. Radkau, *Zeitalter der Nervosität*, 428.
27. Wolfgang J. Mommsen (ed.), *Kultur und Krieg: Die Rolle der Intellektuellen, Künstler und Schriftsteller im Ersten Weltkrieg* (Munich, 1996).

28. Uwe M. Schneede (ed.), *Max Beckmann. Briefe*, vol. 1: *1899–1925* (Munich, 1993), 90 (letter of August 13).

29. 'We young are longing for war.' Ernst Toller, *Eine Jugend in Deutschland. Gesammelte Werke*, vol. 4 (Munich, 1978), 36.

30. Quoted in Matthias Eberle, *Der Weltkrieg und die Künstler der Weimarer Republik: Dix, Grosz, Beckmann, Schlemmer* (Stuttgart, 1989), 31; see also Dietrich Schubert, 'Otto Dix zeichnet im Ersten Weltkrieg', in Mommsen (ed.), *Kultur und Krieg*, 179–193.

31. Quoted in Wolfgang J. Mommsen, *Max Weber und die deutsche Politik*, 2nd edition (Tübingen, 1974), 206.

32. Steffen Bruendel, *Volksgemeinschaft oder Volksstaat. Die „Ideen von 1914" und die Neuordnung Deutschlands im Ersten Weltkrieg* (Berlin, 2003), 58.

33. Barbara Beßlich, *Wege in den "Kulturkrieg". Zivilisationskritik in Deutschland, 1890–1914* (Darmstadt, 2000).

34. Johann Plenge, *Der Krieg und die Volkswirtschaft* (lectures on war at the University of Münster, winter semester 1911–12) (Münster, 1915).

35. See Bruendel, *Volksgemeinschaft*, chap. 3, 93–141.

36. Hermann Bahr, 'Ideen von 1914', *Hochland*, 14 (1917), 431–448.

37. See Rüdiger vom Bruch, 'Aufruf der 93', in Hirschfeld et al., *Enzyklopädie*, 356f.; Jürgen von Ungern-Sternberg and Wolfgang von Ungern-Sternberg, *Der Aufruf 'An die Kulturwelt'. Das Manifest der 93 und die Anfänge der Kriegspropaganda im Ersten Weltkrieg* (Stuttgart, 1996); Kurt Flasch, *Die geistige Mobilmachung. Die deutschen Intellektuellen und der Erste Weltkrieg* (Berlin, 2000).

38. Jürgen von Ungern-Sternberg, 'Wissenschaftler', in Hirschfeld et al. (eds.), *Enzyklopädie*, 169–176.

39. See Verhey, *Spirit of 1914*, chap. 3, 72–114.

40. Wolfgang J. Mommsen, 'Kriegsalltag und Kriegserlebnis im Ersten Weltkrieg' in Mommsen, *Der Erste Weltkrieg. Anfang vom Ende des bürgerlichen Zeitalters* (Frankfurt, 2004), 137–154, at 139; see also Mommsen, *Bürgerstolz und Weltmachtstreben. Deutschland unter Wilhelm II., 1890–1918* (Propyläen Geschichte Deutschlands, 7, 2) (Berlin, 1995), 564–581.

41. Gerd Krumeich, 'Hoch die Herzen. Das Augusterlebnis: Wie begeistert waren die Deutschen, die in den Ersten Weltkrieg zogen?', *Süddeutsche Zeitung*, 24 July 2004, 13.

42. Bernd Ulrich, 'Die Desillusionierung der Kriegsfreiwilligen von 1914', in Wolfram Wette (ed.), *Der Krieg des kleinen Mannes. Eine Militärgeschichte von unten* (Munich, 1992), 110–126.

43. Verhey, *Spirit of 1914*, 108–112.

44. All quotations from Matthew Boden, *Richard Strauss* (Vienna, 1999), 397.

45. Karl Hampe, *Kriegstagebuch*, ed. by Folker Reichert and Eike Wolgast (Munich, 2004).

46. 'The German Revolution had its beginning in those August days of 1914. … There in the western and the eastern trenches this people found itself again; the grenades and the mines asked not whether a man was high-born or low-born, whether rich or poor, to which denomination and which estate he belonged, but rather here was the great, resounding test of the meaning and spirit of community.' Thus Robert Ley in a speech given to the diplomatic corps on 1 March 1934 in Berlin, quoted in Tim Mason, *Sozialpolitik im Dritten Reich. Arbeiterklasse und Volksgemeinschaft* (Opladen, 1977), 26.

47. Kurt Tucholsky, 'Der Geist von 1914', *Die Weltbühne*, 20/2, no. 38, 7 August 1924, 204–210.

4

Construction and Deconstruction of the Idea of French 'War Enthusiasm' in 1914

Nicolas Beaupré

The aim of this chapter is not to present once again 'how the French entered the war', to use the title of the famous and pioneering thesis by Jean-Jacques Becker.[1] In fact, no serious study on the subject has ever contradicted this key work, and it would be presumptuous and dangerous to seek to do so in a single essay. In any case, my own research dedicated to a category of French people – the soldier-writers[2] – has not contradicted his thesis in any way at all.

So, the object here is rather to try and understand how and why the idea of French 'collective enthusiasm' in August 1914 – an idea rightly disparaged by Jean-Jacques Becker – managed to establish itself over the years like a biblical truth about how the French entered the war, to the extent that even today it has not entirely disappeared. This idea of French collective enthusiasm in July–August 1914 has indeed dominated historiography and the way these events in France are represented for a very long time, and it still recurs at times in the most diverse cultural settings like the cinema, literature, comics etc.

So what does Jean-Jacques Becker's revision consist of? In 1977 he published an abridged version of his doctoral thesis entitled *1914: comment les Français sont entrés dans la guerre,* with the subtitle *Contribution à l'étude de l'opinion publique, printemps-été 1914.* The main achievement of this work, based on a most precise and detailed study of public opinion, was, quite rightly, to demonstrate that the supposed collective enthusiasm of the French was nothing but a myth. It was sometimes referred to by the catch-phrase 'la fleur au fusil' (the flower in the gun), due to the weapons adorned with flowers carried by certain soldiers in photographs of the time.[3]

According to Becker, this myth bore very little relation to reality, and was actually a 'complete misinterpretation'.[4] His work seemed to be so 'rigorous and definitive'[5] that since then research on France during that period – for example Gerd Krumeich's *Armaments and Politics in France on the Eve of the First World War* of 1980, or more recently work by Jakob Vogel in 1997 – have concentrated on the years leading up to 1914.[6] For 1914 and the French entry into the war one could also mention Thomas Raithel's work of 1996,[7] which approaches the subject from a comparative perspective with the case of Germany. Given all this, it would be almost impossible today to talk of a genuinely 'new French historiography of the entry into the war'.

The questions posed by Becker's work, and the iconoclastic responses he brought to the period, were ultimately transposed to other national contexts. Indeed (though admittedly with some delay), his work undoubtedly inspired studies on the German[8] and Belgian[9] entries into the war, to name but two examples. A comparative conference on the entry of various countries into the war was also held at Péronne at the Historial de la Grande Guerre in 1994, but the proceedings were not published. The results of all this research that followed Becker's pioneering work (of which only a few examples have been given) were then integrated into vast syntheses that tried to present a European or global image of these entries into the war. The most recent example is Hew Strachan's *To Arms!*, published in 2001.[10]

Just as Becker set about dismantling this myth, we will attempt here to understand how the myth was created, crystalised and consolidated after 1914, and indeed how it was able to change in meaning or function. In order to do so I shall concentrate on certain actors – namely the soldier-writers and witnesses to the war who did so much to forge the collective memories of the conflict[11] – on the methods they used to create this myth of the 'fleur au fusil', and also on the functions it may have had. I shall also try to outline the effects this myth brought with it.

To start I shall give an impression of the atmosphere in France at the moment of entry into the war, before demonstrating the crystallisation of the idea of collective and individual enthusiasm – including voluntary enlistment by intellectuals – and finally looking at the meaning and functions of this myth after the conflict.[12]

The Atmosphere in France at the Moment of General Mobilisation and Entry into the War

Even without Jean-Jacques Becker's work on the chain of emotions during those particular days in July and August 1914, we know that the bellicosity of the French was relative. Even if the nationalist milieux, in particular those of the royalist Action Française, sometimes exerted considerable influence, particularly in times of crisis – one thinks, for example, of the Dreyfus Affair – it would be an extreme exaggeration to speak of a France devoured by resentment and a spirit of revenge that would somehow have favoured plunging into war. If one had to make sense of the assassination of Jean Jaurès even before he had clearly expressed his views on the impending war, one would have to say that it no doubt reflected the heating-up of spirits in the face of uncertainty, rather than the elimination of the last bulwark of peace by a bellicose consensus that had somehow armed the hand of that extreme-right crank, Raoul Villain. There are the most bizarre theories circulating about his death, including the German conspiracy.[13]

Even the question of Alsace Lorraine barely gave rise to any mobilisation. Gundula Bavendamm, for example, has shown in a recent work that before the conflict erupted there was hardly any except on the extreme fringes of French nationalism. Léon Daudet and the Action Française regarded the Alsatians, in an atmosphere poisoned from the very first days and weeks of the war by spy mania, more as potential spies than as French brothers to be saved from the clutches of the Germans.[14]

This does not mean, however, that France is a country of pacifists. Gerd Krumeich has demonstrated how animated the discussion was about three-year military service and Jakob Vogel has shown the extent to which military folklore – military festivals, parades etc. – became a key feature of the Third Republic, binding the masses together. The divisions that could cut across opinion were real and deep, and the opinions entrenched. At the end of July 1914 patriots and pacifists were again wrangling on the streets of the capital. On 27 July, syndicalists, socialists, anti-militarists and workers demonstrated. Two days later thousands of demonstrators waited at the station for President Raymond Poincaré to return from his trip to Russia and followed him, cheering, onto the streets.

On 1 August, L'Illustration, a high-circulation periodical, published more photographs of the demonstration to welcome the president and asked whether the looming conflict was going to remain a purely local affair or would spread out.[15] So above all it was surprise that dominated French emotions when the entry into the war was announced. Bear in mind at the time the public was preoccupied by the trial of Mme Caillaux, wife of the politician and president of the radical party, Joseph Cailllaux. It was front-page news and covered on a good many inside pages as well.[16]

So the feeling of surprise was the first to manifest itself and undoubtedly weighed on the atmosphere of the first days of war at least as much, if not more, than the longer trends of pacifism or revanchist bellicosity that could stir up certain sections of the population.[17] This feeling of surprise was followed by one of resignation, quickly succeeded by one of determination.[18] Thus Becker's conclusion was in accord with the observation made by the historian Marc Bloch: 'The picture presented by Paris during the first days of mobilisation remains one of my most beautiful memories of the war. The city was peaceful and rather solemn. The traffic was slow, the absence of buses and the scarcity of taxis made the streets almost silent. That sadness at the bottom of people's hearts did not overflow: it was just that many of the women's eyes were swollen and red. … Most of the men were not cheerful. They were resolute, which is more important.'[19] Another observer, the anarchist and soldier-writer Leon Werth, gave a fairly similar description of Paris: 'There was no sense of uprising in the Paris air. And the people in the street seemed to be without emotion. Those who were going to be soldiers did not dream of demonstrating on the streets. They said their farewells and spent 'one last evening'. They were going to war. This was enough to calm their imagination and steady them before an event so vast as to be beyond comprehension.'[20] While Pierre Mac Orlan noted: 'The soldiers were wearing blue cap bands. They spoke very little. Otherwise no one spoke at all.'[21] And this is how Etienne Létard described the small town of Senlis: 'Senlis is, perhaps, emotional, but well-balanced, untouched by the transports felt in cities that are young and powerful; and indeed, it has seen so many wars that one more is not going to make it tremble; besides, the place is humble and the population not very large. … On all the faces I admire courageous efforts to retain a perfect serenity.'[22] These examples show that even in large or medium-sized towns the feeling of seriousness was just as dominant as in the countryside where the 'Tocsin of the first of August, the tocsin heavy with suffering'[23] rang out. The tocsin is also at the heart of a poem by Adolphe Gysin, a future Breton soldier.[24]

These examples that resound with the bells of mobilisation echo the simple words of a Breton peasant-woman quoted by Jean-Jacques Becker, words that reflect the feelings aroused in the countryside by the sound of the tocsin: 'That is the knell sounding for our boys.'[25] They also show that not all intellectuals, some of whom really were war enthusiasts, lose their senses and see 1 August purely in terms of joy and enthusiasm, as Pierre Loti did: 'We sing the Marseillaise, we dance, we throw our hats in the air, we cry: to Berlin! We are almost delirious with joy and enthusiasm.'[26]

It must also be said that impressions could change from one hour to the next. It must have been particularly difficult for the witnesses, under the weight of emotion, to recapture their real impressions, and those of the people around them, to reconstruct those days of 1914 with the aid of language. In Loti's case, he evokes his own feelings just before describing the street scene quoted above: 'War! For two weeks now we have lived in anguish, waiting for it to come, but nonetheless with hope. And now this nightmare has become reality. And it will be a war of extermination, more atrocious than any we have ever seen.'[27] If, perhaps, the length of the wait (two weeks here) might be in doubt, the release of tension after it, and the anguish that followed, were certainly real, possibly amplified by news of the mobilisation of his son, Samuel, and of his imminent departure to join his regiment. So, one can perhaps understand how the enthusiasm and joy of the crowd was perceived as a sort of counterpoint – real or literary – to his own fears. Moreover, the places and situations into which the witnesses were tossed also had considerable influence on how they perceived things. Thus, François Porché, in a poem dedicated to the entry into the war, draws a distinction between those mobilised in the towns and in the countryside, finding the latter to be calmer.[28]

In an atmosphere of universal surprise, anguish, resignation, yet resolution, certain places inside the towns could themselves give way to demonstrations of momentary patriotic enthusiasm, for example crossroads, cafés or once again stations, even though, in general, the distinction put forward by Porché was, perhaps, exaggerated. Victor Boudon, for example, describes the departure of a train: 'Soon the train packed with youth bubbling with enthusiasm sets off surrounded by cries of joy.'[29]

But he says nothing of the other noises also resounding at the moment of departure. It is also true that some German shops, or shops thought to be German such as those of Maggi, the Swiss brand, were attacked, ransacked and looted. According to a widespread rumour, Maggi's advertisements for its stock cubes represented a particularly cunning means of espionage. They were thought to contain information for the German army in some sort of secret code.[30] So they were systematically destroyed. The mixture of rumours – another sign of distress – and genuine information, which, as Marc Bloch observed, was a constant feature during the war,[31] further added to the confusion and made it even more difficult for the witnesses to do justice to the emotional kaleidoscope of the first days of the war.

Moreover, these sometimes contradictory emotions could evolve with the passing of time, day by day, virtually hour by hour. Pierre Loti, who wrote on 1 August of his distress, which contrasted with the enthusiasm on the streets, says the next day that a disconcerting calm reigned in the house and on the street: 'And, in the end, this excessive calm is horrible, it bodes ill, it disconcerts you and weighs you down. We would have preferred agitation, cries, fusillades.'[32] On the following day he goes by train to La Rochelle to take leave of his son who is going off to the front. The train is packed with soldiers and reservists: 'Everyone is singing. All along the route … women come running up with flags to salute the train as it passes by. At La Rochelle, in the artillery quarter, indescribable crowds and disorder. … One might say a town having a great celebration. The quays are packed with reservists and sailors.'[33] On 8 March, he writes that he and his family live day and night with the distress of this horrible war of extermination, and this despite the fact that his son has not yet left, and despite the good news that Mulhouse has been taken and the first British troops have arrived. He would have liked to set off as a reserve officer, but clearly he is not wanted: 'This inaction and this waiting get on your nerves! On the other hand, the town of La Rochelle still has its "air of celebration".'[34]

Another witness, Jacques Brunel de Pérard, who went off to war, wrote on 7 August, the day of his departure, that this day was one 'of serious matters' and he wrote in his notebook: 'I have been to confession and have made my will.'[35]

A week later, the news is certainly not good: 'A fifteenth of August gloomy and oppressive. We live in anguished anticipation of the great battle.'[36] Morale remains generally low until 8 September, when the first news of the Battle of the Marne starts to arrive. This gradual evolution of morale and feelings, with all its variations, is also mentioned by Jean-Jacques Becker in his study. For the witnesses it was undoubtedly difficult to reconstruct this tumult of emotions after the event, or even at the time. This tumult can, in part, explain how, in the confusion of feelings, enthusiasm ultimately subsumed all the other emotions. All the more so since certain intellectual milieux that exerted great influence on the war narrative were genuinely enthusiastic and projected their personal feelings onto the population at large. Thus an enthusiasm typical of these intellectual milieux, projected onto the narratives and poems, was able to compete with critical and refined observation of the real feelings before the entry into the war. For a while the representations oscillate between these two poles, for it falls to the intellectual minority, often genuinely enthusiastic, to paint the collective picture of the start of the war. The poet Paul Géraldy is well aware of this tension. He describes the difference in mood between his father and himself: 'Going off to war. I was very excited. He was not, but calm as usual.'[37]

There is all the difference in the world between an already elderly man who stays behind and knows he has nothing to do but wait for the return – or death – of his son, who perhaps, as a child, has lived through the war of 1870, and the enthusiasm of an intellectual, even though, at nearly thirty years of age, he himself is no longer a fiery adolescent.

But on the other hand this confusion does not explain why it was enthusiasm, and not some other feeling like determination, for example, that was to dominate descriptions of the first days of the war for such a long time. The reasons are to be found in the functions that this sort of narrative could assume. But before we come to that, we also need to ask ourselves about the way in which this paradigm prevailed.

How the Paradigm of Collective Enthusiasm Crystallised and Prevailed as a Discourse on the Entry into the War

This is a well-known fact: the modern mass media played an important role in the crystallisation and diffusion of French collective enthusiasm. We all remember the photographs and films of departing soldiers – where they are singing, flowers in their guns. The graffiti on the trains taking soldiers to the front, likewise photographed, also nurture this idea.

Articles in the daily press did just as much to fix the idea of enthusiasm in the collective memory, after the war years, which at the same time gave them a symbolic value – one unique photograph was felt to represent the entire entry into the war – and disseminated the idea amongst a broad public. Since then academic and literary works have often taken up this idea again and have played their part in its long-term dissemination. Even amongst the witnesses one can sometimes perceive a slow – or indeed quick – evolution of feelings about the entry into the war, at the same rate as the event became more distant, or because the context weighed the witness down. A particularly striking instance of this is that of the soldier-writer – and later deputy – André Fribourg.

On 4 August, as his regiment is about to depart, he tries to keep a faithful record of his impressions and the atmosphere of the moment, from hour to hour. Thus he writes at 3 PM: 'How serious and resolute they are!' Half an hour later, still: 'No clashes, no cries.' It is not until the evening, around 6:30, that: 'Enthusiasm swelled in our hearts, deep, instinctive, unreflected, almost wild.' And that: 'Others are singing solemnly, religiously.'[38]

Even when he seeks to evoke the enthusiasm, it is 'deep', and manifests itself in solemn and religious songs; so it does not differ at all from his initial impressions. When he published his notebook in 1917 he added a preface which gives the impression that he had not re-read the text itself. Indeed he now sees the entry into the war in a completely different way, strongly influenced by the ready-made formulae about the enthusiasm of the early days. The emphatic, even bombastic style actually reveals the stereotype behind the formula: 'This was the hour of sublime enthusiasm where we suffered … the pain and anguish of departure founded on moral splendour and immense hope.'[39]

The three war years between the entry into the war and its re-interpretation in the preface have already fixed the idea of enthusiasm. The idea seems to have been so strong that it is as if he had forgotten he had lived through these events himself. The same applies to Jean Galtier-Boissière, who after the war recalls above all the 'fleur au fusil', though at the time he actually remarked: 'All along the path the women of the district were crying on the doorsteps.'[40]

So this topos of collective enthusiasm had already become entrenched during the war. It must be said that it fitted in well with that of the Union Sacrée.[41] But this is not enough to explain everything, because determination could have fitted in with it just as well. During the conflict and just after it the two ideas sometimes still cohabited, even merged in one and the same work, one and the same description. Thus in his second war novel, *Clarté*, published in 1919, Henri Barbusse evokes a 'surge of enthusiasm and determination'.[42]

At the start of the war, during the conflict, even just after it, these two discourses were not necessarily mutually exclusive. Determination was still present as well, because it was likewise a means of expressing a patriotic discourse:

that of defending the fatherland in the face of the German invasion and the need to do one's duty. Thus Antoine Rédier wrote in 1916: 'I serve my country. I am at my post, in my correct place. It is good. If I am killed I will have done my duty.'[43] Other semantic fields are associated with enthusiasm. It is certainly not incompatible with the idea of duty or with the defensive dimension – so essential during the war – of patriotic combat. It always means something else as well.

One function of enthusiasm, for example, can be to symbolise the collective experience, the spontaneous response to the surprise entry into the war. For the soldier-writer André Pavie, this enthusiasm was even a way of proclaiming victory. In terms of mobilisation and the entry into the war it did indeed evoke an 'atmosphere of triumphant gaiety'.[44] In a way, the supposed enthusiasm for war was already a precursor of the enthusiasm that was to take hold of the victors of that war. It also represented a sort of threshold, entry into another era that was very soon to be called the 'Great War'. Guillaume Apollinaire expresses this feeling very well in 'La petite auto', a poem about the entry into the war, which is, quite rightly, often quoted.[45] The upheaval caused by the collective emotion about entry into the war also made it possible to present the 'Union Sacrée' not as a political calculation or a deal between political parties, but as if it emanated from the people themselves.

All these dimensions make enthusiasm into a performative representation that can explain how it was able to establish itself so quickly, even during the war. In the specific case of war literature the soldier-writers added another dimension, that of the enthusiasm, in this case genuine, of intellectuals who mobilised for war.[46] Before trying to understand why and how representation of collective enthusiasm for war prevailed once again in the post-war period, even though its functions had largely ceased to exist, we must now take a closer look at another form of enthusiasm, this time individual.

From Collective to Individual Enthusiasm: Voluntary Enlistment and its Construction in Literature

It was, perhaps, Ernst Jünger who best summed up the dual dimension, both ideological and actual, of voluntary enlistment, when he wrote that to enlist was, ultimately, to melt into a 'great body burning with enthusiasm'.[47] He invites us to compare this with the French case.

More prosaically, the war littérateurs sometimes resorted to pre-dating their enlistment so that they could try to portray the entry into the war. My research amongst a fairly large number of enlisted men[48] has shown, in fact, that the proportion of French soldier-writers who enlisted voluntarily is around 15 per cent.[49] What is more, this act was immediately reflected in the literature and even in the press, where it was sometimes justified by intellectuals who were already famous, and who commented on their enlistment, knowing the effect it would have on public opinion. All the more so if they were too old or debilitated and should have stayed behind. Jean Cocteau, for example, was rejected on several occasions for being too unfit, yet he eventually joined the Red Cross and was sent to the front as a nurse.

So voluntary enlistment is sometimes presented as entry into the war par excellence by the intellectuals, who thereby also demonstrate political commitment. In addition, there is the particular case of foreigners who enlist for France, even if, according to one of them, the American poet Alan Seeger, 'little is known about their case'.[50] This generally refers to foreigners who have committed themselves to the service of France, such people as Guillaume Apollinaire and Blaise Cendrars, of course, but also the Italian Ricciotto Canudo, the American Alan Seeger and the Swiss Gustave Binet-Valmer. Evocation of foreign volunteers serves, of course, to highlight the universality of the French cause when confronted by an enemy uniquely motivated by particular interests. Proof of a 'pure love of France',[51] this was also to become proof of the greatness of its cause.

As early as 29 July, Blaise Cendrars, Ricciotto Canudo, Jacques Lipschitz and their foreign artist friends publish a manifesto which says nothing else; in an outburst almost premonitory for Cendrars, they call on the foreigners to 'open their arms' for their 'second fatherland' and to regroup into a 'solid bunch of wills dedicated to serving France'.[52] From 3 August Canudo and Cendrars match their words by their deeds and sign up. Their will does not falter when they have to confirm their enlistment, which they do definitively a month to the day later. All in all, almost eighty-eight thousand foreigners follow in their footsteps.

Those intellectuals who enlisted utilised diverse justification strategies. Henri Barbusse,[53] born in 1873, already belonged to the world of letters, due as much to the esteem earned by the books he had written as to his bourgeois marriage to Hélyonne, the daughter of one of the princes of letters of the day, Catulle Mendès. He enlists on 2 August and a week later he writes an open letter, which has since become famous, to the editor of *l'Humanité*. The periodical publishes it on 9 August 1914:

> Please count me among the anti-militarist socialists who are enlisting voluntarily in the present war. ... This war is a social war which will take our cause a great step, perhaps the definitive step, forward. It is directed against our old enemies ... : militarism and imperialism, the sword, the jackboot and, I would add, the crown. Our victory will be the destruction of the main den of caesars, Kronprinzen, lords and old soldiers who imprison one people and would like to imprison others. The world can only emancipate itself by opposing them. If I sacrifice my life, and if I go joyfully to war, it is not only as a Frenchman, but above all as a human being.

As a preamble Barbusse takes care to site his enlistment within his own militant context. Thus he confirms that he is not renouncing his commitment, and then explains how it is that his physical enlistment in the conflict is a quite logical step. He thereby rejects in advance any possible reproaches that pacifists might make. He goes on to describe the war as 'social', thereby superimposing patriotic imperatives on social and political struggles: to promote social justice and democracy. In the second part of the piece Barbusse already uses images and expressions which correspond to the war culture that was about to emerge. He emphasises the fact that he has enlisted physically, not just intellectually, and that he is prepared, in the most classical of nationalist rhetoric, to 'sacrifice his life joyfully'. He portrays the enemy by enumerating derogatory terms and by oxymorons linking the 'old soldiers' to 'princes'. The aim is clear: 'destruction of the den of thieves' which will liberate the Germans willingly or by force, and which should, above all, free the whole world from the cruel ambitions of the Germans. The last phrase, which could be understood as humanist engagement going beyond patriotism, can also be read as the engagement of a human being against inhumanity, against those who are not human: the enemies. Subsequently, during the war, without ever renouncing the ultimate goal expressed in this text, in which he never doubts, Barbusse modifies his positions, making them less nationalist, always insisting on the moral and humanist imperative of his action; but he could never be described as a pacifist, at least not until 1918. He never renounces his enlistment of 14 August, even though he removes it to the context of mobilisation.

The evolution of the discourse on enlistment during the war reveals a progressive slide towards the point where it no longer represents the individual and deliberate enlistment of an intellectual, but is the product of an alienating context, a shift which presages a change in the enthusiasm itself. Thus, though enlistment more or less goes without saying in 1914, this is no longer the case later on. This evolution is often no longer the consequence of pacifist condemnation of the war, but of a realisation of the intellectual's specific role in society. Yet this fact is rarely discussed. Individual doubts sometimes emerge and find expression in the correspondence. Guillaume Apollinaire who said in his poem 'A Nîmes' that he 'enlisted under the most beautiful of skies',[54] writes to his friend Jean Mollet on 3 January 1915: 'It is not our business to wage war or the human spirit will be gone. There was war throughout the 17th century, but Corneille, Racine, Malherbe did not fight, nor did Pascal or Bossuet. We do our duty just as well as the others, but it really should be elsewhere. To each, his own.' Apollinaire does not, however, completely renounce his act of enlisting. The one who moves the furthest away from his position at the start of the war, and with the greatest lucidity, is undoubtedly Léon Werth. He notes: 'One could say that the war spontaneously creates the ideas it needs.'[55] Amongst these particular 'ideas', he gives pride of place to that of enemy aggression. In an extremely powerful way, this allows both actual and figurative mobilisation of both body and soul, and gives them immediate entry into an interior relationship with the war. By consenting to this binary representation of reality, of a world divided between agressees and aggressors, the man at war implicitly accepts in advance the only real fault-line of that war, and undoubtedly of all wars, the one between himself and his enemy. Publishing as a pacifist in 1919, Werth exposes himself a posteriori to criticism of the ideas dominant in 1914, criticism which takes on the tone of the pamphlet against 'les nouveaux doctrinaires du catholicisme et de la patrie': against Maurice Barrès, described as a 'delirious old man' 'in an asylum'.[56] But, in a second movement, he admits that the most widespread 'ideas' of the 'earth and the dead', of the syncretic fusion of patriotism and religion, of the theme of small fatherlands, of the peoples' spirit, are those that prevailed in August 1914 and functioned like a well-oiled machine. It is only afterwards 'while reading and writing', that one might be tempted to add that the writer turned pacifist perceives how the idea of the fatherland and that of aggression mutually nourish one another, and how 'the idea of the fatherland ... legitimises war'.[57] Unlike many of his colleagues who constantly reconstructed the war, hiding their own consent and that of those like them, or conveniently replacing it with enthusiasm or the peoples' universal deception, Leon Werth, bitter, lucid and disillusioned 'questions, himself, his own consent and, over and above this, the intellectual's enlistment for a cause'.

But finally it is perhaps a young German poet who provides the key to understanding why enthusiasm has remained intact in the master narrative of the entry into the war, created, amongst other authorised narratives, by the soldier-intellectuals. The experience of the young expressionist poet Rudolf Leonhard[58] is exemplary in this respect. Once the war has started he publishes a collection of patriotic poems and matches his deeds to his words by enlisting like his friend Walter Hasenclever. In 1919, now ranked alongside the spartacists, he publishes a collection that regroups his war poems. He does not wipe out his enlistment and his patriotic poems from his biography, but tries to justify them a posteriori in order to give meaning to his biography. The volume was already largely complete in 1917 and was not published until after the war. In August 1917 he writes a preface to the collection:

> There is only one aim in all this, to confess a bad conscience. There are a certain number of poems from the first phase, republished for the first time since then, which I would no longer write, which I could no longer write, and which I regret having written.

> From a certain point of view I don't think this is inexcusable. Until then, a sentimental sceptic, I had not bothered much with politics. When war was declared, I didn't know the political situation. I assessed it wrongly. I was not easily-influenced, but naive.[59]

This preface is a perfect illustration of the autobiographical reconstruction, not always confessed so openly, with which we are confronted. Within a relatively short time, but a time marked by brutal chronological caesuras (entry into the war, victory, defeat …), these ruptures oblige individuals to take a stance and, in elaborating on their personal stories, to return to historical events that may have become biographical wounds and then scars. So after the war voluntary enlistment was turned on its head: a sign of consent during the conflict, it was transformed into a sign of naivety and manipulation of the masses. The youth, real or supposed, of those involved authorises this seesaw effect. Many of these life stories were re-worked in the period after 1918 and reveal something that became an easy-to-use archetype: enlistment, disillusionment in the trenches, pacifism, a reconstructed biographical model, which leaves little room for understanding the motives behind enlistment in the context of 1914. On the other hand it allows us to recognise how, in these individual and collective biographies, it was possible to re-invest enthusiasm with new meaning after the conflict.

The Meaning of Enthusiasm in the Post-war Period and the Reasons why it Prevailed: Some Hypotheses

As I have shown, the fact that enthusiasm endured and prevailed could be attributed quite simply to projection. The intellectuals, particularly the soldier-writers whose narratives, due to their presence at the front line, had become the authorised ones[60] and who were regarded as entitled to talk about the war, had projected their own enthusiasm – sometimes translated into voluntary enlistment – onto society as a whole. Yet this explanation is undoubtedly incomplete since it does not explain why, in the long-run, the idea of enthusiasm endured, even when the initial enthusiasm of the authorised narratives had disappeared or disintegrated, and especially considering that in any case it had only existed up to a point. What is more, once the war was over, it no longer had to fulfil the political functions related to the context of the war.

Nonetheless, it survived and took root. I would suggest that the reasons are to be found in the state of mind of French society in the post-war period. Antoine Prost, in his thesis dedicated to former soldiers in French society, has demonstrated that most of them were inspired by a principal pacifism, which was not necessarily militant but was also not incompatible with patriotism.[61] In this context, in order to be preserved, the enthusiasm of the start of the war had to be invested with new meaning, which would be compatible with the state of mind that was to become widespread throughout French society. It really is this re-investment that made it possible to preserve the representation of the start of the war as a moment of enthusiasm, a version that triumphed over all others, effacing, for instance, the idea of determination, which during the war sometimes competed with that of enthusiasm, while at others it was its concomitant.

After the war, enthusiasm, which had, amongst other things, served to signify the consent of the various populations to the war,[62] now did the reverse, obliterated it. At the time, it was easier to attribute collective enthusiasm, like individual voluntary enlistment, to a passing feeling of exultation, essentially motivated by external causes – the release of built-up tension, for instance – than to political manipulation that was particularly successful at the start of the war, but which would have been exposed in due course. Now, in its new pacifist connotation, enthusiasm was attributed to the naivety of a people manipulated by its elites. This version of the facts coincides with the one Romain Rolland has already put forward in *Au-dessus de la mêlée*. He excuses the enthusiasm of the young people who enlisted, but blames the elites – religious, political, intellectual – who, according to him, incited them to it. Romain Rolland's famous article opens, in fact, with these words: 'O young men that shed your blood with so generous a joy for the starving earth! O heroism of the world! What a harvest for destruction to reap under this splendid summer sun.'[63] A little later on he addresses the people's elites, to accuse them:

> Let us be bold and proclaim the truth to the elders of these young men, to their moral guides, to their religious and secular leaders, to the Churches, the great thinkers, the leaders of socialism. ... What ideal have you held up to the devotion of these youths so eager to sacrifice themselves? Their mutual slaughter! A European war! A sacrilegious conflict which shows a maddened Europe ascending its funeral pyre, and, like Hercules, destroying itself with its own hands.[64]

Thus in this type of account enthusiasm is disconnected from all consent. Rather it wipes out consent to the war by reducing it to blindness when the war started. The reason for the success of this paradigm is surely to be found here. Fundamentally, enthusiasm exculpates, because it rejects responsibility for the war except on the part of a few members of the elites. It makes it possible to say that the masses were, perhaps, naive, but were not responsible for the great carnage. This version perfectly suited French society in the inter-war period because it was in keeping with both its preserved patriotism and its post-war pacifism. Without doubt, this exculpatory aspect also explains why it is still often present in popular culture, despite Jean-Jacques Becker's revision. In the hour when the 'victims' have become the central figures in Western societies,[65] it is easier to see the 'poilus' as 'victims' of their own naivety, of their enthusiasm and of their elites, than as actors playing a full part in an atrocious conflict.

Conclusion

So, Jean-Jacques Becker's thesis, which revisited the idea of French war enthusiasm, was doubly subversive. The myth of collective enthusiasm was, in fact, a Janus-head. Becker's work was surprising, firstly, because it showed that the supposed nationalism of the French did not lead to their enthusiasm for entry into the war. In fact it relativised both pre-war nationalism and collective enthusiasm with the same epistemological stroke. The initial response to his work underlined this aspect without seeing that it was calling into question not just enthusiasm as a statement of fact, but also as an element in a 'master narrative' of the conflict. Indeed, by demonstrating the determination of the French to defend themselves against 'aggression', it opened up new perspectives which were not pursued until later, when the question of the soldiers' 'consent'[66] to the war was posed and debated.

In this context, the aim of this chapter was not to revise Becker's revision, but rather to try, by means of quasi-genealogical research, to return to the origins of the myth and its triumph before, during and after the war. This reflexive dimension applied to one of the numerous master narratives of the war also calls for international comparisons, specifically of the genesis and development of these master narratives.

Notes

1. Jean-Jacques Becker, *1914, Comment les Français sont entrés dans la guerre* (Paris, 1977). For the author and his influence on historiography see Stéphane Audoin-Rouzeau et al. (eds.), *La politique et la guerre. Pour comprendre le XXe siècle européen. Hommage à Jean-Jacques Becker* (Paris, 2002).
2. Nicolas Beaupré, *Ecrire en guerre, écrire la guerre. France-Allemagne 1914-1920* (Paris, 2006).
3. This expression is also the one chosen in 1928 by Jean Galtier-Boissière, soldier-writer and editor of the journal *Le Crapouillot*. See Jean Galtier-Boissière, *La fleur au fusil* (Paris, 1928).
4. Antoine Prost and Jay M. Winter, *Penser la Grande Guerre. Un essai historiographique* (Paris, 2004), 213.
5. Ibid.
6. Gerd Krumeich, *Aufrüstung und Innenpolitik in Frankreich vor dem Ersten Weltkrieg* (Wiesbaden, 1980). English translation: Krumeich, *Armaments and Politics in France on the Eve of the First World War* (Leamington, 1985). Jakob Vogel, *Nationen im Gleichschritt. Der Kult der 'Nation in Waffen' in Deutschland und Frankreich (1871–1914)* (Göttingen, 1997).
7. Thomas Raithel, *Das Wunder der inneren Einheit, Studien zur deutschen und französischen Öffentlichkeit bei Beginn des Ersten Weltkrieges* (Bonn, 1996).
8. Christian Geinitz, *Kriegsfurcht und Kampfbereitschaft. Das Augusterlebnis in Freiburg. Eine Studie zum Kriegsbeginn 1914* (Essen, 1998); Jeffrey Verhey, *The 'Spirit of 1914':*

Militarism, Enthusiasm and Myth in Germany 1914–1945 (Cambridge, 2000). See also Gerhard Hirschfeld's essay in this volume.

9. Benoit Majerus, 'La guerre commence – Bruxelles en août 1914 et en mai 1940', in Nicolas Beaupré, Anne Duménil and Christian Ingrao (eds.), *L'ère de la guerre*, vol. 1: *Violence, mobilisations, deuil (1914–1918)* (Paris, 2004), 85–106.

10. Hew Strachan, *The First World War*, vol 1: *To Arms!* (Oxford, 2001). For other examples see Prost and Winter, *Penser la Grande Guerre*.

11. For the soldier-writers and the construction of their entitlement to talk about the war see Beaupré, *Ecrire et combattre*; Almut Lindner-Wirsching, *Französische Schriftsteller und ihre Nation im Ersten Weltkrieg* (Tübingen, 2004).

12. Gerd Krumeich has shown that in the German language there is a subtle, but vital, difference between the terms *Begeisterung* and *Enthusiasmus* which can be applied to how people felt about the entry into the war. This distinction does not really exist in French. See Gerd Krumeich, "Gott mit uns!' La Grande Guerre fut-elle une guerre de religions?' in Beaupré, Duménil and Ingrao (eds.), *L'ère de la guerre*, 117–130.

13. Becker, *1914*, 246–247.

14. Gundula Bavendamm, *Spionnage und Verrat. Konspirative Kriegserzählungen und französische Innenpolitik, 1914–1917* (Essen, 2004), 52–70.

15. *L'Illustration*, Saturday, 1 August 1914.

16. Becker, *1914*, 131–134.

17. There is still no new and serious study specifically dedicated to the memory of the 1870–71 war that might verify this. On this subject see the already rather outdated work by Claude Digeon, *La crise allemande de la pensée française 1870–1914* (Paris, 1959); and more recently Wolfgang Schiwelbusch, *Die Kultur der Niederlage. Der amerikanische Süden 1865, Frankreich 1871, Deutschland 1918* (Berlin, 2001).

18. This is the essence of Becker's thesis.

19. Marc Bloch, 'Souvenirs de guerre' in Bloch, *L'Histoire, la Guerre, la Résistance* (Paris, 2006), 119–120.

20. Léon Werth, *Clavel soldat* (Paris, 1919; reprinted 1993), 28–30.

21. Pierre Mac Orlan, *Les Poissons morts, la Lorraine, l'Artois, Verdun, la Somme* (Paris, 1917), 19.

22. Etienne Létard, *Trois mois au premier corps de cavalerie* (Paris, 1919), 3–4.

23. Max Begouën, *Quelques poèmes à la gloire de l'armée française* (Toulouse, 1917), 9.

24. Adolphe Gysin, *Jusqu'à la Marne, Bataille de la Marne* (Landerneau, 1916), 7.

25. Becker, *1914*, 295.

26. Pierre Loti, *Soldats bleus. Journal intime 1914–1918* (Paris, 1998), 39. Entry for 1 August 1914. At that time he is in the provinces, in the little town of Rochefort, not far from La Rochelle.

27. Ibid.

28. François Porché, *L'arrêt sur la Marne* (Paris, 1916), 41–43.

29. Victor Boudon, *Avec Charles Péguy, De la Lorraine à la Marne, Août-Septembre 1914* (Paris, 1916), 6.

30. Bavendamm, *Spionage und Verrat*, 53–57; Becker, *1914*, 505–513.

31. Marc Bloch, 'Réflexions d'un historien sur les fausses nouvelles de la guerre', ibid.

32. Pierre Loti, 'Le chant du départ', in Loti, *Soldats bleus*, 42.

33. Ibid., entry for 3 August.

34. Ibid., entry for 8 August, 42–43.

35. Jacques Brunel de Pérard, *Carnet de route* (Paris, 1915), 26.

36. Loti, *Soldats bleus*, entry for 15 August, 43.

37. Paul Géraldy, *La Guerre, Madame* ... (Paris, 1916), 77.
38. André Fribourg, *Croire. Histoire d'un soldat* (Paris, 1917), 37–40.
39. Ibid., 9.
40. Jean Galtier-Boissière, *En rase campagne. 1914. Un hiver à Souchez. 1915–1916* (Paris, 1917), 3–4, 293.
41. Raithel, *Das Wunder.*
42. Henri Barbusse, *Clarté* (Paris, 1978, first edition 1919), 97.
43. Antoine Rédier, *Méditations dans la tranchée* (Paris, 1916), 1.
44. André Pavie, *Mes troupiers* (Tours, 1917), 6.
45. Guillaume Apollinaire, 'La petite auto', in *Calligrammes,* in *Œuvres poétiques* (Paris, 1965), 207, and notes 1085–1086. The poem was most probably written at speed during the night of 31 July–1 August 1914.
46. Christophe Prochasson and Anne Rasmussen, *Au nom de la Patrie. Les intellectuels et la Première Guerre mondiale (1910–1919)* (Paris, 1996); Martha Hanna, *The Mobilization of Intellect, French Scholars and Writers during the Great War* (Cambridge, MA, 1996).
47. Ernst Jünger, *Orages d'acier* (Paris, 1970; first edition, Hannover, 1920), 14.
48. This is taken, in part, from my thesis: Nicolas Beaupré, *Ecrire en guerre...*, see esp. chap. 1.
49. From 239 reconstructed biographies of soldier-writers I have been able to establish that 35 enlisted voluntarily. Given that it is not always possible to know for certain, if the deed is not specifically mentioned, the proportion is undoubtedly somewhat greater. My comparative study of the German solder-writers produced a similar proportion.
50. Alan Seeger, *Alan Seeger, le poète de la Légion étrangère* (Paris, 1918), 26.
51. Anonymous preface to Alan Seeger, 10.
52. Quoted by Miriam Cendrars, *Blaise Cendrars* (Paris, 1984), 280f.
53. Henri Barbusse has been the subject of numerous books, for example: Philippe Baudorre, *Barbusse, le pourfendeur de la Grande Guerre* (Paris, 1995); Jean Relinger, *Henri Barbusse écrivain combattant* (Paris, 1994).
54. Apollinaire, *Calligrammes,* 211.
55. Werth, *Clavel soldat,* 28–29.
56. Ibid.
57. Ibid.
58. See his unedited autobiographical notes of 1917, DLA, A: Dresdner Verlag.
59. Rudolf Leonhard, *Das Chaos* (Hannover, 1919), 1–2: 'So hat dieses hier keinen anderen Zweck als den, ein böses Gewissen zu bekennen. Es hebt sich vor einigen Gedichten des ersten hier wieder abgedruckten Zyklus' Gedichten, die ich nicht mehr schreiben würde, schreiben könnte, und die geschrieben zu haben ich bedaure. In einer Hinsicht glaube ich nicht unentschuldigt zu sein: ich hatte mich, bis dahin ein empfindsamer Skeptiker, nur ausnahmsweise mit Politik abgegeben; ich kannte bei Kriegsausbruch die politische Lage nicht, ich sah sie falsch, und war nicht beeinflussbar, aber leichtgläubig.'
60. On this aspect see, for the case of Germany, Wolfgang G. Natter, *Literature at War. 1914–1940. Representing the 'Time of Greatness' in Germany* (New Haven/London, 1999); and on the legitimacy of these new authors Nicolas Beaupré, 'New Writers, New Literary Genres (1914–1918): The Contribution of Historical Comparatism (France, Germany)', in Pierre Purseigle (ed.), *Warfare and Belligerence. Perspectives in First World War Studies* (Leyden, 2005), 323–346.
61. Antoine Prost, *Les anciens combattants et la société française,* 3 vols. (Paris, 1977).

62. Annette Becker and Stéphane Audoin-Rouzeau, 'Violence et consentement: la "culture de guerre" du premier conflit mondial', in Jean-Pierre Rioux and Jean-François Sirinelli (eds.), *Pour une histoire culturelle* (Paris 1997), 251–271.

63. Romain Rolland, 'Au-dessus de la mêlée' (15 September 1914), in Rolland, *Au-dessus de la mêlée* (Paris, 1915), 21, quote after the English translation by Charles Kay Ogden, *Above the Battle* (Chicago, 1916), S.37.

64. Ibid., 40–41.

65. Jean-Michel Chaumont, *La concurrence des victimes: Génocide, identité, reconnaissance* (Paris, 1997).

66. The debate amongst historians, sometimes heated, has now arrived in the public space, as is shown by Jean Birnbaum's two articles, '1914–1918, guerre de tranchées entre historiens' and "Au cœur de la mêlée, l'enjeu des témoignages', *Le Monde,* 10 March 2006.

5

The Mood in Britain in 1914

Hartmut Pogge von Strandmann

Recent historical scholarship has put Britain's decision to join the war in 1914 under renewed scrutiny. The question as to whether the mood of the British people in July and early August 1914 forced the liberal government into war or whether it was the government which, by its decisions, influenced the mood in Britain has occupied publicists and historians for the last ninety years.[1] Contemporary British politicians were well aware of the fact that a war could not easily be declared if public opinion was set against it and ultimately a cabinet would have had to resign if this gap could not have been bridged. As public opinion polls did not yet exist, the assumption about the public mood was largely based on press reports which themselves relied on speeches, sermons, demonstrations and other gatherings as well as interviews. That these press reports and a variety of related articles in turn influenced the public was well-known to politicians who were also aware of the fact that the journalists tried to express what they assumed their readers liked to see/read, guided by what they called their instinctive feelings. A leading liberal politician, Reginald McKenna, told the editor of *The Times*, Geoffrey Dawson, early on 2 August 1914 that the government was in a difficult position as it was powerless 'unless the people are behind them and the people are against war'.[2] However some politicians exploited the public in a different way. When the chancellor, Lloyd George, moved to back the war on the evening of 2 August, he told Walter Runciman, then president of the Board of Agriculture, that 'he had enough of standing out against a war-inflamed populace'.[3] Now it was a belligerent public which was going to force the cabinet's hand. Thus Foreign Secretary Grey, who was very sensitive to public opinion, said in looking back some months after the outbreak of the war: 'One of his strongest feelings [had been] that he himself had no power to decide policy and was only the mouthpiece of England.'[4] Grey's assertion was shared by Lloyd George, who after the war justified the cabinet's decision to go to war by referring to 'warlike crowds demonstrating for war against Germany whilst the cabinet was deliberating on the alternative of peace or war'.[5] This is not to say that the decision for war was made in the streets of Westminster but it may indicate how much politicians like to react to and occasionally hide behind or even invent popular attitudes regardless of whether they had really been swayed by the public or not.

So what do we know about the public's reaction to the threat of war? And how did the press reflect or manipulate the mood of the people? Recent research has shown that the so-called 'August enthusiasm' can no longer be taken as a given fact.[6] A very differentiated picture has emerged which has ranged from opposition, rejection, scepticism and unwillingness on the one hand to some sort of excited reaction on the other. The interaction between public opinion, the press and the politicians has proven to be much more complex than the old pronounced adage: 'The newspapers got us into war'.[7] In the case of Britain, as in other countries, special attention has to be paid to chronology, social groups and regions. A distinction has to be made between the pre-war mood and the public reaction after war had been declared. There is also a brief transitory period of short duration which has been specifically investigated and which may be the key to the development of popular attitudes in Britain just before and immediately after 4 August when Britain had declared war against Germany.

Obviously there is, so to speak, a give and take between the press and public opinion. The press often reported public mood swings, but on other occasions newspaper articles helped to create and foster public reactions. In any case the editors would see to it that the leader articles would express opinions which they believed their readership would like to read. The crude yardstick for this editorial policy was the sales success of the paper. The chance to boost these figures was generally welcomed. And news about a pending war in which Britain might be involved provided a business opportunity not easily to be missed. However there was no room for cheap sensationalism in this respect. The campaign of the radical press objecting to Britain's involvement in a European war saw to that.

For the historian there is a dynamic field to study which is marked by public opinion, the influence of the press and the reactions and initiatives of the policy makers. The picture which has emerged in the recent historical literature so far no longer supports the impression of a public keen on war. There were papers and political groups which pressed for British intervention, but there was also vociferous opposition. It was only after 4 August that war seems to have become more widely accepted. Yet there remained an influential minority which had objected to being stampeded into the war by Prime Minister Herbert Henry Asquith and Foreign Secretary Grey and which founded a new peace organisation, the Union of Democratic Control.[8] The Radicals firmly believed that the Liberal-Imperialist government had acted dishonourably, and thanks to the Grey-Asquith-axis too little was done to restrain Russia and France, let alone Germany. Accordingly, Parliament and cabinet were not properly consulted and the public not well-informed.[9]

It is generally assumed that the improvement of Anglo-German diplomatic relations after 1911, known as détente, was also reflected in British press reports. Generally speaking this may have been the case; however there were several areas where anti-German articles appeared unabated. Panikos Panayi has demonstrated that hostile opinions against Germans in Britain had existed for some time and continued to be published, although the concerns about the German navy tended to ease after 1912.[10] Germans living in England had been accused of acting 'as spies in the service of the enemy', for some time, an accusation which was upheld after 1911.[11] German clerks had been accused of stealing economic and technical details before the turn of the century. This economic hostility changed after the South African War when papers such as the National Review under Leo Maxse targeted all Germans living in Britain and accused them of working for the Kaiser and the overthrow of the British state. Leo Maxse belonged to a group of MPs and journalists who disliked Germany and were also strong anti-semites. During the First World War he attacked Jews because they worked for 'our German enemies'. There is no need to go into further detail about the link of anti-Germanism to anti-semitism and to a German Hidden Hand which tried to control Britain. But from this rather vague criticism it was only a small step to the accusation that Germans and Germany were spying and becoming involved in general and especially military espionage once the political and naval rivalries had become more serious. By 1900 the *Daily Mail* had for example decided that all spies in England were now German.[12] Despite protestations from more reasonable people spy and invasion mania gripped the reading public in England to an astonishing extent. But it must be added here that it was especially the *Daily Mail* which was preoccupied with the idea of a German threat right from its founding days. It displayed animosity towards the Germans during the Boer War in reciprocity to German Anglophobia during that time. After the end of the South African conflict the paper warned its readers: 'England will never forget the [hostile] attitude of the German people during the Boer War.'[13] The paper's warnings against Germany led it to focus on the construction of a German battle fleet: the Germans 'do not conceal what they intend to do with that fleet when occasion serves. Great Britain is to be overthrown'.[14] Spy mania, threat of invasion and a direct German naval menace made a heady mixture which had its effects on the British reading public. The *Daily Chronicle* warned its readers not to exaggerate the German threat by pointing out: 'Jingo journals of the baser sort have frankly given themselves over to the now familiar game of making the impressible Englishman's flesh creep with sensational stories of German invasion.'[15]

The German concern of some newspapers like the *Daily Mail* is well-documented. It sometimes even amounted to an obsession with Germany. What is less well-known are the books written about a perceived German threat, a German invasion and subsequent German rule in Britain. It all started with General George Chesney's story of the Battle of Dorking published in 1871 after Germany's victory over France.[16] His tale which was republished in several editions and translations describes a successful German invasion of England, culminating in the rout and defeat of the British army at Dorking, southwest of London. The purpose of the story was to warn Britain of a false sense of security and general lack of military preparedness for any threatening developments on the Continent. The author achieved what he wanted. As a consequence annual army manoeuvres were introduced and Chesney himself earned a knighthood, fame and a seat in the House of Commons. But in the following years the German danger was replaced by a French and Russian threat. In 1894 William Le Queux, one of the most successful and influential hack writers of invasion and spy books, published the *Great War in England* in which the island was invaded this time by France and her ally Russia.[17] During the Fashoda Incident of 1898 Le Queux published another invasion account introducing for the first time two new elements, the spy and the fifth column who would prepare the way for an invasion force.[18] The effects of this book led to some farcical developments. Groups of continental cyclists near the sea were reported to the police because it was suspected that they mapped England in order to be ready for an invasion.[19] What is interesting to note here is that each time the newspapers dealt with international issues and some special concerns some writers were so inspired to follow up the concern or scare and write stories about potential threats to England and publish them in book form. The passing of the second German navy bill and the Boer War became the turning point in the press reports about Germany. Thus the conservative *Morning Post* echoed the *Daily Mail*: 'There is a [new] menace growing up in the East which cannot be ignored.'[20] The *Times* followed suit, but the liberal papers did not share its concern. Generally speaking it had not taken a number of British newspapers long to have become suspicious of German politics and it has been argued that one of the first successes of the British press campaign was to force the Balfour government to abandon the Anglo-German plan of cooperation in building the Baghdad Railway.[21]

At about the same time the first well-known story in which the French danger is substituted with a German peril is Erskine Childers's by now famous novel *The Riddle of the Sands* which was recently made into a television film in Germany.[22] His book became a bestseller and initiated a new wave of invasion and spy stories concentrating this time entirely on Germany. Childers, who also wanted to warn against the potential danger of the new Germany, must have been pleased when the naval staff, in following public pressure, had to undertake a feasibility study of the invasion plan published in Childers's novel. The judgement was however crushing: 'As a novel', the Admiralty wrote, 'it is excellent, as a war plan it is rubbish.'[23] But this did not stop more stories of this genre being published. The fictional anticipation of a war with Germany gained in significance as time went on. There were many other books, such as R. W. Cole's *Death Trap*, A. J. Dawson's *The Message*, Oppenheim's *A Maker of History*, W. Wood's *The Enemy in our Midst*, Captain Curtie's *While England Slept*, Le Queux's *The Invasion of 1910* and his second successful novel *Spies of the Kaiser* and finally, just before the outbreak of World War I, Saki's (Hector Hugh Munro) *When William Came*.[24] Saki's novel is the culmination of this genre as he does not deal with the German threat or defeat of invasion, but with life in England after a successful German conquest, occupation and annexation. A plethora of other titles appeared which have not been mentioned so far such as *The Great Raid* or *The Invaders*. To this topic must be added stories which dealt with the enemy in the midst of Britain such as Phillip Oppenheim's *The Secret*. There were also short stories, poems, plays and schoolboys' magazines which dealt with a future Anglo-German war.[25] Ignatius Clarke has listed a number of these stories published in England, Germany and France and has concentrated on the British ones.[26] According to Clarke it was an obsessive mania which also led to caricatures and satires although P. G. Wodehouse's *The Swoop!* cannot match the successive sales of war and spy stories. In any case so many versions of the expected conflict were published that it would have been difficult to have avoided reading a 'war story' somewhere, some time.

We do not know the exact effect of these stories on the British public, but it has been stated that the number of all of these publications together went into millions. In Germany these stories caused some concern and as a result an article, entitled 'The invasion of England seen through English eyes', was published in the *Marine Rundschau* in 1908 stating that a German invasion was completely unfeasible and hoping that the 'fear of German espionage and invasion may vanish'.[27] Even the Kaiser's assurances after Le Queux's successful publication of *The Invasion of 1910* that Germany was not even contemplating an invasion had little effect on the British public.[28] Thus Field Marshal Frederick S. Roberts's allegation made in the House of Lords that there were eighty thousand Germans in Britain ready to help a German invasion force was discussed seriously.[29] When a number of voices in Britain, including the British Admiralty, pointed to the absurdity of this genre of literature it was in fact the British Foreign Office, that is to say Eyre Crowe, Charles Hardinge and Edward Grey, who noted that the Germans were studying and working on invasion plans.[30] Even the secretary of war, Richard Haldane, firmly believed that German espionage existed in Britain on a grand scale yet he ridiculed the assertion made in Parliament that trained German soldiers in England, who in peacetime had posed as barbers, cycling photographers and clerks, would form the vanguard of a German invasion force, even whose Mauser rifles were hidden in British cellars. The nervousness of the British public combined with the growing strength of the German navy forced Prime Minister Arthur Balfour in 1903 to set up the Committee of Imperial Defence which was to study invasion possibilities for the first time.[31] The committee found that the Royal Navy had plenty of time to prevent an invasion force of an estimated strength of seventy thousand. What is interesting is not so much the outcome of these proceedings, but, as Thomas Boghardt made clear in his unpublished thesis, the precedent that the government had bowed to public pressure on invasion threats.

Le Queux's famous *The Invasion of 1910,* which sold well over one million copies in book form, was planned in such a way that the invasion in the book was to pass through every sizeable town near the eastern coast in order to boost the sales of the *Daily Mail,* whose editor backed Le Queux and serialised his story in 1906. The advertisement campaign for the book included a march down Oxford Street by hired veterans who had been put into spiked helmets and Prussian-blue uniforms carrying sandwich boards with advertisements for the story. Apparently it was during these advertisement campaigns that the word *Hun* was used for the first time to describe Germans. The term is supposed to have sent a chill down the readers' spines because of the atrocities the German invading force was committing.[32]

The invasion scare caused by Le Queux's book had a direct consequence. It led Charles à Court Repington, the military correspondent of the *Times,* and Lord Roberts, the former commander-in-chief of the British army, to found the National Defence Association for the introduction of conscription in Britain. The purpose of Roberts's campaign was not only to develop a strong defending force but also an army which would be strong enough to fight a war of intervention on the Continent. But the latter aspect did not figure prominently in the publicity campaign. In fact it concentrated on the invasion threat and it has been argued that 'invasion became almost the sole justification for conscription.'[33] The publicity campaign exerted more pressure on the government and so a second subcommittee of the CID was formed to investigate once more the likelihood of invasion. In spite of the fact that there were firm believers in the invasion threat even within the ranks of the government, this subcommittee repeated what the first committee had concluded, namely that as long as Britain retained naval supremacy, invasion would be virtually impossible. But it made a plea for a strong territorial army which could prevent any strong foreign incursion into Britain. Lord Roberts, who did not accept defeat easily, put a motion before the House of Lords demanding a defence force of a million men and scared the House by pointing out that there were eighty thousand Germans in England who were waiting for the moment when they could assist the invader. His motion was carried in a House which was dominated by

Conservatives. The editor of the *Unionist Standard,* H. A. Gwynne, believed most of these stories and compared Germany with a burglar 'who is just waiting until the policeman, i.e. the navy, turns his back, in order to break in and steal'.[34] The concern the spy and invasion stories expressed was supported by some more serious political writers such as the socialist Robert Blatchford. He firmly believed in 1909 'that Germany is deliberately preparing to destroy the British Empire; and … we are not able or ready to defend ourselves against a sudden and formidable attack'.[35] Blatchford's book which was first published in the form of articles in the *Daily Mail* fitted in well with Lord Northcliffe's (Alfred Harmsworth) own concerns. Northcliffe, who occasionally became a victim of his own obsessions, wrote in a letter, from one of his many tours in Germany, to Herbert Wilson, his assistant editor of the *Mail:* 'We [Northcliffe and his wife] were amazed at the vast industrial strides made in practically every town we come to. Every one of these factory chimneys is a gun pointed at England, and in many cases a very powerful one.'[36]

Once the invasion scare had somewhat subsided, the fear of foreign spies and agents was raised not only within the public sphere but also by the intelligence departments. Le Queux's new work *Spies for the Kaiser* was matched by James Edmonds's account of Germany's spy network in Britain. He took over the army's tiny MO 5. He himself did not believe that Germany would be able to invade Britain but believed that the Germans wanted to frighten Britain off from sending troops to France. Edmonds was convinced that Germany, rather than invading, would plant a spy ring in England and accused the Germans of running a network of agents in England. In his unpublished memoirs he told the story that he himself had once recognised a German artillery captain acting as a headwaiter at the Burlington Hotel in Dover whom he had met before at the table d'hote of the *Europäischer Hof* in Metz. Once he had confronted him in Dover, he apparently disappeared. Effective counterespionage was that easy. Edmonds referred to another incident when a former British military attaché saw one of the Eulenburgs watching landing exercises at Clacton from a dinghy.[37] Eventually Edmonds was able to persuade Haldane to convoke a third subcommittee, this time to counter German espionage. All this should not have caused any serious action by any government but it was believed that 'a great deal of German espionage was undertaken in Great Britain'. Therefore a Secret Service Bureau was set up in 1909 initially only for two years but later extended to keep a tab on German aliens. The Official Secrets Act of 1889 was amended and an Aliens Restriction Act was prepared which came into force at the outbreak of the war. A. J. A. Morris has concluded that by late 1909 the public had been saturated with spy and invasion stories and enough were on the market to keep the issue alive.[38]

However, behind the scenes the newly created Secret Service Bureau kept working. Its director continued to be alert to the danger of German invasion and by 1913 had compiled a register of all aliens, mainly Germans, and kept all German clubs and other institutions under some form of observation.

There were other issues which kept the potential of the German menace alive. The navy carried out manoeuvres in 1912 and in 1913 which were designed to stop a potential German landing force in North England. In both cases the defenders failed to prevent a landing and when the news about this was leaked to the press it was used by those who advocated conscription and a larger army to criticise the liberal government for not doing enough for the defence of Britain in case of war, particularly as a war was expected in the not too distant future despite the general improvement of Anglo-German diplomatic relations after 1911.[39]

While Germans working in Britain attracted some animosity there were numerous efforts made to improve Anglo-German relations in general. Günter Hollenberg and Stuart Wallace are two historians who have followed the fate of various Friendship Committees / Societies, Anglo-German Foundations, Anglo-German newspapers and the Anglo-German Understanding Conference in London in 1912.[40] In addition there were more localised efforts in Oxford, Manchester and Bradford. In Oxford the Anglo-German Hanover Club was established in University College which had regular meetings between May 1911 and spring 1913. By the autumn of that year diplomatic relations between the two countries had improved sufficiently so there was no acute need to fend off a crisis and the current generation of students who had supported the Hanover Club had left Oxford. The next generation of students seemed to have different concerns. The Hanover Club was not matched by anything similar in Germany, but it was interesting that even at the club's student level attempts were made to reduce Anglo-German tensions. It is not known what its members thought in July 1914 but the majority joined their national forces and 25 per cent were killed in the war.[41] There are other critical voices. The Navy did not accept the invasion scares nor the spy stories. Some of the journalists raised objections to an anti-German hysteria and the Oxford Union defeated a motion 'that in view of the existing European situation a rapprochement between England and Germany is an unrealisable idea'.[42] In May 1914, a few weeks before the outbreak of the war, the Union passed a motion with a majority of 61.5 per cent criticising 'the Triple Entente as embodying both an unnecessary and unnatural policy'.[43] However the motion did not lead to a condemnation of Grey's foreign policy or to an anti-war attitude later on. It only supports the assumption that at this stage most people were not keen on a conflict with Germany.

These attempts by some more-educated members of the public to improve relations between the two countries did not lead to sustained efforts to prevent the outbreak of war. The mood in 1914 was more influenced on the British side by those who had seen a danger in Germany than those who had been keen to underline the many links between the two people. Panayi rightly emphasizes the pre-war peaks in denouncing Germany as the source of the 'hostility during the years of armed conflict', but he does not want to go as far as seeing the animosity in pre-war Britain 'as a steadily growing plant which bore fruit in 1914'.[44] As far as the mood in 1914 is concerned the alarm bells which had been rung over Germany's ambitions may have prepared the public to accept war, as the mood of July and August 1914 was not only shaped in the last few weeks before the beginning of hostilities. What appeared in July and early August was a mixture of pre-war anxieties and fears and ad hoc considerations as the July Crisis unfolded. As the sales figures of the invasion and spy stories indicate, the reading public must have devoured their contents. But little is known about the press's reaction to these sensational accounts. The critical reaction of the *Times,* which in other respects was weary of Germany's political and military intentions is relatively well known but neither the attitude of the other national papers nor the regional ones have been subjected to any scrutiny.

If we assume that a large proportion of the reading public must have absorbed the spy and invasion stories, only limited evidence has emerged to indicate to what extent the public's reaction has been formed by these accounts. Only a small number of studies have dealt with the public's reaction but what they reveal is, as one might expect, a great variety of opinions and attitudes. The majority of analyses has concentrated on the politicians and the scene in Whitehall and Westminster. Therefore not much is known about the public before the war. One of the few historians who has analysed the mood of the public rather than merely the manifestations caused by writers and public figures is Adrian Gregory. He has come up with the suggestion that the 'evidence for mass enthusiasm at the time is surprisingly weak'.[45] He has criticized for instance Kenneth Morgan for stating that the Welsh people 'threw themselves into war with gusto'. According to Gregory the Welsh language press appeared to be sceptical, full of foreboding and certainly not enthusiastic. But after the war had been declared 'Wales as a whole did come round quite quickly', partly because the Welsh Liberals remained loyal to their government in London and partly because the South Wales Miners who initially did not respond to calls to cut short their annual holidays or work longer finally rallied as late as 1 September by which time it looked as if higher pay for soldiers and higher separation allowances were forthcoming.

The so-called crowds in London appear at closer inspection less war enthusiastic than hitherto assumed. The local London papers describe the people on 3 August as a typical Bank Holiday crowd rather than a mob baying for war.[46] Even tones of misery rather than enthusiasm seem to have been pervasive. In some areas the usual bank holiday mood was observed and the *Islington Daily Gazetteer* even suggested that the international crisis had added to some sort of amusement. Somebody overheard a conversation on a bus: 'What do you reckon England will do? … Why stick up for her friends as soon as they're set upon – France in particular. Quite a little applause greeted the speaker's conclusion.'[47] This did not amount to enthusiasm but stood in contrast to the pro-neutrality and anti-war rallies. The most famous one was the socialist demonstration in Trafalgar Square on Sunday, 2 August 1914.[48] Even that did not attract large crowds, but generated in the press a number of articles which differed according to the bias of the papers. The resolution the meeting passed called upon the government to prevent the spreading of the war and the country being dragged into conflict. Middle-class youths and clerks had tried to disturb the meeting but without great success. Gregory has pointed to photographic evidence which showed that more 'boaters' than 'cloth caps' were amongst the various relatively small gatherings.

The national press reflected and influenced the general mood in the days after 23 July, the day Austria handed over its ultimatum to Serbia. Before that it was the *Morning Post* and the *Times* which advocated British intervention in an expected European War, the *Morning Post* on 21 July and the *Times* a day later. After that the two papers were joined by the *Pall Mall Gazette* which published pro-British intervention articles day after day. They were joined by the *Daily Telegraph* and the *Globe*. All these papers were suspicious of German pretensions and believed that it was in Britain's interest to join the conflagration against Germany in the name of strategic interest, duty and honour. The *Times* also put forward a new reason for an early entry into the war.[49] It would be cheaper to intervene early because Britain would join the other powers fighting Germany. If France were defeated then Britain might have later to face Germany alone, an effort which would be financially ruinous. It is interesting to note that a number of journalists who wrote pro-interventionist articles had also been involved in supporting the invasion and spy mania in previous years. So there is some continuity between the anti-German line then and the later pro-interventionist stance. However not all Unionist papers followed the lead of the *Times* and the *Pall Mall Gazette*. Especially at local level Unionist papers had expressed a preference for neutrality. It is difficult to estimate how representative the *Times* was in reflecting and shaping the mood of its readership. Undoubtedly its letter section was regarded as important by virtually all politicians. A good example was 1 August. First, the Oxford historian J. A. R. Marriott, later a conservative MP, thanked the *Times* 'for the lead it has given' over the last few days in its pro-interventionist articles.[50] Most of these articles had been written by J. W. Flanagan whose leaders were praised by the editor Geoffrey Dawson.[51] Secondly, Norman Angell protested against a war favouring Russia which had only 'a very rudimentary civilisation.'[52] Finally, the *Times* published the by now famous 'Scholars Protest Against War with Germany'[53] which also appeared in the *Manchester Guardian* and apparently in some northern papers. The proclamation was sent from Cambridge and signed by nine scholars of whom one was an historian, F. J. Foakes-Jackson from Jesus College, who was the *spiritus rector* behind the protest. The signatories of this letter argued that it would be 'a sin against civilisation … to be drawn into the struggle with a nation so near akin to our own and with whom we have so much in common'. The protest caused quite a stir and also raised objections. One such letter was sent by the Oxford historian, Stuart Jones, from Trinity College, which was printed by the *Times* soon afterwards.[54] He accused the signatories of the Scholars' Protest of naivety in praising German culture without referring to the militarist and expansionist traditions. He also objected to the notion that Germany had rendered intellectual services to the world. Stuart Jones seems to have written to several papers criticising non-interventionists. In a letter to the *Tees-Side Weekly Herald* he lambasted Norman Angell for assuming that German power was less aggressive and more benevolent than it was generally assumed.[55] We do not know what the reaction was to Jones's intervention in the North, but the signatories of the Scholars' Protest could not reply to Jones's challenge because of the outbreak of war between Germany and Britain. In any case this might have been difficult because in their letter they had made clear that if Britain found itself involved in war, then patriotism would suppress any objections they had raised. Before that happened, however, a number of radical MPs attacked the Tory press and the *Times* 'as if they are the voice of England'.

The Radical MPs were not alone. The interventionist views were opposed by many liberal papers. The *Manchester Guardian,* the *Westminster Gazette,* the *Nation* and the *Daily News* formed the vanguard with arguments that the Balkans were of little interest to England, that a war between Serbia and Austria was regrettable, but not a disaster and that Serbia ought to be towed to the middle of the ocean and sunk. The Daily News wrote on 1 August that 'if we crush Germany in the dust and make Russia the dictator of Europe and Asia, it will be the greatest disaster that has ever befallen Western culture and civilisation'.[56] The *Manchester Guardian* published reams of letters all denouncing the forthcoming war while other papers expressed preference for Germany over Russia and accused those who supported Russia of following a mission against the forces of civilisation. There were even some letters in these papers which advocated neutrality irrespective of a German invasion of Belgium or not. On the one hand papers which endorsed the arguments in favour of neutrality tried to persuade the government to act as mediator in order to save Europe from disaster. On the other hand the peace movements also called upon the government to do everything possible to prevent Britain from joining the war. They mobilised the international peace movement in Brussels and founded two new organisations in London. One was the Neutrality Committee backed by Hobson and Wallas and a number of liberal historians and the other was

Norman Angell's Neutrality League. The latter was quite active in the two days before the war. It distributed half a million leaflets, 362 sandwich-men walked the streets of London and 10,000 posters were printed and distributed. But it expressed clearly its opinion that any infringement of Belgian neutrality would change the League's position.[57] The same was true for the Independent Labour Party and the British Socialist Party for which it became a duty after 4 August to defend Western states and to defeat German imperialism.

The lack of knowledge about the planned intervention of the British Expeditionary Force in Northern France was not the only weakness of the anti-war groupings. They could also not cope easily with the speed of events. In any case the public appeared very much divided and it is difficult to know which side commanded a majority in the run up to the British declaration of war. Furthermore it was not clear whether anti-German sentiments were stronger than anti-war reactions. There were also pro-German sentiments, but they were quite different in scope from the anti-war feelings. Furthermore it looks as if there was widespread sympathy for France but not for Russia. And Serbia was generally condemned by Unionist and Liberal papers. Even Horatio Bottomly, the editor of the right-wing journal *John Bull*, published a leader under the headline: 'To Hell with Serbia.' Bottomly, no friend of the German side, repeated his condemnation a few days later. Later in the war Serbia was not mentioned any more and Bottomly directed his ire against Germans and their influence in Britain.[58]

It has generally been assumed that some sort of war enthusiasm made itself heard after 4 August in London. It was, as Gregory has pointed out, inspired to some extent by the hearty send-off of the mobilising troops.[59] The feelings of these well-wishing crowds were noticed more than the voices of dissent and actual opposition. The *Labour Leader* published the headline: 'Down with War.' The Independent Labour Party organised anti-war demonstrations in Glasgow asking for an armistice and lower food prices.[60] Together with some Quaker organisations war was opposed by members of the Labour movement. R. MacDonald, E. D. Morel, C. P. Trevelyan and Norman Angell formed a new peace organisation, the Union of Democratic Control, which whilst it gained support during the war, could ill defend itself at the beginning of the war from being branded as treacherous.

Apart from these organisations a wealth of private sources has come to light which gives evidence to the reservations people had about the war. During the first few days of the war recruitment figures seemed to support these reservations and only by the time the call for pro-war solidarity had made its impact did a substantial enlisting take place. Thus between 4 and 8 August only ninety-three joined the colours, but by 22 August the numbers had swollen to over one hundred thousand. However the real push came after the defeat at Mons on 25 August. Adrian Gregory has recently made the point that this rather belated rush indicated less an enthusiastic motive, rather the 'expectation for a desperate fight for national defence'.[61]

Yet on the whole there seems to have been widespread ambiguity which was also reflected in some of the regional papers. The papers in the northeast of England, as a recent study has shown, did not follow party lines or the London press in their reaction to the developing crisis in the Balkans. Already on 25 July Unionist and Liberal papers warned that 'Europe stands on the brink of war'.[62] The calls for mediatory efforts by the government and the preservation of British neutrality were echoed, but some papers put forward the view even before Austria's declaration of war against Serbia that the conflict would end in a general European war. With regard to Germany it was the liberal press which expressed concern about Germany and her war-like intentions whilst the Unionist papers believed that Germany desired mediation and would not necessarily aid Austria-Hungary if war broke out. As it turned out the conservative press was not as anti-German in the July crisis as it had been in previous periods. Thus it is not surprising to find in the Liberal *North-Eastern Daily Gazette* that Austria had been plotting for war, with the support of Germany, since the assassination of Archduke Franz Ferdinand. At the very end of July the Liberal northern papers became very critical of Austria's actions against Serbia encouraged by Germany and together with the conservative newspapers adjusted their frame of mind to meet the growing public concerns about a general European war. Up to that time there had hardly been any mention of active British involvement in a war which was expressed in letters to the editor, editorials and reports covering protest meetings. According to Patrick Esposito: 'All major political parties found supporters who argued against British intervention.'[63] And pro-German statements still prevailed. Especially the editorials and reports from the *Carlisle Journal* emphasize an anti-interventionist stance. On 3 August the paper reported an anti-war meeting in that town which passed a resolution in favour of neutrality to be sent to the government. The assembled crowd was not quantified but seemed to represent a cross-section of the population of Carlisle. When a Mr. Lowthian, prospective Labour candidate for Carlisle, made a supporting speech for the resolution the paper commented 'that he was not often seen in a company of this kind, but, of course, terrible danger made strange bedfellows'.[64] Similar meetings were organised in other towns of the north. In Scarborough a similar resolution was sent to the Foreign Secretary Grey. Even in the last hours before Britain's declaration of war the Yorkshire Miners' Association tried to bring pressure upon the government for the preservation of peace.

Even some editors of northern papers came out in favour of neutrality. The *Barrow Guardian* criticised the *Times* for its pro-war line and British involvement. The renowned Unionist editor of the *Yorkshire Post* concluded in an editorial: 'We are by no means of the opinion that the British Government should hasten to join in an European war, on one side or the other.'[65] Another argument for non-intervention was that German expansion was inevitable and the future in Europe belonged to her. On the side of the pro-war camp the *Yorkshire Herald* noted that it was reassuring to know that the nation was ready for war. And the *Scarborough Evening News* and *Daily Mercury* observed that 'the public mind is less peaceful than it was [a few days ago]'.[66] Whereas a war for the preservation of the balance of power was mentioned by some papers the argument that Britain must prevent the destruction of France drew much greater support.

The papers were critical of Austria, but the liberal press still entertained hopes of Germany's peaceful intentions in the present crisis. This view changed on 3 August when the conservative papers began to attack Germany openly and the German nation was regarded as hostile. It was accused of having goaded Britain into war. This view that Germany sought war with Britain revived and intensified the clichés which had abounded at the time the invasion and spy stories had peaked. Thus the *Northern Weekly Gazette* alluded to the German intention to sack London which had been the theme of one of the invasion books. And the *Newcastle Daily Journal* wrote: 'While the Kaiser was talking of peace, his generals were doing their best to make war inevitable. They must have known of the Austrian ultimatum to Serbia long before it was issued, and, realising that Russia was bound to intervene, they began their war-like preparations before other countries knew that a crisis was imminent. While the Germans were protesting against Russian mobilisation, they were actively mobilising themselves.'[67] It took the liberal papers a few days to follow suit. On 4 August the liberal *Carlisle Journal* still regretted that England had joined the war and added that there was 'little doubt that the majority of Englishmen regard the prospect of being dragged into this war with feelings of amazement and horror'.[68] After that all the papers seemed to be imbued with a sense of solidarity and agreement with the government's policy. The claim that Britain's cause was just was very strong. In all the papers letters appeared criticising the work of the neutrality groups and their campaign to keep Britain out. By this stage those who still opposed Britain's intervention were in a much weaker position. The key to the rallying of the northern papers was Germany's disregard for Belgian neutrality. There was sympathy for a 'little' and peaceful country which was being invaded and a feeling of identity even grabbed the liberal press because the innocent Belgian people were compared to the innocent British people upon whom the conflict had also been forced.

Closing ranks in the press and declaring solidarity with the government should not necessarily be confused with 'war enthusiasm'. Although there must have been some excitement in some of the crowd appearances, some papers would tend to exaggerate that aspect in order to strengthen further the nation's resolve. This intention was probably stronger in Fleet Street than in the north as the *Times,* the *Morning Post* and the *Pall Mall Gazette* had pleaded for British intervention from mid-July onwards. It is difficult to find out what mark the papers left on the opinion of the public. There are some letters and diary entries which refer to newspaper articles but the number is very small and difficult to verify. It is possible that other groups of opinion-makers might have wielded more direct influence such as priests and possibly even academics who could claim to have a more independent judgement, but again it remains difficult to assess to what extent they helped to shape the mood of the public. Clergy of various denominations expressed concern but this did not lead to opposition or to a lack of loyalty to the government cause once war was declared. Thus the bishop of Lincoln warned his congregation on 2 August of the brutalities in war and prayed 'to God to keep our people from war'.[69] Other clergy men followed in painting a picture of misery and bloodshed. However the archbishop of Canterbury anticipated redemption on 2 August.[70] He declared the crisis to be the 'work of the Devil, not of God's' and believed that Britain's active involvement would be for Britain's own good. The coming redemption of Britain became a constant theme for Anglicans whereas the nonconformist denominations were much more vigorous in their anti-war positions. It looks as if the upper clergy of the Anglican Church became firmly committed to the British war effort and regarded it, as the bishop of London did, as a 'Holy War'.[71]

Yet as with the trade union movement and meetings of the Independent Labour Party there was a reluctant acceptance of war, should it come.[72] This basic feeling strengthened the resolve of those members of the cabinet who had decided to resist Germany, a decision which was made easier the moment Germany started to invade Belgium, although it was the position of France which figured prominently in the debate before 3 August. Academics and especially historians were very much part of the polarised debate between interventionists and 'neutralists'. Very few seem to have been keen on war but stood by the government once war was declared. Some of them understood that it was important to explain to the public why Britain had joined the war. From here it was only a small step to an active 'self-mobilisation' in the forthcoming propaganda war during the first few months of the war.

So what can we conclude? The British mood in 1914 up to the beginning of the war has been very much shaped by a vigorous public debate for and against intervention. At the height of the invasion and spy stories it was assumed that a possible war would result from a direct confrontation between Britain and Germany. What emerged in the July Crisis was different from the general expectation. Now a conflict between two power coalitions developed which in early August turned into a war between these two groupings. Britain was dragged into the conflict as a result of Austrian and German military actions and mainly entered the war to protect and maintain the entente with France and Russia, to defend its security interests in northern France and to resist being overpowered by Germany. Until 2 August most liberal MPs and members of the cabinet favoured staying out. It is difficult to say whether the public would have gone along with their earlier position. It looks as if a narrow majority might have opted for war, but that is difficult to prove. The violation of Belgian neutrality provided the public rallying cry for intervention. The vital point was not the Belgian issue, 'but that Germany was the invader'.[73] If Germany were to be successful the expected German domination of Western Europe was regarded as dangerous to Britain and its political interests. Whereas Grey and Asquith followed a cautiously interventionist line the change of opinion in the cabinet depended on Lloyd George who, in following Colonial Secretary Harcourt, swung behind Grey.[74] For the time being Lloyd George accepted the foreign secretary's concern to uphold political credibility in foreign and domestic politics and the gradually emerging majority in the liberal cabinet was backed by a swing of public sentiment towards acceptance of war but without enthusiasm, once the German ultimatum to Belgium became known. The speed with which a probable pro-war majority emerged can be explained by a deep-seated suspicion of German intentions nourished lavishly by the spy and invasion literature of previous years as well as by the conservative press and one socialist paper, the weekly *Justice* which had consistently warned against German power ambitions. If the public had come out strongly against British intervention then Asquith and Grey would have had to resign, an option which was never considered by any German politician or military leader at the time. If the German and British decision-making of the last days of July and early August is compared it is interesting to note that in both countries the decision for war was made by a very small group of people who were in the centre of politics, but there the similarity stops. In Britain neither the military nor the King were seriously involved whereas in Germany the equivalent men played a vital role. What proved to be essential for the final decision in London was the growing consensus in the cabinet, the acceptance of war in Parliament and the approval by a majority of the public. Despite all the peaceful and positive signs of Anglo-German relations in general the mood in the public had mentally geared itself up to accept war with Germany should that state do something which had made all the warnings come true. The invasion of Belgium proved to be such an instance. An agent of the intelligence department of the German general staff had reported to Berlin that the British 'army and navy are mobilising since 3 August. ... The popular mood was against the war, but swung round following the news from Belgium'.[75]

Notes

1. See for this I. F. Clarke (ed.), *The Great War with Germany, 1890–1914* (Liverpool, 1997); J. Charmley, *Splendid Isolation? Britain, the Balance of Power and the Origins of the First World War* (London, 1999); C. Gade, *Gleichgewichtspolitik oder Bündnisp-*

flege? Maximen britischer Außenpolitik (1909–1914) (Göttingen, 1997). H. Strachan, *The First World War*, vol 1: *To Arms* (Oxford, 2001); J. Leonhard, 'Construction and Perception of National Images: Germany and Britain, 1870–1914', *The Linacre Journal* 4 (2000), 45–67. See also the recent thesis (2008) by Catriona Pennell, 'A Kingdom United: British and Irish Popular Responses to the Outbreak of the War', July to December 1914, PhD thesis Trinity College Dublin, which will be published as a book shortly.

2. A. J. A. Morris, *The Scaremongers. The Advocacy of War and Rearmament 1896–1914* (London, 1984), 361.

3. K. Wilson, 'Britain', in Wilson (ed.), *Decisions for War 1914* (London, 1995), 179.

4. G. C. L. Hazlehurst, *Politicians at War. July 1914–May 1915* (London, 1971), 52.

5. D. Lloyd George, *War Memoirs*, vol. I (1938), 39. A. Gregory, 'British "War Enthusiasm" in 1914. a Reassesment', in G. Braybon, *Evidence, History and the Great War. Historians and the Impact of 1914–18* (New York/Oxford, 2003), 68–89.

6. Ibid., 67–69; N. Ferguson, *The Pity of War* (London, 1998), 174–185. See also C. Pennell, 'A Kingdom United', 57–64.

7. D. Geppert, *Pressekriege: Öffentlichkeit und Diplomatie in den deutsch-britischen Beziehungen (1896–1912)* (Munich, 2007). See also his article, '"The Foul-Visaged Anti-Christ of Journalism"? The Popular Press between Warmongering and International Co-operation', in Dominik Geppert and Robert Gerwarth (eds.), *Wilhelmine Germany and Edwardian Britain. Essays in Cultural Affinity* (Oxford, 2008). See also B. Rosenberger, *Zeitungen als Kriegstreiber? Die Rolle der Presse im Vorfeld des Ersten Weltkrieges* (Cologne, 1998), 33.

8. P. Laity, *The British Peace Movement 1870–1914* (Oxford, 2001), 226; F. L. Carsten, *War against War. British and German Radical Movements in the First World War* (London, 1982), 31–32. Catriona Pennell has convincingly demonstrated in her recent thesis that 'opposition to the war was not widespread in August 1914'; C. Pennell, 'A Kingdom United', 66.

9. D. Newton, '"This Black Horror of Inconceivability"': British Radicals and the Descent into War, July–August 1914', unpublished manuscript, 2005. See also M. Swartz, *The Union of Democratic Control in British Politics during the First World War* (Oxford, 1971).

10. P. Panayi *The Enemy in our Midst. Germans in Britain during the First World War* (New York, 1991), 5–45.

11. Ibid., 29–32.

12. Morris, *Scaremongers*, 149.

13. *Daily Mail*, 13 January 1902.

14. *Daily Mail*, 31 May 1902.

15. *Daily Chronicle*, 22 March 1909. See F. Wolff, *Die Reaktion der britischen Presse auf die deutsche Flottenpolitik vor dem Ersten Weltkrieg*, unpublished MA thesis, Münster, 2003.

16. I. F. Clarke, *Voices Prophesying War. Future Wars, 1763–3749*, 2nd edition (Oxford, 1992), 27–41; Clarke, *The Patterns of Expectation 1644–2001* (London, 1979), 94–95, 103, 183.

17. W. Le Queux, *The Great War in England in 1897* (London, 1894). Clarke, *Voices*, 58, 62.

18. W. Le Queux, *England's Peril: A Story of the Secret Service* (London, 1899). See T. Boghardt, *German Naval Intelligence and British Counter-Espionage, 1901–1918*, unpublished DPhil thesis, Oxford, 2001, 57–105.

19. Morris, *Scaremongers*, 101–102.

20. *Morning Post*, 20 February 1903.
21. M. Egremont, *A Life of Arthur James Balfour* (London, 1980), 164–165.
22. L. U. Scholl, 'London unter den Hohenzollern. Saki und die Kriegsantizipation vor 1914', in T. Stamm-Kuhlmann et al. (eds.), *Geschichtsbilder. Festschrift für M. Salewski zum 65. Geburtstag* (Wiesbaden, 2005), 225.
23. Boghardt, *Intelligence and Counter-Espionage*, 64.
24. Clarke, *Voices*, 41, 106, 124–126. See also for excerpts of these stories Clarke, *The Great War with Germany 1890–1914. Fictions and Fantasies of the War-to-come* (Liverpool, 1997); Scholl, 'London unter den Hohenzollern', 228–230.
25. Clarke, *Voices*, especially his chapter 'Politics and the Pattern of the Next Great War, 1880–1914', 93–130; see also Ferguson, *Pity of War*, 1–15.
26. Clarke, *The Great War*, 313–323.
27. Boghardt, *Intelligence and Counter-Espionage*, 67–68.
28. Ibid., 69, quoting an 'Immediatvortrag' of 26 June 1906.
29. Ibid.; Morris, *Scaremongers*, 145.
30. Boghardt, *Intelligence and Counter-Espionage*, 70.
31. Clarke, *Voices*, 122–129.
32. Morris, *Scaremongers*, 107–110; S. Hynes, *The Edwardian Turn of Mind* (Princeton, 1968), 43; Boghardt, *Intelligence and Counter-Espionage*, 72.
33. Ibid., 74.
34. Panayi, *The Enemy*, 36.
35. R. Blatchford, *Germany and England* (London, 1910), 3.
36. Northcliffe to Wilson, 19.5.1909, British Library, Lord Northcliffe Papers, Add. MS 62201.
37. See for these two stories, Boghardt, *Intelligence and Counter-Espionage*, 82.
38. Morris, *Scaremongers*, 160–162.
39. Ibid., 144–145, 329–337, 380. See also S. M. Lynn-Jones, 'Détente and Deterrence. Anglo-German Relations, 1911–1914', in S. Miller, S. M. Lynn-Jones and S. Van Evera (eds.), *Military Strategy and the Origins of the First World War* (Oxford, 1991), 165–194; F. Kießling, *Gegen den "großen Krieg"? Entspannungen in den internationalen Beziehungen 1911–1914* (Munich, 2002).
40. See G. Hollenberg, *Englisches Interesse am Kaiserreich. Die Attraktivität Preußen-Deutschlands für konservative und liberale Kreise in Großbritannien 1860–1914* (Wiesbaden, 1974); S. Wallace, *War and the Image of Germany: British Academics 1914–1918* (Edinburgh, 1988).
41. K. Plöger, 'Griff nach der Freundschaft', *Frankfurter Allgemeine Zeitung*, 23 June 2004; T. Weber, *Our friend, the Enemy. Elite Education in Britain and Germany before World War I* (Stanford, 2007).
42. Ibid. The date of the motion was 7 March 1912.
43. Ibid.
44. Panayi, *The Enemy*, 41.
45. Gregory, 'British "War Enthusiasm"', 69.
46. Ibid., 71.
47. Ibid., 73.
48. Carsten, *War against War*, 25.
49. H. Pogge von Strandmann, 'The Role of British and German Historians in Mobilizing Public Opinion in 1914', in B. Stuchtey and P. Wende (eds.), *British and German Historiography 1750–1950. Traditions, Perceptions, and Transfers* (Oxford, 2000), 338.
50. Ibid.
51. Morris; *Scaremongers*, 344, 358–361.

52. H. Hanak, *Great Britain and Austria-Hungary during the First World War: A Study in the Formation of Public Opinion* (Oxford, 1962), 39.
53. Ibid., 39–40; Morris, *Scaremongers*, 360; Pogge von Strandmann, 'British and German Historians in 1914', 338–339.
54. von Strandmann, 'British and German Historians in 1914', 340.
55. P. Esposito, 'Public Opinion and the Outbreak of the First World War: Germany, Austria-Hungary, and the War in the Newspapers of Northern England', unpublished MSt thesis, Oxford, 1996, 37.
56. Carsten, *War against War*, 24.
57. Laity, *British Peace Movement*, 220.
58. A. Gregory, 'British Public Opinion and the Descent to War', unpublished manuscript, Cambridge University, 1996.
59. Gregory, 'Evidence, History and the Great War', 79.
60. Carsten, *War against War*, 28.
61. Gregory, 'Evidence, History and the Great War', 80.
62. Esposito, *Public Opinion*, 16.
63. Ibid., 23.
64. Ibid., 25.
65. Ibid., 27.
66. Ibid., 29.
67. Ibid., 32.
68. Ibid., 33.
69. Gregory, 'Evidence, History and the Great War', 75.
70. Archbishop Randall Davidson, sermon, 2 August 1914 – 'The Eve of a Great War, Westminster Abbey', quoted from P. Porter's unpublished DPhil thesis, Oxford University, 2006.
71. Ferguson, *Pity of War*, 209.
72. Gregory, 'Evidence, History and the Great War', 77.
73. D. Stevenson, *The First World War*, 33.
74. Wilson, *Decisions for War*, 178–182.
75. Boghardt, *Intelligence and Counter-Espionage*, 166.

6

The First World War in the History of the Weimar Republic

Gerd Krumeich

It was Erich Ludendorff who coined the sinister dictum that politics is or should be the continuation of war by other means.[1] This reversal and perversion of Carl von Clausewitz's paradigm of the constraint politics should exercise on war is like a symbol of the devastation the Great War left on the politics of the post-war period. This war, which lasted for four and a half years, was fought with such commitment that it was impossible for reason, rather than the (temporary) exhaustion of one side, to bring it to an end and hand matters over to the political order of the day, as Clausewitz would have wished. What is often overlooked, however, is that nearly a hundred years before the First World War Clausewitz had sketched an essential phase of this development when he warned against absolute war: war, according to him, has no limit in itself; one thing leads to another, and it is the task of politics to set the limit. If politics itself becomes immoderate, then war will become 'absolute'.[2] This is a clear prediction of what happened in the First World War and what Ludendorff's dictum quoted above formulates as precisely as it does brutally.

For these reasons, research on the First World War and its ramifications for Germany has long pondered the consequences and deformations in German politics brought about by the war. Kurt Sontheimer's analysis of anti-democratic thought in the Weimar Republic was innovative,[3] taking as its subject not only 'thought' but also the forms and styles of expression of political intercourse. In the 1960s Sontheimer's observations and theses brought forth a series of enduring studies on post-war military associations and 'military nationalism' in general.[4] Yet it was not until the 1980s that the concept of the 'brutalisation' of German politics in the 1920s by the experience of the war,[5] introduced by George L. Mosse, gave a real impetus to the history of mentalities in this area. Mosse's book appeared on the market at exactly the time when the turn to the history of mentalities and (later) to cultural histories was beginning everywhere in historical research, including research on the First World War.[6]

In spite of everything that this new approach has developed in the past twenty years, it must be said that the guides to the Weimar Republic, the great historical compendiums by H. Mommsen, H. A. Winkler, H. Schulze, Detlev Peukert and Eberhard Kolb,[7] do not really make the experience of the First World War and its absorption their fixed starting-point for analysis and judgement. Karl-Dietrich Erdmann's thesis of 1955, that all study of the Weimar Republic must be seen in terms of the causes of the Republic's collapse, is now as then invariably stressed as guiding research.[8] 'Versailles' constantly appears as an important initial event, mainly accompanied by the participants' rejection or rebuke, whether mild or severe. The sharpest commentator is Heinrich August Winkler, who expressly criticises contemporaries' lack of insight: 'Versailles was hard. But hardly anyone in Germany realised that everything could have been much worse. … It required only a sober insight into the new situation. … But sobriety was seldom to be seen in Germany in the summer of 1919.'[9]

Above all the generation of historians that lived through National Socialism and the Second World War as children and young people have sought long-term explanations for the calamity and refused to be fobbed off with the older generation's view that 'Versailles' and the world economic depression at the end of the 1920s adequately account for the German catastrophe. And in addition to the search for traditions of 'illiberalism' (Fritz Stern) in Germany, there was the experience of Konrad Adenauer's Federal Republic and the anxious question whether 'Bonn' would meet the same fate as Weimar. In both sets of questions about Weimar, however, what is missing is actually the most obvious, namely the 'localisation' of the Weimar Republic in the mental structures and upheavals which were the unambiguous legacy of the Great War. Only the social consequences of the war have been studied since the 1970s, for instance by W. J. Mommsen and Gerald D. Feldman.[10] Recently, however, Hans-Ulrich Wehler, in the fourth volume of his *Deutsche Gesellschaftsgeschichte,* has presented the total syndrome with admirable precision. He has done a great service in pointing, much more boldly than has hitherto been the case in works of this kind, to further problems treated more closely here. The First World War was, according to Wehler, a 'pressure chamber for the radicalisation' of rightist and leftist totalitarianism. The 'irritated nationalism' of the post-war period had a potential that reached across classes and could therefore become a political religion.[11]

The Versailles Treaty of 6 June 1919 marked the writing on the wall for the failure of the Weimar Republic – and still does so to this day. Yet the statesmen assembled at Versailles were by no means possessed only by intentions of revenge or an interest in wreaking economic harm and moral humiliation on Germany.[12] Virtually forgotten today is the fact that Article 1 of the treaty created a League of Nations to ensure peace, to which, interestingly, an International Labour Organisation belonged and still exists today. This measure arose from the conviction that nationalism and war were the result, among other things, of economic distress and depression. The treaty was burdened, however, from the outset and in general, by the demand that the losers should take responsibility for the gigantic and ruinous costs of the war to the victors. The Hun will pay, *le boche payera*, became a saying in France and a slogan capable of producing consensus in the elections for the 'Chambre bleu horizon' of 1919.[13] The 'Huns' were even prepared to pay a certain sum (100 million Mark), but they were shocked at the hatred with which they were met at Versailles. The French prime minister, Raymond Poincaré, addressed the delegates of the victorious nations at the opening of the peace conference on 18 January 1919 as follows (the losers were not admitted until April): 'What gives you the authority to make a just peace is the fact that none of the people represented by you had any share in this crime that led to a hitherto unknown calamity.'[14] And in June 1919 Georges Clemenceau, the French president, handed the Germans the draft of the treaty with these words: 'The conduct of Germany is virtually unprecedented in the history of mankind. The terrible responsibility that weighs on it may be encapsulated in the fact that at least seven million dead lie buried in Europe, while more than twenty million survivors bear witness by their wounds and suffering to Germany's wish to satisfy its passion for tyranny through war.'[15] There was unanimous indignation in Germany at what were called the 'war-guilt paragraphs', Article 231 of the Versailles Treaty, which read: 'The Allied and Associated Governments affirm and Germany accepts the responsibility of Germany and her allies for causing all the loss and damage to which the Allied and Associated Governments and their nationals have been subjected as a consequence of the war imposed upon them by the aggression of Germany and her allies.'[16]

For Germans in 1919, this charge of criminality was the worst thing that could have happened to them. The absurd conviction that for four years they had been fighting a defensive war in France and elsewhere[17] had been engrained in their minds by years of propaganda and served, following the unexpected defeat, as a means of basic self-protection. Surely defeat itself was already hard enough to bear given the one and half million fallen soldiers and the economic distress. What should be borne in mind, however, though it is generally overlooked, is that most Germans were convinced this distress derived from the greatest crime of the war, namely the British 'hunger blockade', which was not suspended after the end of the war and was to claim more than ten thousand victims in Berlin alone.[18] That all these sacrifices were not only senseless but also the result of a crime was a thought that was collectively unbearable. Hitler's propaganda profited from nothing more than the promise to erase the 'ignominious peace' of Versailles. In my father's generation and in the discourse of the Federal Republic of the 1950s and 1960s, it was still a matter of course to identify 'Versailles' and the world economic crisis of 1929 as the causes of National Socialism. The questionable response to this in the historiography of the 1970s (of a piece with the 1968 revolution) was vehemently to impugn such a connection, as I have already mentioned.

From the point of view of the history of mentalities, it should be noted that after 1919 the question of war guilt dominated all other 'factual issues', reparations, etc. The indignation in Germany over the war guilt verdict was unanimous, but had many different strands. Unlike France after 1871, national solidarity could not be forged from national dishonour. From the outset the Right accused the Left of having 'stabbed Germany in the back' with strikes and revolutions, therefore bearing the guilty for having forced acceptance of an 'ignominious peace' with a heavy heart.[19] It was not only Adolf Hitler's extremist ideology that thrived on this accusation. Indeed, Hitler was only expressing somewhat more radically ('Jewish Bolshevism') what the entire Right said and thought: Communism was responsible for the German collapse and the ignominious peace. And, depending upon the degree of radicality, moderate MSPD politicians like Friedrich Ebert and Philipp Scheidemann could also be perceived as helpers of 'Jewish Bolshevism', for had they not stopped the war, signed the truce, and helped the revolution to victory in the shape of the Republic? Accurate distinctions were useless against such hate-filled and resentful ideas, which not only dominated the political Right but, more importantly, also the organisations of front soldiers, especially the 'Stahlhelm' with its millions of frustrated veterans.[20]

Franz Schauwecker, an important poet and front-line soldier at the time, though now largely forgotten, captured the syndrome in an interesting paradox: 'We had to lose the war in order to gain the nation.' Here a quotation from his then much read but today ridiculous-seeming 'lived' prose:

> A being rises in the far distance. A mass comes forth, grey, densely thronged, filling the field of vision, endless ... endless. They approach and separate into ordered troops ... and I see the German host of the Great War, which rises up, comes forth, whose march is like the powerfully swelling breath of a colossal breast. All the thriving force of youth breathes in these grey, endless platoons; the heart of the people beats in their bodies; battle thuds in the heavy fall of their tread; it ripples in the folds of the flags and standards. ... They approach, inexorable and tremendous as the flood of the sea. A voice rises above them, a voice of bronze and steadfastness, of inflexible earnestness and gnashing defiance against the world, a voice that cries of pain, booming with the fierceness of battle like the crash of a heavy cliff'.[21]

Out of defeat an extreme nationalism emerged, which, in its radicality, exclusivity, lust to kill and fantasies of destruction, eclipsed everything that had previously been called nationalism: a nationalism of revenge and hatred, in which the most extreme form of this hatred was not so much xenophobic as of a domestic political nature. And the radicality with which the Freikorps dealt with alleged and actual revolutionaries was stamped with this boundless hatred. Also contempt: the symbolic casting of corpses into the river, of which the dead bodies of Rosa Luxemburg and Karl Liebknecht were not the only examples.[22]

In the 1920s the American Carnegie Foundation 'for the establishment of international peace' began an extensive programme for the intellectual appraisal of the world war, which produced several seminal studies. The study by Otto Baumgarten, Wilhelm Flitner and others, published in 1927, on the 'intellectual and moral effects of the war in Germany' is still particularly well known.[23] The first part of this interdisciplinary study (which included historians, psychologists, educationalists and others) treated the 'effects of the world war on the psychological life of the German people' and noted a general 'shock to the sense of reality', an 'emotional brutalisation' and 'dissipation in the area of sex' (chapter 4). This study laments, among other things, that 'still today' (1927) leading minds are convinced that 'the enemy would have submitted to German superiority if only we had held out for a short time more'. It analyses the incapacity 'honestly to take the facts into account': 'Precisely the best, noblest, and patriotic part of the nation constantly demands that the nation pull itself together for the most active possible resistance to the dictates of the pitiless foe. When one demands of them proof that the possibility of success exists, one is silenced by loud outbursts of feeling and fantasy.' Among such 'outbursts of fantasy', incidentally, the expert report includes both communist and nationalist putsches, for example Hitler's putsch in 1923. The concluding sentence of the Carnegie report still gives pause today: 'The conduct of the war over many years against a world of enemies was possible only by dint of a habituation to an idealistic, ideological, and delusory refashioning of reality, which must have left deep and lasting traces in the popular psyche.' In general, the Germans underwent an 'emotional brutalisation'; they had become a 'people of wrath'.[24]

Wrath, fury and hatred are, in fact, the terms that shaped the political conflicts of the 1920s, in which political opponents became deadly enemies virtually over night. I have maintained that this hatred was less of a xenophobic than domestic-ideological kind. This is quite astonishing and needs special explanation. Perhaps the situation in Germany would have developed differently had the Freikorps, which arose spontaneously after the war, not been predominantly deployed in the civil war (and as law enforcement agents against communist uprisings). Initially there had been other options: the Freikorps, which varied in size (from four hundred to four thousand men), were also deployed by the Republic as border guards, especially in the border disputes with Poland, for instance, in the then famous battle at the Annaberg when they attempted to regain militarily the area appropriated by Polish troops where (according to the Versailles Treaty) elections were to be held. But the Freikorps were dissolved by order of the Allies, so that the doubly frustrated soldiers had to look on as military interventions were carried out all over Europe and in the Near East, and the post-war world order was only now established definitively by force of arms. The specific interventions by the Great Powers, out of which the international post-war settlement grew, are quite unknown today in Germany; here are a few examples:

In 1919 French troops fought in Russia against the Bolsheviks; General Foch and Georges Clemenceau energetically supported the 'White Russians' in order to construct a new front against Germany. There were also other massive interventions. In December 1918 a French division landed in Odessa and General Berthelot prepared a contingent of 150,000 French soldiers to be sent to Russia.

There were further interventions of a colonial sort and others that were connected to compliance with the Versailles Treaty. Thus in the 'pacification' of Morocco, in the so-called 'Rif War', aeroplanes and tanks were deployed. General Pétain fought here until 1924 with 100,000 men. The division of the Arab territories of the Ottoman Empire into French and British mandates, agreed in the Versailles Treaty, also led to further war. In order to exercise control over Syria, larger military actions had to be undertaken. France used military means to prevent the formation of an Arab state, including the bombing of Damascus in 1925.[25]

Today nearly forgotten, but then crucial, was the experience of the Russian civil war after the Bolshevik putsch and the October Revolution. This conflict, which lasted three years and was often conducted with the most extreme brutality, spanned the entire country, from the Baltic to the Pacific. The fighting came to an end only in 1923. Historical works published in the Soviet Union concocted a conspiracy myth out of the events that is not unlike the phantasmagorical ascriptions of guilt on the part of the Nazis. According to this story, traitors within the country itself were bought with foreign money. The capitalist enemy, above all France, Great Britain and the USA, invested hundreds of thousands of roubles in the overthrow of the Soviet system and bribed all the Russian parties. In 1918–19 alone, according to the *Illustrated History of the Civil War* of 1929, there were 344 revolts against the Soviet government, and more than 400 counter-revolutionary organisations were uncovered and destroyed. In the Soviet literature of the 1920s the struggle against the 'Whites' became a direct continuation of the Great War. A glance at the enormously bloody reciprocal revenges between the Red and White Russians in post-war Finland in particular shows that in many parts of Europe after 1919 there was not even an armed peace, but rather open war and civil war.[26]

In Germany, too, war returned. This was particularly true of the occupation of the Ruhr in 1923, which unlike the 'contractual' occupation of the Rhineland in 1919, and the occupation of Düsseldorf, Duisburg and Ruhrort in 1921, which was simply accepted, led to a genuine 'war in peace'. For former German front soldiers, Freikorps fighters and storm troopers of every sort, it was the climax of humiliation to have to look on powerlessly as the invasion of Belgian and French troops was carried out in the form of a regular wartime occupation. On 12 January, 6,000 men with heavy equipment, including tanks, moved into Essen. In the following days two cavalry divisions and one infantry division started from Düsseldorf, until in March there was an approximately 100,000-man-strong occupying force on the ground in the Ruhr region. Field courts-marshal were set up by both the Belgian and the French occupying armies to deal with Germans who had been arrested and handed over to them for refusing to obey orders, for protests or acts of violence.[27]

The Germans understood quite well the symbolic character of this large-scale deployment. The metaphor of war was rolled out in the appeal of the German President 'To the German People' on 10 January 1923; evidently he wished to create a mood like that of 'August 1914'. In dramatic formulations, he condemned the 'storming' and the 'blow of the French fist'. The appeal also evoked the 'coming suffering under foreign rule', but advised prudence in spite of the 'renewed breach of peace and law'. It invoked the 'firm standing together of the entire people'. Chancellor Wilhelm Cuno speculated on: 'A strong wave of national feeling. This wave must be made serviceable to the State, not left to itself and allowed to fall under the sign of the swastika [sic] or the black-white-red flag, but so guided that from the outset it serves unification and conciliation among the German people.'[28] In the imagery of truce and war employed by middle-class and conservative groups in Germany in 1923, however, calls to revolt, sabotage and some extension of 'passive' resistance played no part. These actions were reserved to a small minority of activists. Partisan activities like the blowing up of bridges or railway installations remained, in fact, the great exception. This is rather surprising and can be explained only by the fact that the population and political groups knew physical resistance was possible only in the shape of pure desperado actions. The military superiority of the French was as crushing as had been the German occupation of France during the war.

On the day of the invasion, Adolf Hitler, then a popular Munich circus and beer-hall speaker indulged by the Bohemian world, took a stance on the events in the Ruhr. They were only a consequence, he declared, of the policy that had begun with the revolution and that had deliberately made the German people defenceless. The dagger in the back of the victorious army had been thrust deeper with the disarmament of the German population and the Freikorps. It was meaningless now to make patriotic noises and forge a new truce with the traitors. 'The German rebirth in the world will be possible only once the criminals have been made accountable and given over to their just fate. Down with the traitors to the Fatherland: an *army of revenge* shall bring us the hour of the rebirth of honour and freedom and a truly German Reich everlasting.'[29] Revenge and hatred were the principal terms of National Socialism and the ideology was deeply bound up with the experience of the world war and the never-acknowledged defeat of 1918. This is the element of Nazi ideology and propaganda that, beyond the crude anti-Semitism and 'folkish' delusions, found the most support in German society, crossing classes and generations. If the Nazi party was really a 'people's party' of negation, as Jürgen Falter has rightly observed,[30] then this was primarily because it expressed, hyper-radically but in a way intelligible to everyone, the trauma of Versailles and promised a remedy.

In retrospect Sebastian Haffner expressed this fundamental mood:

A psychological organ had been removed from an entire generation of Germans: an organ that expressed itself, as the case may be, as conscience, reason ... morality or fear of God. An entire generation had learned ... that things work without [this] ballast. The previous years had been a good preparatory school for nihilism. 1923 prepared Germany – not specifically for Nazism, but for every fantastic adventure. ... Evidently experiences of this kind lie beyond the bounds of what people who have not suffered psychological damage can bear.[31]

Important ingredients of this 'madness' were profound hatred and collective embitterment. Interestingly, Hannah Arendt broaches the phenomenon of collective embitterment on the first page of her *The Origins of Totalitarianism*, where she develops the theme that one of the main catastrophes of the First World War was the emergence of ever larger groups who found themselves living in exceptional circumstances, conditioned by the war.

It was precisely the seeming stability of the surrounding world that made each group forced out of its protective boundaries look like an unfortunate exception to an otherwise sane and normal rule, and which filled with equal cynicism victims and observers of an apparently unjust and abnormal fate. Both mistook this cynicism for growing wisdom in the ways of the world, while actually they were more baffled and therefore became more stupid then they ever had been before. Hatred, certainly not lacking in the pre-war world, began to play a central role in the public affairs everywhere, so that the political scene in the deceptively quiet years of the twenties assumed the sordid and weird atmosphere of a Strindberg family quarrel. Nothing perhaps illustrates the general disintegration of political life better than this vague, pervasive hatred of everybody and everything, without a focus for its passionate attention, with nobody to make responsible for the state affairs – neither the government nor the bourgeoisie nor an outside power.[32]

The similarity of this analysis to Haffner's diagnosis quoted earlier is interesting.

What has so far not been analysed sufficiently, however, is the National Socialists' promise of peace. It is well known that following the seizure of power, the National Socialists acquired some sympathy and credit abroad by their constant vows of peace. French front fighters' organisations, which had a great influence in French politics, even assumed that the Nazis took seriously the famous German-French front fighters' vow of peace at the 1936 Olympics, and therefore energetically opposed French armament.[33] But the 'peace record' (as Hitler called it in 1937), cynically played again and again by the Nazis, was credible because of the tradition in which it stood. We must assume that the 'Never Again War' movement, which for a short time at the beginning of the Weimar Republic attracted vast masses of people (in contrast to all shades of pacifist organisations) and in 1924 mounted demonstrations with tens of thousands of participants, was not a movement only of the democratic Left, but also retained a quite ambivalent link to the Centre and the Right. This is a subject for further research. At any rate, the 'Never Again War' movement originated not in the pacifist organisations but in the mass circulation, middle class-democratic *Berliner Volkszeitung* of 3 August 1919. The Veterans' League for Peace (*Friedensbund der Kriegsteilnehmer*), founded at this time, organised annual mass demonstrations, beginning in 1924, on the anniversary of the outbreak of the First World War, in which two hundred thousand people in Berlin alone and approximately half a million throughout Germany took part.[34] Perhaps this was a repetition of what (as I remarked at the beginning) had been so effective in the propaganda for the First World War, namely the hope that the Great War would ultimately lead to a Great Peace. And so powerful was this idea that even the Nazis attempted to make use of it. I have in my possession a Nazi brochure of 1923 with the title 'Never Again War', which refers to the French writer Jean Jaurès and to Philipp Scheidemann, and heavily underscores the idea that no one except the capitalists of the stock exchanges and the banks wanted the world war, 'not the German people and not the other peoples of the earth'.[35]

Perhaps the long-term effect of the war trauma on the culture and politics of the Weimar Republic may be better approached if we look more closely than has been the case so far at the claims laid on the First World War by the National Socialists. Curiously, there is a gigantic gap in research here. We know much about Hitler and his experience of the war, but up to now I have seen no study of the question as to how the Nazis exploited and ideologically transformed the world war for their purposes.[36]

There is, indeed, no study on the form in which Nazi leaders and institutions (for instance, the Hitler Youth) drew on the world war and how they attempted through their actions to contribute to healing the trauma.[37] 'And so you have yet triumphed' reads the inscription on a big poster from 1940 referring to the victory over France. It shows a Wehrmacht soldier of 1940 passing the Reich War Flag to the soldier of 1916, still holding his position in the trenches.[38]

The radicalism with which, from the outset, the National Socialists directed their political doctrine towards the revision of the Versailles Treaty, and to a far greater degree than the other right-wing parties defined the guilty and the traitors in a manner which today seems grotesque, found an echo in a defeated and traumatised German society that has still not been sufficiently studied.[39] Historians have long been aware that the extreme hooliganism of the NSDAP, and in particular the SA, was strongly tempered in the eyes of the political Right and moderate dignitaries by the (false) opinion that the healthy nationalist element in Hitlerism could be used to repulse the 'revolution'. Dirk Blasius's new work on the civil war of 1930–33 has treated this with great pithiness.[40] But how could conservative dignitaries take Nazi hooligans for guardians of law and order? Political and socio-historical aspects cannot account for this. My thesis is that here, too, the trauma of 1918 played a prominent role – it was not an accident that in his speeches during the civil war of 1930–33 Hitler constantly invoked the revolutionary situation of 1918 and the betrayal by the elites at that time. Was it a coincidence that Hitler, at least in Goebbels's opinion, had, since the early 1930s, surrounded himself with ever more celebrities of the First World War, in order to build the confidence of middle class dignitaries and the Reichswehr? It also seems to me that Hitler's *ceterum censeo* that he would free Germany from dishonour and wipe out its defeat did much to build public confidence in the years before the seizure of power. That he succeeded in doing this became one of the main pillars of the Hitler myth, as Ian Kershaw has strikingly shown.[41]

In conclusion, a few further facts about Nazi political practices may illustrate the general questions broached here. As Sabine Kienitz has shown, Hitler was given immense acclaim by the masses of war invalids because he promised to give their heroic sacrifice due recognition in a National Socialist state. Actually, after 1933 Hitler abolished many social benefits that the Republic had granted invalids (for example, free travel by rail), but he gave them seats of honour in the Olympic Stadium and many similar signs of recognition. Such symbolic re-stagings of World War I heroism resulted in the false, but widely held conviction that only Hitler had redeemed the moral claims of war invalids in German society.[42] Another example concerns the Nazi policy on war monuments, which has likewise been insufficiently studied so far. Here it appears that, beginning in 1933, the National Socialists simply adopted 1920s war monuments as long as they were 'militant' or revanchist in character, without introducing any specifically National Socialist ideology. A good example of this is the monument to the traditional Lower Rhenish regiment '39', built after 1935 on the Reeserplatz in Düsseldorf. In this war monument there is not the slightest Nazi symbolism. This was a Nazi monument that derived completely from the tradition of the First World War and rendered further 'monopolising' superfluous.[43]

In sum, National Socialism was (like the 'great hope'[44] of Communism) deeply bound up with the experience and events of the First World War. The lost peace of 1919 was the beginning of the final downfall of the old Europe of nations and nationalism, and the descent into the barbarism of the Second World War.

Notes

1. Erich Ludendorff, *Kriegsführung und Politik* (Berlin, 1922), 23.
2. Carl von Clausewitz, *Vom Kriege*, 16th edition (Bonn, 1952), chap. 1.
3. Kurt Sontheimer, *Antidemokratisches Denken in der Weimarer Republik. Die politischen Ideen des deutschen Nationalismus, 1918-1933* (Munich, 1962).
4. Especially Volker Berghahn, *Der Stahlhelm. Bund der Frontsoldaten 1918–1935* (Düsseldorf, 1966); Kurt G. P. Schuster, *Der Rote Frontkämpferbund 1924–1929* (Düsseldorf, 1975); Karl Rohe, *Das Reichsbanner Schwarz-Rot-Gold* (Düsseldorf, 1966); Hagen Schulze, *Freikorps und Republik 1918–1920* (Boppard, 1969).
5. George Mosse, *Fallen Soldiers: Reshaping the Memory of the World Wars* (New York, 1993), see esp. chap. 8, 159–181. For further discussion of the 'Mosse thesis', see Anette Becker and Stephane Audoin-Rouzeau, *Understanding the Great War* (New York, 2002), 14–18; Antoine Prost, 'Les limites de la brutalisation', *Vingtième Siècle* 81 (2004), 5–20; Benjamin Ziemann, 'Republikanische Kriegserinnerung in einer polarisierten Öffentlichkeit', *Historische Zeitschrift* 267 (1998), 357–398.
6. Cf. Ute Daniel, *Kompendium Kulturgeschichte*, 3rd edition (Frankfurt, 2002); cf. also my earlier research report in G. Hirschfeld, G. Krumeich and I. Renz, *Keiner fühlt sich hier mehr als Mensch…. Erlebnis und Wirkung des Ersten Weltkriegs* (Frankfurt, 1996), 11–29.
7. Hans Mommsen, *Aufstieg und Untergang der Republik von Weimar 1918–1933*, 2nd edition (Munich, 2001); Heinrich A. Winkler, *Weimar 1918–1933: Die Geschichte der ersten deutschen Demokratie* (Munich, 1998); Hagen Schulze, *Weimar – Deutschland 1917 – 1933*, 2nd edition (Berlin, 1983), 413; Eberhard Kolb, *Die Weimarer Republik*, 6th edition (Munich, 2002), 155; Detlev Peukert, *Die Weimarer Republik* (Frankfurt, 1987).
8. Cf., e.g. Schulze, *Freikorps*, 418f., with the surely incorrect thesis that opposition to 'Versailles' unified Germans.
9. Heinrich August Winkler, *Der lange Weg nach Westen* (Bonn, 2002), 402. Had Winkler consulted contemporaries instead of reproving them, he would have found the most reflective and intelligent would probably have responded that the world had become so mad that one could not remain sober. Cf. Martin H. Geyer, *Verkehrte Welt. Revolution, Inflation und Moderne: München 1914–1921* (Göttingen, 1998).
10. Wolfgang J. Mommsen (ed.), *Die Organisation des Friedens. Demobilmachung, 1918–1920* (Göttingen, 1983) (Geschichte und Gesellschaft, 9), Gerald D. Feldman, *Vom Weltkrieg zur Weltwirtschaftskrise. Studien zur deutschen Wirtschafts- und Sozialgeschichte* (Göttingen, 1984).

11. Hans-Ulrich Wehler, *Deutsche Gesellschaftsgeschichte*, vol. 4: *Vom Beginn des Ersten Weltkrieges bis zur Gründung der beiden deutschen Staaten* (Munich, 2002), 536, 544f.

12. Cf. Klaus Schwabe (ed.), *Quellen zum Friedensschluß von Versailles* (Darmstadt, 1997); and the short and pregnant account by Eberhard Kolb, *Der Frieden von Versailles* (Munich, 2005).

13. Cf. Jean-Jacques Becker and Serge Berstein, *Victoire et Frustrations, 1919–1929* (Paris, 1990) (Nouvelle histoire de la France contemporaine, 12).

14. R. Poincaré, *Messages, discours, allocutions*, vol. 2 (Paris, 1920), 133ff.

15. Clemenceau on 16 June 1919; quoted in Schwabe (ed.), *Quellen*, 357ff.

16. *The Versailles Treaty*, official text, Berlin 1924 (2. Aufl.). The official German translation, however, is toned down. The legally valid French text reads 'aggression' (not 'attack' [*Angriff*]) and 'originator' (*Urheber*) appears in the more vague than correct form of 'cause'; for details cf. Gerd Krumeich (ed.), *Versailles 1919* (Essen, 2001), 53–64.

17. Cf. Gerd Krumeich, 'Die Somme in der deutschen Erinnerung', in Hirschfeld, Krumeich and Renz (eds.), *Die Deutschen an der Somme*.

18. Cf. Charles Paul Vincent, *The Politics of Hunger* (Athens/Ohio, 1985).

19. Cf. Gerd Krumeich, 'Die Dolchstoß-Legende', in H. Schulze and Etienne François (eds.), *Deutsche Erinnerungsorte*, 3 vols. (Munich, 2001), vol. 1, 585–599.

20. Cf. in general Boris Barth, *Dolchstoßlegenden und politische Desintegration. Das Trauma der deutschen Niederlage im Ersten Weltkrieg 1914–1933* (Düsseldorf, 2003).

21. Franz Schauwecker, *Im Todesrachen. Die deutsche Seele im Weltkriege* (Halle [Saale], 1919); also published under the title 'Gedenke' in the then widely circulated collection edited by Gustaf v. Dickuth-Harrach (ed.), *Im Felde unbesiegt. Der Weltkrieg in 24 Einzeldarstellungen*, 4 vols. (Munich, 1921), here vol. 2, 311.

22. On the problem of violence in the Weimar Republic, see Bernd Weisbrod, 'Gewalt in der Politik. Zur politischen Kultur in Deutschland zwischen den beiden Weltkriegen', *Geschichte in Wissenschaft und Unterricht* 43 (1992), 391–404; Dirk Walter, *Antisemitische Kriminalität und Gewalt. Judenfeindschaft in der Weimarer Republik* (Bonn, 1999); Eve Rosenhaft, 'Links gleich rechts? Militante Straßengewalt um 1930', in Thomas Lindenberger and Alf Lüdtke (eds.), *Physische Gewalt. Studien zur Geschichte der Neuzeit* (Frankfurt, 1995), 238–275.

23. Otto Baumgarten et al. (eds.), *Geistige und sittliche Wirkungen des Krieges in Deutschland* (Stuttgart/Berlin/Leipzig, 1927) (Wirtschafts- und Sozialgeschichte des Weltkriegs, Deutsche Serie, edited by James T. Shotwell).

24. Ibid., 25.

25. Cf. for a survey, Jean-Jacques Becker, 'Frankreich und der gescheiterte Versuch, das Deutsche Reich zu zerstören', in Krumeich (ed.), *Versailles 1919*, 65–70.

26. See Dittmar Dahlmann, 'Krieg, Bürgerkrieg, Gewalt. Die Wahrnehmung des Ersten Weltkriegs und des Bürgerkrieges in der Sowjetunion in der Zwischenkriegszeit', in Jost Dülffer and Gerd Krumeich (eds.), *Der verlorene Frieden* (Essen, 2002), 91ff.

27. Cf. in addition G. Krumeich and Joachim Schröder (eds.), *Der Schatten des Weltkriegs. Die Ruhrbesetzung 1923* (Essen, 2004).

28. Ibid., 17.

29. Account of the speech of 13 January 1923, in Eberhard Jäckel and Axel Kuhn (eds.), *Hitler. Sämtliche Aufzeichnungen 1905–1924* (Stuttgart, 1980), 782f.

30. Jürgen W. Falter, *Hitlers Wähler* (Munich, 1991).

31. Sebastian Haffner, *Geschichte eines Deutschen* (Stuttgart, 2000), 54f.

32. Hannah Arendt, *The Origins of Totalitarianism* (New York, 1951), 266–267.

33. Cf. Antoine Prost, *Les Anciens combattants et la Société française*, 3 vols. (Paris, 1977), especially vol. 3; a dissertation by Holger Skor (Düsseldorf) on the relation between

National Socialism and the anciens combatants will be published shortly; cf. the account by Helmut Dieter Giro, *Die Remilitarisierung des Rheinlandes 1936* (Essen, 2006).

34. Reinhold Lütgemeier-Davin, 'Die Nie-Wieder-Krieg-Bewegung in der Weimarer Republik', in Helmut Donat (ed.), *Die Friedensbewegung. Organisierter Pazifismus in Deutschland, Österreich und in der Schweiz* (Düsseldorf, 1983).

35. Archives of the Bibliothek für Zeitgeschichte (Stuttgart).

36. Thomas Weber, *Hitler's First War* (Oxford and New York, 2010). Naturally individual aspects have been studied cursorily: Gerhard Paul, *Bilder des Krieges – Krieg der Bilder* (Paderborn, 2004); Sabine Behrenbeck, *Der Kult um die toten Helden. Nationalsozialistische Mythen, Riten und Symbole 1923–1945* (Vierow b. Greifswald, 1996); and Christine Beil, *Der ausgestellte Krieg: Präsentationen des Ersten Weltkriegs 1914–1939* (Tübingen, 2005).

37. I am studying this set of questions in a project sponsored by the Gerda Henkel Foundation; dissertations are being prepared on the Hitler Youth (Arndt Weinrich), the front veterans organisations (Anke Hoffstadt) and Nazi war novels (Caroline Glöckner), and MA projects on, among other subjects, the First World War in Nazi films.

38. Reproduced in Susanne Brandt, *Vom Kriegsschauplatz zum Gedächtnisraum. Die Westfront 1914–1939* (Baden-Baden, 2002).

39. Cf. Volker Berghahn, *Europa im Zeitalter der Weltkriege. Die Entfesselung und Entgrenzung der Gewalt* (Frankfurt, 2002), whose survey is the only overall account of the inter-war period that discusses this aspect; cf. the new study by Dirk Blasius, 'Karl Schmitt und der Heereskonflikt', *Historische Zeitschrift* 281 (2005), 659–682.

40. Dirk Blasius, *Weimars Ende. Bürgerkrieg und Politik 1930–1933* (Göttingen, 2005).

41. Ian Kershaw, *Der Hitler-Mythos. Führerkult und Volksmeinung* (Stuttgart, 1999).

42. Sabine Kienitz, 'Beschädigte Helden. Zur Politisierung des kriegsinvaliden Soldatenkörpers in der Weimarer Republik', in Krumeich and Dülffer (eds.), *Der verlorene Frieden, 199–214.

43. Gerd Krumeich, 'Denkmäler zwischen Mahnmal und Schandmal', in Jörg Engelbrecht and Clemens von Looz-Corswarem (eds.), *Krieg und Frieden in Düsseldorf. Sichtbare Zeichen der Vergangenheit* (Düsseldorf, 2004), 219–232.

44. Jean Fourastié, *Die große Hoffnung des 20. Jahrhunderts* (Munich, 1954).

7

Fascism and the Legacy of the Great War

Angelo Ventrone

Interventionism and the Origins of Fascism

The First World War brought about a profound rupture in Italy, altering not only the way people led their lives, but changing the way in which the country was politically governed.[1] Between 1914 and 1918, a new political mentality came into being. This grew out of a desire for a different political model, an alternative to the liberal-democratic system, the proponents of which had been accused of mishandling the transformations which the war had brought about. What made this new mentality so particularly original was the way in which it militarized politics and demonised its adversaries.

The leading protagonist of this transformation was the 'interventionist' movement, an organisation which had been created with the distinct objective of ending Italy's neutrality, proclaimed in August 1914. The movement included both individuals and groups, with many diverse political objectives. In it, we find nationalists who were authoritarian and monarchist; we also find branches of the revolutionary trade union movement along with anarchists, all of whom sought war in order to bring about a social revolution. The movement also boasted republicans, radicals and reforming socialists. The latter wanted to bring down the great Empires, end the military build-up in Europe and liberate the oppressed countries. The movement was also embraced by dispersed liberal groups, each of which was seeking an opportunity to bind Italy together as a nation and marginalise the socialist movement. We even find a minority group of the Catholic Church which sought moral renewal both through war and the concomitant acts of sacrifice, sobriety and reciprocal solidarity that the war would bring.

Despite the interventionist movement's composite nature, the different elements within it were obliged to put their differences aside. Only in this way could they take the country into war and keep it united until that war was won. Such a policy led to a great deal of blending and when war eventually broke out many interventionists experienced 'protracted contact with nationalists, either in the militant squads (*fasci*), in the committees of public salvation (*comitati di salute pubblica*), or in the patriotic unions', and as a result they 'allowed themselves to be progressively assimilated, assuming a nationalist psychology', a psychology that would eventually 'become apparent both to themselves and others in the hour of victory'.[2]

At a time when the other European countries were already at war, the interventionist movement was quick to comprehend that they would need to mobilise all of Italy's human and material resources and that they would effectively be fighting on two fronts, one domestic the other military.[3] The complete militarization of the nation now became a primary objective, while the army itself became the role model for the country as a whole.[4] In order to intensify the cohesion of the nation's politics, violence and repression were forged together, becoming indissolubly linked. From now on, all forms of dissent, in particular from those opposing Italy's entry into the war, were to be effectively constrained and reduced to silence. The dissenters, referred to as *neutralisti*, consisted of socialists and liberals (the latter recognised Giovanni Giolitti as their leader), although a large section of their support also came from the Catholic Church.

In the first months of 1915, public demonstrations, similar to those that had already been seen between July and 14 August in the German, French and British cities, began to occur in Italy as well. In the streets and piazza, rallies and parades resounded to the sound of people joyously proclaiming the coming of the long-awaited event.[5] The situation deteriorated during the course of the so-called 'radiant month of May' (*maggio radioso*), in which street mobs mobilised in support of Salandra, who was attempting to force Parliament – up until now largely neutral – into war. Exasperated and burning with a patriotism that had been stoked-up by the inflammatory speeches of Gabriele D'Annunzio, groups of interventionists began a 'witch hunt' in the cities to root out all those in favour of neutrality. On 15 May, an attempt was made to storm the Parliament, which, although poorly organised, still had an important symbolic effect.[6]

Thus the Parliament now found itself falling increasingly under the influence of the mobs. It was now the people in the piazza who were going to decide how the country was run.[7] Concerning the 'radiant month of May', the republican Costanzo Premuti wrote:

> It is the exaltation of the believers on a pilgrimage to Lourdes, it is a form of ascetics degenerating into frenzy, it is the madness of the masses, it is the most illogical thing that one has ever imagined … and yet, to all those who revel in it, it is pure bliss and our lives and those of our loved ones appear such a poor offering in com-

parison. When the bell atop Campidoglio sounds with its thunderous boom … the knees buckle as if some titanic hand weighs upon our shoulders, forcing us all to fall in adoration before the Great Destiny of Italy.[8]

In the days following 15 May, a 'great fervour' swept across the country. From one end of the peninsula to the other, people 'could see swaying and hear something squeaking'.[9] The nation, which was supposed to have been regenerated by the war, rapidly began assuming the characteristics of a transcendent entity, capable of assuring the well-being of its citizens or imposing eternal damnation upon them. As an entity, the nation had now been positioned beyond history, beyond all will, beyond the existential horizons of the individual. The individual now represented nothing more than a simple temporary incarnation, whose limited existence was inconsequential compared to the grand designs of the state.[10] Before such a divinity even Mussolini is supposed to have bowed. Upon arriving at the banks of the Isonzo – the 'Sacred River!' – he is supposed to have bowed down before fighting, drinking the water 'with devotion'.[11]

The communal project of national regeneration through war meant instilling a sense of order and discipline into the life of each and every citizen. This meant social contexts too, to the extent of even controlling pastimes and sexual habits, the aim being to ensure that energy that was precious for the state was not siphoned-off towards individual ends.[12] In many ways, the project anticipated everything that a totalitarian regime would have imposed, had it come to power, even if in the case of the latter – and this was certainly a major difference – the measures requested would have depended more upon constraint than upon the good will of the people.[13]

In this perspective, enemies, whether internal or external, were placed under the same rubric and treated as one. The main internal enemy was of course the Socialist Party. Their formula of 'neither support nor impede', adopted at the outbreak of hostilities, together with their role in promoting the socialist congresses of Zimmerwald (September 1915), and Kienthal (April 1916), and their repeated appeals for a cessation of hostilities, was interpreted by the interventionists as an act of treason, a plot hatched behind the backs of the combatants.[14] Given the slogans contained within the socialist manifestos themselves – 'Death to the Kingdom of Death', 'Soldiers desert!', 'Workers revolt' – the party's opposition to the conflict was never in any doubt.

Apart from being labelled a bloodthirsty bourgeoisie, the socialists were also saddled with the accusation of being an 'antinational enemy'. Not only were they accused of being in the pay of the Germans, they were actually accused of becoming Germans themselves. Their MPs were accused of collaborating with the followers of Giovanni Giolitti in order to obstruct the government and obtain a separate peace deal that would have precluded both winners and losers.

Because of this, the Socialist Party, the so-called 'official' party (referred to as PSU, in order to distinguish them from those socialists who were favourable to military intervention, such as Mussolini), was sneeringly labelled 'Pus' in the propaganda of their adversaries. The name was still in use in the 1920s. 'Pus' was considered to be a dangerous vehicle of infection that was festering within the social body; as such it had to be eliminated at all costs.

Proposals were presented to create concentration camps in which to intern all the foreign- born citizens present in the country – a policy adopted by other countries involved in the war.[15] Such camps ought, ideally, to be located in the most distant colonies, such as Benadir or Eritrea. In addition, there were those, such as General Cadorna, head of the General Staff, who proposed the implementation of the same measures against the internal enemies. In his opinion, all that was needed was to 'arrest a few hundred community leaders and propagandists, extradite them to the Eritrean or Somalian coast and suppress the poisonous newspapers and pamphlets' that the government had failed to clamp down on.[16] According to others, those guilty of subversion ought to be placed in a 'single concentration camp' in Southern Italy and kept there until six months after the conflict had ended.[17]

The political isolation in which the interventionists found themselves during the war had come about by what they considered to be a perverse alliance, an alliance that had been forged between the socialists and the majority of pro-Giolitti MPs in the house. The feeling of political isolation was such that it prompted many interventionists to accuse the Parliamentary institutions of actually adopting a subversive role, a role, which to them, was seditious, since it ignored the real will of the country.[18] In such a way, the whole question was turned around – it was now the Parliament that was seditious and subversive, not those who were plotting against it. Parliament was thus accused of being a 'pestilential boil', a boil that was slowly poisoning the 'blood of the nation' and that ought to be lanced as quickly as possible.[19]

By 1916, the situation was such that people of the most diverse ideological beliefs were beginning to perceive Cadorna as the only true duce that the country could rely on. To them, he was the man who could bring to the nation the same iron discipline, unshakeable faith and force of will, which – free, in effect, from all political control – he was applying with success on the military front.[20]

On 17 August, demonstrations against the elevated cost of living in Turin were brutally repressed by the army.[21] At the end of October, when news of the rout at Caporetto began to break, accusations against the clerics, the socialists and the followers of Giolitti became more serious than ever. According to the interventionists, the routing of the army had occurred because of all the 'perfidious ideas' the socialists had been putting inside the soldier's minds, ideas which had convinced them that with a 'general laying down of arms' they could end the war immediately. In the interventionists' view, the defeatists now had to be halted at all costs. They had to be taken away, removed from the country and if necessary even shot. In order to carry out such a mission, special battalions of volunteers were drawn up.[22] Given the deep rancour and the bitter hostility towards all those who were opposed to the war, the measures taken against them could only get more extreme.

Violence and Politics

During the turbulent months of Italy's neutrality, nearly all of the various groups forming part of the interventionist movement had resorted at one time or another to the systematic use of violence in order to harass their political opponents.[23] However, the situation was becoming increasingly volatile. Since the government's handling of the war was judged incompetent, the interventionists had begun drawing up precise plans to overthrow the establishment. At the beginning of June 1916, the newspaper *Popolo d'Italia* began threatening to create committees of public salvation (*Comitati di salute pubblica*), which were to replace the legitimate authorities, if the latter failed to pursue the conflict with the requisite level of severity.[24] Interestingly, in the post-war period, the interventionists would once again use fascist squads, organised and coordinated by secret committees composed of local maximalist officials, in order to seize the cities in north and central Italy.[25] Such secret committees became frequent in the towns of central and northern Italy from the end of 1916 onwards.

From the ranks of the interventionists, calls were now coming for the Parliament to be adjourned for the whole duration of the conflict. Others actually wanted to dissolve it and substitute it with a war cabinet composed of only non-members of Parliament. An article published in the weekly *Fronte Interno*, which rapidly went from being a democratically orientated newspaper to a ferociously nationalistic one, was categorical on the question: 'When a Parliament loses all sense of discipline, it falls out of touch with the nation and has to be coerced back into line. ... The country cares nothing for its legal right to govern, its laws are not their laws. ... The country hungers for authority, the Parliament no longer represents authority in any way or form. The executive power has to exert its own authority, since this is the only one that counts.'[26] In the first months of 1918, Mussolini – anticipating to some extent what he effectively did when he came to power – wrote of the need to suppress all the newspapers and to substitute them with a 'single newspaper', under the control of the government and charged with the responsibility of keeping the public informed.[27]

Police informants were now speaking of the existence of potentially subversive ideas, ideas that were circulating even on the military front. Indeed, in the spring–summer of 1917, information obtained by the *Ufficio Centrale di Investigazione* signalled that a committee of public salvation (*Comitato di salute pubblica*) had been created in Rome. This was apparently composed of twelve of the most eminent members of the Masonic lodge of Palazzo Giustiniani and had the precise aim of deposing the monarchy and proclaiming a constituent assembly; the reformist socialist Leonida Bissolati was to be its president.[28]

Particularly hated, especially for his tolerance of the PSI, was the interior minister, Vittorio Emanuele Orlando. As a consequence, some members of the committee of public salvation had proposed assassinating both him and his assistants. Nor was King Victor Emmanuel III safe from terrorist attack. Here too, allegations were made that the organisation was plotting to capture all the members of his family and assassinate the sovereign during one of his regular visits to the front.[29]

More revolutionary plots began to emerge throughout the year. At the beginning of November, after the rout of Caporetto, a police informant revealed the creation of a secret association, which had its grassroots support in the northern and central regions of the peninsula. Although the organisation's main supporters were to be found in the *carbonari* of central Italy, the organisation included activists of all political persuasions, from anarchists to Masons, from the nationalists of Enrico Corradini to the revolutionary trade unionists of Alceste De Ambris. Following in the footsteps of the late–nineteenth-century sectarian associations of Guiseppe Mazzini, such groups were known by the name of *centurie* and *sotto-centurie* (or *decurie*), and could count on the support of many soldiers and even some high-ranking officers.[30]

Officially known as the Red Legions, the mission of these 'stout hearted warriors of the home front', was to carry out terrorist attacks in the capital and then to extend their activities, through the help of the Masons, to the other cities in the peninsula. One of their objectives was to assassinate their 'opposite numbers', i.e. the leaders of all parallel movements working against them. These included the principal heads of the PSI – Filippo Turati, Claudio Treves, Giuseppe Modigliani, Bruno Maffi, Mauro Ferri – and those within the Parliamentary faction of Giolitti, including Giolitti himself. Orlando who, after the defeat of Caporetto, had become prime minister was once again pencilled-in for assassination. Intelligence from the prefects reveals that the formations were even able to use the printers of *Popolo d'Italia* in order to publish booklets and pamphlets.[31]

At the end of the year, the members of the Red Legions – for the most part republicans and anarchists – numbered between one hundred and three hundred. Bound to secrecy, they attended meetings with black-hooded faces, swore oaths upon a dagger and skull and were ruled by a strict code of discipline that required absolute obedience to their leaders, who were armed with a knife and a revolver.[32] The Red Legions were effectively disbanded just before the end of the war, although a promise to continue their operations was made in order to keep the interventionists united.

Some of the initiatives of these groups prefigured the strategy that would later be adopted by the fascist squads in the post-war period. If in December of 1917, for example, the socialist leader Emanuele Modigliani was beaten up in Rome,[33] in Milan at the same time another incident occurred which was similar to the systematic attacks on the organisations and symbols of the Socialist Party, occurring between 1919 and 1922. In the case of Milan, a wagon belonging to the party newspaper *Avanti!* was ransacked and the newspapers it was transporting thrown into the water courses round about – the same thing would happen again in April 1919, when the Socialist Party headquarters in Milan was gutted, an event considered by Mussolini to be the 'first chapter in the civil war'.[34]

During the period of the war itself, the PSI had to confront the growing aggressiveness of its adversaries. The requests for resignation, issued by the communal administrations in answer to the demands of the interventionist movement, prove it. In some cases, the prefects did not hesitate to back up such demands, taking over the communal administrations that were accused of boycotting the war effort.[35]

Even the groups of volunteers that were formed in order to spy upon and eventually repress their 'internal enemies' appear to have made little, if any, distinction, between the war and the post-war period. For such groups, violence had become an essential, if not indispensable part of their politics. The characteristics of this new *mentality,* as it was eventually termed, were effectively summed up by Giuseppe Bottai, the futurist *Ardito* who rapidly became one of the principal intellectuals of the fascist regime. For him, the *Arditi* ('the braves') – the elite assault group drawn up in the spring of 1917, who had even inspired the Red Legions – did not necessarily represent a general desire to make war, but a desire 'to conduct it in a certain way'. According to Giuseppe Bottai, this meant 'lightening out and out war, taken to its most extreme consequences ... waged in such a way on two fronts, the external and the internal, against all enemies, both inside and out'. This was one of the ways in which many young men, such as Bottai himself, were able to enter into politics via the militant rank and file.[36]

Such thinking was a pointer to where the increasingly violent tendencies were leading, both on the military front – with the loss of civility and the brutality engendered by the need to assure one's own survival at the expense of others, not to mention the cult of heroic deeds,[37] and on the home front, where attitudes to the war were completely divided – i.e. the socialist opposition to the war on the one hand and the nationalistic one on the other, where a militarization of civil life was called for.[38] Such a state of tension was a huge burden for the country to bear. In the end, something had to give and it was not long before it did – in 1919–1921, the launching of the so-called 'red biennial' was followed by wave after wave of fascist violence. If it is possible to attribute a 'secret' to the fascist successes, it was not just their promise to inaugurate a 'restoration' of order and social harmony, it was also their capacity to provide an outlet for all the violent tensions that had been accumulating during the war.[39]

Midway through the twenties, the former revolutionary trade unionist Sergio Panunzio made a compelling synthesis of how the war had altered perceptions of society. In his opinion, the whole state had been transformed into a 'great army, a disciplined mass, a living hierarchy'. By now, not only soldiers but 'all citizens from the highest to the low' were 'soldiers and combatants'.[40] If the world was a place where countries now had to fight for domination – as the First World War had just dramatically shown – from now on it was only going to be possible for Italy to survive if the whole country became more ordered and compact, resolved to march as one beneath the command of an elite, created to guide them. Only in such a way could the forces of defeatism, desegregation and the 'monsters of decadence' be definitively destroyed.[41] This was the only path by which the sacred unity of the nation – achieved by the resistance on the Piave and the triumph of Vittorio Veneto – could become permanent and definitive.

In was thus during the First World War that the concept of brotherly hierarchy came to the fore. Emphasised by the totalitarian regime, the culture encapsulated not only moral unity, but also national cohesion, both of which were maintained through a linking together of social justice, discipline, military camaraderie and a 'faith' in the capacity of the elite to guide them.[42] The importance attributed to the figure of the manufacturer – and of the cooperative model that the regime itself had conceived – formed part and parcel of this thinking.[43] Every citizen was, in fact, considered to be a bearer of his own fundamental social rights. As a result, each citizen was perceived to be a link in a harmonious network of solidarity, but – for this very reason – he was also considered to be the bearer of collective responsibility to which he had to submit consciously and whole-heartedly. Between 1919 and 1920, the concept was gradually perfected, the authoritarian aspect being progressively emphasised to the detriment of the social one, the key stone of the original programme.[44]

The Legacy of the War

Once the war was over, people realised that the country had radically changed. '1919', it was written, 'was an unhappy year, but everyone was convinced that a new and better epoch was just around the corner.' In effect, this period cannot really be understood without taking into consideration this sort of 'nineteen nineteen-ism' and 'spasmodic recourse to radical solutions'.[45]

At the end of the war a strong wave of political unrest struck the country. The discontent was strongest in the central and northern regions of Italy, although the south of the peninsula and the islands were affected too.[46] Between 1917 and 1922, following the Russian Revolution, the European ruling classes were constantly seeking ways of impeding the spread of political subversion and revolutionary ferment that was spreading all over the continent.[47] But it was only in Italy that the political system actually buckled under the pressure. A great deal of this was due to the transformations brought about by the First World War and in particular the bitter feuding between those who had declared themselves favourable to the conflict and those who had been against it. Contrary to the measures that had been adopted in other countries, such as Britain and France, Italy had abandoned the politics of persuasion and had opted for out and out coercion in an attempt to remain united both on the domestic and military front. Indeed, since the state had failed in its attempts to secure satisfactory levels of justice and equity, social tensions in the country were constantly rising. Just when Italy needed strong government, the liberal-democratic culture had been exposed as weak. Continually marginalised and humiliated by the invasiveness of the army, the governing institutions had shown that they had failed to win the loyalty and consensus of large sectors of the population.[48]

How the conflict ought to be commemorated by those who had survived it was bitterly contested. By now, every town had its own local committee – composed of gentry, aristocrats and the affluent bourgeoisie – whose sole purpose was to honour the fallen 'heroes' and the 'martyrs of the new Italy' through the construction of monuments. In many cases, such organisations faced fierce opposition from the local socialist administrations. Not only did the latter often decide not to allocate resources to the construction of war memorials, but very often they openly boycotted such manifestations. On the rare occasions that they did promote commemorations in remembrance of the dead, the plaques condemned their 'futile' sacrifice.[49]

The widespread protests convinced the militants and indeed many socialist leaders that they had the support of the majority of the population and that the ruling classes were heading towards defeat. In December 1918, the leadership of the PSI set out the following objective: socialist Republic or dictatorship of the proletariat. The congress of Bologna in October of the following year officially sanctioned the plan, decreeing their adhesion to the Third International.

'The beautiful haven of concord and harmony which we, the combatants and invalids, had dreamed of building after the brilliant victory of October 1918 was now falling apart before our very eyes', wrote Mussolini a few years later. 'I felt myself shudder at the decadence and destruction.'[50]

Hopes of a rapid socialist upheaval grew enormously after the latter's success in the elections of 1919. Indeed, on the basis of a maximalist programme, the

PSI had, in fact, quadrupled the number of its MPs and was confirmed as the largest national party. While the members of the *Confederazione generale del lavoro* continued to grow at a heady rate (from approximately three hundred thousand before the war to more than two million in 1920), the party continued to pull in yet more votes, attaining 32.3 per cent. This success, together with that of Luigi Sturzo's newly created *Partito Popolare* (20.6 per cent,), which opposed the bellicose rhetoric of the interventionists and was Catholic in nature, convinced patriotic public opinion that Italy was once again descending into a country of squabbling factions. Moreover, the party that was gaining a major advantage from this situation was the PSI, the very party which, for the whole duration of the conflict, had represented the anti-nation as its antonomasia.

The boldness of many local leaders, militants and workers was now out of control. Sensing that they were close to obtaining power, they were keener than ever to make the 'lords' pay for all the suffering of the war. In the committees activists were now chanting: 'We rule the street, down with the war! Down with the government! The king has lost, burn him, dethrone him.'[51] It was now becoming normal practice for militants to disrupt their adversaries' meetings, to heckle the speakers, to burn the national flag and manifest hostility towards such social groups – most of all the officers – as were deemed responsible for the 'carnage' of which the workers had been the principal victim. Many of them were tried in kangaroo courts, menaced, clubbed, injured and occasionally even lynched.[52]

Moreover, the protests against the scarcity of food and the inflated cost of living, which reached new peaks in the summer of 1919, were often accompanied by widespread looting: bakeries, shops, warehouses, even the residences of landowners. Despite the imposition of lower prices on the shopkeepers, the violence continued, not only against the landowners, but also against the other workers, in particular those who were not enlisted with the socialist organisations, those who refused to vote and even those who went to church.[53]

In the confusion of the moment, numerous working-class organisations were formed. Some were quite spontaneous, others were more organised. These were coordinated by the work bureaux, or by the town halls along with other groups linked in some way to the PSI, or even occasionally to the Republican Party or some other alliance within the constantly shifting democratic spectrum. All the organisations had the task of coordinating the protests, fixing prices or even authorising the sequestration of goods. To many contemporaries such groups, which were often self-defining, or referred to as *soviet,* were proof that the socialists had finally taken over[54]; the alarm that this caused was enormous.

In many bourgeois circles, such events provoked a rebellious backlash. Slow in starting, it became more pronounced in the autumn of 1920, when, after the administrative elections, the PSI succeeded in extending its control over many of the communes of the Valle Padana and over much of the central part of the country. The worry engendered by the spreading influence of the PSI was exacerbated by continued strikes in the public services and by several incidents of mutiny within the army. In June 1920, several units of light infantry (*bersaglieri*) refused to leave their barracks in Ancona and put down the revolt against the Italian occupation of Valona in Albania. Explicit revolutionary projects concocted by the most ideologically informed sectors of the working class also played upon public fears. In Turin, such revolutionary plans led to sit-ins in the factories during the following August–September.[55] From this moment on, many entrepreneurs began organising private militia in order to protect their holdings. While the fascist movement that was still a minority, the entrepreneurs found support in anti-Bolshevik paramilitary clubs.[56] During the congress of Bologna, the leader of the socialist reformists, Filippo Turati affirmed with lucid foresight that 'Violence is nothing other than the suicide of the proletariat. … Today [our enemies] do not take us seriously enough, but when the time eventually comes for them to do so, our call to arms will be met by [them], and they will be one hundred times better armed than we are and when that happens we can all wave goodbye to Parliamentary government, to economic stability and the Socialist Party!'[57] The fact that the militants were now calling into question the very authority of the state created deep unease within the affluent classes. In the cities, associations began to be formed in an attempt to keep public order. The same associations were used to break strikes and temporarily substitute striking staff, in particular the public sector workers such as postmen, railway workers and street cleaners.[58] Promoters or financers of such associations were very often the principal victims of such waves of protest. As landowners and shop owners, they felt threatened by the competition of the socialist cooperatives.

The new worries of the property-owning classes and of the middle classes concerning the antisocialist – or anti-Bolshevik – polemic helped support the struggle against the 'enemy within' of 1914–1918. Thanks in part to the interventionist movement, men of the most varied political persuasions were now in a position to offer their services as a new governing class. During the process of mobilisation for war, such men had refined their knowledge of the politics of the masses, they had theorised and were familiar with the exercise of violence and had succeeded in obtaining the necessary means of controlling the consensus and suppressing any potential dissent.

The first clear sign of the high tensions that had been simmering, not just among the common people, but also within the Italian institutions themselves, occurred in September 1919. Under the command of Gabriele D'Annunzio, a hotchpotch army – composed almost entirely of units that had either previously mutinied, or were drawn from various genres of nationalists and interventionists – revolted against the state and occupied the city of Fiume in

Dalmatia. This open act of rebellion by sections of the army revealed just how far the movement still lacked broader objectives, i.e. to take Rome and drive out the old ruling class.[59]

It was in this very frontier zone, only just sequestered from the Austro-Hungarian empire, that the real squad-based offensive began. In many cases, the squads operated with the explicit support of the army. The first episode was the burning of the Balkan Hotel in Trieste on 20 July, which was the seat of various Slovak politico-trade union organisations. The motto of the squad from Trieste – 'Ready to kill and ready to die' – was exalted by the newspaper *Popolo d'Italia* and diffused throughout the rest of the country.[60] Henceforth, with the excuse of defending the Italian culture of these regions, attacks began even against the organisations belonging to the workers movements, which were accused of being anti-Italian and pro-Slav.

The example that had been set on the eastern frontier was rapidly copied in the central and northern regions, where the danger of communist subversion was greater. Even in the rural areas of central and northern Italy, leagues of resistance composed of armed squads were being set up. Their purpose was twofold: to protect the strike-breakers from the menace of the socialist leagues and to protect those people and their belongings who were being boycotted. Not surprisingly, in the ensuing politico-trade union conflicts, the number of fatalities began to rise.[61]

Clashes between National Fascists and Anti-Fascists

During the war, over and above the sabre-rattling of the most radical branches of the interventionist movement, the political infighting was essentially limited to brawls that resounded to the sounds of slaps, punches and clubs; firearms were rarely involved. In the post-war period, however, the violence escalated. The escalation was due to a combination of factors. Firstly, from the very beginning of the conflict, the need for violent action had been emphasised, since it was perceived as the only way of resolving the political controversies. Secondly, the October Revolution had ignited strong political passions on both sides, while arms had become a great deal easier to obtain. Thirdly, the suffering engendered by the First World War had exasperated many of those who had lived through it, while the delusion of the results of the peace treaty had diffused a strong sense of humiliation amongst patriotic public opinion. Referred to as the 'mutilated victory',[62] the peace treaty confirmed in the eyes of many the failure of the liberal ruling class to achieve what had been the original objective of interventionism: i.e. to create the 'Greater Italy'. As Italo Balbo, a member of one of the most militant fascist squads, recalled in his diary: 'The present regime is our sole battle objective. We want to destroy it together with all its venerable institutions.'[63] But to do so, younger more audacious politicians were needed, preferably those who had survived the hell of the trenches. According to a clear, effective neologism of Mussolini, the moment had come to set up the 'trenchocracy'.[64]

In the post-war period, the circulation of arms (hand grenades, revolvers and daggers, the preferred weapon of the *Arditi*, not to mention the infamous cudgel) increased as the number of paramilitary squads multiplied. The *Arditi*, who were disbanded a year after the war was concluded, ended up supplying many of the more aggressive elements of these squads. From the very beginning, veterans of the *Arditi* helped constitute part of Mussolini's bodyguard and formed part of the editorial team of the *Popolo d'Italia*. As early as September 1918, i.e. two months before the First World War actually ended, Mario Carli, one of their leaders, spelled out what their 'mission', or 'divine work', actually was: to save Italy 'from all her enemies' and to kill all 'the monsters, both at home and abroad' who were ravaging her.[65]

Successive governments were accused of remaining passive while the situation deteriorated. These include the governments of Francesco Saverio Nitti, of Vittorio Emanuelle Orlando (June 1919) otherwise known as the government of Victory, of Giolitti (June 1920), of Ivanoe Bonomi (summer of 1921) and the two governments of Luigi Facta, which remained in power until the March on Rome. But the accusations of passivity are not completely founded. Nitti mobilised the units of the Royal Guard with the express purpose of repressing civil unrest. Even Giolitti did not remain inert. After the agreement of Rapallo, decreeing Fiume a 'free state', he drove D'Annunzio out of the city (24 December 1920) in the so-called 'Bloody Christmas'.[66] In addition, he also implemented the so-called *Blocco Nazionale* policy, which attempted to set up coalitions with other political groups (bourgeois forces and ex-servicemen's associations) which in general opposed maximalist socialism. The tactic was applied in the administrative elections of the autumn of 1920 and on an extended scale in the main political elections of 1921.

The political strategy executed by Giolitti had paradoxical effects. Although the intervention of the army at Fiume increased the rancour of the nationalist forces against him, his coalition strategy actually helped legitimize his position institutionally. But another problem was looming – how could he ask the prefects and the other representatives of the institutions to halt the violence of those to whom they had allied themselves in order to defeat the growing wave of socialism? The conviction of the Piedmont statesman that he could 'constitutionalise' fascism, just as he had succeeded in doing with the republicans and socialists in previous decades, was to be proven wrong by events.

The loyalty of important sections of the country's institutions was now beginning to waver. A growing percentage of the armed forces, in particular the officers, were becoming increasingly close to the fascist squads, arming and equipping them, wearing their badges and singing their songs, even actively participating in some of their violent acts. But it was other members of the same institutions that set the country on a course for disaster. During the course of 1920, a colonel, under the orders of the Ministry of War no less, traversed the entire peninsular in order to build up units of officers whose sole objective was to impede socialist subversion. In the words of the officer concerned, the units were composed of 'a militia of idealists, made up of the most expert, valorous, strongest and most aggressive of us all'. The disturbing objective of these squads was to execute 'acts destined to quell local fervour in those places where the subversive fury had most taken hold'.[67]

However, to use the words of the same officer, the army commanders pushed themselves well beyond the preparation of 'punitive local actions'. In a circular dated 24 September 1920, expedited to the head of the intelligence office of the general chief of staff, the colonel, Camillo Caleffi, openly affirmed that, in the light of the 'not insignificant importance' of the militant paramilitary squads (*fasci*), the latter should be considered 'active forces that could eventually be used to counterbalance any anti-national or subversive element'.[68] One month later, Giolitti's minister for war, the socialist reformer Ivanoe Bonomi, issued another circular stating that those officers in the process of being demobbed (circa sixty thousand) were to be sent to the large agglomerations with the obligation of taking over and commanding the militant paramilitary squads.[69] In effect, a great many of the leaders of the fascist movement would later be drawn from such squads.[70]

After the overtly partisan stance of the army, which from this perspective was 'the most polluted of all the state organs', came that of the local authorities themselves. The majority of them now revealed that they too shared a fundamental fascist assumption – that subversive socialism could not be considered an expression of the will of the nation, even if the election results indicated the contrary.[71]

Of course, it should not be forgotten that the maximalist criticisms of the liberal government had contributed to discrediting the latter in the eyes of a large part of the population. Moreover, the socialist aversion for the armed forces, especially the *carabinieri* and the army, had created irreparable divisions.[72] On this point a socialist from Umbria, who later turned to communism, quite frankly asked: 'But are we really being serious, is there really any point in asking those [the police] who give matches to pyromaniacs [the fascists], to put out the fire?'[73]

An important sign of the reorganisation of the anti-socialist front came from the numbers of new recruits now swelling the ranks of the militant paramilitary squads (*fasci*). Created in Milan in the first months of 1919, the squads were, in reality, off-shoots of the interventionist movement. It was in Milan, in fact, that the *Fascio rivoluzionario d'azione internazionalista* was formed.

Inaugurated on 29 October 1914, the squad was created out of two subgroups of parties belonging to the extreme left.[74] In January of 1915, even Mussolini himself played a prominent role in the squad's activities, to the point of erroneously taking credit for its creation.[75]

From that moment on, the use of the term *fascist* became increasingly frequent. It no longer indicated the adherents of one of the many political organisations or trade-union movements which were two a penny at that time, but referred precisely to *that* particular movement. After the rout of the Italian army at Caporetto at the end of 1917, the creation of the *Fascio parlamentare di difesa nazionale* reinforced this tendency, the latter being an 'anti-parliamentary movement', comprising all the interventionist MPs, who were also known as 'fascists'.[76] As a consequence, during the post-war period the term *fascism* was already charged with meaning, being explicitly linked to the legacy of the First World War.

Even as late as 1919, the basic structure of the fascist movement was made up of former trade unionist revolutionaries, who were now members of the revolutionary squad of 1914. The most prominent were Michele Bianchi, Umberto Pasella, Cesare Rossi and Giovanni Marinelli, but it also included the futurist Filippo Tommaso Marinetti and the *Arditi*, led by Ferruccio Vecchi and Mario Carli. Their first official act – if we may call it that – was the destruction of the Milanese headquarters of the newspaper *Avanti!*, already referred to, and carried out barely a month after the squad's formation. Right from the very beginning, the militant paramilitary squad had anticipated the need for armed units, co-ordinated in such a way as to back up the legal activities of the organisation. As such, they were a clear expression of the militarization of politics which had been steadily developing since 1914.

The attack, owing more to the *Arditi* and the futurists than to fascists, was executed with military precision, as Mussolini himself recalled a few weeks before the March on Rome: 'The members of the Milanese squad went into the assault on *Avanti!* as if they were attacking an Austrian trench. They surmounted walls, cut nets, broke down doors, all the while dodging the hail of burning lead that the defenders were firing down upon them. ... This is the violence that I approve of, this is the violence that I exalt.'[77] Notwithstanding the importance of the episode, up to the second half of 1920, the militant fascist squads remained just one of the many patriotic organisations of the time. But from this moment onwards, the group began to grow dramatically: from circa 20,000 members at the end of 1920, to 250,000 a year later and over 300,000 in May 1922, thus making it the largest political party in Italian history up to that date.[78]

The social composition of the new recruits was extremely mixed. As has already been underlined, one cannot overly insist 'on considering the political and ideological inclinations as a true reflection of the socio-economic situation', especially in a period when political passions were running so high.[79] The socialist success in the elections of 1919 and 1920 demonstrated not only the hold the party had over the proletariat, but also the influence they wielded over the wide band of 'middle classes'. In the fascist squads, however, from the 1920s onwards, wealthy share-croppers came into the movement, counter-balancing the poorer share-croppers who were now under the protection of the socialist leagues. Day labourers and the rural unemployed also joined the fascist squads, especially those who were not inserted into the socialist organisation, or who, after having lost their jobs through the post-war economic depression, had difficulty in supporting the collective discipline imposed upon them by the leagues. The fascist squads also picked up all those who were afraid of losing their jobs in the event of a socialist election victory, or who were scared by the latter's promise to socialise the land. The fascist squads also took in the unemployed and the common delinquents, all of whom were ready to take advantage of the chaos and gain some personal advantage. But they were not alone; alongside them in the fascist ranks were teachers, students, lawyers, tradesmen, doctors, public and private workers, local industrialists, merchants and craftsmen. The principal aim of this group was to take the control of the masses out of the hands of the PSI and the other working class parties (which were considered to be insufficiently patriotic, for instance, the Catholics, who were accused of applying "white bolshevism"). In other words, to take control of the PSI's organisations in the hope of guiding them towards solutions compatible with the existing social order. It was perhaps no coincidence that this varied social group had already represented the most important social classes during the campaign for the patriotic mobilization for war.

The rapid rise of the militant fascist squads was due to a number of factors. As we have just seen, their political legitimisation was largely due to Giolitti's national coalition, while their numbers continued to swell through the influx of large groups of demobbed soldiers and young students. Although the latter had been too young to take part in the First World War, they had, nevertheless, been brought up believing in the myth of the armed defence of the homeland and of the struggle against the enemies both at home and abroad.[80] Very often, murders and other acts of great cruelty were carried out by such adolescents, who were often between the ages of sixteen and eighteen. In 1921, the socialist leader, Giacinto Menotti Serrati, wrote a dramatic speech addressing this very question:

> What really torments us is that such a reaction, so difficult to imagine, does not come from the state, nor from any of the public authorities, it comes from below, sinking to the level of arbitrators, criminals and thugs. Armed with revolvers, daggers, rifles and hand bombs, the dregs of society have all been enrolled and are now maintained with twenty or thirty lira a day and live by hunting down socialists. And

now the youngsters from our schools have actually gone and joined them. Drunk with romanticised ideas of war, their heads full of patriotic hot air, they see in us the 'Germans', the traitors, and they attack us with zeal, just as if they were fighting for their country, just as if they were soldiers fighting for their lives in the trenches. Students of 18 to 20 years old are now drawn up amongst criminals and they are brawling with the workers as if they were our foreign enemies.[81]

Mussolini and the leaders of the militant paramilitary squads soon realised that the balance was tipping in their favour. Although they were still guarded about the rural fascist movement's aspirations to autonomy, financed by the landowners of Emilia, Tuscany and Umbria, they clearly understood the advantages that this brought them. In fact, rural fascism not only furnished the movement with a solid base of supporters, through its violent protagonist stance, it had also helped them win a central position on the national political scene. It was an unexpected comeback, but all the more important given the delusion of the 1919 elections, in which none of the fascist candidates had won a seat.

That being said, the large influx of new members was profoundly altering the movement itself. As noted by Renzo De Felice, not only was the social composition of the organisation being deeply transformed, but its political composition was too. The new levy that grafted itself onto the original interventionist nucleus was 'politically rougher and more immature and much readier to resolve issues through violence and brute force'.[82] In order to avoid a dangerous fragmentation of the movement, Mussolini and the other exponents of fascism in Milan decided to set up a centralised and hierarchical structure. Although this went against the opinion of various provincial squad leaders (the so called 'ras'), such a course of action, soon proved successful in the battle with the socialists. The re-structuring was made definitive at the Congress of Augusteo (7–10 November 1921), when the movement became officially known as the National Fascist Party.

The increase in membership occurred in the very places where civil unrest was most bitter, i.e. the Valle Padana, Tuscany, Umbria and some of the more developed provinces of the south, where socialism had succeeded in taking root. In the majority of the southern regions and on the islands, where the socio-economic transformations had been less incisive and where the radicalism of the PSI had been tempered, fascism nearly always came later, taking root only after the battle had already been won.

After the events in Trieste, another outbreak of political violence occurred in Bologna on the very day that the socialist administration was supposed to take up office after its victory in the elections of 20 November. In the pitched battle that followed, ten socialists were killed. The only local nationalist councillor to be killed – a mutilated First World War veteran – was immediately selected by the fascists as their martyr. The capitulation of the socialists led to a prefectorial commissar being made head of the town council. The event actually served to promote the cause of the fascist movement, since the public now perceived them as the most credible and decisive opponents of the communist peril, able to confront them *manu militari*.[83]

Faced with the new strong-arm tactics of their adversaries, many socialists just tended to put their heads in the sand. Refusing to organise a common plan of action, the socialists continued operating with the same provincial mentality that had always characterised their movement. In stark contrast, the fascists had already begun to coordinate their actions, first on a provincial scale and then on a wider inter-regional scale with the mobilization of hundreds, sometimes thousands of squad members who, after devastating one zone, would rapidly descend upon another.

In order to terrorise their opponents and, indeed, raise the conflict to the ultimate pitch, the fascists adhered to the axiom of kicking their opponents as hard as possible, even when they were down. To this end they set in motion a terrible phase of reprisals and counter reprisals. These included the disruption of town and provincial councils, the redaction of statements under the menace of violence and the destruction of political and trade union headquarters (later including those of the republicans and Catholics as well). Other targets for attack included the branch offices of the other working-class parties, the newspaper offices, the cooperatives, right down to their adversaries' private dwellings. Other abuses involved preventing local MPs from returning to their constituencies to canvas support, kidnappings, murders, muggings, lynching, clubbing, even obliging political opponents to walk around with nooses around their necks, or coercing them into signing declarations of resignation. Other forms of intimidation included the organising of parades in which their victims were bound to the back of cars and driven round like a trophy or even dragged for miles along the ground until they were reduced to a bloody pulp. A more subtle form of aggression involved the use of laxatives, such as castor-oil, to publicly humiliate their unfortunate victims. This method was initially applied to individuals but was eventually taken up and proposed as a solution to a much larger problem – namely to 'purge' the entire nation of its 'swarms of subversives'.[84]

In the political elections of May 1921 the freedom to vote was heavily compromised. Nevertheless, the PSI still managed to obtain a good result, with 24.7 per cent of the votes and 123 MPs (to whom another 15 were added from the Italian Communist Party, created after the split of January 1921). Where the violence had been more systematic, the drop in the number of people turning up to vote was much more apparent. Moreover, it was in this very period that fascism began moving from a selective form of violence – what Mussolini actually defined as a *surgical* form of violence, employed against the socialist leaders – to a more indiscriminate form, which was aimed against all those who were even suspected of sympathising with the 'enemy'.[85] Only now did the projects and the long-term plans drawn up during the war begin to take shape. The political game-plan of the liberals now appeared completely inadequate. Indeed, groups of private individuals openly aspired to take control of the state, convinced that they were now the exclusive representatives of the *real* interests of the nation.

In the fascist squads, the prestige attributed to combat experience was extremely high, as can be seen by the manner in which they decorated their toughest and most courageous members. One Venetian, for example, wounded during a mission in Treviso, was awarded a gold medal – 'struck in the forehead by a rifle round' the latter 'bound the wound, took up arms and returned to the fray, displaying notable valour through his exemplary behaviour and indomitable courage, obtaining complete success despite the grave situation'.[86] Even the funeral prayers composed in honour of the squad members who had been ambushed or killed in action followed a schema which, through innumerable commemorations, was gradually built upon during the course of the war. More often than not, such events were celebrated not just by the families, but by the entire community as a whole.[87]

Although the socialist leaders had ordered their own militants to ignore the provocations, during the spring of 1921, a notable intensification of the violence led to the first signs of an organised reaction. The most significant response involved the formation in June of the *Arditi del popolo*, a paramilitary organisation founded by Argo Secondari, an officer of the *Arditi*. The group's main aim was to oppose the fascists for as long as the latter continued 'assassinating their fellow workers and for as long as they continued pursuing the fratricide war'.[88]

The fear of remaining isolated pushed Mussolini into a move which, in his own words, avoided plunging the country into a 'chronic' civil war. On 3 August Mussolini signed the Pacification Pact with the PSI and the CGL, which foresaw the end of all violence and established the reciprocal respect of each party's symbols.[89]

However, some of the most prestigious leaders of the provincial squads, such as Piero Marsich, Dino Grandi, Italo Balbo and Roberto Farinacci, refuted the treaty outright. Such a decisive rejection forced Mussolini to perform an about-face and accept with great pomp the renewal of 'punitive missions'. A proclamation opposing the peace, circulated in the province of Modena, aptly summed up the mood:

> When will we disarm?
>
> When the socialist party renounces:
>
> 1 – criticising the war, denigrating the victory and deriding the combatants,
>
> 2 – menacing the revolution . . . .

3 – adopting a stance which is exclusively anti-Italian,

4 – continuing the scandalous boycott and the violence against our workers who decline to enrol in their organisations

Until these conditions are met, the fascists will continue to come down hard on all those who oppose them, battling without reserve, without scruples and without quarter.[90]

The rejection of the Peace Pact on the part of the most extreme elements of the fascist movement threw into the spotlight the divisions existing between the '19th group' from Milan and the new levies who had entered the movement in 1920–21. Such a change in direction provoked the many prominent ex-interventionists of the Left, such as Pietro Nenni, Alceste De Ambris, Mario and Guido Bergamo, to move away, now finding themselves caught between the anti-socialism of the war years and the condemnation of the systematic use of violence as a means of gagging the working class.[91]

Bonomi, who, as an ex-interventionist, could not help but sympathize with fascism (he was elected at Mantua on an electoral slate that included members of the militant fascist squads), attempted nevertheless to respect the law and bring the violence to an end. The first step, in accordance with the terms of the Peace Pact, was repression of the *Arditi del popolo*. In effect, the latter had by now been renounced both by the PSI, who had ended all military clashes with the fascists, and also by the Communist Party, who now accused the group of only wanting to fight against fascism, not bring down the bourgeois state.[92] On 15 December 1921, Bonomi took the next step – he issued a decree, classing the cudgel an offensive weapon. The week after that he ordered the disbanding of all organisations known 'to be armed and organised in a militarily fashion'. In reply, the PNF, through a number of directives published the very next day by *Popolo d'Italia*, declared that the political sections of the party and the 'militant paramilitary squads' formed an 'indivisible whole' and as a consequence, to disband one would mean having to outlaw the other. A few days later, the constitution of the PNF formally confirmed the existence of the militia of the party, or better still the 'party-militia' as official.[93]

During the first months of 1922, military expeditions multiplied against the cities of northern and central Italy: Ferrara, Bologna, Cremona, Viterbo, Novara, Rimini, Ravenna, Milan, Ancona, Bolzano, Trento and many more.[94] Once the defenders had capitulated, they were obliged to parade around the streets draped in the national flag. Some were made to kneel down and kiss it. After being forced to shout fascist and patriotic slogans, some prisoners were forced to declare before the entire community their adhesion to the fascist trade union organisations. Others were marched off to the local First World War monuments where they were forced to chant patriotic slogans such as: 'I love my country and a thousand times I say with true heart: long live Italy!'[95]

In order to cleanse the hostile cooperatives of their subversion, some captives were coerced into paying for the construction of war monuments as a tangible sign of their 'conversion'.

Finally, the most high-profile leaders, such as the trade unionists, the councillors and the heads of the leagues, all of whose names had been compiled in 'proscriptions' and then published by the fascists, were banished from the community. Harried by chants, insults and burlesque funerals, they were escorted to the nearest train station and warned never to return, on penalty of death. Many of them had little choice but to go into exile.

As has already been noted, the role played by the forces of order in aiding the fascist cause was crucial. But they were not alone, both the army and the local authorities lent a hand. Even the Church played a part, especially after the rout of Caporetto, taking up and linking nationalist and anti-socialist propaganda. Pro-fascist activities by the forces of order included the destitution of the socialist councils by the prefects, the arrest of the trade unionists and councillors, the halting of clashes only when the socialists appeared to be getting the upper hand, even their arrest and prosecution. Indeed, whenever fascists were accused of crimes, the magistrates ensured that their cases were rapidly dismissed. Although the methods employed were clearly questionable, in the eyes of the patriotic public such manoeuvres came across as an admirable example of the state being defended against the danger of subversion.

Equally important of course was the open support of the press. As has already been noted, the papers tended to dampen down the 'civil war', referring to it as if it was merely a problem of public order or just 'bad news'. A similar situation existed in Parliament where the socialist accusations gained little support.[96] Even when fascist aggressions were discussed, the violence was judged to be a temporary measure, something that was both necessary and legitimate in order to bolster the state and reintroduce 'prerogatives and obligations'.[97]

The last signs of resistance came in the form of the *Alleanza del lavoro,* created out of an amalgamation of the CGL and other trade union organisations, together with the Communist, Republican and Socialist parties (the latter being somewhat reluctant). In August 1922, the *Alleanza del lavoro* organised a 'constitutional strike' as a protest against the fascist attacks. Too late, the anti-fascist stance began to be perceived as a common ground upon which to construct a response to the aggression. In fact, the strike had the paradoxical effect of making the objective which the interventionist movement had not been able to attain actually look almost attainable – i.e. replace once and for all the impotent liberal ruling class. A communication issued by the leaders of the PNF and timed to coincide with the beginning of the strike, made the following threat: 'We give 48 hours to the state to demonstrate the proof of its authority over all those who are answerable to it and over all those who menace its existence. When the time is up, Fascism will claim free liberty of action and will *substitute the state* which once again will have demonstrated its impotence.'[98] The ending of the strike on 3 August did nothing to stop the last and definitive fascist offensive against the subversives. A violent wave of repression and the storming *manu militari* of the workers centres in the north wiped out any illusion that the socialists might somehow react. There were only a few sporadic episodes of successful resistance, these occurring in Parma and Bari. Despite the fascist offensive, the opposition was still incapable of organising a strong united front. If anything, the tensions within the socialist movement were becoming more fraught than ever and at the beginning of September, during the course of the 19th national congress in Rome, the maximalist majority expelled the reformist minority.

The moment was now ripe to take the capital and on 28 October, the plan was executed.[99] On the afternoon of the same day, a special edition of *Popolo d'Italia* published the manifesto, announcing that Benito Mussolini had been given responsibility for forming a new government. Citing almost to the letter a passage of the famous communication with which General Diaz had announced victory over the Austro-Hungarians, in November 1918, the announcement affirmed: 'Fascists! … The battle that you have engaged and conducted with unequalled spirit of sacrifice has now come to its victorious end. … The remnants of the enemy forces are retreating back up the valleys, harassed by our brave militia, ruling out any return to the past.'[100] The struggle that had begun in the autumn of 1914 and had been concluded four years later now appeared to have been won decisively.

Political Violence and Modernity

Intransigent champion of the absolutist state, demonising all those who refused to associate themselves with it, fascism also sustained that violence had a profoundly moral, regenerating role. Such contradictory elements had already been debated by intellectuals: the themes had been confronted in the avant-garde literature of the early twentieth century; they were taken up again by the interventionists and were discussed and accentuated in the post-war period.[101]

Fascism was the embodiment of all of these elements. According to Luigi Freddi, leader of the *Avanguardie studentesche fasciste*, if the adversary could not be convinced by words, beating him up saved a great deal of time and guaranteed the outcome: 'The fist is a synthesis of many things. … Since it interacts directly upon the body of the adversary in a manner which is short and sharp, it cannot be ignored. … And nothing is more synthetic than the bullet of a revolver. … It is most efficacious since it effectively stops the discussion ever recurring – maximum economy, rapidity and fluency.'[102] But the reasoning behind the cult of violence went even deeper than this. In October of 1922, an article appearing in the *Gerarchia* affirmed significantly:

> Fascists exalt courage and physical force, they nurture gymnastics and every form of sport, disdaining intellectual decadence. ... Fascists accept the value of discipline and recognise the need for a hierarchy. They instil in their young recruits a sense of responsibility and through the order of the squads they exalt and build up the military spirit. Through their ceremonies, they gave a new lease of life to traditional rites that the dull uniformity of democracy has always tended to suppress.[103]

The fascist exaltation of activism and their defiance of death – explicit in the names assigned to their squads (Desperate, Indomitable, Who cares) – were particularly visible in fascist ceremony and pomp. One has only to consider the pennons in the wind, the black shirts, the helmets, the hymns, the fasces, the roman salute, the appeal to the dead, the pagan feasts, the solemn oaths, the military parades etc. Such rituals were all expressions of an attempt at 'heightening the sentiment' and in so doing oppose the intellectualism which characterised the traditional political class.[104]

Herein lies the principal reason why fascism, from its very earliest beginnings, was so keen carefully to nurture all its ritualistic elements. Far from being an extemporaneous exercise, or a simple means of manipulating the conscience, fascist ritual was above all a research of the senses, an aesthetic, an experience linked to perceptions and sensations, something that could return emotive intensity to everyday life, reinstating everything that modern secular society had taken out of it. Such an approach could be captivating, especially to the younger fascists. One of them would later recall how they had all been moved by 'indefinable motives, all too often incomprehensible to historians'. Such motives included: 'proving ones courage, doing away with stalemates and compromises and eradicating from society all those who were vile, slothful, slow, treacherous, fat and lazy.'[105]

With this new liturgy and exaltation of the memory of the First World War, the new recruits, or the 'base' as Mussolini referred to them later, were actively encouraged 'to believe in the sanctity of the sacrifice of our dead. By establishing continuity between the epos of war and the drama of the revolution, interventionism and fascism have [in fact] become indissolubly linked. In such a way, we have shown that we were ready for our destiny'.[106] As early as 1917, the future duce was already prescribing rites 'of remembrance and purification' in order to remind the young of the sacrifices made in war.[107]

The quest for a more 'human' society, a society that was truer, less artificial and more dynamic, was thus one of the motives that succeeded in capturing the interest of a great many people, people who, in the society of the masses, saw a rare opportunity for social ascension, but who, at the same time, felt menaced by the very processes of levelling, homogenising, impersonalising that the same dynamic was producing.[108]

The absolutism of its very own ideology, the conviction of representing the will of an entire nation and the expulsion of dissenters, were all expressions of an attempt to rebuild the nation in a totally different way and to assure complete social cohesion. As Dino Grandi explained in a reference to the fascist movement during a Parliamentary sitting of 1921: 'We are not a faction of the state, because we ourselves feel that we are the state.'[109] In his diary, Italo Balbo underlined the same fact: 'There is only one truth and whoever believes they possess it should defend it with their life. And those who do not believe in having the absolute and total truth within them cannot be a fascist, they cannot defy death.'[110]

Fascism has often been interpreted as the very peak of 'infinite negation' – anti-socialism, anti-parliamentarianism, anti-liberalism, anti-materialism etc.[111] But, as has already been seen, its negative aspects aside, fascism also liked to consider itself a positive force, as the very persecutor, in fact, of the elements which appeared to be threatening Italy itself – materialism, decadence, individualism, egoism, etc. – counteracting them with policies which had been perfected and refined during the First World War.

Within this vision, the words of the future duce are particularly apt: in order to make the Italians a disciplined race, it would first be necessary to convince them that he who 'marches does not grow weaker … , but grows stronger through all those who march with him.'[112] The fascist exaltation of war, the war-like spirit, combined with respect for military organisation and violence, all went in the same direction, that is, offering the possibility to every individual to enlarge and expand their own 'I', learning at the same time, to march together as one.

To a certain extent, one might say that fascism was generated by a confluence of different political projects, all of which aimed at restoring to the country that aura of sacredness and absoluteness that the process of secularisation had taken away.[113] When all is said and done, the real enemies of fascism, against whom its proponents vigorously campaigned, were the erosion of traditions, moral decay, heterogeneity, relativism and the complexity that characterised the modern bourgeoisie, and which the fascists pledged to replace with transparent and instantly comprehensible social ties. To bring this about they introduced the concepts of militarization, order, discipline, hierarchy and force, emphasising the quality of the elite as opposed to the quantity of the masses.

Notes

1. For an overview, see Mario Isnenghi and Giorgio Rochat, *La Grande guerra 1914–1918* (Florence, 2000); Roberto Vivarelli, *Storia delle origini del fascismo. L'Italia dalla grande guerra alla marcia su Roma* (Bologna, 1991); and Walter L. Adamson, 'The Impact of World War I on the Italian Political Culture', in Aviel Roshwald and Richard Stites

(eds.), *European Culture in the Great War. The Arts, Entertainment, and Propaganda, 1914-1918* (Cambridge, 2002).

2. Cleanto Boscolo, "Ognuno al suo posto!", *L'Unità*, 1 February 1919. Giovanna Procacci, 'La politica interna italiana, la Rivoluzione di febbraio e l'involuzione politica dell'interventismo di sinistra', in Procacci, *Dalla rassegnazione alla rivolta. Mentalità e comportamenti popolari nella Grande Guerra* (Rome, 1999).

3. Concerning the blurring of the civil and military spheres during the First World War, see Andreas Hillgruber, *La distruzione dell'Europa. La Germania e l'epoca delle guerre mondiali (1914-1945)* (Bologna, 1991), 121. A comparative study can be found in John Horne (ed.), *State, Society and Mobilization in Europe during the First World War* (Cambridge, 1997).

4. For the stance of Benito Mussolini, the future fascist duce, on these themes, see 'Disciplina di guerra', *Il Popolo d'Italia*, 9 November 1917, now in Mussolini, *Scritti e discorsi. Dall'interventismo al fascismo (15 Novembre 1914-23 Marzo 1919)* (Milan, 1934), 283-284, and for the post-war period, see 'L'instaurazione dello Stato Fascista nel pensiero e nei propositi di Mussolini', *Il Popolo d'Italia*, 2 January 1923.

5. A general picture can be found in Martin Gilbert, *The First World War: A Complete History* (New York, 1994), 16-34.

6. Angelo Ventrone, *La seduzione totalitaria. Guerra, modernità, violenza politica (1914-1918)* (Rome, 2003), 75-80, but also Brunello Vigezzi, 'Le "Radiose giornate" del maggio 1915 nei rapporti dei Prefetti', *Nuova rivista storica*, September-December 1959 and January-April 1960.

7. On the tradition of subversion which was inaugurated for the occasion, see Luigi Salvatorelli, *Nazionalfascismo* (Turin, 1977; 1st edition, 1923), 26-28, 48-49.

8. Costanzo Premuti, *Come Roma preparò la guerra* (Rome, 1923), 335.

9. Francesco Paoloni, *I nostri "boches": il giolittismo, partito tedesco in Italia*, with a preface by Benito Mussolini (Milan, 1916), 61.

10. On this theme, see Emilio Gentile, *La grande Italia* (Milan, 1997).

11. Mussolini, *Il diario di guerra (1915-1917)*, in Mussolini, *Scritti e discorsi*, 77.

12. Giovanni Calò, *Doveri del cittadino in tempo di guerra* (Milan, 1915).

13. On this subject, see Ruth Ben-Ghiat, *La cultura fascista* (Bologna, 2001), 207, 214-215.

14. On the demonizing of political adversaries, see Angelo Ventrone, *Il nemico interno. Immagini, parole e simboli della lotta politica nell'Italia del '900* (Rome, 2005).

15. Stéphane Audoin-Rouzeau and Annette Becker, *14-18, retrouver la Guerre* (Paris, 2000).

16. The passage is taken from his memoirs written after the war, cit. in: Piero Melograni, *Storia politica della Grande guerra* (Milan, 1998; 1st edition, 1969) 319-320.

17. Ventrone, *La seduzione totalitaria*, 225-226. On the position of the PSI, Alberto Malatesta, *I socialisti italiani durante la guerra* (Milan, 1926).

18. „Il Fronte interno" *durante la guerra* (Rome, 1918), 15-17.

19. Benito Mussolini, 'Abbasso il Parlamento', *Il Popolo d'Italia*, 11 May 1915, now in Mussolini, *Scritti e discorsi*, 35-36.

20. Concerning the birth of the myth of Cadorna, see Gioacchino Volpe, *Il popolo italiano nella Grande guerra (1915-1916)* (Rome, 1998), 170-173; on the likely manoeuverings towards a military dictatorship, see Melograni, *Storia politica della Grande guerra*, 312-319.

21. Forty-one people were killed and around two hundred injured, see Alberto Monticone, 'Il socialismo torinese ed i fatti dell'agosto 1917', in Monticone, *Gli italiani in uniforme 1915/1918: intellettuali, borghesi e disertori* (Bari, 1972).

22. This explains the existence of the unsigned pamphlet, entitled *I responsabili del disastro. Socialisti e clericali*, in Archivio centrale dello Stato, Ministero dell'Interno, Direzione generale di Pubblica sicurezza, Divisione Affari Generali e Riservati, A5G – Prima guerra mondiale (henceforth referred to as ACS, A5G PGM), b. 96, f. 212, Florence, stf. 10, in. 2 and also the speech by Alceste De Ambris at a meeting of the *Unione sindacale italiana* of Padua, ibid., *Relazione del prefetto di Firenze*, 29 January 1918.

23. Premuti, *Come Roma preparò la guerra*.

24. 'For victory. Government do something!', *Il Popolo d'Italia*, 2 June 1916.

25. Italo Balbo, *Diario 1922* (Milan, 1932).

26. 'Parlamento – Partiti – Convinzioni e convenzioni – Un atto risoluto – S'invoca che diventi metodo, finalmente, di governo', *Il Fronte Interno. Organo centrale dei Comitati d'azione*, 17 March 1916.

27. Benito Mussolini, 'Un po' di verità nel paradosso. I giornali sono necessari?', *Il Popolo d'Italia*, 11 February 1918.

28. The convocation of a constituent assembly was constantly requested by various sectors of the interventionist movement in the post-war era, see Roberta Suzzi Valli, *Le origini del fascismo* (Rome, 2003), 21–22. For an analogous project, supported by the anarchists, the *Arditi* and various other military corps in the summer of 1919, see Ferdinando Cordova, *Arditi e legionari dannunziani* (Padua, 1969), 83–85.

29. Archivio centrale dello Stato, Ufficio Centrale d'Investigazione, b. 23, f. 470 Massoneria, *Complotto contro S.M. il Re*, 21 March 1917.

30. Ibid., b. 41, f. 77, *nota firmata Cillario*, s.d., 61–64. Even post-war fascism was organized in a similar way with the *squadre*, the *centurie* and the *legioni*, see Emilio Gentile, *Storia del partito fascista, 1919–1922. Movimento e milizia* (Bari, 1989), 516–517 and 534–535.

31. ACS, A5G PGM, b. 119, f. 242, stf. 3, ins. 4, „Sette terroriste di repubblicani carbonari", note of 29 November 1917 and 12 December 1917.

32. Even in the post-war period, other paramilitary organizations continued to make use of analogous rituals, as in the case of the Knights of Death (*Cavalieri della morte*), created in 1921 by a splinter group of the militant paramilitary squads (*fasci di combatimento*) of Venice, see Giulia Albanese, *Alle origini del fascismo. La violenza politica a Venezia 1919–1922*, on behalf of Mario Isnenghi (Padua, 2001), 160.

33. ACS, A5G PGM, b. 96, f. 212, stf. 10, ins. 2, *Relazione del prefetto di Firenze*, 22 December 1917.

34. *Continuando*, ibid, b. 106, f. 225, stf. 16, ins. 3, manifesto attached to the *Relazione del prefetto di Milano*, 17 January 1918. On the attack on the *Avanti!* on 15 April 1919 and the quote by Mussolini, see Renzo De Felice, *Mussolini il rivoluzionario. 1883–1920* (Turin, 1995; 1st edition, 1965), 519–523; for the destruction of the printing house in Rome belonging to the newspaper, 21 July 1920, ibid., 624.

35. The socialists did the same thing immediately after the war against the 'bourgeois' administrations, who were accused of financial corruption and pursuing their own personal interests; for example, Hubert Corsi, *La lotta politica in Maremma 1900–1925* (Rome, 1987); and Roberto Bianchi, *Bocci-Bocci. I tumulti annonari nella Toscana del 1919* (Florence, 2001).

36. Giuseppe Bottai, preface to the *XXVII Battaglione d'assalto* (Milan, 1937), 5–7. For the history of the special assault groups, see Cordova, *Arditi e legionari dannunziani*, and Giorgio Rochat, *Gli arditi della grande guerra. Origini, battaglie, miti* (Milan, 1981).

37. On this subject, see the classic Eric J. Leed, *No Man's Land. Combat & Identity in World War I* (Cambridge, 1979); and George L. Mosse, 'The Brutalization of German Politics', in Mosse, *Fallen Soldiers: Reshaping the Memory of the World Wars* (Oxford, 1990).

38. An in-depth study on the relationship between politics and violence can be found in Eduardo Gonzales Calleja, *La violencia en la política. Perspectivas teóricas sobre el empledo deliberado de la fuerza en los conflictos de poder* (Madrid, 2002).

39. Adrian Lyttelton, 'Fascismo e violenza: conflitto sociale e azione politica in Italia nel primo dopoguerra', *Storia contemporanea*, a. XIII, n. 6, December 1982, 972–973.

40. Sergio Panunzio, *Che cos'è il fascismo* (Milan, 1924), 16.

41. Benito Mussolini, *La mia vita* (Milan, 1999), 68; the autobiographical account, actually written for the most part by his brother Arnaldo, was serialized in the *Saturday Evening Post* of Philadelphia in May of 1928.

42. Ventrone, *La seduzione totalitaria*, 270ff.

43. For the writings of one of the protagonists upon this theme, see Angelo Oliviero Olivetti, *Dal sindacalismo rivoluzionario al corporativismo*, introduction by Francesco Perfetti (Rome, 1984); and for an analysis of the debate both before and after the war, see Zeev Sternhell, Mario Sznajder and Maia Asheri, *Naissance de l'idéologie fasciste* (Paris, 1989). On the figure of the manufacturer, Francesco Perfetti, *Il sindacalismo fascista. Dalle origini alla vigilia dello Stato corporativo (1919–1930)* (Rome, 1988); and Giuseppe Parlato, *La sinistra fascista. Storia di un progetto mancato* (Bologna, 2000).

44. Adrian Lyttelton, *The Seizure of Power. Fascism in Italy 1919–1929* (London, 1973), in particular the paragraphs entitled *L'antipartito* and *I „fascisti della prima ora“*.

45. Salvatore Lupo, *Il fascismo. La politica in un regime totalitario* (Rome, 2000), 40.

46. On the occupation of the land by the associations representing the dispossessed, see Giovanni Sabbatucci, *I combattenti nel primo dopoguerra* (Bari, 1974), 184–198.

47. Charles S. Maier, *Recasting Bourgeois Europe. Stabilization in France, Germany and Italy in the Decade after World War I* (Princeton, 1975).

48. A general overview can be found in Horne (ed.), *State, Society and Mobilization*.

49. Gianni Isola, *Guerra al regno della guerra: storia della Lega proletaria mutilati, invalidi, reduci, orfani e vedove di guerra (1918–1924)* (Florence, 1990).

50. Mussolini, *La mia vita*, 66ff.; also 'Contro la bestia ritornante', *Il Popolo d'Italia*, 18 February 1919.

51. Serafino Giulietti, 'Fascio fascisti e antifascisti. Fossombrone 1919–1929', in Paolo Giannotti (ed.), *La provincia di Pesaro e Urbino nel regime fascista* (Ancona, 1986), 13.

52. A fascist interpretation of these events can be found in *Barbarie rossa. Riassunto cronologico delle gesta compiute dai socialisti italiani dal 1919 in poi*, preface by Benito Mussolini (Rome, 1921).

53. Luigi Preti, *Le lotte agrarie nella Val Padana* (Turin, 1955), 298ff.; and Alessandro Roveri, *Le origini del fascismo a Ferrara, 1918–1921* (Milan, 1974).

54. Pietro Nenni, *Storia di quattro anni. 1919–1922* (Milan, 1976; 1st edition, 1946), 50ff.

55. Paolo Spriano, *L'occupazione delle fabbriche. Settembre 1920* (Turin, 1964).

56. As testified by one of the future members of the fascist quadrumvirate, Cesare Maria De Vecchi di Val Cismon, *Il quadrumviro scomodo* (Milan, 1983), 26–27.

57. Cited in Jens Petersen, 'Il problema della violenza nel fascismo italiano', *Storia contemporanea*, a. XIII, n. 6, December 1982, 994–995. For a similar evaluation, see Giovanni Zibordi, *Critica socialista del fascismo* (Bologna, 1922), now in Renzo De Felice (ed.), *Il fascismo. Le interpretazioni dei contemporanei e degli storici* (Bari, 1998).

58. Consider for example the coining of the nationalist slogan 'Ever-ready for the homeland and the king' in Bologna, or even the characteristic blue shirts, the Young Explorers (*Giovani exploratori*) and the Ladies of the Red Cross (*Dame della Croce Rossa*).

59. De Felice, *Mussolini il rivoluzionario*, 545–599.

60. *Popolo d'Italia*, 15 October 1920. On the role of the army, see Marco Mondini, *La politica delle armi. Il ruolo dell'esercito nell'avvento del fascismo* (Bari, 2006).

61. Concerning the bourgeois reaction, see Italo E. Torsiello, *Il tramonto delle baronie rosse* (Ferrara, 1921); and Concetto Valente, *La ribellione antibolscevica di Bologna* (Bologna, 1921).

62. The celebrated definition derived from an appeal of Gabriele D'Annunzio, 'Our victory will not be mutilated', *Corriere della Sera*, 24 October 1918.

63. Balbo, *Diario 1922*, 30.

64. Benito Mussolini, 'Trincerocrazia', *Il Popolo d'Italia*, 15 December 1917.

65. 'Primo appello alle fiamme', *Roma futurista*, 20 September 1918, reproduced in Cordova, *Arditi e legionari dannunziani*, 208–209. The failure of a possible agreement between the *Arditi* and the socialists in the first months of 1919, was attempted in the name of the struggle against the ruling classes, who were considered to be 'mean, incapable and dishonest', see ibid., 46–56, 60–61.

66. According to the terms of the treaty (Trattato), Italy obtained the city of Zara and a few Dalmatian islands, but renounced Dalmatia itself.

67. Angelo Tasca, *Nascita e avvento del fascismo* (Bari, 1976; 1st edition, 1938), 159–161.

68. Cited in Giorgio Candeloro, *Storia dell'Italia moderna*, vol. VIII: *La prima guerra mondiale, il dopoguerra, l'avvento del fascismo* (Milan, 1989; 1st edition, 1978), 347–348.

69. Tasca, *Nascita e avvento del fascismo*, 161.

70. Concerning the myth of war amongst members of the intellectual middle class, who in large made up the one hundred thousand reserve officers, see Mario Isnenghi, *Il mito della grande guerra* (Bologna, 1989). Only later, after numerous splits and differences, when the fascists' dictatorial stance had become explicitly clear, did some branches of the *Arditi* and the *Associazione nazionale combattenti* decide to distance themselves from the fascist movement, see Cordova, *Arditi e legionari*, 158–159; and Sabbatucci, *I combattenti*, 369–375.

71. Lupo, *Il fascismo*, 101.

72. *Querimonie e rimedi*, 'Il Corriere della Sera', 28 April 1921.

73. Francesco Alunni Pierucci, *1921–1922. Violenza e crimini fascisti in Umbria. Diario di un antifascista* (Milan, 2004; 1st edition, 1960), 16.

74. Ventrone, *La seduzione totalitaria*, 47–52; the name of the *Fascio* was altered slightly over the course of time.

75. This explains the famous entry in the *Enciclopedia Italiana*, concerning the fascist doctrine, written at the beginning of the 1930s (Rome, 1932; 2nd edition, 1949), 851.

76. For a historical account of the group and its activities, see Francesco Lorenzo Pullé and Giovanni di Vegliasco Celesia, *Memorie del Fascio Parlamentare di Difesa Nazionale (Senato e Camera)* (Bologna, 1932). On the March on Rome, see Giulia Albanese, *La marcia su Roma* (Bari, 2006).

77. Benito Mussolini, 'Il discorso alla "Sciesa" di Milano', *Il Popolo d'Italia*, 4 October 1922.

78. For the data, see De Felice, *Mussolini il rivoluzionario*, 511. For some regional case studies, see Francis J. Demers, *Le origini del fascismo a Cremona* (Bari, 1979); Paul Corner, *Il fascismo a Ferrara 1915–1925* (Bari, 1975); Frank M. Snowden, *The Fascist Revolution in Tuscany, 1919–1922* (Cambridge, 1989) and Paolo Giovannini, „*Tutto da abbattere, tutto da creare". Le origini del fascismo nella provincia pesarese: 1919–1922* (Bologna, 1993).

79. Lupo, *Il fascismo*, 88.

80. Antonio Gibelli, *Il popolo bambino. Infanzia e nazione dalla Grande guerra a Salò* (Turin, 2005), 179–199; on the contribution of the young to the fascist movement, see Paolo Nello, *L'avanguardismo giovanile alle origini del fascismo* (Bari, 1978), Jens Petersen, 'Elettorato e base sociale del fascismo italiano degli anni Venti', *Studi storici*

3 (1973), 627–669; and Roberta Suzzi Valli, 'The Myth of *squadrismo* in the Fascist Regime', *Journal of Contemporary History*, (April 2000), 131–150. An in-depth discussion on the generational revolt in the post-war period can be found in Maurizio Degl'Innocenti, *L'epoca giovane. Generazioni, fascismo e antifascismo* (Manduria-Bari-Rome, 2002), in particular 69–107.

81. Cited in Antonio Gibelli, *La grande guerra degli italiani 1915–1918* (Milan, 1998), 326–327. On the awareness of the central role of the young and the very young in the construction of a 'New Italy', see Ferruccio Vecchi, *Arditismo civile* (Milan, 1920), in particular 80ff.

82. De Felice, *Mussolini il fascista. La conquista del potere (1921–1925)* (Turin, 1995; 1st edition, 1966), 114, 505–506 and 593–590.

83. Nazario Sauro Onofri, *La strage di Palazzo d'Accursio. Origine e nascita del fascismo bolognese, 1919–1920* (Milan, 1980).

84. An impressive description of the violence, nearly five hundred pages long, can be found in *Fascismo. Inchiesta socialista sulle gesta dei fascisti in Italia* (Milan, 1963; 1st edition, 1922). A fascist version can be found in Mario Piazzesi, *Diario di uno squadrista fiorentino* (Rome, 1980). Fire was also a good natural means of purification, as demonstrated by the systematic burning of the headquarters of their rivals along with the houses of their leaders.

85. Benito Mussolini, 'In tema di violenza', *Il Popolo d'Italia*, 25 February 1921.

86. Albanese, *Alle origini del fascismo*, 140.

87. Consider the prayer cited in ibid., 239. Concerning the cult of the fallen soldiers in Italy, see Claudio Canal, 'La retorica della morte. I monumenti ai caduti della Grande guerra', *Rivista di storia contemporanea* 4 (1982); and for a European perspective, see Jay Winter, *Sites of Memory, Sites of Mourning. The Great War in European Cultural History* (Cambridge, 1995).

88. Cordova, *Arditi e legionari*, 90–91; and Eros Francescangeli, *Arditi del popolo* (Rome, 2000). After Bloody Christmas (*Natale di sangue*), even the legionary veterans of Fiume distanced themselves from the fascists; see Cordova, *Arditi e legionari*, 113ff. The maximalist leaders of the PSI invited their followers to ignore the provocations, advocating tolerance and kindness, their aim being to deprive their opponents of vendettas and pretexts to fight, while the fascist wave passed; see 'Un messaggio di Filippo Turati ai contadini pugliesi', *Avanti!*, 4 May 1921, now in Filippo Turati, *Socialismo e riformismo nella storia d'Italia. Scritti politici 1878–1932* (Milan, 1979), 426.

89. The text is reproduced in De Felice, *Mussolini il fascista*, 753–755.

90. A photographic reproduction of the document can be found in Mimmo Franzinelli, *Squadristi. Protagonisti e tecniche della violenza fascista 1919–1922* (Milan, 2004).

91. Enzo Santarelli, *Pietro Nenni* (Turin, 1988), 50ff.; Livio Vanzetto (ed.), *L'anomalia laica. Biografia e autobiografia di Mario e Guido Bergamo* (Verona, 1994); and A. De Ambris and R. De Felice (eds.), *La Carta del Carnaro nei testi di Alceste De Ambris e di Gabriele D'Annunzio* (Bologna, 1973).

92. Cf. Cordova, *Arditi e legionari*, 94–107.

93. Franzinelli, *Squadristi*, 95, 101. For the fascist document, see 'Programma del PNF', *Il Popolo d'Italia*, 27 December 1921. On 3 October 1922 the same newspaper published the disciplinary rules of the militia. Concerning the 'party-militia', see Emilio Gentile, *La via italiana al totalitarismo. Il partito e lo Stato nel regime fascista* (Rome, 1995).

94. The data concerning the number of casualties incurred during the clashes remains uncertain. Estimates range from twenty-five hundred to three thousand deaths.

95. Alunni Pierucci, *1921–1922*, 58, 74. For the cult of the nation during the fascist era, see Emilio Gentile, *Il culto del littorio. La sacralizzazione della politica nell'Italia fascista* (Bari, 1994).

96. Petersen, *Il problema della violenza*, 996–997.

97. See Enrico Decleva, „*Il Giornale d'Italia" (1918–1926*); and the contributions in *La Tribuna, L'Italia e Il Corriere della Sera*, in Brunello Vigezzi (ed.), *1919–1925. Dopoguerra e fascismo. Politica e stampa in Italia* (Bari, 1965).

98. The document is reproduced in Giorgio Alberto Chiurco, *Storia della Rivoluzione fascista*, vol. 4 (Rome, 1929), 193 (the italics are mine).

99. The plan for the military occupation of Rome can be found in Balbo, *Diario 1922*, 195–198. Concerning the military preparations behind the event, see also Curzio Malaparte, *Tecnica del colpo di stato* (Florence, 1994; 1st edition, 1931), 193–205.

100. *Il Popolo d'Italia*, 28 October 1922. The original text of Diaz's communication affirmed: 'The remains of what was once the most powerful army in the world, retreats in disorder and without hope back up the same valleys they had once descended with proud self assurance.'

101. Other than the works already cited, see for a European perspective Vincenzo Calì, Gustavo Corni and Giuseppe Ferrandi (eds.), *Gli intellettuali e la Grande guerra* (Bologna, 2000). An analysis dealing with a longer time period can be found in Daniel Pick, *War Machine. The Razionalisation of Slaughter in the Modern Age* (New Haven/London, 1993); in addition, see George L. Mosse, *Nationalism and Sexuality: Middle-Class Morality and Sexual Norms in Modern Europe* (Madison, 1988); and Mosse, *The Image of Man: the Creation of Modern Masculinity* (New York, 1996).

102. Cit. in Gentile, *Storia del partito fascista*, 497–498.

103. Giacomo Lumbroso, 'La genesi ed i fini del Fascismo', *Gerarchia*, October 1922.

104. Ibid.

105. Marcelo Gallian, *Il Ventennale. Gli uomini delle squadre nella Rivoluzione delle Camicie nere* (Rome, 1941), 61–62. On this theme, see Barbara Spackman, *Fascist Virilities: Rhetoric, Ideology, and Social Fantasy in Italy* (Minneapolis/London, 1996). An interesting case of the political translation of this existential activism, even if prevalently libertarian in tone, can be found in Claudia Salaris, *Alla festa della rivoluzione. Artisti e libertari con D'Annunzio a Fiume* (Bologna, 2002).

106. Yvon De Begnac, *Taccuini mussoliniani* (Bologna, 1990), 199.

107. 'Battisti', *Il Popolo d'Italia*, 12 July 1917, now in Mussolini, *Scritti e discorsi*, 259. Concerning the ritualistic dimension of fascism, over and above the works already cited, see also Simonetta Falasca-Zamponi, *Fascist Spectacle: The Aesthetics of Power in Mussolini's Italy* (Berkeley, 1997).

108. A collection of these studies can be found in Sergio Luzzatto, 'La cultura politica dell'Italia fascista', *Storica*, 12 (1998).

109. Cited in Franzinelli, *Squadristi*, 126.

110. Balbo, *Diario 1922*, 19.

111. De Felice, *Mussolini il fascista*, 114–115.

112. Emil Ludwig, *Colloqui con Mussolini* (Milan, 1932), 122–123.

113. On the relationship between modernity and the crisis of sacredness, see Marshall Berman, *All that is Solid Melts into Air. The Experience of Modernity* (New York, 1982), in particular chap. 3. An in-depth analysis on the relationship between fascism and modernity, dealing with a longtime perspective, can be found in Roger Griffin, *Modernism and Fascism: The Sense of a Beginning under Mussolini and Hitler* (Hampshire & New York, 2007).

8

The French Desire for Peace and Security in the 1920s

Jean-Claude Allain

At the end of the First World War France is in a peculiar position. Though one of the three great victors, it is the country most affected by the war: 1.35 million dead, that is, 3.4 per cent of the French (metropolitan) population and 10.4 per cent of the working men (in Germany, 2.9 per cent and 9.8 per cent respectively); and 1.1 million wounded and invalids, amongst them 10 per cent mutilated, specifically those with damaged faces (*gueules cassées*). In the combat area 17,600 public buildings and more than 500,000 houses are destroyed or damaged, miles and miles of streets and railway tracks are in need of repair, and more than 2 million hectares of rich agricultural land have been laid waste by trenches and grenades.[1] It took four years to regain the production level of 1913.

These human and material losses – beyond all statistics – are experienced most intimately by the soldiers and the civilian population at home (*l'Arrière*) and so the armistice of 11 November is a huge relief: it brings to an end an interminable and murderous war and at the same time gives rise to the joy of victory. The British and French governments were well aware of the public's strong and diverse expectations. They chose an immediate ceasefire[2] instead of pursuing their strategic advantage into Germany. This, as we know, is to influence German perceptions of defeat. But relief meant neither forgetting nor forgiving. Most people are convinced, without recourse to Article 231 of the Treaty of Versailles, of Germany's responsibility, since it declared war and attacked in 1914. In other words, in France there is no question of 'war guilt', but a twofold desire: to punish Germany thoroughly, in order to prevent another war from unfolding, and to establish a new international order that would secure a lasting[3] peace and ensure that the war just endured would be the 'last of the last'.[4]

Thus the outcome of the war has two faces, complementary despite their differences: on the one hand glorification in a just and deserved victory, on the other an ongoing desire for peace, sometimes to the point of rejecting the principle of war. Parallel to this, outside the leadership circles, the ordinary citizens reflect on the peace. These feelings, widespread in post-war French society, can, depending on the conjuncture of the 1920s, determine or support the policies of the governments, which, by their speeches and deeds give them an official, visible character. Yet they elude large sections of public opinion because of their 'dumb existence' (they were later called the 'silent majority'). They are only perceived via facts of society or communication, pertaining to socio-cultural milieux with variable contours and with no direct link, sometimes even contradictory ones, to official policy. Only a few perceptible aspects of this feeling for peace amongst the French will be mentioned here.

The Exultation of Victory

This first found expression in the elections of 1919, with the success of the 'Bloc national', which, thanks to the system of proportional representation, gained 336 Deputies as opposed to 195 by the radical and socialist Left.[5] This comes to be known as the 'Blue Horizon Chamber', after the colour of the uniforms of the 'Poilus' (from 1915), but its character of former fighters, which it was electorally 'correct' to emphasise, was promoted as much by the Right as by the Left, for whom 43 per cent of the electorate voted. However, it was divided over what attitude to take towards the Bolshevik Revolution, which had determined Russia's retreat and thus betrayed France in 1917. Then the patriots and nationalists made their voices heard: the first criticism of possible responsibility on the part of Poincaré and Nicholas II for the outbreak of war finds little response, except a negative one designed to repudiate it.[6] History books intended for junior schools are written in a bellicose and extremely hostile spirit towards Germany, which is responsible for the war and is guilty of atrocities against the civilian population or wounded soldiers, and of 'barbaric' destruction. This has been generally known about since the beginning of the war, e.g. the library at Louvain or Reims cathedral. Engravings or photographs, still rare in schoolbooks, sometimes illustrate these accusations. Henceforth, logically, '28 June 1919 (signing of the Versailles Treaty) becomes the day of reckoning.'[7] Of course, this accusatory and vengeful message depended on how it was used by the school teacher in the classroom. Very often he himself is a former soldier but he has not automatically learnt this lesson from the war, since a running criticism of these aggressive schoolbooks emerges from 1920 onwards, though without much echo until 1924–26. The study of schoolbooks undertaken by the Carnegie Foundation for International Peace between 1921 and 1923 comes to much the same conclusions. In senior schools the history of the war, removed from the official syllabus by ministerial order in 1920, is not taught in the final year until 1929 (decree of 1925) and until then depends on the initiative and interpretation of the school councils.[8] However, in the course of these years a certain calming of spirits, the emergence of pacifist ideas, and dissemination of the first academic studies on the origins of the war, the first one appearing in 1925, can influence this teaching.[9] The first half of the twentieth century thus seems to be marked by a patriotic, if not nationalist spirit, which coincides with the official memory.

This memory is constructed and then maintained by public commemorations. It should be remembered that the Unknown Soldier was buried beneath the Arc de Triomphe on 28 January 1921 and that the flame was not lit there for the first time until 1923, on 11 November, a day which the former front-line soldiers had managed to have declared a national holiday. But at a regional and local level the memorial ceremonies, as in the case of the war of 1870, involve the erection of monuments to the dead. The choices made by the municipal councils and the frequent appeals for public subscriptions have a direct effect on the population. Virtually all French communities have dead or missing, which motivates the construction of such monuments. The wave of inaugurations (which creates, incidentally, a veritable market in monuments to the dead) goes on until 1926–27. Once it has been inaugurated the monument becomes the focus of regular memorial ceremonies in which veterans, families, and often local schoolchildren take part. Speeches are made by the administrative and political authorities, which must, in strong words and in the theatrical and declamatory style practised by the orators of the Third Republic[10] (perhaps even the Fourth), celebrate the sacrifice and glory of 'those who died for France'.[11]

These ceremonies are always ambivalent. On the one hand they pay homage to the war heroes, but at the same time they remind the survivors and their families of the realities of war and reveal to the next generations the terrible human consequences. Around the flags stand wounded, amputees, mutilated men who bear physical witness. The pain of the grieving families (600,000 widows, 750,000 orphans[12]), whose names are written on the monument, can only be reawakened by it all. It is by no means certain that these silent spectators, especially as the years go by, experience a feeling of hatred and vengeance towards the former enemy; soon they would rather condemn the war and wish for guaranteed peace, which would give some meaning to their parents' sacrifice. Whatever the case, the form of the monuments (all of a figurative realism) very often evoke pain and suffering, be it of women (wives and mothers) or of soldiers, rather than the heroic and exultant pose of the victorious 'poilu'.[13]

The Desire for Peace

This feeling tends to have various dimensions, expressed by the French vocabulary: the word *pacifique* (peaceable) describes a naturally peaceful temperament that hopes for peace amongst the nations. The word *pacifiste* (pacifist) denotes a doctrinaire choice of peace combined with a systematic rejection of all war. In the 1920s the borderline between these two attitudes remains unclear in authors writing about the peace[14] but various social and cultural presentations express or imply this longing for peace.

The view of the image and landscape of the war starts to change. A different message from the one that prevailed during the war is received or perceived. The sense of the war-images presented in the cinema can be reversed. The exit from the trenches and the assault, captured by the army Film Service (founded in 1915) for projection in cinemas, especially in Paris, no longer inspire public admiration and patriotic ardour when Abel Gance, in his first version of *J'accuse*, of 1918, (he was to rework this in 1934) shows the dead of Verdun standing up again en masse for peace. Although this film sequence reached a limited audience, hundreds of thousands of war postcards were produced showing partly destroyed famous monuments (the cathedrals of Reims, Amiens, Noyon, the belfry of Arras etc.), villages and urban quarters in ruins, rural landscapes decimated (by fallen trees). During the war these must have aroused anger against the enemy; after the war they did as much, if not more, to make people deplore war and wish for a secure peace that would prevent any repetition of such destruction. The same ambivalent feeling is evoked by the series *Guides illustrés des champs de bataille* which the Michelin brothers published (up to 1929)[15] in order to arouse patriotic memories. Their narrative was supposed to facilitate a memorial re-visiting that was educational for the new generations, and to be a pilgrimage for the veterans, but their descriptive and explicatory narrative produced less emotion than the direct view of the devastated sites – or what nature had left of them – which gave rise to contemplation of the war that had produced them.

During the war, and because of it, various artists and writers felt obliged to question the aesthetic norms, and beyond that those of society. Germany saw the upsurge of expressionism, and in and around Dresden there is no getting away from Otto Dix. The France of the 'avant-gardes' (long since cubism) embraces Dadaism, born in Switzerland in 1916, and later (1922) surrealism in literature (André Breton, Paul Eluard etc.) and in art (Hans Arp, Max Ernst etc.). This aesthetic and social questioning can range from the classical challenge to the establishment, to a sort of nihilism inspired by the culture of death, the spectacle of which has been made universally accessible by the war,[16] via the hope of global revolution, expressed by Soviet Russia. This evokes enthusiasm (and leads to membership in the French Communist Party) in several French writers (Breton, Tzara), until their deep disillusionment in the early 1930s.[17]

This artistic milieu, far removed from the aesthetic taste of the public at large, is, certainly, fairly small and is paid little attention. On the other hand, the book as a medium reaches a much larger public that is culturally and regionally more diverse. The war gives rise to the mass production of memoirs, witness accounts, studies in newspapers, periodicals and in publishing houses.[18] Tales of the war, fictitious but based on true stories,[19] are published even before the war is over. The most famous is *Le feu* by Henri Barbusse, first published as a feuilleton, then as a book in 1917, whose account, indeed the very fact of its publication, are not without ambiguity.[20] Other authors do not raise such problems: Roland Dorgelès with *Les croix de bois* (1919) and, in particular, Maurice Genevoix, also a former soldier, who after demobilisation wrote a series of memory-novels, the first in 1916, *Sous Verdun,* then *Nuits de guerre* (1919), *La Boue* (1921), *Les Eparges* (1923), in the immediate aftermath of the war. These books describe the everyday life of the soldiers in the trenches or at the Front, in general, without adopting the epic or exulted tone of a Barrès; they show the extraordinary hardship and constant mortal danger, highlight the soldiers' devotion to their country, but also evoke more compassion than vengeance towards the enemy. This image of the war environment, endured as an accepted constraint,[21] does not lead to its glorification, but to the hope of a lasting peace that will prevent it from happening again. In 1929, *Témoins* by Norton Cru and *A l'ouest rien de nouveau* by Erich Maria Remarque are published but in a different context.

The desire for peace also manifests itself in changes affecting the way of life, especially in towns. New forms of sociability, either products of the war or imported from abroad, appear in Paris society and spread to the provincial towns, less so to the countryside, by means of fashion magazines, department store catalogues and popular periodicals, which are more and more frequently illustrated.

A fierce desire for life and distraction is expressed in the reaction to the constraints and deprivations of the war, which people want to or try to forget by enjoying the present to the full. The '*années folles*' follow, with the war bracketed in-between, the years of the 'Belle Epoque', which can perhaps still evoke a certain nostalgia, but which cannot return in the new environment. Thus, for example 'dancing', with the imported rhythms of the Charleston and American Jazz[22] or the Argentinian Tango, replaces the popular folk-ball of former times – the '*bal musette*' to the sound of the accordion.

The liberation of women enters a new phase; the independent woman 'à la George Sand' is no longer an exception. Even more numerous are those who, as men have habitually done, choose their own profession and lifestyle, particularly to remain single. The novel by Victor Margueritte, *La garçonne*

(1922), popularises this affirmation of female autonomy and fashion works in the same direction with a specific haircut named after the novel. The phenomenon is neither general nor sudden: it embodies certain aspects of an evolution in the woman's condition during and after the war. We know that male conscription meant that women had to take their places in industry, where they had previously been employed only rarely, and in public and private services, where there had been a few more of them. This contribution did not, however, bring them the recognition of the right to vote, and the return of peace and the demobilised men sent them back to 'house and home'. The losses that hit the generations between twenty and thirty years of age seem to have reduced the possibilities of marriage or remarriage: at the end of the war there are 20 per cent more women than men. Nonetheless, statistically, the percentage of single people is not much different from that of the pre-war period. The demographic structure exercised a constraint, though not in this sense, but in that of adapting to earlier marriage strategies. 'So it is a myth that the war created a generation of old virgins.'[23] The novelty would not be society's choice, but the particular attention paid to this social fact.

In these aspects of social life reference to the war is only negative, without producing any reflection on the peace which is experienced, if one can put it that way, only in its immediate everyday effects. Only a small section of the civilian population is able to do this: namely those who have an above-average education, critical observers of national and international politics, though without personal commitment, who have mastered the art of writing. They belong to the intellectual and university milieux and that of the 'free' professions.

'Citizens' Reflection' on the Peace

The treaties of 1919 created, at the initiative and request of President Woodrow Wilson, the first permanent international organisation charged with safeguarding the peace, firstly by seeing that the treaty conditions were implemented. This was a considerable advance compared to congresses convened in the past to end or resolve conflicts, or to the permanent court of arbitration in The Hague (1902), which states could use for resolving conflicts if they so wished. The idea of a League of Nations had been discussed during the war and at the peace conference, i.e. at governmental level. After 1920 the political community will continue to debate it: was it an unacceptable infringement of national sovereignty or a generous utopia, granted by political necessity to the president of a state that had refused to ratify the treaties?

A broad spectrum of opinions was expressed. The Right remained sceptical, if not hostile, to the organisation, which it presumed to be both dangerous and ineffectual. The Left, out of conviction, defended it as a means of guaranteeing peace, while at the same time wishing to increase its powers, specifically by making recourse to arbitration obligatory, combined with the adoption of a security arrangement that would permit disarmament as an option (1924).

These questions also concern those citizens who have no official responsibility, as individuals or as members of private associations for peace and liberty, who, as before the war, publish brochures or books in very small print-runs, pass into obscurity and remain unknown to historians, especially because they have had no influence on the governments. Nonetheless, they are witness to reflection, call it 'citizens' reflection', on safeguarding the peace, at least in Europe, and on the expected, or hoped-for contribution of the League of Nations. This found expression at the time of the competition for the peace prize in 1924.[24]

In 1924 an American industrialist, Edward Filene, decides to launch a public prize in France, Italy, England and Germany: for means that will 're-establish security and prosperity in Europe through international cooperation'. He is inspired by a similar prize, this time specifically for peace, introduced in the United States in 1923 by Edward Bok: having donated a prize of 100,000 US dollars, he received more than 22,000 applications. The French prize will share out 200,000 francs among the main winners, chosen by a jury of prominent personalities (such as Léon Bourgeois, Henry de Jouvenel, Marie Curie, Charles Richet etc.). The summary report on the 5,139 applications received confirms, as far as security is concerned, global confidence in the Treaty of Versailles, rejection of the systems of alliances (as existed before 1914) in favour of open multilateral diplomacy within the framework of the League of Nations, and sometimes also the suggestion of a reduction in armaments and the prospect of forming a United States of Europe. Those taking these moderate positions seek to be realistic, taking account of the new European order created by the Treaty of Versailles, but also French security concerns vis-à-vis Germany.[25] They are less robust than those of the Americans who, far removed from any direct threat, can envisage a disarmed peace and even an international fighting force to maintain it. In September 1924, the first prize (one hundred thousand francs) was awarded to Fernand Maurette, professor of geography at the Ecole des Hautes Etudes Commerciales in Paris. He underlined the strong will for peace, recommended a European League of Nations working closely with the United States, which would remain outside the League, and judged that this European co-operation would be the prelude to global co-operation.

French civilian society wants peace, like any society that has not been indoctrinated by a totalitarian and bellicose power. Yet those who bear witness to this reveal a degree of uncertainty as to the manner of safeguarding it by means of collective security which, though much-desired, so far remains only virtual. This hope can be seen as justified by the first peace settlements achieved by the

League of Nations (from Silesia to Corfu) or disappointed by the recourse to force against Germany (1921–23, Ruhr Affair) and by its failure to match up to international realities until 1925–26. Édouard Herriot's preliminary protocol on arbitration and the Locarno agreements seemed to usher in a new era of expected peace, but, as the former head of the government, Joseph Caillaux, put it in 1927: 'It is a difficult task to transform an asthmatic peace into a real peace.'[26] The illusion is to be short-lived. The desire for peace, beyond the wait-and-see attitude of the majority, becomes more radical in two opposite directions: firstly, in the direction of pacifism, though in order to be efficient this path requires (more than socialism in 1914) international co-ordination and action that are slow to organise. The modalities of action for rejecting war are hotly disputed and this orientation, present at an early stage – as we have seen – amongst teachers, develops but slowly before 1930 compared to that manifested by the Anglo-Saxons and Germans.[27] From this point of view the other direction is easier, because it concentrates on the national space: nationalist groups, very often formed from old soldiers' associations, are founded. They want to revive enthusiasm for victory, and by orders and authority, to strengthen the nation and its security against attack, presumed to come from Germany. This verbal activism, made accessible by various street demonstrations, emerged precisely in the years 1924–25.[28] It is only after this time that those 'leagues' are in the ascendancy whose goals are initially domestic (the 'Croix de feu' is founded in 1928) in the new political, diplomatic and above all economic, context of the 1930s. Henceforth the desire for peace and the safeguarding of peace are well and truly compromised.

Notes

1. Cf. Alfred Sauvy, *Histoire économique de la France entre les deux guerres,* vol. 1 (Paris, 1965), chap.1.
2. Given appropriate guarantees since 'les troupes qui auront déposé les armes, ne les reprendront pas', note of the French general staff, 12 October 1918. Cf. P.-M. de La Gorce, *La Premiere Guerre mondiale,* vol. 2 (Paris, 1991), chap. 28: 'Les armistices de 1918'. Was the armistice premature? This question was disputed after the war, and later by historians.
3. This word – very topical – is in the title of the book by August Schvan, *Les bases d'une paix durable* (Paris, 1917).
4. 'We want it to be the last war', Marcel Sembat.
5. Georges Lachapelle, *Les élections législatives du 16 novembre 1919. Résultats officiels* (Paris, 1920).
6. For example Fernand Gouttenoire de Toury, *Poincaré a-t-il voulu la guerre?* (Paris, 1920); or Mathias Morhardt in the Société d'études documentaires et critiques de la guerre, whose book *Les preuves* was not published until 1924, like that of Alfred Fabre-Luce, *La victoire.*
7. Ernest Lavisse, *Histoire de France* (Colin, 1920).

8. Hubert Tison, 'La mémoire de la guerre 14–18 dans les manuels scolaires français d'histoire (1920-1990)', *Guerres et cultures 1914–1918* (Paris, 1994), 295–299.

9. Pierre Renouvin, *Les origines immédiates de la guerre, 26 juin–4 août 1914* (Paris, 1925).

10. Cf. recordings of this period in the former 'Phonothèque française', in the INA and ECPAD (Ivry).

11. Stéphane Tison, *Guerre, mémoire et traumatisme. Comment Champenois et Sarthois sont-ils sortis de la guerre (1870–1940)?*, PhD in history submitted to the Sorbonne Nouvelle in January 2002. Cf. his article, 'Traumatisme de guerre et commémorations (1870–1940)', *Guerres mondiales et conflits contemporains* 216 (2004), 5–30; and Alexandre Niess, 'Monuments aux morts et politique: l'exemple marnais', *Guerres mondiales et conflits contemporains* 212 (2004), 17–32. Bruno Cabanes, *La victoire endeuillée. La sortie de guerre des soldats français (1918–1920)* (Paris, 2004).

12. For example, Stéphanie Petit, 'Le deuil des veuves de la Grande Guerre : un deuil spécifique', *Guerres mondiales et conflits contemporains* 198 (2000), 53–66.

13. Cf. Jacques Bouillon and Michel Petzold, *Mémoire figée, mémoire vivante. Les monuments aux morts* (Paris, 1999). Inscriptions decrying the war are very rare; the ones always quoted are the monuments of Gentioux (Creuse) and Equeurdreville (Manche).

14. Observation by Norman Ingram.

15. Cf. Antoine Champeaux, *Mémoires de la Grande Guerre. Témoins et témoignages* (Nancy, 1989); and his thesis 'Michelin et l'aviation', vol. 2, submitted to the Sorbonne in July 2003.

16. Following François Géré, *Les volontaires de la mort* (Paris, 2003), 78.

17. With certain exceptions, such as Eluard.

18. For example Plon or Payot with the series 'Mémoires, études et documents pour servir à l'histoire de la guerre' from 1920.

19. Other, more profitable ways of combining the picturesque with espionage were also pursued: e.g. the series of novels by Louis Dumur (from *Nach Paris,* 1920) or by Charles Lucieto, though not until the end of the 1920s.

20. A volunteer in the name of freedom, as he puts it, wounded and demobilised in 1917, Barbusse is published without censorship in *L'Oeuvre* from August 1916: was his much-vaunted pacifism overshadowed by his anti-German tone? Eberhard Demm has pointed out this ambiguity: 'Barbusse et son *Feu*: la dernière cartouche de la propagande de guerre française', *Guerres mondiales et conflits contemporains* 197 (2000), 43–64; Barbusse's pacifist reputation endures for Geneviève Colin and Jean-Jacques Becker in 'Les écrivains, la guerre de 1914 et l'opinion publique', *Relations internationales* 24 (1980), 482–484.

21. There is room for discussion about these two words, depending on how much weight is attached to 'war culture' (Stéphane Audouin-Rouzeau and Annette Becker, Historial de Péronne) or the repressive environment (Fréderic Rousseau), but the question as to whether these feelings and attitudes endured after the war that gave rise to them remains open.

22. *La revue nègre* with Joséphine Baker was a huge success in 1925.

23. Cf. Antoine Prost and Jay Winter (who demonstrated this for England in 1986), *Penser la Grande Guerre* (Paris, 2004), 227.

24. Carl Bouchard studied this aspect of public opinion in his doctoral thesis, 'Projets citoyens pour une paix durable en France, en Grande-Bretagne et aux États-Unis (1914–1924)', written under the joint supervision of Samir Saul (Montreal) and J.-C. Allain (Sorbonne Nouvelle) and submitted to the University of Montreal in October 2004. The following is from chapter 6 on the competition for the peace prize.

25. Or, on the contrary, the projects presented demand removal of the treaty's constraints, if not of the treaty itself.

26. Discourse of 16 October 1917 in Joigny, quoted in Jean-Claude Allain, *Joseph Caillaux*, vol. 2: *L'oracle (1914–1944)* (Paris, 1981), 450.

27. See the overview by Dieter Riesenberger, 'Zur Geschichte des Pazifismus von 1800 bis 1933. […] 3. Die Friedensbewegung in der Zwischenkriegszeit', in C. Rajewsky and D. Riesenberger (eds.), *Wider den Krieg* (Munich, 1987), 220–226.

28. In 1924, 'Les jeunesses patriotes', in 1925, 'Le faisceau', the periodical '*Le nouveau siècle*' (26 February) parallel to the royalists of the 'Action française', founded well before the war and then in crisis.

9

Britain in the Wake of the Great War

Jay Winter

This chapter points to the contradictions of the immediate post-war years in Britain. On the one hand, the war had been won and demobilization proceeded relatively smoothly. The paradox of the war economy was that noone had predicted it would perform so well. That very success lulled leaders from Lloyd George to Winston Churchill to imagining a prosperous future. On the other hand, labour militancy at home, violence in India and civil war in Ireland threw Britain and its empire into an uncertain state. The Versailles settlement was a pyrrhic victory for Britain, bringing neither peace nor stability. By mid 1920 Britain had begun its long-term decline to the position of a nation with diminishing resources, declining exports in the old staple trades of coal, textile and shipbuilding and increasing commitments overseas it could no longer afford. That turn of affairs increasingly cast doubt on whether the human and material price of the war had been too high.[1]

The mournful victory ceremony at the Cenotaph on 19 July 1919 captured this uncertain mood. The nation and empire had seen the deaths of one million men in the war; the illusions of victory could not conceal the reality of staggering losses, and to what end? Edwin Lutyens's design, without Christian notation or any note of triumphalism, embodied the somber mood of the moment when the full weight of the war came home to the British people.

The ceremony at the Cenotaph was echoed by the interment of the Unknown Soldier in Westminster Abbey a year and a half later. By presenting the choreography of mourning in these two events, it is possible to see how early and how deeply etched in British popular culture was a view of the war as a disaster. That view has dominated British remembrance of the Great War ever since, and it marks British historical literature on this period as well.

We historians have been buoyed along on a current of interest in the Great War, but one which is quite distinctive from that of the other major combatant countries. This chapter attempts to explore this landscape in two ways. The first is with respect to the major commemorative moments of 1919 and 1920; the second is with respect to the British approach to the historiography of the Great War and its immediate aftermath, an approach at variance with other national reconfigurations of this period.

La Prise de la Parole: Reconfiguring the Symbolic Landscape

One of the most striking features of the immediate post-war period in Britain is the shriveling of triumphalism in public about winning the war. Too many men had died and for too obscure a purpose to enable the survivors to preserve the echoes of the victory celebrations on November 1918. Six months later, that swagger was gone, and in its place, a more somber, more sober set of performative acts marked the ways in which war remembrance became imbricated within British cultural life.

Here indeed, is a meditation on what Pierre Nora has termed 'sites of memory'. In London, public space turned into a cemetery – a symbolic cemetery for all those who died on active service in the Great War.[2] This cemetery had two foci. The first was in Westminster Abbey, where the Unknown Warrior was buried on 11 November 1920; here was the Christian site of hierarchical worship. The second was half a mile away on Whitehall, where the 1919 Cenotaph of Sir Edwin Lutyens was unveiled in permanent form. It was a pre-Christian form, one which deeply disturbed traditional clergymen but which clearly appealed to the masses.[3]

For this reason, it was the Cenotaph which was at the heart of this 'symbolic cemetery' right in the center of the city. Hundreds of thousands of ordinary people who came to London chose it. On 12 November 1920, a unique set of events transformed the heart of London. This was the day after the interment of the casket of the Unknown Soldier in Westminster Abbey. The next day, after the official ceremony had closed, another event took place, both similar to and very different from the official events of the previous day. On 12 November 1920 and in the following days, a massive pilgrimage continued to pass through Whitehall just as the captains and kinds had done the day before. But the pilgrimage was different: it was anonymous, civilian and massive. Estimates vary, but in the week following 11 November, perhaps one million people filed past the Cenotaph.[4]

By doing so, they affirmed the centrality of that monument in British commemorative practice and history. They voted with their feet for this site as a sacred one, and by doing so, created a symbolic cemetery right in the middle of official London, adjacent to Downing Street, the Houses of Parliament and ministries of state.

The official ceremony had all the hallmarks of aristocratic, formal, static, inegalitarian, male Britain. Then the next day, the same space was reconfigured into a national/imperial ceremony with democratic, informal, mobile, egalitarian, mixed-gendered elements describing the world of mourners who flowed like a river into the city. The space between Trafalgar Square and Parliament Square became the nation's, indeed the empire's cemetery, and into that space came a population of visitors much larger and more anonymous than any similar group the city had ever seen before. The comparison to Lourdes showed the spirituality of the pilgrimage; the evidence of spirit photography showed the overflow of emotion and the capacity of individuals to profit from it.[5] The fog added mystery to the already and always present mystery of the absence of nearly one million men from the lives of the pilgrims, and the absence or distant location of graves of most of them. In addition, many areas in which the Imperial War Graves Commission (IWGC) was engaged in constructing cemeteries were closed to visitors, since such areas were still littered with unexploded ordnance.[6] Even when relatives knew where their loved-ones lay, at this time, they could not get there. London was the surrogate site chosen by hundreds of thousands of people in which to mourn in public.

The weekend of 12–14 November formed a unique moment in the history of London. Nothing like this had ever happened in the metropolis before; nothing like it happened in Berlin, to be sure, or in Paris, where the ceremony of 14 July had retained the Republican element, tinged with sadness by the presence of *les grands mutilés de guerre*. Characteristically in the capital city of a country without a tradition of compulsory military service, and without much of a tradition of militarism, the center of the ritual were civilians, not soldiers, the anonymous mass, not the political or military leadership of the nation.

The uniformity of the headstones being erected by the IWGC at the same time as the ceremony at the Cenotaph was held also showed the resistance of those in authority to individualizing forms of commemoration. No crosses or different notation would be allowed.[7] Thus the tension between elite views and the collective representation of loss of life in wartime was reproduced in the ceremony of interment of the Unknown Warrior, and the mass pilgrimage to the Cenotaph, en route to his place of burial at the entrance to Westminster Abbey. The stop chosen in the Abbey was right at the entrance: anyone going in had to go around the unknown warrior: all the other eminent figures could be approached or not, according to taste and choice, but the Unknown Soldier could not be evaded. He stood in the path of history.[8]

Both Westminster Abbey and the Cenotaph were sacred sites, and together represented an amalgam of hierarchy and universality in the language of British commemoration in 1919. The people of Britain – over one million in the course of the week following 11 November 1920 – came to London to mark this moment, and by doing so, transformed it. Thus one of the city's most celebrated public thoroughfares, the home of the machinery of state and empire, was the site of a public negotiation of the symbols of remembrance. There in the heart of Whitehall, a symbolic cemetery was placed, and it was to this site that millions came to pay their respects and to remember.

Put yourself in the shoes of these pilgrims. In November 1920, the economic slump had begun; hopes of a new order in international affairs were gone; the Wilsonian moment was over. Civil war in Russia and Ireland and violent repression in Egypt and India all showed what the post-war world had come to – ideological strife and anti-colonial violence.[9] Here was the setting for the London pilgrimage of 1920, and for the framing of the meaning of the war as a pyrrhic victory.

The Great War: Between History and Memory

That notion of war as a pyrrhic victory has dominated British perceptions of the conflict ever since. The late poet laureate Ted Hughes had it that the war was a defeat around whose neck someone had hung a victory medal. He was referring in particular to an uncle of his who never recovered from shell shock, but who wore his victory medal nonetheless. Still the wider reference of this notion is evident through the inter-war years and beyond. It might be useful to point out how much at variance this British set of 'unspoken assumptions', in James Joll's terminology, is with notions about what the war was all about, notions which emerged in the immediate aftermath of the conflict, and to a degree, are with us still. From the outset of the inter-war years, the war was constructed in discrete national terms. Indeed every nation created its own Great War.

This national or imperial framework was what the ceremonies in Whitehall were all about. Firstly, the global perspective is absent. The war mobilized men all over the world: nearly a million Indians were under arms; perhaps half a million French colonial troops also served. The peace conference at Versailles elicited huge hopes and equally powerful disappointments, with far-reaching consequences, as in the case of China. These colonial or dependent nations were treated as secondary or marginal to the major discussions of the day. Most of the time, they were simply ignored, and when acknowledged, they were located within an imperial story of a nation unfolding its *mission civilisatrice*.

Historical accounts of the war were produced from the outset of the conflict, and continued to appear in the immediate post-war years. The key framework in which they operated was national. The enemy, from ordinary citizens to the high command, constituted one pole, and the allies, another. Bringing them together was a way of deepening national history by measuring the relation between the central national case, and the others. Other countries at war were configured in terms of the national case with which historians started and in which they were primarily interested. Popular understandings of the war effort unfolded, therefore, from the interplay of these similarities and these differences. The historian considered other countries, but he saw them in the mirror of his own.

This domination of national perspectives has several sources. The first, and perhaps the most fundamental, is inherent in the subject: war is imbricated in the history of the nation; war is even its affirmation. Raymond Aron defined the nation state as an autonomous subject in international law by its indivisible right to be the sole judge of its vital interests and to go to war to defend them.[10] The tie between war and the nation is strong, fundamental, constitutive. In this sense, Jean Jaurès was entirely right in saying that a nation carries war in its flanks the way a cloud carries a storm. War is the destructive apotheosis of the nation. From this perspective, the very idea of a war which would not be national is something of a paradox.

The second source of the power of the national perspective arises out of the fact that all history is written from a particular point of view, of which historians may not be fully aware. Why? Because we are formed by the very evidence we are trying to understand. It may be useful at this point to refer again to James Joll's phrase and to speak of the unspoken assumptions on which rest the construction of historical writing. In the last two decades, the linguistic turn in historical study has habituated us to the exploration of those pre-suppositions which pre-form and pre-structure narratives. The point is, though, that these assumptions differ in each country.

Any historian who would begin a course of lectures in France on the Great War with the remark that the war of 1914–18 was not a victory would stun many of his students. In France, the assumption that France won the war comes from within. The 'natural' question to pose is why did she win the war and lose the peace? Over the last few years, and during a period when the very existence of the nation state in Europe has been contested and its authority blunted by the development of the European Union and European citizenship, this assumption has appeared to be less self-evident. It was even possible to hear the president of the French Republic state that three million French and German soldiers had died during that war for nothing,[11] an affirmation unthinkable in 1920 or even in 1980.

But not for the British. On the other side of the English Channel, the national interest was less directly challenged in the war; the national territory had not been invaded and part of the country had not been cut off by an enemy army. The sense that all these dead men who fell in the war had died for nothing, that the war had been useless, even absurd, invaded soldiers' accounts even before structuring historical inquiry. The Italian and German cases are different as well, given the elision between war and fascism. But it is evident that we cannot treat in a comparative perspective a war which is at one and the same time deemed a victory and an absurdity. From the very beginning of the 1920s, such a distinction between British and other perspectives is evident.

In addition, right from the start, each national culture has developed narrative models through which they characterize their national history and in particular their history of the Great War. British irony, that sense of a cultivated detachment and distance between one's self and the world developed systematically in the finishing schools of the dominant social class, as much as the internalized practices of understatement, pre-formed British narratives of the war. It is there in soldiers' letters home and in their trench journals. It is there in the gallows' humour which accompanied troop movements up the line; it is there in music hall and popular song which basked in the glow of nostalgia for a world the war had blown apart.

This sense of irony as a way of life is also deeply ingrained in later historiography. Consider the prominent role played by a number of American anglophiles, like Paul Fussell, whose vision of the Great War is profoundly strange to French students of the field.[12] Perhaps this is one reason why the pioneering work of Fussell on 'modern memory' has never been translated into French. His definition of the war as ironic makes little sense to French readers, who would be equally scandalized by A. J. P. Taylor's *Illustrated History of the First World War*.[13] In this book, both text and captions offer a withering and – from a French perspective – inappropriate irony, like jokes at the bedside of a dying man. And yet Taylor's paperback edition of this book was a best-seller, with over 250,000 copies sold; it is still in print and going strong. The extreme contrast between anticipation and outcome, the tendency not to take anything too seriously, created this ironic distance among soldier-writers. Just consider the titles of two of them: *Goodbye to All That* and *Journey's End*. The soldiers' tale, as Samuel Hynes has termed it, tells the story of a war set in motion by leaders who had no idea what they were doing.[14] From this assumption it is easy to see why so many British observers from 1914 onwards termed the conflict as the quintessence of futility; the world *futility* does not even exist in French; how then can they respond to the time-honoured British understanding of the war as a mixture of the useless and the absurd.

In France, no one jokes about the Great War. It was experienced intensely as a drama in which the stakes were the survival of the national collectivity. This is remote from the way British soldiers saw it, and this initial perception has durably marked British approaches to the war ever since. French education valorizes a positivist, or rather a scientific, approach to problems – which foreigners all too quickly attribute to the Cartesian tradition – an approach in which it is difficult to think about results without thinking about causes. What happened had to have its causes. British observers of the Great War, then as now, had their doubts.

German historiography has developed much later than the other two bodies of historical writing on the war. The gap is palpable. Gerd Krumeich notes that the great German historians of the 1920s kept their distance from historical writing on the war.[15] It was a professional soldier, Alfred von Wegerer, who took on the mantle of the specialist, but the dominant characteristic of whose history is not its objectivity.[16] In fact, it would take generations before German scholars would write the history of this lost war. The very disputed character of the defeat is part of the reason for the delay, since for many Germans, 1918 was not a defeat. The Armistice intervened before combat had reached German soil; the army had indeed been beaten in the field, but they still stood on enemy soil on 11 November, and certainly did not know defeat the way the French army did in 1940. They marched home and paraded in military order before the families and friends they had left behind years before, as if they had been victorious. And there was more. In general, after a defeat, the losers seek to learn something from their adversity. This is what happened in Prussia after Jena, in France after 1871, but nothing of the kind happened in Germany in 1918. The defeat was not accepted; it was denied. The stab-in-the-back legend led them to escape from reality.[17] To write the history of the war, it was necessary to bring a kind of reality back into the historical conversation about it. It would take time before this would become possible.

To think historically about the war, finally, is to integrate it into a relevant chronological structure. The problem is that different national historical schools have adopted different periodizations in which to set the war. The French chronology starts in 1871 and unfolds around the pivotal years of 1914–18, 1939–40 and 1944. The German chronology cannot terminate in 1918 but in 1933 or 1945. The Russian and American chronologies begin in 1917. These different forms of periodization have meant that each national school stands alone.

I have noted that the very act of imagining the war has varied in different countries due to the power of different national assumptions and frameworks. These arose because the collective experience of the war was historically very different: a defeat denied in Germany; a painful victory in France; an exercise in futility in Britain. But these variations also reflect different cultural traditions: British irony, French cartesianism and Weberian sociology do not go together easily. History is always pre-formed by assumptions which define possible interpretations. It is evident that assumptions underlying historical accounts of the Great War are defined in national terms. It is not possible to imagine the Great War as a European war if one starts from nationally structured frameworks.

Conclusion

Right from the outset, the way the Great War was configured took on distinctly national inflections. Why is this so? In part the reason is the sheer volume of the sources an historian has to command about the immediate post-war years. Whatever his or her linguistic gifts, an historian surveying the archival materials and published sources available on the war decade in any one country requires promethean energy; to do so in two countries is even more daunting.

But another part of the reason is the language available in which to frame these accounts. One of the oddities of the British story is the centrality of war poetry in framing accounts of the conflict from 1914 on. Why did verse matter so much in Britain, and why does it matter still? I can only offer a few surmises in this brief rumination I call a conclusion.

The first is that the role of the King James's Bible in the people's English has been underestimated. Secularization of practice yes; secularization of language, maybe not. Scripture was alive and well in non-conformist Britain, and it was this language which ties together British families with soldiers at the front and those from Canada or Australia. The music in their voices and in their letters was different from that of the French or German equals. And then there is Shakespeare, a national institution, whose ribald classics were more widely performed than the tragedies, and certainly more than the histories. Remote cousins of Falstaff and Malvolio peopled dozens of music hall romps and theatrical ventures aimed at the Victorian and Edwardian masses. It does not take a Shakespearean scholar to hear the echoes of the Bard in songs and tales and accounts of war up to and including 1914–18.

Here are two enormously rich pools of cultural reference, out of which came the readership for war poetry from the war years and beyond. Much of it was trivial, but nonetheless important for that. Some of it was enduring. What these varied verse forms shared though was the elegiac tone so evident in London on 19 July 1919 and 11 November 1920, as I have tried to show earlier. A pyrrhic victory, one the price of which eclipsed whatever benefits accrued to the so-called victors, was a conflict fit for the economy and rhythmic ruminations of verse.

I cannot claim to have mastered the French and German poetry of the war, but my hunch is that it mattered less in framing the post-war conversation about the war than it did in Britain. Politics mattered more in both cases than it did in Britain; that is, the political struggle over what the war meant was deeper and more profound in France and Germany than in Britain, where politics and society have always been separated to a degree unknown on the continent. Poetry can be mobilized into political discourse only with difficulty. It does not preach or exhort; it ministers and meditates.

Such poetic ministries and meditations have taken on iconic form in Britain, and did so from very early on. The first school texts using war poetry to teach English literature in London's elementary schools were issued in 1919. They were edited each year. A glance at their contents shows the two motifs I have tried to sketch in this chapter: elegy and irony. Anger is there too; so is a warning. Consider this fragment from a poem of 1919 written by the British nurse Charlotte Mew: It is entitled 'On the Cenotaph (September 1919)', and was included in the English literature texts available in London and Cambridge (and perhaps many other county school systems I have not yet had time to check on) throughout the inter-war years.

Not yet will those measureless fields be green again
Where only yesterday the wild sweet blood of wonderful youth was shed;
There is a grave [the Cenotaph] whose earth must hold too long, too deep a stain,
Though for ever over it we may speak as proudly as we may tread.
But here, where the watchers by lonely hearths from the thrust of an inward sword
    have more slowly bled,
We shall build the Cenotaph: Victory, winged, with Peace, winged too, at the
    column's head.
And over the stairway, at the foot – oh! here, leave desolate, passionate hands to
    spread
Violets, roses, and laurel, with the small, sweet, tinkling country things
Speaking so wistfully of other Springs,
From the little gardens of little places where son or sweetheart was born and bred.
In splendid sleep, with a thousand brother
        To lovers – to mothers
        Here, too, lies he:
Under the purple, the green, the red,
It is all young life: it must break some women's hearts to see
Such a brave, gay coverlet to such a bed!
Only, when all is done and said,
God is not mocked and neither are the dead
For this will stand in our Marketplace – [Whitehall, the seat of power, in between
Parliament and 10 Downing Street, adjacent to the War Office and Horse Guards
Parade, the center of British history, in which the cadences of the universal will be
mixed with the mundane]
Who'll sell, who'll buy
        (Will you or I
Lie each to each with the better grace)?
While looking into every busy whore's and huckster's face
As they drive their bargains, is the Face
Of God: and some young, piteous, murdered face.[18]

Glancing at the Cenotaph helps draw out the different levels of meaning in the ways I have tried to describe Britain in the wake of war. A wake is a moment of uncertainty, where in the presence of the dead, the living let go of their loved ones. To a degree, that moment of uncertainty never really ended. It described the beginning of a harsher world, one remote from the certainties of 1914. One from which, a century later, we have yet to extricate ourselves.

Notes

1. For an account of Britain in this period see for instance Zara S. Steiner, *The Lights that Failed: European International History 1919–1933* (Oxford, 2005), chap. 4; and Martin Kitchen, *Europe between the Wars: A Political History* (London, 1988), chap. 8.
2. Pierre Nora, 'Entre mémoire et histoire', in Nora (ed.), *Les lieux de mémoire*, vol. 1: *La République* (Paris, 1984), xv–xlii.
3. Jay Winter, *Sites of Memory, Sites of Mourning: The Great War in European Cultural History* (Cambridge, 1995); see also Jane Ridley, *Edwin Lutyens: His Life, His Wife, His Work* (London, 2003); and the website of the Edwin Lutyens Trust, www.lutyenstrust .org.uk, which contains a bibliography of works about Lutyens.
4. Alex King, *Memorials of the Great War in Britain* (Oxford, 1998), 141–149.
5. King, *Memorials*, 21.
6. Philip Longworth, *Unending Vigil: A History of the Commonwealth War Graves Commission, 1917–67* (London, 1967); King, *Memorials*, 187.
7. King, *Memorials*, 187.
8. King, *Memorials*, 139.
9. See for example David E. Omissi, *Air Power and Colonial Control: The Royal Air Force, 1919–1939* (Manchester, 1990); David George Boyce, *Nationalism in Ireland* (London, 1982); Ewan Mawdsley, *The Russian Civil War* (Boston/London, 1987).
10. See Raymond Aron, *Paix et guerre entre les nations* (Paris, 1962), esp. 294–300.
11. Conférence de presse à l'Office fédéral de Presse, Berlin, 27 June 2000.
12. Paul Fussell, *The Great War and Modern Memory* (Oxford, 2000, 1st edition 1975).
13. A. J. P. Taylor, *The First World War: An Illustrated History* (London, 1963).
14. Samuel Hynes, *The Soldiers' Tale: Bearing Witness to Modern War* (London, [1997] 1998), xii–xiii.
15. Gerd Krumeich, '80 ans de recherche allemande sur la guerre de 14–18', in Jules Maurin and Jean-Charles Jauffret (eds.), *La Grande Guerre 1914–18: 80 ans d'historiographie et de représentations* (Montpellier, 2002), 27.
16. Alfred von Wegerer, *Wie es zum Großen Kriege kam* (Leipzig, 1930).
17. Gerd Krumeich, 'La place de la guerre de 1914–1918 dans l'histoire culturelle de l'Allemagne', in Jean-Jacques Becker et al. (eds.), *La très grande guerre* (Paris, 1994), 36–45.
18. Charlotte Mew, *Complete Poems* (London, 2000), 61–62; also see the discussion in Tim Kendall, *Modern English War Poetry* (Oxford, 2006), 76–77.

10

Germany

War without Public Backing?

Hans Mommsen

Unlike 4 July 1914, when the German population greeted the outbreak of war with exuberant rejoicing, the invasion of Poland on 1 September 1939 was received in Germany with reticence and apprehension, and there was scarcely any enthusiasm for war. This was astonishing in view of the fact that for years the government had given top priority to re-armament of the Wehrmacht and at the same time carried on extensive propaganda about making the German people capable of 'defending' itself. How a great majority of Germans could, on the one hand, welcome Adolf Hitler as chancellor and concur with his active foreign policy, and, on the other, shrink from the consequences of this policy and hope that the Polish conflict would remain a mere episode, is not easy to explain.

The ambivalent attitude of the German population emerged visibly in September 1939. In many respects it can be traced back to the constellation that appeared at the end of the First World War. In spite of the heavy burdens that the war had placed on them, the great majority of the people was susceptible to the agitation of the political Right, according to which only a *Dolchstoß* (a stab in the back) by the Social Democrats had brought about the military collapse and robbed Germany of certain victory. At the same time the German Supreme Command, under Paul von Hindenburg and Erich Ludendorff, succeeded in shrugging off responsibility for the military defeat and blaming the Republican politicians for the harsh conditions of the truce. Even the moderate wing of the Social Democrats inclined, out of misguided patriotism, to highlight the responsibility of the military leadership and to urge its dismissal.

German public opinion therefore never admitted that the war had been lost, that is, never admitted the military defeat, and fortified itself with the illusion cultivated by the revisionist parties that the defeat of 1918 could be made good by military means at some point in the future. This was possible because the majority of the population held the territorial, economic and military provisions of the Versailles Treaty to be manifestly unjust, and in desperate need of revision. Adolf Hitler's ascent to power was facilitated in no small measure by the Nazi propaganda claim that he would expunge the 'ignominious peace treaty' of Versailles and lead Germany back into the ranks of the great powers.[1]

At the same, during the Weimar Republic and in spite of the difficult economic developments, the leading military figures managed to circumvent the disarmament regulations of the Versailles Treaty and pursued extensive illegal re-armament that would later play into the hands of the Nazi war policy. This was done without exceeding plans for the strength of the army until the beginning of the Second World War. Without these preparations, the extent of German re-armament after 1933 would not have been possible.[2]

The Republican parties of Weimar made repeated attempts to uncover the 'illicit re-armament' (*schwarze Aufrüstung*) and to bring the activities of paramilitary nationalist groups and the Freikorps under control. Pacifist authors like Erich Maria Remarque, whose novel *All Quiet on the Western Front* was furiously attacked by the Nazis, and Julius Gumbel, who led the pacifist movement, opposed the literature of militaristic nationalism represented by Ernst Jünger's *Storm of Steel*. But the more these paramilitary organisations lost in military importance, the more they were able to influence the political culture of the late Weimar Republic. NSDAP propaganda exploited the cult of violence fostered by sections of the population, for instance by reporting the recurrent public clashes between the SA and the Red Front Fighters' League.[3]

In many respects this climate of ready violence aided the rise of the National Socialist movement after 1929, but its success in January 1933 rested on Hitler's alliance with conservative dignitaries around the aged President Paul von Hindenburg. The attitude of the Reichswehr leadership was vitally important here since they valued Hitler's promise to re-introduce compulsory military service and hoped to use the SA to supplement the 100,000-man army whose expansion was long overdue. The Reichswehr therefore supported Hitler's cabinet from the beginning.[4]

Hitler was determined to carry on re-arming the Reich and to overcome the armament restrictions of the Versailles Treaty by every means, but outwardly he let himself be called the 'Chancellor of Peace'. Whereas in a meeting with the commander of the Reichswehr on 3 February 1933 Hitler stated his resolve to use military means,[5] his public statements, for instance the 'Appeal To the German People By the Government of the Reich' of 1 February, were shaped by his promise 'to stand up for the maintenance and consolidation of peace'.[6] In the statement accompanying the passing of the Enabling Act on 23 March, which was given out as a 'peace speech', he spoke of a new war as 'utter madness' and declared that the new government was resolved to place itself in the service of peace.[7] He was reluctant, however, to go out on a limb about the armament question. It was the army leadership who, against Hitler's initial misgivings, pushed through Germany's withdrawal from the League of Nations disarmament conference in October 1933, thereby paving the way for compulsory military service.[8]

Hitler, supported by Goebbels's propaganda, adhered to this basic line until 1939. The withdrawal from the League of Nations was garnished with avowals of peace whose tactical significance was to hinder French intervention, and the propaganda took the same approach to other individual foreign policy decisions of the Reich, ranging from the Anglo-German Naval Agreement, to the occupation of the de-militarised Rhineland, to the return of the Saar. The Reichswehr Law of 1935 was given out as an act of 'German self-defence', the re-building of the German armed forces as a 'component of peace'.[9] All this was also a systematic deception of the German public, who were not informed until much later of, for instance, the role played by the Condor Legion in the Spanish Civil War.

The turning point in the issue of the armed forces came in 1937. The propaganda now highlighted the role of the Wehrmacht in the fight against Bolshevism and emphasised pride in 'the German army of peace'. On the other hand, it made no mention at all of any intended use of military force. It declared the German invasion of Austria a 'friendship visit'.[10] The propaganda campaign against Czechoslovakia, which began in May 1939 and was the psychological preparation for military intervention, also avoided the idea of war.[11] As is known, Hitler failed in his intention to crush Czechoslovakia in a swift, isolated campaign. He reluctantly accepted Chamberlain's intervention and agreed to the arrangements of the Munich conference, by which extensive areas of Czechoslovakia were ceded to Germany, but Hitler was restricted from continuing military operations already under way.

On 27 September 1938, when Hitler ordered a motorised division to march through the government district of Berlin in order to test the people's readiness for war, a mute and hostile crowd in front of the Chancellery failed to give the usual applause[12] (William L. Shirer called this the most impressive demonstration against war that he had ever seen). Conversely, news of the Munich Agreement and the prevention of war was greeted by the population with rejoicing and enthusiasm. The peaceful solution of the Sudeten question was acclaimed everywhere and eased the people's concerns about the maintenance of peace.[13] Before this, however, the mood of the population was markedly critical and threatened to cause a collapse in Hitler's popularity.[14]

The Führer's 'new bloodless European victory' 'extraordinarily strengthened' the trust and faith in him, according to a representative public mood report. The Munich Agreement earned Hitler a 'nearly legendary reputation'.[15]

Paradoxically, he was celebrated above all for having gained crucial foreign policy successes (in the Saar, in Austria and now in the Sudetenland) without spilling blood. In early 1939 this reflex meant that when Czechoslovakia was crushed and the Memel territory annexed without involvement in a war, these were attributed to the unique 'genius' of the Führer. 'Faith in the Führer and his foreign policy has become so strong that fear of war does not exist.'[16] Had Hitler then resigned his position, he would have gone down in history as the 'Chancellor of Peace'.

Undoubtedly Hitler's foreign policy successes in the last years before the war played a vital part in his popularity amongst broad sections of the population. They engendered a naive underestimation of the dangers bound up with continuing a policy of expansion. Yet there was isolated resistance. The view was expressed, for example, that it was not worth risking a war for the Memel territory. Nevertheless, Hitler was now firmly set on sorting out the question of Poland. The propaganda directed against the Polish Republic exaggerated Polish conflicts with the resident German minority. At the same time Goebbels's propaganda encouraged the wishful thinking that Great Britain and France would stay out of a possible conflict and that, thanks to the 'statesmanship of the Führer', 'this goal [would be] achieved by peaceful means', as the district president of Upper Bavaria wrote in his report of 10 July 1939.[17] At any rate, the majority of the population still did not believe that war was imminent in the summer of 1939, expecting, at most, a localised campaign. To the end, they clung to the hope that war could be avoided and, especially after the German-Soviet Non-Aggression Pact, that Great Britain and France would not enter a war. 'The predominant majority of the population [believe]', wrote the district president of Lower Bavaria at the beginning of August 1938 in a confidential communication, 'that the Führer will again succeed in achieving his goals without war'.[18]

In a secret speech to about four hundred journalists and publishers on 10 November 1938 – that is, during the events of *Reichskristallnacht* – Hitler radically changed course and demanded the reorientation of propaganda to the preparation of the Germans for war. He admitted that the line previously pursued was purely a deceptive tactic: 'For *decades,* circumstances forced me to speak only of peace', for only 'by continually stressing the German will to peace and peaceful intentions' had the previous foreign policy achievements been possible. 'But now the view has become dangerously fixed in the minds of many people that the present regime is *as such* identical with the resolution and will to preserve the peace in *any and all* circumstances.' It is necessary 'that the German people be psychologically reoriented and should gradually realise' that certain things 'must be achieved by means of force'.[19]

Public mood reports of the pre-war years show quite clearly that fear of war and longing for peace were the predominant attitudes amongst the German population, and also the ineffectiveness of the many individual steps taken to increase their acceptance of the use of force. Evidently a great majority of the people were prepared to believe that the extensive measures taken in these years to strengthen German armaments and to prepare the civilian population for mobilisation were taken in pursuit of exclusively defensive goals. The Sudeten Crisis temporarily shattered the German public's dreams of peace. In October 1938 public mood reports registered the existence of a widespread war psychosis. The anxiety about a new war temporarily abated after the Munich Agreement, only to come to the fore again in the early autumn of 1939. Thus the goal of government propaganda, to produce war enthusiasm comparable to that of August 1914, had completely failed, as Wolfram Wette has pointed out.[20]

Before 1 September, the term *war* was avoided in propaganda, out of consideration for the German people's fears, and it continued to be avoided until the beginning of the Polish campaign. The announcement of a Party Conference for Peace for September 1939 was along the same lines. Even after the invasion of Poland the propaganda sought to play down the fact of the war and to dismiss the action as an episode to be swiftly concluded. At the same time its attacks were directed against the Western powers, which were accused of pursuing a deliberate policy of encirclement. This served to support the claim that Germany found itself 'in a just war that had been forced upon it'.

The concluding of the German-Soviet Non-Aggression Pact, in spite of the ideological about-face which it represented, was greeted by the broad public as a guarantee that the attack on Poland would remain an isolated episode. The declaration of war by Great Britain and France took them by surprise. Even after the Polish campaign Hitler's image as a peacekeeper remained intact. The spectacular defeat of France (in contrast to the First World War) was felt to be a singular triumph. Hitler stood at the zenith of his popularity and was praised even by many who had previously kept their distance from the 'nationalist camp'. The promised swift end of the war, however, did not come about. The myth of Hitler's 'statesmanship', reinforced by his bloodless successes, began to fade, even if the German population was ready, under the influence of anti-British propaganda, to hold Great Britain responsible for the rejection of Hitler's peace offer on 19 July 1940. Meanwhile, a blatant sullenness took hold as it became clear that there would be no swift end to the fighting and a second winter of war was in the offing.[21]

Nevertheless, it was the Führer cult that again and again bridged the gap created by the people's growing pessimism. The war enthusiasm that had arisen in the phase of swift victories further decreased and gave way to scepticism. The invasion of the Soviet Union on 20 June 1941 then caused a widespread 'cushioned shock'.[22] Anxiety over an arbitrary prolongation of the war, after the first hopes of bringing the campaign to an end in late autumn were shattered, contributed to the progressive worsening of the popular mood. German casualties and setbacks and indeed underestimation of the strength of the Red Army, which could no longer be kept secret, now also played a role here. However, criticism was mainly directed against the Nazi Party and its representatives, while Hitler was exempted from the worst charges with the formula 'If only the Führer knew that' – a sign of how strong the attachment to Hitler still was as a result of his early foreign policy and military successes.

Meanwhile the public mood reports revealed that many of Hitler's followers had no understanding of his war goals in the East, partly because they still thought in terms of the German nation state, and partly because the Eastern expansion was over-extending German forces. The enthusiasm for the early successes of the Russian campaign gave way to doubts, certainly not unfounded, about whether it was right to involve Germany in a war on multiple fronts, which initially seemed to have been avoided by the defeat of Poland. From this point on, memories of the First World War became somewhat ambivalent, and it was in this context that the Nazi leadership, recalling the trauma of 9 November 1918, committed itself to preventing a collapse on the 'home front' and organised its domestic policy accordingly.[23]

Letters from the Eastern front reflected not only the worsening military situation but also the loss of a frame of meaning for soldiers pushed to the limits of their strength.[24] Defence of the homeland became increasingly farcical for the soldiers since, given the Allied carpet bombings of Germany, it no longer served to protect their own families. The efforts of Nazi propaganda, including those geared towards a 'military education', could not prevent the cumulative war-weariness, and the introduction of National Socialist Guidance Officers, an innovation copied from the Soviet commissars, could do nothing to change this. The idea advanced by the Head of the General Office of the Wehrmacht, General Reinecke, of mobilising the troops ideologically 'so that believing soldiers write home in a believing spirit and so make the front a forceful appeal to the home front' was absurd, but reflected the escalating scepticism at home.[25]

In the course of the Russian campaign Nazi war propaganda progressively lost its credibility after its premature reports of an imminent 'total' victory. The German population preferred other sources of information to the official propaganda, including the reports by front soldiers and Allied broadcasts. By 1942 Goebbels could no longer effectively combat the sceptical attitudes that had established themselves on the Eastern front. The temporary bright spots of occasional military successes 'were only breathing spaces between periods of dejection'.[26] The population also no longer accepted the official government picture of the Soviet adversary. An unofficial opinion emerged that clearly deviated from official information. It forced Goebbels to abandon propaganda that spoke only of victories and to permit more realistic reporting.

The first great change of mood occurred in November 1941 when the proclamation about the final 'crushing of Bolshevism', released only a few weeks before, was followed by reports of 'unexpectedly tough Russian resistance' and an appeal for winter clothing to be collected for the German troops. The subsequent disillusionment was directed not least at the person of the Führer himself. The expectations of 1940, 'the experience of new national community and of a national triumph', were projected above all on to the figure of the dictator', and the shattering of this dream 'made him more and more into an unreal figure'.[27] Hitler himself shunned the public. He made fewer and fewer public appearances and speeches – to Goebbels's distress. However, it was not until the defeat at Stalingrad that the Führer myth really started to disintegrate, even though Hitler remained a decisive factor, as shown by reactions to the attempted assassination of 20 July, and his importance only began to fade in the final months of the war.

After the defeat at Stalingrad, at the latest, the previously pro-war mood of the public collapsed completely and the desire for the war to end intensified, even without a complete German victory. This reflected the profound disillusionment felt, above all, by members of the older generation. In many Germans a 'dull faith in fate'[28] now replaced their former confidence. For a time they clung to the hope that the war would take a favourable turn. But by the time of the Ardennes offensive in 1944 a mood of dejection had set in which neither the promise of a 'miraculous' new weapon nor the illusory hope of repelling the Allied Normandy landings could overcome.

The 'Dispatches from the Reich', the public mood reports collected by the Security Service, reported on 8 February 1942: 'The question today is no longer how long the war will go on until we win, but rather how long we can still hold out with the prospect of a favourable outcome. A third winter of fighting in Russia, under the same conditions as the first two, particularly considering the combat strength of the adversary, is inconceivable.'[29] And the reports by the Security Service, which were ultimately discontinued because of their attempts to give a realistic picture of the situation, registered only a section of popular opinion. The growing silent majority were left out of the picture.

Accordingly, the government altered the prescribed terminology. At the beginning of 1942 Nazi Party headquarters proclaimed: 'It has been shown, especially in recent weeks, that more decisive than the popular mood is the posture of the population, which now as before is borne by confidence in the Führer and faith in final victory'.[30] The popular mood did, in fact, change from mere despondency to self-adjuration, according to which 'we must win the war because otherwise all is lost'.[31] On the other hand, it was still the Hitler cult that bridged all these grievances and ensured a relative stability amidst the chaos.

The question why the Germans submitted to these impositions requires a complex answer. One important factor was the defence against Bolshevism, and here the regime's longstanding anti-Communist propaganda had its effect.

However, the picture of Russia stamped in the minds of the population was to change. Contact with Russian prisoners of war and forced labourers, and also a new, positive assessment of the Russian solider, forced Goebbels to remove the catchword of the Russian *Untermensch* from his propaganda. Once the crimes perpetrated by the Germans in the occupied areas of the Soviet Union and the murder of the Jews became known, however, fear intensified that defeat would lead to extensive retaliation against Germany.

The pressure exerted by the machinery of terror, which sought to compel fighting to the last man by threatening the fiercest reprisals, should not be underestimated. The calamitous effect of military jurisdiction, the drumhead courts-martial, the appointment of special courts in the defensive zones, and SS units operating independently, defies normal imagination. The murderous orgies continued until the final hours of the Reich, so that resistance only emerged once the Wehrmacht and SS had withdrawn. In addition, there were the murders committed by the Gestapo and the Security Service in the last weeks of the regime.

Manfred Messerschmidt has recently described in depth the ruthless suppression of all opposition within the Wehrmacht.[32] More than 25,000 death sentences were imposed, of which at least 18,000 were carried out. More than 100,000 members of the Wehrmacht were placed in penal camps in the field or in probationary battalions and were often put to death. 5,000 to 8,000 court-martial sentences were carried out. All this explains why, in the final days of the war, soldiers allowed themselves to be forced into a hopeless fight. Between July 1944 and May 1945 more perished than in all the previous years: 2,700,000 men altogether, amounting to more than 8,600 casualties per day.

By early 1945 it was clear to the vast majority of the German people that the war had been lost militarily, and that responsibility lay not with the population at large but with the political and military leadership. Their thinking was dominated by the justified criticism that the leadership had dangerously underestimated the military power of the Soviet Union. A public mood report by the Security Service in March 1945 admitted that the population regarded the situation as hopeless and that, apart from the continuing effect of a 'residue of faith in miracles which has been nourished by adroit and purposeful propaganda about new weapons', they were convinced that a catastrophe could no longer be averted by the methods previously employed. The people 'no longer have faith in the leadership'.[33]

This was the culmination of a development that began no later than the defeat of the German armies outside Moscow in December 1941. It had its high and low points, but its inner logic led to a complete loss of faith in the government. It had been presaged in the mounting criticism of the NSDAP, its corruption and authoritarianism, and also of the actions of the SS, though initially the person of Adolf Hitler had been exempt from this verdict. This began to change in the summer of 1944, but until that time the Hitler cult had held together, despite the drifting and disintegrating political system.[34]

Notes

1. On the agitation against Versailles, see Ulrich Heinemann, *Die verdrängte Niederlage. Politische Öffentlichkeit und Kriegsschuldfrage in der Weimarer Republik* (Göttingen, 1983), 151f., 238ff.
2. On re-armament, cf. Michael Geyer, *Aufrüstung oder Sicherheit. Die Reichswehr in der Krise der Machtpolitik 1924–1936* (Wiesbaden, 1980); Geyer, 'Das zweite Rüstungsprogramm 1930–1934', *MGM* 17 (1975), 125–172.
3. Bernd Weisbrod, 'Gewalt in der Politik. Zur politischen Kultur in Deutschland zwischen den beiden Weltkriegen', *GWU* 43 (1992), 391–404; Hans Mommsen, 'Militär und zivile Militarisierung in Deutschland 1914–1938', in Ute Frevert (ed.), *Militär und Gesellschaft im 19. und 20. Jahrhundert* (Stuttgart, 1997), 265–276.
4. Klaus-Jürgen Müller, *Das Heer und Hitler: Armee und nationalsozialistisches Regime 1933–1940* (Stuttgart, 1969), 35ff.
5. Notes of Lieutenant General Liebmann on Hitler's visit to General Freiherr von Hammerstein Equord on 2 March 1933, printed in Klaus-Jürgen Müller, *Armee und Drittes Reich 1933–1939* (Paderborn, 1987), 264.
6. Max Domarus, *Hitler. Reden und Proklamationen*, vol. 1 (Munich, 1963), 193.
7. Wolfram Wette, 'Ideologien, Propaganda und Innenpolitik als Voraussetzungen der Kriegspolitik des Dritten Reiches', in *Das Deutsche Reich und der Zweite Weltkrieg*, ed. by Militärgeschichtliches Forschungsamt, vol. 1 (Stuttgart, 1959), 115.
8. On Germany's withdrawal from the disarmament conference, see Wilhelm Deist, 'Die Aufrüstung der Wehrmacht', in *Das Deutsche Reich und der Zweite Weltkrieg*, vol. 1, 397 f.
9. Ian Kershaw, *Der Hitler-Mythos. Volksmeinung und Propaganda im Dritten Reich* (Stuttgart, 1980), 113f.; Wette, *Ideologien*, 16.
10. Wette, *Ideologien*, 132.
11. Cf. E. K. Bramstedt, *Goebbels und die nationalsozialistische Propaganda 1925–1945* (Frankfurt, 1971), 241ff.
12. Helmut Krausnick, 'Vorgeschichte und Beginn des militärischen Widerstandes gegen Hitler', in *Vollmacht des Gewissens* (Frankfurt, 1960), 265.
13. S. Marlis and G. Steinert, *Hitlers Krieg und die Deutschen. Stimmung und Haltung der deutschen Bevölkerung im Zweiten Weltkrieg* (Düsseldorf, 1970), 76.
14. Kershaw, *Hitler-Mythos*, 122.
15. Steinert, *Hitlers Krieg*, 79; Kershaw, *Hitler-Mythos*, 122 f. The judgement of both is that the repercussions of the Munich Agreement were disastrous and strengthened Hitler's prestige.
16. Steinert, *Hitlers Krieg*, 81.
17. Ibid., 84.
18. Quoted in Kershaw, *Hitler-Mythos*, 125.
19. Wilhelm Treue, 'Die Hitler Rede vor der deutschen Presse vom 10. November 1938', *VfZ* 6, 1 (1958), 82f.; cf. Wette, *Ideologie*, 133f.
20. Wette, *Ideologie*, 141f.
21. Cf. Kershaw, *Hitler-Mythos*, 150ff.

22. Steinert, *Hitlers Krieg,* 206.
23. Cf. Jutta Sywottek, *Mobilmachung für den totalen Krieg. Die propagandistische Vorbereitung der deutschen Bevölkerung auf den Zweiten Weltkrieg* (Opladen, 1976).
24. Steinert, *Hitlers Krieg,* 227f., 273f.
25. Jürgen Förster, 'Geistige Kriegsführung in Deutschland', in *Das Deutsche Reich und der Zweite Weltkrieg,* vol. 9, 1 (Munich, 2004), 570f.; cf. Steinert, *Hitlers Krieg,* 278.
26. Cf. Aristotle A. Kallis, 'Der Niedergang der Deutungsmacht. Nationalsozialistische Propaganda im Kriegsverlauf', in *Das Deutsche Reich und der Zweite Weltkrieg,* Bd. 9, 2 (Munich, 2005), 222.
27. See Kershaw, *Führer-Mythos,* 172.
28. See Steinert, *Hitlers Krieg,* 424.
29. *Meldungen aus dem Reich. Die geheimen Lageberichte des Sicherheitsdienstes der SS,* vol. 9 (Herrsching, 1984), 338.
30. Quoted in Steinert, *Hitlers Krieg,* 339; cf. directive A 91/42 from the Head of the Party Headquarters, 1.18.1942; ibid., 320f.
31. Thus the President of the OLG, Jena, on 30 November 1943; quoted ibid., 424.
32. Manfred Messerschmidt, *Die Wehrmachtsjustiz 1933–1945* (Münster, 2005).
33. Cf. the public mood report of the SS Security Service, end of May 1945 (*Meldungen aus dem Reich,* vol. 17, 6734–6740, printed in Norbert Frei, *Der Führerstaat. Nationalsozialistische Herrschaft 1933–1945,* (6th edition, Munich, 2001), 273ff.
34. This development has been analysed at length by Kershaw, *Hitler-Mythos,* 183–191.

11

The French Entry into the War in September 1939

Between Reluctance and Resignation

Barbara Lambauer

The defeat of France in June 1940 was one of the greatest traumas in the history of French foreign policy. Along with 1870 and 1954, it sealed the nation's final descent from a great power to a power of the second rank. In view of this, it is all the more remarkable that French historians (with the exception of Marc Bloch[1]), waited patiently for over thirty years before addressing themselves to the subject. Particular attention was then given to the psychological constitution of French society in the years before the war; the standard work on French foreign policy in the 1930s, by Jean-Baptiste Duroselle, is entitled *La décadence*.[2]

Since the 1970s, French work on the end of the Third Republic has predominantly studied the 1930s as the path leading inevitably to the defeat of June 1940, and underlined in this connection the importance of domestic political and social tensions.[3] It was only in 1990 that Jean-Louis Crémieux-Brilhac (incidentally a former resistance fighter) addressed himself in a highly regarded work to the French frame of mind at the entry into the war; the first volume of his book was significantly sub-titled: *The War: Yes or No?*[4] Drawing a line between the questions as to the cause of the defeat and the state of French society is not easy in most cases. The allegedly insufficient military build-up of the French army is generally explained by unstable political conditions, but also by the advanced ages of the political class. British and American studies, on the other hand, seek to challenge the previously dominant view that there was a direct connection between social crisis and military defeat.[5] In the eyes of Ernest R. Mays, for example, the Allies should actually have emerged victorious from the conflict in the spring of 1940, a thesis that he maintains can be proven by computer simulation.[6] The Franco-British defeat, he argues, is to be explained primarily by the fact that the secret services were not sufficiently involved in the planning of the war and defence, and by the shock effect of the Ardennes offensive, to which the British and French responded far too slowly. Peter Jackson, on the other hand, emphasises the French secret service's false estimation or overestimation of the strength of German armaments and the feeling of military inferiority that this engendered in the French.[7] Nor can Julian Jackson find anything in the thesis that the seeds of the French defeat were sown in the 1930s: apart from the six weeks of the French campaign, the Third Republic could, in his opinion, be seen as 'an extraordinary success story'.[8]

What picture, then, emerges of the French in the period before September 1939? Were they ready for a major war? It is impossible to give an adequate answer to this question without considering the five and a half years that preceded the declaration of war in September 1939. The French journalist and historian Henri Amouroux speaks of the 'melancholy triumph' of Marshal Pétain in the early summer of 1940, which would have been impossible without the general 'bewilderment, de-politicisation, the immense weariness of a people that had been thrown into a badly planned war which they had lost long before they could learn how to wage it'.[9] So in this chapter I shall distinguish between two periods: one of escalating inner tensions and schisms from 1934 to 1938, followed by one of attempts at moral and military build-up.

'Better Hitler than Blum'? France on the Verge of Civil War, 1934–1938

During the second half of the 1930s the French were much less concerned about international security and the threat represented by Hitler's Germany than about the internal state of affairs in their own country. This was marked not only by an extremely unstable political situation but also by violent clashes, particularly between the (extreme) left and the right. This is how Raymond Aron recalled the situation: 'In the thirties, I lived in despair of French decadence, with the feeling that France was preparing to throw itself into an abyss. To all intents and purposes, France no longer existed. [The country] existed only in the feelings of hatred that Frenchmen harboured towards each other.'[10] Feelings of hatred that, in the coming years, were to go so far as to make some middle-class circles, as the Catholic intellectual Emmanuel Mounier noted in October 1938 in the journal *Esprit*, prefer 'Hitler to Blum'.[11] The historian Pierre Laborie proposes the following diagnosis: France found itself in a 'serious crisis of collective consciousness and identity'; the feeling of belonging to a national community gradually went to pieces in the second half of the 1930s.[12] This breaking asunder could be traced to the violent social struggles before the outbreak of the war. The fears and confrontations fomented in the course of the popular front government left wounds that were still felt years later.

The starting-point for the social and political tensions was the economic crisis that hit France with full force in 1932 and could not be cushioned because of the structural instability of the country's domestic politics: between June 1932 and March 1940 there were no less than sixteen different cabinets (seven between June 1932 and February 1934 alone); the average life of a government was thus somewhat less than six months.[13] The resultant political crisis of confidence reached a dramatic climax in the so-called 'Stavisky Affair', a political corruption scandal of huge dimensions that caused right-wing leagues and war veterans to hold a large demonstration in front of the Chamber of Deputies protesting against the 'republic of thieves'.[14] The demonstration degenerated into a riot that lasted for hours and the police opened fire: fifteen dead and more than two thousand injured turned the clash into a decisive event that caused a deep and long-lasting shock. For Raymond Aron it was the beginning of a 'cold civil war'.[15] From this time onwards the political fronts remained irreconcilable. For the Left, it was a question of the dangerous radicalisation of a re-strengthened fascism and a failed coup d'etat. The Right focussed on the corruption of state power.

Foreign policy at this time operated very unsystematically; Duroselle laments the 'lack of seriousness' and the inadequate preparation and competence of the ministers responsible.[16] The man in charge at the Ministry of Foreign Affairs was Alexis Léger, an adherent of Aristide Briand's approach at a time when this was long outdated, the Weimar Republic having turned into National Socialist Germany, which had no intention of observing international agreements. France's customary flight into 'pact mania' could no longer meet the growing threat. Using the ratification of the French-Soviet mutual assistance pact as a pretext, Hitler re-militarised the Rhineland in the spring of 1936. This fait accompli ultimately met with mild protest in France, which had only briefly considered a military response, since new elections were to be held in six weeks. On this the young writer Robert Brasillach, then working for the royalist newspaper *Action Française,* commented sarcastically in his memoirs: 'I do not know whether the French army was prepared or not; I know only that elections were impending, and that in a republic military operations cannot be ordered a few weeks before the polls.'[17] Raymond Aron thought the French descent to the defeat of June 1940 began with this missed opportunity to confront Hitler's breaches of the Locarno Pact: France spared itself the pain of defending 'its only guarantee of peace, which it owed to the lives of 1.3 million of its children'.[18] In this Aron saw a much graver French responsibility for 'abdication' in the face of Hitler's Germany than, for instance, the Munich Conference two and a half years later. The majority of the French, however, could not then distinguish between the now overt National Socialist policy of aggression and the German policy of revision in the 1920s.

The elections of May 1936 brought a radical change in the government: the victorious *Rassemblement populaire,* composed mainly of socialists, radical socialists and communists, formed a government under the president of the council of ministers, Léon Blum, which has gone down in history as the *Front populaire* and still today divides opinion and nourishes debates. The swearing-in of the government was immediately followed by a sweeping wave of strikes: more than 2.5 million workers stopped work until the government introduced collective contracts, two-weeks paid holiday and finally a forty-hour week. The formation of this first Popular Front government under Blum, the first Jew to lead a French government, aroused growing fears in conservative and extreme right-wing circles of the approach of communism, fears whose consequences reached into the Vichy regime. They also left their mark on French society, which became increasing polarised. Extreme parties were given a new impetus, both the Communist Party and extreme right-wing movements.[19] The Popular Front government had dissolved the right-wing political leagues, but this measure was immediately countered by the formation of new extremist parties. The most important example is the *Parti Social Français* (PSF) of Colonel de la Rocque, which became an assembly point for former followers of the *Croix de feu* league. Two months after it was founded it already had more members (over six hundred thousand) than the Communist or Socialist parties. Another example is the *Parti Populaire Français* (PPF) of Jacques Doriot, a renegade Communist, with one hundred thousand supporters.[20] The model for these parties was not national socialism but rather Italian fascism, which was widely admired in right-wing French circles. 'Fascism' (like 'communism' on the Left) became a synonym for 'action' and 'youth cult', and could inspire an enthusiasm against which liberal democracy was barely able hold its own. Extreme right-wing and nationalist publications such as *Gringoire, Candide, Je suis partout, L'Echo de Paris* and *L'Action française* had already made their mark in 1935 as vociferous 'advocates' of Italy's war against Ethiopia.[21] Charles Maurras, leading figure in these circles, expressed himself very clearly: 'Where public opinion rules, no one rules', for democracy 'leads into the abyss', into decadence and, in the case of war, into military disaster.[22] And even Raymond Aron admitted in his memoirs that, in view of the paralysis of the democratic countries, the spectacular rise of Hitler's Germany and the economic growth rates published by the Soviet Union, he himself sometimes thought or said: 'If an authoritarian regime is necessary in order to save France, then so be it; we shall accept it, even if inwardly we profoundly reject it.'[23]

Moreover, the French Right perceived in the effects of the Popular Front government alarming parallels to the Spanish Civil War that had broken out only a few months before. The size of the strike movement made them fear a similar conflict in France. The first indication of this seemed to be the terrorist attacks against the French federation of employers in September 1936. In fact, these were perpetrated by the *Cagoule*, an underground right-wing extremist group, which intended to direct suspicion towards the Communist Party.[24] The resentment of a frustrated bourgeoisie, who, according to Marc Bloch, were finding it difficult to cope with the mutations of the economy, the emergence of a new class of workers and their demands,[25] now became concentrated on the 'Jew' Léon Blum. The bourgeoisie could not forget the 'red flag of the demands' which flew over the factories during the strike.[26] Bloch writes: 'From one day to the next, a long, deep fissure dividing social groups into two blocks ran through French society.'[27] The subsequent attitude of the middle class remained for Bloch 'inexcusable', for it 'behaved stupidly' towards reasonable and preposterous measures alike: they gave up their own country, thereby surrendering it too hastily to the enemy.[28]

There was a remarkable reversal among the traditionally anti-German Right (above all, in *Action française* and the circles related to it) in the years before the war: they abandoned their germanophobic tendencies in favour of an anti-communist course and began gradually to make friends with National Socialist Germany. This, combined with the decisive strengthening of the communist camp and continued social unrest generated a 'pre-civil war climate' (*préguerre civile*), to quote Amouroux,[29] or in Robert Brasillach's words: 'We felt the revolution approaching.'[30] The official and unofficial representatives of Hitler's Germany working assiduously in France for the 'German-French rapprochement' could only congratulate themselves on this change and exploit it for their own ends. It was not, however, their work, as the myth of a 'fifth column' would have us believe in the immediate aftermath of French defeat. By the end of 1935, Ribbentrop's assistant, Otto Abetz, an art teacher now established in the department for para-diplomatic activities founded by the former and later ambassador in Paris, had already persuaded well-known French figures to found a pro-German platform composed of various political tendencies. Until the spring of 1939 this *Comité France-Allemagne* was to give German-French exchange a purely French veneer.[31] Under the roof of the committee, whose strings he pulled behind the scenes, Abetz had managed to unite left-wing as well as right-wing war veterans' associations, 'non-conformist' intellectuals, journalists and writers (such as Drieu La Rochelle, Bertrand de Jouvenel), academics (Henri Lichtenberger) and young followers of *Action française* who had gathered round the journal *Je suis partout*. The chairman of the *Comité France-Allemagne*, Major R. M. L'Hôpital (Marshal Foch's former adjutant), formulated the committee's task as follows: 'To prepare a form of co-existence for the coming generation in which each [country] can achieve its place in the sun through its own efforts.'[32] One of the chief means of persuading the French of both the peaceful intentions and political superiority of the 'new Germany' were organised tours beyond the Rhine, to a country that was, incidentally, in the process of fully re-arming itself. From 1939 onwards, contributors to *Je suis partout* regularly took part in the Nazi Party Conferences in Nuremberg.[33] Shortly before the ratification of the Franco-Soviet mutual assistance pact, Hitler declared in an interview with Bertrand de Jouvenel for the high-circulation daily newspaper *Paris-Soir:*

> There are key moments in the lives of peoples. Today France can, if it wishes, put an end once and for all to the 'German peril' which your children have been taught to fear from generation to generation. You can rid yourselves of this alarming hypothesis that has weighed on French history. The opportunity is yours. Should you not seize it, think of your responsibility towards your children! You stand before a Germany nine-tenths of whose people have placed their trust in its leader, and this leader says to you: Let us be friends![34]

The French attitude towards National Socialist Germany was in fact profoundly ambivalent. On the Left, it was marked by feelings of guilt about the terms of the Versailles Peace Treaty, feelings that Abetz, in particular, deliberately exploited. The previously germanophobic Right re-defined their enemy in the light of the Popular Front government, now focussing on Communism as the main evil, and this allowed their cautious rapprochement with the German dictatorship. This re-definition shaped their so-called 'neo-pacifism', whose chief motive was not the rejection of armed force but rather anti-communism and the fear that an armed conflict in Europe could, with the aid of national Communist Parties, lead to Soviet dominance.[35]

The 1936 Olympic Games furnished an excellent opportunity to showcase a 'new Germany' radiant with strength, dynamism and enthusiasm to an international public. The *Comité France-Allemagne* played an important role in conveying this image to France. A member of the French delegation to the Games, Jacques Benoist-Méchin, was delighted by the enthusiastic welcome given French athletes in Garmisch-Partenkirchen and Berlin, and added that it was absurd to maintain, as some of the French press had done, that this was the work of an 'acclamation brigade'.[36] The Games, he said, were a lesson and an encouragement: 'They show in a concrete and unforgettable manner that understanding between our peoples is possible and that, if we wish, our dream can become reality.'[37]

The mounting threat presented by Hitler's Germany by 1936 was not recognised by the majority of the French, who could not distinguish between the new German policy of aggression and former German demands for revision of the Versailles Treaty in the 1920s. Apart from the factors already mentioned, especially political polarisation and growing anti-communism, a pacifism deeply anchored in society played a crucial role in French foreign policy during this period. The extremely vague term *pacifism* stood for a multiplicity of attitudes, but was generally inspired by, as Pascal Laborie put it, an 'intense longing for peace' that could well be called a 'collective and general will'.[38] It was a strong feeling widespread amongst the population, forming a consensus and rooted in the conviction that, in reality, there was no such thing as an unavoidable war and no fatalistic tendency that inevitably leads to armed force. The rejection of war went so far that a trade union leader openly declared he preferred 'serfdom to war', 'for one can get over being a serf, whereas there is no getting over not returning from a war'.[39] As Aron later expressed it in a conversation:

> The French had the feeling – rightly – that the war, however it turned out, would be a disaster for France. France, nearly bled to death by the First World War, could not afford another blood-letting, even should she prove victorious in the end. ... In 1936 intellectuals wrote one appeal after another. All of them said: 'It was fortunate we did not resort to military measures.' All of them. In 1938 all of them said: 'We have avoided a war, and this avoidance alone is good'. We had [finally] to be so strongly cornered by the course of events that a kind of acceptance of disaster could emerge.[40]

In this connection it should be mentioned that in 1938 40 per cent of the male population were still survivors of the 'Great War': there were about 5.25 million of them, of whom 1.5 million were still eligible for conscription.[41] The majority of the French political and administrative elite belonged to this social group, with Edouard Daladier leading the way.

France and the Approach of War, 1938–1939

The Sudeten Crisis hit France during Prime Minister Edouard Daladier's government, which still counted as part of the Popular Front, but which had already distanced itself considerably from the programmes of the first period. Its most important characteristic was probably the increasing popularity and authority of Daladier himself, who seemed to be responding more and more to the call for a 'strong leader' and to be ruling by ordinances without convening Parliament.[42] Although Daladier, like his predecessors, could be dismissed by Parliament, the fact remained that he had the majority of deputies behind him.[43] We shall return later to his ambivalent efforts to prepare the country for the war that was clearly looming, while at the same time crucially accelerating the division of French society.[44] All in all, he seems to have been quite close to the 'soul of the French people', as Julian Jackson has observed: 'He was neither an unconditional *appeaser* like [his Foreign minister Georges] Bonnet nor a convinced *belliciste* like [his Finance Minister Paul] Reynaud. Thus, he was well placed to sell peace in 1938 and war in 1939.'[45]

In France his participation in the Munich Conference and his signing of the resultant agreement met with virtually unanimous acclaim. A few days after the conference, Antoine de Saint-Exupéry commented as follows on the fundamental dilemma it had precipitated:

> We have decided to save the peace. But by saving the peace, we have harmed our friends. And without a doubt there were many among us who would have been prepared to risk their lives for the duties of friendship. They felt a kind of dishonour. But had they sacrificed the peace, they would have felt the same dishonour, for then they would have sacrificed mankind. … For this reason we swayed back and forth between this view and the other. When peace seemed to us to be threatened, we discovered the dishonour of war. When the war seemed to us to be threatened, we felt the dishonour of peace.[46]

The majority of the French, still considerably influenced by a first partial mobilisation of troops (750,000 reservists and 25,000 officers were engaged[47]), were in favour of the agreement, or as Jean-Pierre Azéma put it, were 'très munichois'.[48] In the Chamber of Deputies only the Communists and two renegade deputies voted against Munich, so that there were 537 votes for and only 75 votes against. One of the first opinion polls conducted by the recently founded *Institut français d'opinion publique* confirmed this basic mood: in October 1938, 57 per cent of the French were satisfied with the result of the conference (though 37 per cent were dissatisfied with it). The answer to the second question asked on the same occasion is not without significance. Asked 'Do you believe that France and England will now have to oppose every new demand by Hitler?', no less than 70 per cent of those questioned answered 'Yes', and only 17 per cent 'No'.[49] The French were quite aware that although they had escaped by the skin of their teeth this time, any further crisis must inevitably lead to war.

For the time being, a great wave of relief swept through the country; the popular celebrations to mark Daladier's return were impressive, and were echoed in the major newspapers. In *Le Figaro,* for instance, the well-known journalist Wladimir d'Ormesson emphasized the 'plebiscite' that had 'prevailed throughout the whole world'.[50] Significantly, the right-wing press celebrated a victory over 'international Communism' and 'Jewry' rejoiced at what it regarded as the obvious 'disappointment of Moscow and Israel'.[51] Louis Marin, formerly an adamant opponent of Germany and now especially hostile to the Agreement, had to admit: 'We cannot afford to treat the world every 20 years to a Battle of the Marne'.[52] Léon Blum was divided between 'deep joy' at the catastrophe so narrowly avoided and 'deep pain' for the 'allied and stalwart nation' whose integrity and part of whose independence had had to be sacrificed for the sake of 'Europe's tranquillity'.[53]

These few comments already point to the diversity of motives that existed within the pro-Munich camp. For if to be 'antimunichois', to oppose the agreement, was perforce the same as assenting to a new war, the motives and goals of the agreement's defenders were anything but unitary. The divisions between supporters and opponents cut across all political camps; the single exception was the Communists. The party most shaken by internal discord over Munich was undoubtedly the Socialists, who were henceforth divided between the followers of Blum and those of Paul Faures (an unconditional pacifist). Schematically speaking, it could be said that the defenders of the agreement were divided into two clear groups: proponents of the British policy of appeasement,[54] and converted 'neo-pacifists' from the formerly germanophobic, extreme right-wing camp. To be distinguished from these was a temporising tendency that simply aimed to gain time, a motive which has also been ascribed to Daladier and to which a certain number of independent radical socialists, socialists and several factions of the nationalist Right belonged.[55]

A striking characteristic of the French situation was the indignation focussed on the Communist Party, which vehemently opposed the agreement because the USSR had been excluded from the negotiations. The Party's position, which sought to blur the boundaries between democracy and dictatorship and repeatedly raised the issue of the class struggle (for instance, it referred to the '200 families' that profited from the agreement[56]), was unconvincing. It thereby gave its opponents ammunition in the battle against communism, a battle which, Henri Amouroux observed, replaced 'the war that we were not fighting against the Germans'.[57] In the weeks following the Munich Conference, several newspapers conducted veritable hate campaigns against the so-called 'red menace'. The Communists were accused of seeking to send the bourgeoisie and peasants to the slaughterhouse, that is, to the front, so that back home they could establish a dictatorship of the proletariat, who would have stayed behind to work in the factories.[58]

The Munich Agreement is usually said to have created the misleading impression that peace had once again been saved at the last minute. To the government in Paris, however, it was plain that the agreement could only serve to delay the inevitable and that a decisive military build-up was urgently needed. Not for nothing had Daladier been acting minister of war since 1936. At the end of August 1938 he had already drawn public attention to the need to relax the forty hour week in order to boost armaments production in view of the mounting international threat. The trade union movement, less concerned about considerations of foreign policy than about the fierce conflicts with employers that had been going on since 1936, had no intention of conceding a triumph of any kind to the government and rejected overtures to this effect out of hand.

The inauspicious combination of decreased production, initially due to the cut in working hours, with a flight of capital, connected with refusals to invest on the part of employers, had in fact led to a significant price rise since 1936. The demands for corresponding wage increases coupled with the simultaneous refusal to relax regulations about working hours further nurtured the already far-reaching tensions between workers and employers. By 1937, the situation in the factories (especially the larger ones) was explosive. The 'daily renewed guerrilla war characteristic of the time of the Popular Front' culminated in 1938 in a test of strength between employers and workers which ultimately revolved around the simple question: 'Who takes the decisions at the workplace?'[59] The historian Antoine Prost has underscored that, for the employers, this confrontation was rather a question of 'their social position and authority than their income', whereas for the workers it was a question of defending the freedom they had won in 1936 from the factory hierarchy. In the end, it was the new international situation created by the Sudeten Crisis that enabled the government to strike the crucial blow against the French trade union movement, bringing victory to the employers and political Right. The impetus was given by a regulation initiated by the new minister of Finance, Paul Reynaud, on 12 November 1938, which proclaimed an exception in the extension of working hours that was practically tantamount to abolishing the forty hour week. What is more, the employers decided on a very broad interpretation of the text, which inevitably gave the impression that the workers had been the victims of 'collective chicanery'.[60] In the Renault factories, for example, the forty hour week was spread over six days instead of five (as it had been before), and the trade union leader was sacked. Another factory in a Parisian suburb introduced a seven-hour working day from Monday to Sunday, with the exception of Saturday, when it was to be nine hours. The government's response to the first local strikes was to clear the occupied factories and there were mass dismissals (twenty-eight thousand, for instance, at Renault). The trade union answered with a call for a general strike on 30 November.[61]

This was to go down in history as a great failure, for the government did not hesitate to crack down: there were numerous arrests and dismissals. They were implemented primarily against the trade union leaders and works councils: by January 1939 more than ten thousand had been definitively sacked and barred from other work because of their participation in the general strike. By February 1939, there were 1,731 criminal prosecutions; 806 resulted in prison sentences, 103 for a period of longer than two months; 94 people were still serving sentences then.[62] Daladier, who had clearly come down on the side of the employers, emerged from the conflict stronger than before, whereas from now on the Socialists, and indeed the Communists, were to find themselves politically isolated. Trade Union membership declined drastically; the records of the Ministry of Labour show no further strikes for 1939.[63] By the spring of 1939 at the latest, the public mood had moved to the Right, but without strengthening the extremists.[64] Daladier had succeeded, so to say, in lowering the 'anti-Communist fever' in France; in the words of Julian Jackson, the cry 'Better Hitler than Blum' became 'Why Hitler when we have Daladier?'[65]

According to the historian Talbot Imlay, the Daladier government's overt support for the employers was to have 'tremendous consequences for France's war effort':

> By allying with industry, the government ensured that economic mobilization for war was pursued along laissez-faire, economic liberal lines. Yet preparations for a possible war demanded greater economic direction and co-ordination. ... With the state abnegating responsibility in the economic realm, inefficiency and chaos resulted. ... Finally, the isolation of organized labour, a direct result of the government's alliance with industry, exacerbated the sense of general crisis by fostering the perception of a disgruntled and alienated working class dangerously susceptible to the PCF's revolutionary designs.[66]

In the aftermath, anti-communism became the real basis of a new social consensus, whose concept of the enemy included even the moderate Left. Reynaud could pursue a liberal financial policy, which did in fact gradually lure capital back into the country and lead to a clear improvement in the economic situation.[67]

With regard to its foreign policy at this time, the French government remained remarkably discreet and ready to compromise. When there was a brutal pogrom against the Jews in Germany on 9 November 1938, after the assassination in Paris of Ernst vom Rath, the response of the French press was largely guarded and cautious. The pogrom was reported only briefly and soberly, mainly on the middle pages. As Georges Bidault noted with clear amazement in the newspaper *L'Aube,* the reporters were obviously 'sweating with fear of offending the public': 'But why should we keep silent about the sorrow and abhorrence we felt yesterday when reading the Parisian press?'[68] The constraint is all the more astonishing in view of the fact that the assassination took place in Paris. It can undoubtedly be explained by Paris's desire to avoid new tensions with Berlin at all costs and its primary objective was to gain time against Germany. In this connection, the new French ambassador presented his credentials to the German government on exactly the same morning as the American ambassador was recalled from Berlin in protest against the pogrom.[69]

In November 1939 France was also in the midst of a two-week long commemoration of the end of the 1914 war, which was celebrated with solemn torchlight processions and to which considerable political significance was evidently attached. The commemoration of the truce was accompanied by carefully prepared events and was supposed to comply with the wish, also frequently expressed by war veterans, to surmount social and political obstacles and to re-connect with the 1914 spirit of national unity, while avoiding any expression of satisfaction at the German defeat as it could have been taken as a provocation by Berlin.[70]

Parallel to this France and Germany were preparing to sign a joint declaration, which Joachim von Ribbentrop had to postpone supposedly because of international indignation at the treatment of Jews in the Third Reich.[71] The event was officially announced in Paris on the same day as the visit of Prime Minister Neville Chamberlain and his Foreign Secretary Lord Halifax was scheduled. The strange balancing act of French foreign policy, ogling, as it did, both of its neighbours, did not escape alert observers. Thus Georges Bidault noted: 'One document is added to another, to the Briand-Kellogg Pact, for example, which Hitler's Germany has not renounced and the importance it means to attach to which one could see in September. … It is not, alas, the first time that the stance adopted by Paris must end in disorienting British and American opinion at a time when it has begun to become particularly well-disposed towards us.'[72] The futility of the international policy of appeasement became evident, at the very latest, when German troops entered Prague. Did the French government now clearly address the population and prepare it for the danger of an imminent war against Germany? Although it did respond to the fresh crisis by intensifying the military build-up, politically the country seemed more divided than ever, despite the official discourse that never wearied of appealing to a sense of national unity. In this connection Pierre Laborie regards it as characteristic of France immediately before the war that there was no concrete designation of the enemy. Weekly newsreels, for example, addressed the subject of national defence at length (Laborie quotes here General Weygand's 'famous and unfortunate declaration' of July 1939, according to which the French army was equipped 'with material of the highest quality, fortifications of the first order, an extraordinary courage and a remarkable high command'[73]). But what authorities did not mention, is against *whom* France would have to defend itself. Laborie detects here a systematic 'drift into irrationality', bred by a diffuse discourse that revolved around the so-called 'decadence' of French society: 'The long slide from reason to unreason, the ease with which false, demonological explanations gradually replace the analysis of the complex causes of a crisis and fuse into a succession of certainties – or at least of assumptions presented as certainties'. Part of this was, for instance, the allusion to allegedly malevolent (foreign or occult) forces working to corrode the nation, and also the search for scapegoats and the call for a strong leader – Edouard Daladier. Political debates conformed to flagrant stereotypes and generalisations along the lines of: 'If one is *against* the war, one is *for* fascism', or 'Anti-Fascists are automatically warmongers and conscious or unconscious agents of the "Bolshevik revolution"' (from which must follow that opponents of Bolshevism basically agree with actions undertaken to maintain peace).[74]

The progressive and deep-reaching dissolution of social cohesion that followed from this was undoubtedly an important factor in the thoroughly ambivalent character of the French entry into the war in 1939, and indeed in the ease with which the Pétain regime was established in summer 1940.

An event that illustrates this state of affairs is the celebration for the 150th anniversary of the French Revolution in July 1939, a few weeks before the outbreak of the war, which turned out to be a failure. The mounting danger of an international war served as a pretext to steer the celebrations clear of any show of 'passion'; the storming of the Bastille seemed to have been completely forgotten.[75] The government's indifference to the occasion was already clear in the planning stage, and apart from the Communist Party (which sought to monopolise the anniversary for itself and its own revolutionary ideas) no other political group wished to appear in public as co-organiser: 'Cabinet ministers were no more inclined than the elected representatives to turn their attention to the [pre-] history of the regime [the Third Republic] so as to illustrate its defence.'[76] Thanks to the doggedness shown by the organisers of the *Ligue des droits de l'homme* and the *Ligue française de l'enseignement,* the planned events did take place and were publicly subsidised, but they were overshadowed by a 'double crisis, both domestic and international'. Participation by official representatives and the French public turned out to be merely nominal.[77] 1939 was obviously not the year in which to mobilise the French for republican values; it seemed easier for the government to associate itself with the extreme Right than with the Left.[78] The single exception was the military parade with the theme 'The Fourteenth of July Marks the Recovery of France', which lured one and a half million spectators and in which four companies of English Grenadiers took part.[79] Photographs of the parade were, incidentally, also published in the *Deutsch-französische Monatshefte,* the organ of the *Comité France-Allemagne.*[80]

The idea of France's new 'recovery' became a major theme of official propaganda, to which Daladier attached increasing importance. This was made clear by the appointment of the first general commissioner for information in the person of the writer Jean Giraudoux, a good acquaintance of Otto Abetz. In 1935 he had written a play entitled *The Trojan War Will Not Take Place,* in which he imagines how the Trojan War could have been avoided had Hector decided in favour of peace and sent Helen back to the Greeks. In the summer of 1939 Giraudoux published a book entitled *Pleins pouvoirs,* in which he expresses his concerns about contemporary France. In his opinion, the temptation to trace the 'present French problem' to the international situation was too great, and would be mistaken: 'To think that the struggle we must wage is a struggle of democracy against tyranny means to accept a dangerous confusion. It means to ascribe responsibility to Germany and Italy, who are not to blame, for a fatal but internal trouble, which we have sought out of unconscious or feigned stoicism, or else out of weakness, to conceal by all means behind projected states of fear.'[81] The core of the 'French problem' lay, in his view, in the 'decline of the French race'. Among the reasons for this Giraudoux counted the unchecked influx, 'under the cloak of every revolution, ideological movement and persecution', of 'all the outcasts, maladjusted, greedy and impaired' of Europe, among whom were 'hundreds of thousands of Ashkenazim that had escaped Polish or Rumanian ghettos' whose 'spiritual values, though not particularism', they rejected.[82] Even after the French declaration of war, on 11 November, Giraudoux addressed a speech to French draftees in which he invoked the idea of an inner change in France.[83]

How did the majority of French see the situation in their country in 1939? They seemed at any rate to be gradually preparing themselves for the imminent war; the crucial change had begun with the shock of the German invasion of Prague. Even Frenchmen who wished to show understanding for German aims, such as Félix Bérard of the *Comité France-Allemagne* in Lyon, revealed their incomprehension. In 'The Swastika Flies Over Prague … We No Longer Understand', he wrote: 'Now, in contrast to our view of the spirit of Munich, it seems that the politics of the *fait accompli* and the fist hammering a table has gained the upper hand. That is alarming and will put the nerves of old Europe to a hard test. … The true friends of Germany do not know how they can defend her in their own country.'[84] French opinion polls in July 1939, that is, in the midst of the Danzig crisis, show that 45 per cent of those questioned thought a war in the same year was probable (50 per cent among those aged between twenty and thirty years). By comparison, in April 1939, following the German entry into Prague, it was only 37 per cent. However, in July 1939, 34 per cent were still optimistic about the chances of preserving the peace (in contrast to 47 per cent three months before).[85] To the question whether, if a war did not occur by October, there was still danger of a later war, 67 per cent replied with 'yes'. And in contrast to the neo-socialist Marcel Déat, who on 4 May 1939 had questioned whether the French should 'be dying for Danzig', 76 per cent of those questioned were of the opinion that Germany must be prevented from taking Danzig by force. Many authors admit, however, that this mounting national solidarity against Hitler's Germany probably arose from an illusion, namely that if the French took a hard line Berlin could be held in check before events led to a war.[86]

A decisive event, which strengthened the nation in its attitude and enabled Daladier to join the British declaration of war at the beginning of September, was the Hitler-Stalin Pact and the shock it triggered in France. Significantly, with this pact the French Communist Party became 'Enemy Number 1',[87] for the government seized the opportunity to start persecuting communists. Only two days later the communist newspapers *Ce soir* and *L'Humanité* were impounded and banned, and the first arrests ordered; the Party started on its long path into the underground.[88] 'The pact with Moscow, a disaster for the democracies at a military level, gives Daladier's government a psychological advantage: it can shift the responsibility for the declaration of war to Russian treachery and National Socialist irrationality.'[89] France responded to the German invasion of Poland on 1 September 1939 with a general mobilisation of its army and, a day later, with the Chamber of Deputies' authorisation of war credits. A vote on the declaration of war itself, supposed to follow on 3 September, was never to take place. In his speech, which stood under the shadow of July 1914 (adhering to the main points of the speech of then head of government[90]), Daladier emphasised: 'I have tried everything to avoid the worst. The world bears witness that this has happened contrary to the will of France.'[91] On 4 September, he again addressed his compatriots: 'Frenchwomen and Frenchmen, we are waging war because we have been forced to wage it.'[92] Was he prepared for war? Numerous historians have questioned whether he was; years later the economist Alfred Sauvy, advisor to Paul Reynaud, pointed to Daladier's greatest error, the greatest that a head of state can commit in times of hostilities: 'to proclaim that under no circumstances would he seize the offensive initiative. In contrast to Clémenceau, *he waged no war.*'[93]

The French thus entered the war of 1939 with a marked reluctance and resignation, but at the same time with the certainty that they must 'make an end of it'[94] with Hitler's Germany:

> From socialists to conservatives, the initial reaction was basically the same. France had never wanted another war; this war was instigated by the new barbarians, the Nazis, headed by Hitler. France is doing her elementary duty in defending civilization against the onslaught of barbarism. It is symptomatic that the French press in expressing public opinion laid no stress on patriotic, strategic, and economic goals, nor on any other French interest. These were rarely mentioned, the motive stressed being that there was no choice, the crusade must be carried out.[95]

The memory of 1919 was still vivid and caused fear that France might not be equal to a new conflict. A crucial role was played by the feeling of weakness and inner discord which was also kindled by the government: in spite of the belated preparations for war which had been going on since the autumn of 1938, the French were not really ready for a war *against Germany,* either militarily or psychologically. As General Maxime Weygand, by now a friend of truce, said at the end of May 1940: 'France committed the immense blunder of entering a war for which it had neither the necessary material nor the necessary military doctrine'[96] – an observation that was meant to refer to the army, but would probably also be valid for French society. Who was France's real enemy? Even as the Wehrmacht advanced on Paris, the fear of a communist rebellion was still greater than the fear of a German victory. In this connection Julian Jackson quotes the American ambassador William Bullitt who reported to Washington at the end of May 1940: 'Everyone believes that once the government leaves Paris, the Communists of the industrial suburbs will seize the city and will be permitted to murder, loot and burn for several days before the Germans come in.'[97] The latent fear of civil war and the previously described inner discord were therefore by no means fires that appeared and were fanned only during the subsequent German occupation or at the time of the liberation. They were already bitter reality at the end of the thirties and moved historian Marc Bloch, for example, to make a detailed analysis in which neither French society, politics nor economy were spared. So, too, François Mitterrand, stationed at the front, wrote home in a letter of November 1939: 'What would really bother me, would be to die for values (anti-values) in which I don't believe.'[98]

Notes

1. Marc Bloch, *L'étrange défaite* (Paris, 1946; here I cite the 1990 edition).
2. Jean-Baptiste Duroselle, *Politique étrangère de la France: La décadence 1932–1939* (Paris, 1979).
3. Henri Amouroux, *Le peuple du désastre, 1939–1940, La grande histoire des Français sous l'Occupation*, vol. 1 (Paris, 1976); Jean-Pierre Azéma, *De Munich à la Libération, 1938–1944* (Paris, 1979); Elisabeth Du Réau, *Edouard Daladier, 1884–1970* (Paris, 1993); Pierre Laborie, *L'opinion française sous Vichy. Les Français et la crise d'identité nationale 1936–1944* (2nd edition; Paris, 2001); Alfred Sauvy, *Histoire économique de la France entre les deux guerres,* 3 vols. (Paris, 1984); René Rémond and Janine Bourdin (eds.), *Edouard Daladier, chef de gouvernement, avril 1938–septembre 1939* (Paris, 1977); Rémond and Bourdin (eds.), *La France et les Français en 1938–1939* (Paris, 1978).
4. Jean-Louis Crémieux-Brilhac, *Les Français de l'an 40,* vol. 1: *La guerre oui ou non?,* vol. 2: *Ouvriers et soldats* (Paris, 1990).
5. Julian Jackson, *The Fall of France. The Nazi Invasion of 1940* (Oxford, 2003); Peter Jackson, *France and the Nazi Menace. Intelligence and Policy Making, 1933–1939* (Oxford, 2000); Ernest R. May, *Strange Victory. Hitler's Conquest of France* (New York, 2000).
6. May, *Strange Victory,* 6.
7. P. Jackson, *France,* 207.
8. J. Jackson, *The Fall,* 196. Jackson's book provides a highly informative chapter on the historiography of the French defeat of 1940 (188–197).
9. Amouroux, *Le peuple,* 11.
10. Raymond Aron, *Le spectateur engagé. Entretiens avec Jean-Louis Missika et Dominique Wolton* (Paris, 1981), 74.
11. Quoted in *Journal de la France et des Français* (Paris, 2001), 2049–2050.
12. Laborie, *L'opinion française,* 70–71.
13. Duroselle, *La décadence,* 15.
14. Quoted in Pierre Milza, *Les Fascismes* (Paris, 1985), 288.
15. Raymond Aron, *Mémoires. 50 ans de réflexion politique,* vol. 1 (Paris, 1983), 209.
16. Duroselle, *La décadence,* 16–17.
17. Robert Brasillach, *Notre Avant-Guerre* (Paris, 1941; here 3rd edition, 1981), 198.
18. Aron, *Mémoires,* 189.
19. On the veritable 'explosion' of PCF membership figures beginning in 1936, see Philippe Buton, 'Du parti légal à l'organisation clandestine', in Jean-Pierre Rioux, Antoine Prost and Jean-Pierre Azéma (eds.), *Les communistes français de Munich à Châteaubriant (1938–1941)* (Paris, 1987), 19–20.
20. Dominique Borne and Henri Dubief, *La crise des années 30, 1929–1938* (Paris, 1989), 178–179.
21. Amouroux, *Le peuple,* 30–31. Cf. Robert Brasillach's memories concerning these matters (*Notre Avant-Guerre,* 172–177).

22. In *Action française,* 11 January 1937, quoted in Crémieux-Brilhac, *La guerre oui ou non?,* 110. On the 'lust for fascism' felt by the editorial staff of *Je suis partout,* see Jeannine Verdès-Leroux, *Refus et violences. Politique et littérature à l'extrême droite des années trente aux retombées de la Libération* (Paris, 1996), 89–104.
23. Aron, *Mémoires,* 208.
24. J. Jackson, *The Fall,* 110.
25. Bloch, *L'étrange défaite,* 195.
26. Amouroux, *Le peuple,* 18; Robert Basillach also speaks of the red flags that flew from the windows in the streets of Paris (*Notre Avant-Guerre,* 190).
27. Bloch, *L'étrange défaite,* 197.
28. Ibid., 198–201.
29. Amouroux, *Le peuple,* 32.
30. Brasillach, *Notre Avant-Guerre,* 186.
31. See Barbara Lambauer, *Otto Abetz et les Français ou l'envers de la Collaboration* (Paris, 2001), 89–119.
32. *Deutsch-französische Monatshefte/Cahiers franco-allemands* 1 (1936), 5.
33. Lambauer, *Abetz,* 110; cf. also Brasillach, *Notre Avant-Guerre,* 273.
34. *Deutsch-französische Monatshefte/Cahiers franco-allemands* 4–5 (1936), 168.
35. Laborie, *L'opinion française,* 114.
36. Jacques Benoist-Méchin, 'Evolution de l'Idée Olympique', *Deutsch-französische Monatshefte/Cahiers franco-allemands* 8–9 (1936), 278.
37. Ibid., 279
38. Pascal Laborie, *L'opinion française,* 100.
39. Jean Mathé of the trade union of postal workers at the conference in Toulouse (March 1936), quoted in *Journal de la France et des Français* (Paris, 2001), 2048.
40. Aron, *Le spectateur,* 58.
41. Janine Bourdin, 'Les anciens combattants et la célébration du 11 novembre 1938', in Rémond and Bourdin (eds.), *La France et les Français,* 96–97.
42. See Gilles Le Beguec, 'L'évolution de la politique gouvernementale et les problèmes institutionnels', in Rémond and Bourdin (eds.), *Edouard Daladier,* 56.
43. See also Olivier Dard, *Les années 30. Le choix impossible* (Paris, 1999), 213.
44. See also Elisabeth Du Réau, *Daladier,* 452.
45. J. Jackson, *The Fall,* 119.
46. *Paris-Soir,* 2 October 1938, quoted in Du Réau, *Daladier,* 255.
47. Amouroux, *Le peuple,* 84.
48. Azéma, *Munich,* 18.
49. Yvon Lacaze, *L'opinion publique française et la crise de Munich* (Bern, 1991), 597.
50. *Figaro,* 1 October 1938, quoted in Lacaze, *Munich,* 285.
51. Léon Daudet, *Action Française,* 1 October 1938, in Lacaze, *Munich,* 287.
52. Louis Marin, *Nation,* no. 40, 1 October 1938, 625, in Lacaze, *Munich,* 285.
53. *Œuvre,* 28 September 1938, 244, quoted in Lacaze, *Munich,* 399.
54. For instance, the minister of foreign affairs Georges Bonnet, the right-wing of the radical socialists, the *Alliance démocratique* round Pierre-Etienne Flandin, and the pacifist wing of the Socialist Party round Paul Faure.
55. Azéma, *Munich,* 17.
56. See Lacaze, *Munich,* 595.
57. Amouroux, *Le peuple,* 128.
58. Laborie, *L'opinion française,* 115, who quotes at length the example of the daily newspaper *La Garonne.*
59. Antoine Prost, 'Le climat social', in Rémond and Bourdin (eds.), *Edouard Daladier,* 100–103.

60. Prost's description of the new working conditions (ibid., 105).
61. Ibid., 105–107.
62. Ibid., 108.
63. Ibid., 109–110.
64. Azéma, *Munich*, 27.
65. J. Jackson, *The Fall*, 118.
66. Talbot C. Imlay, *Facing the Second World War. Strategy, Politics, and Economics in Britain and France, 1938–1940* (New York, 2003), 361.
67. Du Réau, *Daladier*, 312–313.
68. *L'Aube*, 'Les scènes de barbarie en Allemagne', 12 November 1938.
69. See the editorial by Georges Bidault, *L'Aube*, 23 November 1938. The new ambassador was Robert Coulondre.
70. Bourdin, 'Les anciens combattants', 99–112.
71. Duroselle, *La décadence*, 384.
72. Georges Bidault, 'Editorial', *L'Aube*, 24 November 1938.
73. Laborie, *L'opinion française*, 129.
74. Ibid., 133–134.
75. Pascal Ory, 'La commémoration révolutionnaire en 1939', in Rémond and Bourdin (eds.), *La France et les Français*, 134.
76. Ibid., 116.
77. Ibid., 117–118.
78. Ibid., 134–135.
79. According to Amouroux, it was the most 'impressive' parade since 1919 (*Le peuple*, 78–79).
80. *Deutsch-französische Monatshefte/Cahiers franco-allemands*, Nr. 8/1939.
81. Jean Giraudoux, *Pleins pouvoirs* (Paris, 1939), 15.
82. Ibid., 65.
83. The speech was published in December 1939 under the title *Le Futur Armistice* by B. Grasset edition.
84. Félix Bérard, 'Das Hakenkreuz weht über Prag. … Wir begreifen nicht mehr. …', *Deutsch-französische Monatshefte/Cahiers franco-allemands*, May 1939, 269–272 (quotation, 271).
85. Quoted in Amouroux, *Le peuple*, 123.
86. Thus Crémieux-Brilhac, *La guerre oui ou non?*, 65.
87. Amouroux, *Le peuple*, 129.
88. See Philippe Buton, 'Du parti legal', 26–43.
89. Crémieux-Brilhac, *La guerre oui ou non?*, 68.
90. Dard, *Les années trente*, 230.
91. Daladier's statement to journalists upon his arrival at a session of the French council of ministers. *Le Jour. L'Echo de Paris*, 2 September 1939 (title page).
92. *Le Jour. L'Echo de Paris*, 4 September 1939 (title page).
93. Alfred Sauvy, *Histoire économique de la France entre les deux guerres*, vol. 2 (Paris, 1984), 20 (emphasis in original).
94. Amouroux, *Le peuple*, 125.
95. Haim Shamir, 'The *drôle de guerre* and French Public Opinion', *Journal of Contemporary History* 11 (1976), 130–131.
96. Weygand, 25 May 1940, quoted in Bloch, *L'Etrange défaite*, 55.
97. J. Jackson, *The Fall*, 133.
98. Letter by François Mitterand from the front, 11 May 1939, quoted in Pierre Péan, *Une jeunesse française. François Mitterand, 1934–1947* (Paris, 1994), 113.

12

Great Britain
Declaring War as a Matter of Honour

Lothar Kettenacker

More than half a century after the end of the Second World War and almost two decades after the end of the Cold War, we may be permitted to pose the question whether the focus of research on the negative attributes of Neville Chamberlain's appeasement politics does justice to the historical reality. Doubts about this way of looking at things already emerged in the critical discussion of A. J. P. Taylor's account of the outbreak of war.[1] Here too it now appears to be time to place the Third Reich in the perspective of history, as Martin Broszat has proposed.[2] The answer to the question as to how it could have come to such a narrowing of perspective should already considerably qualify this research approach. To begin with, we should recall Churchill's long-influential but highly questionable verdict on the Second World War as 'the unnecessary war'. 'There was never a war more easy to stop than that which has just wrecked what was left of the world from the previous struggle.'[3] What war, then, is necessary? Chamberlain could not defend himself against this judgement: he died of cancer in 1940. Today one is inclined to agree with D. C. Watt, who emphasizes the German dictator's implacable will to war, which was not to be broken from outside: 'Hitler wanted, willed, craved war and the destruction wrought by war. He did not want the war he got.'[4] In other words, it is an illusion to assume that there was an effective alternative to the politics of appeasement. Government efforts to recruit the Soviet Union for the defensive front against Hitler also failed miserably in the end. Still, Chamberlain initially succeeded in keeping Mussolini out of the war. After 1945, when the West was now to all appearances confronted by a Soviet dictator lusting for expansion, it seemed wise to heed Churchill's pointedly formulated lesson drawn from recent history and to emphasize the responsibility of the free world not only for that which had been, but also for that which should not be permitted to happen again. Everything may have its political justification in its time. But history also has its own life and a right to be taken seriously per se. And here at last is the indisputable declaration of war, emphatically demanded by press and Parliament, an expression of moral rather than military strength: the reluctant declaration of war by a man who looked upon it as a mark of failure, who sought like no one else to maintain peace to the last, and who, disregarding all criticism of his person, embodied the will to peace of his countrymen and their unbending self-respect. 'Everything that I have worked for', he confessed at the proclamation of the state of war on 3 September 1939, 'everything that I have hoped for, everything that I have believed in during my public life, has crashed into ruins.'[5] Let me mention only one episode that shows how seriously the historian should take this confession: In order to bring about a solution to the Sudeten Crisis, in September 1939 Chamberlain was prepared to board an aeroplane for the first time in his life to visit the much younger German dictator. Once airborne, he was deeply impressed by the view of the densely populated estuary of the Thames. He asked himself, as he later reported to his Cabinet, what protection could be offered to the homes spread out below, only to come to the conclusion 'that we were in no position to justify waging a war today'.[6] Such a man was no good as a war leader, unlike Churchill, who would show no scruple in sending British bombers to attack the German civilian population.[7] But he was, in his manner and in his strengths and weaknesses, far more representative of his country than his charismatic and headstrong critic and successor.

In no other European country did the maintenance of peace and the continuance of the international order stand so much in the foreground of public interest as in Great Britain, the largest, but also the most challenged imperial power of Europe. At no other time was this will for peace coupled with such an aggressively expressed need for security. There are no lack of indications of a general longing for peace: the reduction of armament spending from 766 million pounds per year in 1919–20 to 102 millions in 1932, based on the Ten Years Rule which Churchill also accepted – that is, the assumption that Great Britain would not have to face a serious opponent for at least ten years; the much publicised Oxford Union vote in February 1933 in favour of the pacifist motion, 'This House will in no circumstance fight for King and Country'; finally, the Peace Ballot Movement, nearly all of whose 11 million voters decided in favour of their country's remaining in the League of Nations and of adhering to international disarmament agreements. Twenty per cent of the participants rejected military measures even in the case of an unprovoked attack.[8] At exactly the time when Hitler was starting an intense programme of re-armament with the introduction of compulsory military service, British post-war pacifism reached its zenith with this referendum for peace. Only four years later the British press and Parliament forced Chamberlain into a declaration of war against Hitler. How is this astonishing change of heart to be explained?

Certainly the mind of the population had not fundamentally changed in these four years, including its stance on war and peace. British society had undergone a rather radical sobering up, which ultimately posed the dilemma: either a declaration of war or the loss of national self-respect. The development of public opinion from an unqualified will for peace to the realisation that war was inevitable took place within the existing democratic framework, which was never seriously called into question; there was no polarisation into doves and hawks, democrats, communists and fascists, but rather a quite normal difference of opinion as, for instance, in the question of the approach to be taken towards Italy after its Abyssinian adventure or towards the opposing camps in the Spanish Civil War. The process by which the democratic will is formed set narrow boundaries to the range of political action. Up to the Munich Conference, the great majority of the population and the leading newspapers supported Chamberlain's policy of appeasement.[9] For the opinion-forming elite and the great majority of the population 'appeasement' signified not a cowardly accommodation of the German dictator, but rather the satisfaction of all apparently justified popular political demands by negotiation; in other words, the peaceable revision of the Versailles Treaty, which in retrospect was held responsible for Germany's having gone off course. In 1938 hardly a serious commentator could be found who advocated the rigorous maintenance of the Versailles order. Hitler's polemic against the treaty had proved to be his most successful propaganda hit both at home and abroad. As long as the policy of 'Back into the Reich' amounted to the creation of a German nation-state, as Hitler never wearied of emphasising, Great Britain had no fundamental objections to it. Misgivings were stirred up, however, by the German dictator's methods, which became apparent especially in the final phase of the Sudeten Crisis and fostered the insight that now an accelerated re-armament was on. Even the economic dominance of the Reich in southeastern Europe,[10] the Reichsmark bloc as the counterpart to the Sterling block, was intelligible and accepted. So why should Hitler plot a war when he could have everything that the Reich could demand, as understood by a dominant European Great Power, by peaceful means: if not the return of the German colonies, then at least an 'informal empire' in eastern Europe. This probably corresponded to Chamberlain's view and his pronounced flair for economics. His then Parliamentary Private Secretary, the later Prime Minister and Foreign Secretary Alec Douglas-Home, wrote in his memoirs: 'Germany was strong and sitting pretty. The whole of the Danube basin was economically within her sphere of influence. ... All in all, Hitler's ambitions could have been gained without war, and Germany would have been the strongest power in Europe, with her word carrying authority far and wide outside her borders.'[11] The accent lies of course on 'informal empire', such as the British had first set up in Africa, whereas Hitler had a very different and more archaic idea of empire, and also of the admired

British Empire itself, which in his opinion was ruled by a 'core of the white race'. Hitler lacked any realistic idea of the ruling practices of the British Empire in other parts of the world; he could only cite a litany of statistics and square kilometres and population numbers about its larger colonies and compare them with those of the German Reich.[12] The political autodidact could not conceive of a form of rule other than direct domination.

Yet the British range of perception was also limited. The German dictator's common-sensical political acumen and opportunistic rationality blocked the British decision-making elite's view of the ideological determinants of Nazi foreign policy. After the war A. J. P. Taylor still described the foreign policy successes of the Third Reich as the continuation of Weimar revisionism by other means.[13] For the ordinary man, Hitler was the bully in the European schoolyard, who respected only physical force. Who better to sort out such an enfant terrible than the old schoolmaster Chamberlain? Munich had already been perceived as a personal contest between two men and their principles; and who the victor was remained open. Hitler had by no means succeeded in achieving his demands all along the line. After all, the British Prime Minister could now position himself in the public eye as the bringer of peace. To all appearances, he had successfully asserted the principle that territorial changes in Europe could not take place without the consent of the Great Powers. Revision of the Versailles Treaty was legitimate as long as it was not unilateral and was done in consensus with the Great Powers.

With Hitler's invasion of Prague in mid March this appearance evaporated. Chamberlain took the unilateral action of his adversary as a personal affront; and so too did the British public, with its predilection for the personalising of grand politics. Their Prime Minister, with his habitual top hat, stand-up collar, umbrella and understated manner,[14] the very embodiment of the British nature, had been made to look a fool before the whole world by an underhand continental dictator, a social nobody. Only now did it become clear to everyone that Hitler would not content himself with reclaiming German territory.[15] He had shown himself to be a classic imperialist, a threat to all neighbouring countries. In Chamberlain's words: 'Is this the end of an old adventure or is it the beginning of a new? Is this the last attack upon a small State, or is it to be followed by others? Is this, in fact, a step in the direction of an attempt to dominate the world by force?'[16] This was a new language, and these were rhetorical questions to which everyone in Britain thought they knew the answers. With Hitler's march into Prague, Great Britain once more took on the role it had played in the face of potential continental hegemony since the days of Philip II. Was the man on the street as aware of this as were the leading articles in the *Times* and the *News Chronicle*?

How is the attitude of the population to the events of the last months of peace to be assessed? Much as it was influenced by public, that is, published opinion (by the press, incidentally, more than the BBC), the vox populi cannot be equated with the latter; above all, the sources of popular opinion cannot be so easily ascertained as those of printed matter, such as, for instance, the Parliamentary speeches published in Hansard. For the years 1938 and 1939 only one genre of sources is available to the historian: opinion polls, which were first introduced around this time – the Gallup Polls, which had already been conducted in the USA, and those of Mass Observation, a commercial and politically independent organisation founded in 1937 by two British pollsters, who made it their task to test the mood of the lower classes, especially the 'upper working' and the 'lower middle classes'. On the advisory board of Mass Observation were well-known contemporary figures such as Julian Huxley, J. B. Priestley and H. G. Wells, who were concerned about the tenacity of ordinary people in political crises. They had in mind people who possessed no passport, had never been abroad, had no geographical picture and thought of foreign politics as 'merely crazy'. 'I don't study politics' was a common response, or 'Proper Englishmen should not bother their heads about foreigners.'[17] This apolitical manner of seeing things was very disquieting for many intellectuals, who could see the progress of fascism everywhere in Europe. Could the people be relied upon when the bomber squadrons of the Luftwaffe beleaguered the island? In early 1939 the pollsters came to the conclusion 'that the spirit of the masses of our countrymen at the moment is largely defeatist and depressed'.[18] This was a summons to the government not only to do everything it could to secure peace, but also to realise that it had a good deal of convincing to do in the event of war. Since Munich, people had pinned all their hopes on the government, especially Chamberlain and his efforts to preserve the peace. According to Gallup Polls, the Prime Minister always had the majority of the population on his side; Churchill, who had a reputation as an aggressive politician, could get nowhere against him. In February 1939, 29 per cent of those polled still believed that Chamberlain would secure a lasting peace, while 46 per cent were certain that he would at least keep the country out of war.[19] But in June a majority of 76 per cent already felt that Britain was obliged not to leave Poland in the lurch if war should come over Danzig. Although the international situation in early 1939 (as far as he understood it) worried the man on the street, he was nevertheless not prepared to buy peace with further concessions. In March, after Hitler's invasion of Prague, the majority of the population (78 per cent) did not want to hear anything more about the return of the German colonies; and a still greater portion (84 per cent) declared themselves in favour of a grand alliance with France and Russia.

One may assume that the population came increasingly to adopt the position of public opinion, especially as the Labour Party now acted in concert with the government in regard to foreign policy. Peace could no longer be secured by the satisfaction of justified demands or an appeal to the common sense of the opponent, but now only through a policy of deterrence and the formation of a 'Peace Front', to which the Soviet Union and the United States should also belong if possible. But this policy was rather like a poker game, for without the previously mentioned flanking powers London no longer held any trumps in its hand. On 17 March Chamberlain sent his first serious warning to the German dictator, which seemed to signal the end of the previous policy of appeasement. The British love of peace should not, he said, be mistaken for a sign of decadence; it sprang rather from the insight into the senselessness and cruelty of war. But one should be chary of believing that the nation had so abandoned its will to self-assertion that it would not defy a challenge with all its might.[20] The Prime Minister still preferred not to enter into unspecific obligations, 'operating under conditions which cannot now be foreseen'. But only fourteen days later the government ventured precisely such an undertaking. Alarmed by a secret report from Ian Colvin, the young Berlin correspondent of the *News Chronicle*, according to which Hitler now had his sights set on Poland, on 31 March Chamberlain made an ominous promise: If any action should threaten the independence of Poland and the country should see itself compelled to offer resistance, Great Britain and France would rush to the aid of the Poles. The Parliamentary transcript shows that at this point there was vociferous approval on both sides of the Upper House.[21] D. C. Watt, however, comments on this dramatic step as follows: 'The decision, war or peace, had been voluntarily surrendered by Chamberlain and his Cabinet into the nervous hands of Colonel Beck and his junta comrades-in-arms. It was unprecedented.'[22] It was in fact the greatest bluff in the recent history of Great Britain, for it was plain that the island nation was not in the position to offer Poland effective military support on its own. Sir Alexander Cadogan, the highest Foreign Office official, observed retrospectively in the autumn of 1940: 'We lived on bluff in Europe for the last ten years of the peace, and we have been living on a larger degree of bluff in other parts of the world, e.g., in the far East, for nearly half a century.'[23] The threat of war was a strategy of deterrence whose credibility actually depended on the French army, although the British government had not even consulted Paris before issuing its statement. Only if this army, which was positioned entirely for defence, were prepared to march would the German Reich again be faced by the threat of war on two fronts. A. J. P. Taylor goes so far as to maintain that the primary purpose of the British guarantee was to prevent Poland from slipping into the enemy camp. What is certain is that the British government had become involved in a dangerous game in which they were playing poker with their allies' cards. Of course the cynicism imputed to the government should not be exaggerated. The guarantee was, after all, a desperate attempt to put a stop to Hitler's uninhibited aggression. There is much to be said for the assumption that the Cabinet's decision to draw a clear line was ultimately aimed not only at deterring Hitler, but also at avoiding an ignominious retreat. After the war Cadogan described the situation in which Chamberlain found himself at the time of the crisis in just this way. Naturally the guarantee could not have provided Poland any protection in the event of an immediate German attack, 'but it set up a signpost for himself. He was committed, and in the event of a German attack on Poland, he would be spared the agonizing doubts and indecisions'.[24] The Prime Minister once more enjoyed the status he had regained as the international referee who had shown Hitler the yellow card. The change of mood in public opinion had already been heralded by the response to the *Kristallnacht* in November 1938, when even many national-socialist sympathisers in Britain turned away from Nazi Germany.[25] Now in early 1939 the great majority of the British people were well aware that there was no longer any way in which to get on peacefully with Hitler's Germany. Benny Morris' analysis of the weekly press at the time after Prague and during the Polish Crisis leads him to the conclusion that the nation had now begun to prepare itself for a new war against Germany: 'What had been unthinkable to the great majority of the nation in September 1938 was now accepted, with varying degrees of resignation and despair.'[26] Only now did the word *appeasement* take on its unmistakably pejorative meaning, for up to this point the diplomatic accommodation of upcoming powers was one of the natural instruments of British foreign policy. Chamberlain was so much identified with this policy that the press did not quite accept his new role as 'High Noon sheriff'. As the success of the new strategy of containment, denounced immediately by Nazi propaganda as a policy of encirclement, crucially depended on the steadfastness of the Prime Minister, the British press, with a rare unanimity, saw its chief task in the last months of peace as to sniff out and pillory any signs of a new willingness to concede.[27] Above all the government was pressed into an active policy of alliances so as to lend the deterrence more weight. It may therefore be said that the end of the appeasement policy manifested itself in a conciliation of public opinion.

Time and again not only Chamberlain's opponents but also his supporters presumed that he would retract the guarantee at the last minute. Harold Nicolson reports on 11 May 1939 that an acquaintance overheard the following dialogue between two Tory MPs: 'I suppose we shall get out of this beastly guarantee business?' – 'Of course, thank God, we have Neville!'[28] The doubts about Chamberlain's steadfastness, however, were unfounded. The British Cabinet did not get cold feet in reaction to the Hitler-Stalin Pact; on the contrary, on 24 August Parliament passed in summary proceedings the Emergency Powers Act, a kind of enabling act for wartime, and the following day ratified the mutual assistance pact with Poland.[29] At this point one may again ask whether the guarantee for Poland was ever meant seriously. To this there are two answers: first, probably not on the part of the government; at any rate, only in the sense of a deterrent, which represented a questionable assessment of the real balance of power; and second, very likely on the part of public and popular opinion as far as this was reflected by Parliament, press and opinion polls. Much may be said against A. J. P. Taylor's account, but not that it suffered from a deficient sense of British popular feeling. 'Not that the general public was bubbling over with enthusiasm for Poland, or knew anything about her', he explained in a lecture at the University of Surrey in 1979, 'but in a very grumpy way they would say: "Well, we have given our word, we must stick to it."'[30] The press gave the government complete rear cover, but in the expectation that it would now keep its word. The Prime Minister did not resign, as Hitler had prophesied, and the government and public opinion showed great composure in the face of a war that was now virtually unavoidable. A mood spread in the final days of August that might be described as a feeling of truce amongst all parties in the land. The armed forces were put on alert. In Westminster the doors were caulked against poison gas attack, the windows protected with sandbags: the worst had to be reckoned with. Nicolson described these preparations for the inevitable and summed up the mood of his Parliamentary colleagues thus: 'I think also, that they are proud of themselves for having behaved so well, so calmly, so unitedly today.' And a day later: 'The absolute despair of a week ago seems to have changed into determination, the gloom of anticipation melting into the gaiety of courage.'[31] Not the exaltation of August 1914, but nonetheless the corporative assurance that the nation would spare no sacrifice where its moral self-respect was at stake. Yet it was, and this is important, primarily a matter of self-reassurance, that a test of courage had been passed, and not of the security of Poland.

So when Hitler attacked Poland on 1 September 1939, 3.5 million city-dwellers took themselves and their children off to the countryside. In the expectation of a gigantic German bomber fleet, air-raid protection measures were taken, above all the recruitment of a host of air-raid wardens.[32] All the greater was the incomprehension, even the public indignation, at the government's hesitation to invoke the mutual defence pact and declare war against Hitler. If the mood of the population were the decisive factor, wrote the *Daily Telegraph*, 'the first shot across the Polish frontier would have been the signal for British intervention.'[33] When on 2 September Chamberlain still made do with expostulations and warnings instead of issuing the expected ultimatum, the outrage in Parliament, including that of the ruling party, could no longer be contained. The Cabinet itself tested the water of rebellion and refused to leave the Chancellor of the Exchequer's Parliamentary office until a specific time had been agreed upon for issuing the ultimatum. Desperately, but in vain, the Prime Minister endeavoured to synchronise the decisive step with Paris. The scheming manoeuvres of the French foreign minister, Georges Bonnet, who still hoped for a peace conference initiated by Italy, put the British government in a highly precarious position. The Prime Minister felt compelled to give Paris notice of the fall of the government should the long-awaited ultimatum not follow on the next day, 3 September. Up to the end of the hectic discussions with Paris, Rome and the Swedish mediator Birger Dahlerus, the government refused to be argued out of the condition that negotiations were possible only once German troops had pulled out of Poland.

The dramatic events between 1 and 3 September, when the ultimatum ran out at 11:00 PM, have been researched and described down to the last minute.[34] Here it need only be observed that the collective feeling of the British people at this point was almost eruptive. However, this emotional upsurge remained at first without consequence. On 1 September only a single off-course aeroplane had showed itself in the skies above London, not the German bomber fleet which would, it had been predicted, claim the lives of one hundred thousand Londoners in a few days. Harold Macmillan later recalled: 'We thought of air warfare in 1938 rather as people think of nuclear warfare today.'[35] Nor did Royal Air Force planes set off in the direction of the Ruhr. It was more than a month before the first three British divisions crossed the Channel. Only Churchill, again appointed First Lord of the Admiralty, carried on a serious war at sea. The description 'phoney war' for the period from September to March was originally an American expression; in England it was the 'bore war' or the 'funny war'; for the Prime Minister it was 'this strangest of wars' or 'the twilight war'.[36] But there was no doubt that the war would be a hard test for the government. For all its resolve not to back down, the military activity proved to be demoralising: Poland was left to fend for itself; the French army entrenched itself behind the Maginot Line; and Chamberlain held back his bomber fleet for fear of retaliation and in the hope of a change of government in Germany.

The single point that could be counted to the government's credit during the 'phoney war' was that it had refused all Hitler's overtures since the Polish campaign. To the American ambassador it was disclosed on 26 September that: 'The fate of Poland will depend on the ultimate outcome of the war, i.e., on our ability to defeat Germany, and not on our ability to relieve pressure on Poland at the outset.'[37] This was the internal rationalisation for having been practically incapable of coming to Poland's aid. Officially, the government let it be known that it was prepared for a war that would last at least three years,[38] whereas Chamberlain prophesied to the American ambassador Joseph Kennedy (father of the later president) that the war would end early in the coming year.[39] The majority of the British population (66 per cent) reckoned with a war lasting six months to two years. After the Wehrmacht's defeat of Poland within a few weeks, all attempts at reaching a settlement on the part of the German government were called 'peace offensives' and looked upon as something to be warded off by diplomacy.[40] In other words, all that Great Britain had to oppose Hitler in the first months of the war was the resolve not to grovel.

Amongst the population a patriotic, if naïve, assurance of victory emerged: 87 per cent were convinced that they would beat the Germans; only 12 per cent thought there would be a stalemate.[41] The British Establishment by no means shared this confidence. From Harold Nicolson's diaries we know that they had to fight against a widespread feeling that the war could not be won: 'Yet the fact that this war costs us six million pounds a day and that I am not really certain that we shall win it, fills me with acute sadness at times. We all keep up a brave face and refuse to admit that defeat is possible.'[42] More to be feared than military defeat was moral capitulation. What prevented this was self-respect, pride, the only thing that remained, as Nicolson thought.[43] Hitler may have imagined that if he guaranteed the existence of the Empire, this would remove all reasons for the government to continue the war. For the decision-making elites, however, to receive the Empire as, so to speak, a fiefdom from the hands of a man like Hitler would have meant gambling away their moral role as leaders. And that was exactly the point at issue: moral leadership, a convincing representation of what distinguished the nation and held it together. It was soon clear to all MPs that Chamberlain was not equal to this task. His deadly boring weekly reports were suited rather to spreading defeatism and disconsolateness; as Nicolson noted in his diary: 'The Prime Minister has no gift to inspire anybody, and he might have been the Secretary of a firm of undertakers reading the minutes of the last meeting.'[44] How could it be conveyed to an entire people that the war was a matter of life and death when they were exposed to no enemy attack and did not yet need to save their own skins? Had London already been bombed daily by the Luftwaffe from 3 September 1939 onwards and not only in September of the following year, the question would not, of course, have arisen. In the First World War profane war goals may still have been decisive, such as the territorial integrity of the Empire or the balance of power in Europe; this was not so in the new conflict. No one understood better than Churchill how to invoke the seriousness of the hour and its historical significance for the nation in elevated and solemn words. It was not a question of Danzig or even Poland, he said to the Lower House on 3 September, thus adroitly rationalising Britain's inability to help its ally: 'This is no war for domination or imperial aggrandisement or material gain; no war to shut any country out of its sunlight or means of progress. It is a war, viewed in its inherent quality, to establish, on impregnable rocks, the rights of the individual, and it is a war to establish and revive the stature of man.'[45] With this allusion to Germany's legitimate aspirations to development, Churchill tied in with the readiness of the British government to come, even now, to a peaceful general settlement with a newly constituted Reich government, as Chamberlain had unremittingly, but in vain, attempted in the past years. Yet there could be no peaceful co-existence in Europe with a country that attacked its neighbours by force of arms. That was also the tenor of Chamberlain's speech to the House of

Commons on 12 October, the official response to Hitler's speech in the Reichstag on 6 October, in which he showed no willingness to an accommodation whatsoever and demanded a posture of war. The speech to the House of Commons was an utter indictment of 'Herr Hitler', 'the German Chancellor' and 'the German Government'; he alone stood in the way of a 'a real and settled peace, not an uneasy truce'.[46] The speech was so formulated that it should be plain to everyone in Germany that the removal of Hitler was the simplest path to the re-establishment of peace.

Today one must ask why the British government did not go one step further and in no uncertain terms make Hitler's resignation an absolute condition of peace negotiations. Chamberlain abominated the German dictator and could no longer imagine concluding a peace with him. 'The difficulty is with Hitler himself', he wrote on 10 September to his sister Ida. 'Until he disappears and his system collapses there can be no peace'.[47] That this obvious war goal had been internally discussed emerges from an entry in the diary of Alexander Cadogan: 'The line according to me is to say (and the P.M. hesitates to say this) that we won't make peace with Hitler. Get rid of Hitler: that is my war aim – not peace aim'.[48] In the first days of September the press had not the least doubt as to who had instigated the war. Gannon sums up the reaction of the *Times* as follows: 'That it was one man's war – Hitler's war – alone was now clear beyond doubting'.[49] For the *Manchester Guardian* the goal of the war was already plain: 'the overthrow of this dictator and his system of government'.[50] The vox populi, too, saw in Hitler the real warmonger and villain. Why did the British government shrink from the consequences of its own policy? There were essentially three reasons that explain why the Cabinet had agreed not to commit itself to concrete war goals, and they remained in effect throughout the duration of the war.[51] The French government wanted more than merely the removal of Hitler, namely a guarantee of security. On the British side there were evidently still leading figures who believed that Hitler would ultimately be prepared to negotiate. Moreover, Foreign Secretary Halifax argued in Cabinet that this demand would be politically unwise and that 'a statement of that kind would have the effect of uniting the German people behind Herr Hitler'.[52] One may see here the tacit assumption on the part of the British government that the declaration of war had already effected a certain alienation between the German people and their leadership.

At this point it is perhaps as well to look back at British propaganda addressed to the German people, since (as has been said) the British Prime Minister had deliberately not directed his declaration of war against them. Stephanie Seul has recently shown that British foreign propaganda since Munich and the unstaged, enthusiastic reception given Chamberlain as a peacemaker by the population of the city was directed to winning over the German people for a lasting peace. The Prime Minister could not free himself from the premises of democratic politics according to which the German population, like the British, must somehow have been in a position to exert pressure on their government. Very few British politicians and high officials had any notion of what it meant to live under a totalitarian regime that controlled all aspects of life. Since the beginning of 1939 the Foreign Office had pleaded unswervingly for the government to concentrate its efforts on the most effective means of deterrence: the German population's fear of war and its consequences.[53] This propaganda line was put into practice, but constantly thwarted by the compromise-minded Prime Minister who, following the advice of his ambassador in Berlin, believed that the German dictator should not be provoked. Secret contacts with German resistance circles were therefore out of the question. After the outbreak of the war such considerateness towards Hitler no longer applied. But now Downing Street and the Foreign Office diverged in the question of whether Great Britain could look to a revolt of the German people against Hitler's war policy. Undoubtedly the Prime Minister's longing for peace clouded his sense of reality. Seul comes to the conclusion that, notwithstanding previous experience, 'Chamberlain and a great part of the British government elite' continued to believe up to early 1940 'that the Nazi regime must sooner or later collapse under the influence of the allied blockade and the propaganda addressed to the German civilian population'.[54] All in all one cannot avoid the impression that the British government, confronted by one of the greatest rogues of the twentieth century, who would balk at nothing to achieve his ends, continued to tread the conventional path. Only extraordinary incidents, such as Georg Elser's attempt to assassinate Hitler on 9 November 1939 (he was at first accused of working for the British Secret Service), could now still change the course of history. Elser's declared purpose was to prevent war.[55] Perhaps his would not have been a solitary act had London emphasised in a large-scale propaganda campaign that the removal of the German dictator was the crucial condition for peace. Perhaps certain circles of the Wehrmacht, who were unhappy with the dictator's war policy, would then have pulled themselves together and attempted a coup. D. C. Watt's more than 700-page-long work on the origins of the Second World War ends with the sentence: 'The only people who could have stopped him [i.e. Hitler] permanently were those least conditioned to do so, his Generals and their soldiers, if they had been ready to obey, by a *coup d'état,* or an assassin capable of penetrating the Reich Chancellery from which, in the last days of peace, Hitler never emerged. History knows this did not happen.'[56]

The barometer of opinion constructed by Mass Observation showed that the attitude of the great majority of the British population towards the war was at first rather apathetic. There can be no question of war enthusiasm amongst the general population, much less amongst the recruits. Nevertheless, in September a large majority (77 per cent) rejected the proposal that the government should enter into peace negotiations with Hitler.[57] A narrow majority of those questioned (52 per cent) were even in favour of a stronger use of the Royal Air Force, even if this meant retaliation by the enemy. Government rationing of certain foodstuffs was astonishingly popular. To fight for 'King and Country' was almost never mentioned as grounds for the war; rather simply 'the defence of freedom'.[58] The soldiers drafted into military service, Mass Observation finds, 'do not have a great deal of enthusiasm for war as such and not a great deal of enthusiasm for this war in particular'. There is hardly any hatred felt towards the German people, as was the case in the First World War, but 'Hitler, of course, is generally referred to as a bastard'.[59] None of those who should have known the reasons had made it very clear to those questioned what they were supposed to be risking their necks for. The result was widespread cynicism: 'Patriotism, the Flag and the Empire are a lot of tripe – only that they don't say tripe.' Just as many were of the opinion that they were going to war not for democracy but for British capital. They had little good to say of Chamberlain; Churchill was by far the most popular minister. But, like Chamberlain, most British subjects also hoped that they would be spared a bloody war in the end. Like him, they cleaved to the illusion that, once the British lion had begun to growl, the Germans would wake up and soon get rid of the Führer who had brought disaster upon them. In spite of all the loyalty shown to the Prime Minister in war time, those questioned towards the end of 1939 were not certain whether Chamberlain was the right man for the job. The comments that Mass Observation registered most frequently were: 'A good man, a gentleman, trying his best, not the best man for the job, a splendid chap, he tried for peace, too weak, too ill.'[60] As the war in the west became serious, Churchill was the man of the hour who put an end to all fecklessness, all illusions and all cynicism. Under him the people, the government and public opinion were fused into a unity.

Let me sum up my remarks. If the historian, as he usually does, simply stares at the policy of the British government, at the failed peace strategy,[61] the hectic succession of collective security, appeasement, containment and finally deterrence, then he will not be able to do justice to the social and psychological and, if one likes, democratic causes of Great Britain's entry into the war on 3 September 1939. He will then miss the dimension of the Second World War that was constitutive for the collective memory of the British nation. From the start, the Second World War was 'The People's War', as Angus Calder in his social history of the war has called it,[62] and not only after Churchill took over the government and included the Labour Party. The traumatic genesis of the British declaration of war, which was at first followed by no real war, was an indispensable condition for Churchill's popularity, and Churchill then turned the war into a saga that would be capable of creating a lasting consensus. Like Hitler before him, Churchill gained political capital from humiliation suffered, with, of course, the great difference that he mobilised the noble rather than the base instincts of the nation. He did not have to deal with a people whose very existence had been made insecure since the defeat of 1918. At the end of this epochal struggle, Great Britain had lost its standing as a world power, its empire, its financial resources – everything, except this: its moral integrity, or, to put it in a very old-fashioned way, its honour, which was so much more important to the average citizen than anything else that statesmen and historians might regard as war goals. Great Britain was the only one of the victors of the Second World War to enter the war for the sake of international law, without having been attacked by Hitler. The position that the country assumed in world politics after 1945 rested, as D. C. Watt has rightly pointed out, less on its weight as a political power than on the moral authority that it had acquired at the beginning of September 1939, in the insight that Poland had become a test case 'as to whether the "law of the jungle" or the "law of nations" was to rule Europe'.[63] When it was said in a retrospective in the *Times* in 1982, on the occasion of the two hundredth anniversary of the Foreign Office, that 'influence must now do the work of power',[64] precisely this moral authority was meant, at least within the circle of Britain's allies, for Britain had once proved its loyalty in a spectacular and convincing manner. It is not the purpose of the British Foreign Office to compete with the Vatican. During the war its leadership had certain misgivings about an impulse originating amongst the common people that lacked any consciousness of power and responsibility, because improvement of living conditions seemed more important than armaments. For the higher officials, September 1939 was a question not only of proving Britain's loyalty to its allies, but also its capacity for alliances whose prerequisite is the strength that the nation lacked during the 'phoney war'. 'We have no choice, we must, on the one hand, either have some powerful ally or allies, or cease to be a World Power, and, on the other, we cannot expect to have powerful allies unless we are powerful ourselves.'[65] In other words, moral principles are not just a question of good will; more was needed to satisfy Britain's principles than the mere declaration of war on 3 September 1939.

Notes

1. Cf. Paul Kennedy, 'Appeasement', in Gordon Martel (ed.), *The Origins of the Second World War Reconsidered* (London, 1986), 140–161. On the debate about Taylor, including his own position, see Esmonde M. Robertson (ed.), *The Origins of the Second Word War* (London, 1971).
2. Martin Broszat, 'Plädoyer für eine Historisierung des Nationalsozialismus', *Merkur* (1985), 5, 373–385. See also the Festschrift dedicated to Broszat: Uwe Backes, Eckhard Jesse and Rainer Zitelmann (eds.), *Die Schatten der Vergangenheit. Impulse zur Historisierung der Vergangenheit* (Frankfurt/Berlin, 1990).

3. Winston S. Churchill, *The Second World War*, vol. 1: *The Gathering Storm* (London, 1948), viii (preface).

4. Donald Cameron Watt, *How War Came. The Immediate Origins of the Second World War, 1938–1939* (London, 1989), 623.

5. *House of Commons Debates* (Hansard), vol. 351, cols. 291–292 (3 September 1939).

6. Cabinet protocol from 24 September 1938, CAB 23/95, quoted in Uri Bialer, *The Shadow of the Bomber. The Fear of Air Attack and British Politics 1932–1939* (London, The Royal Historical Society, 1980), 157.

7. Cf. Jörg Friedrich's controversial but very evocative account of the bombing war, which fixes its sights above all on the RAF: *Der Brand. Deutschland im Bombenkrieg 1940–1945* (Munich, 2002).

8. Cf. A. J. P. Taylor, *English History 1914–1945* (Oxford, 1965), still the best history of the period between the wars.

9. According to the Gallup Polls, Chamberlain always had the majority of the population on his side after Munich (1938): *The Gallup International Public Opinion Polls: Great Britain 1937–1945*, vol.1 (New York, 1976), 7–12. See also Franklin R. Gannon, *The British Press and Germany 1936–1939* (Oxford, 1971), 136–229; and Benny Morris, *The Roots of Appeasement. The British Weekly Press and Nazi Germany during the 1930ies* (London, 1991).

10. Cf. Alan S. Milward, 'The Reichsmark Bloc and the International Economy', in Gerhard Hirschfeld and Lothar Kettenacker (eds.), *Der 'Führerstaat': Mythos und Realität. Studien zur Struktur und Politik des Dritten Reiches* (Stuttgart, 1981), 377–413. The author argues, however, that the Reichsmark bloc was not a system of exploitation and that the countries of southern Europe profited from it more than did the German Reich.

11. Lord Home, *How the Wind Blows* (London, n.d.), 65.

12. Illuminating in this connection is Hitler's secret speech at the Ordensburg Sonthofen on 23 November 1937 with its many statistics intended to prove 'that parts of this gigantic structure were held together by an unnaturally small core of members of the white race'; Henry Picker, *Hitlers Tischgespräche im Führerhauptquartier* (Wiesbaden, 1983), 481–490.

13. A. J. P. Taylor, *The Origins of the Second Word War* (London, 1961). See also fn. 1.

14. See Lord Home's characterisation, *How the Wind Blows*, 60.

15. On the basis of secret reports the Foreign Office had already reckoned with this possibility, that is, with Hitler's intention 'to subject Eastern and South-Eastern Europe to Germany's political and economical hegemony, to vassaldom, if not worse'; memorandum of 19 January 1939, TNA, CAB 27/627, quoted in David Dilks (ed.), *The Diaries of Sir Alexander Cadogan 1938–1945* (London, 1971), 131.

16. Speech in Birmingham on 17 March 1939, quoted in Maurice Cowling, *The Impact of Hilter. British Politics and British Policy 1933–1940* (Chicago/London [Phoenix Edition], 1977), 295.

17. Imperial War Museum: *Mass Observation*, Microfilm Archive, File Report Series for 1939, A 16.

18. Ibid.

19. *Gallup Polls*, 13. All further poll results from the following pages.

20. See fn. 16.

21. *House of Commons Debates* (Hansard), 31 March 1939, vol. 345, cols. 2421–2422.

22. Watt, *How War Came*, 186; equally critical are Anita Prazmowska, *Britain, Poland and the Eastern Front 1939* (Cambridge, 1987), 57–79; and Simon Newman, *March 1939: The British Guarantee to Poland* (Oxford, 1976).

23. Comment on a memorandum by Orme Sargent of 28 October 1940, TNA, FO 371/25208/W11399.
24. Quoted in Dilks (ed.), *Cadogan Diaries*, 167.
25. Richard Griffith, *Fellow Travellers of the Right. British Enthusiasts for Nazi Germany 1933–1939* (Oxford, 1983), 331–343.
26. Morris, *Roots of Appeasement*, 166.
27. Cf. Gannon, *The British Press and Germany*, 262–287.
28. Nigel Nicolson (ed.), *Harold Nicolson. Diaries and Letters 1930–1939*, vol. 1 (London, 1970), 394.
29. Text in Prazmowska, *Britain, Poland and the Eastern Front*, appendix 4.
30. A. J. P. Taylor, 'The British View', in Roy Douglas (ed.), *1939. A Retrospective Forty Years After* (London, 1983), 52. Cf. fn. 19.
31. Nicolson, *Diaries and Letters*, vol. 1, 407, 409.
32. Described in the greatest detail by Angus Calder, *The People's War* (paperback edition, London, 1971), 40–88.
33. *Daily Telegraph*, 4 September 1939, quoted in Gannon, *The British Press and Germany*, 286.
34. Recently and in the greatest detail by Watt, *How War Came*, 568–604.
35. Harold Macmillan, *Winds of Change* (London, 1966), 522.
36. Cf. Calder, *The People's War*, 65; also Harold Macmillan, *The Blast of War: 1939–1945* (London, 1967), 4.
37. TNA, FO 371/22946/C15080.
38. *The Times*, 9 November 1939.
39. *Foreign Relations of the United States* 1939/1 (Washington, 1956), 527.
40. Cf. Lothar Kettenacker, *Krieg zur Friedenssicherung. Die Deutschlandplanung der britischen Regierung während des Zweiten Weltkrieges* (Göttingen, 1989), 40–67.
41. *Gallup Polls*, 23.
42. Nicolson, *Diaries and Letters 1939–1945*, vol. 2, 42 (25 November 1939).
43. Ibid., 26 (5 September 1939).
44. Ibid., 31 (20 September 1939).
45. *House of Commons Debates* (Hansard), vol. 351, cols. 295.
46. Ibid., vol. 352, col. 565. See also Kettenacker, *Krieg zur Friedenssicherung*, 40–43.
47. Quoted in Keith Feiling, *The Life of Neville Chamberlain* (London, 1946), 417f.
48. Dilks (ed.), *Cadogan Diaries*, 221 (7 October 1939)
49. Gannon, *The British Press and Germany*, 285.
50. *The Manchester Guardian*, 9 February 1939.
51. Resolution of the War Cabinet on 10 September 1939, TNA, WM 42 (39) 8, CAB 65/1. It was unanimously agreed that a sharp distinction should be drawn between the terms *Germany* and *the German people* on the one hand and *the German government* on the other, a distinction that was given expression in Chamberlain's speech on 12 October 1939.
52. Cabinet protocol of 10 July 1939, TNA, WM 40 (39) 7, CAB 65/1.
53. Cf. Stephanie Seul, *Appeasement und Propaganda. Chamberlains Außenpolitik zwischen NS-Regierung und deutschem Volk*, vol. 1, dissertation, Florence, European University Institute Department of History (2005), 333–352.
54. Ibid., vol. 2, 1328.
55. It is only since the research by Anton Hoch that Georg Elser has been rehabilitated after the war: 'Das Attentat auf Hitler im Münchner Bürgerbräukeller 1939', *Vierteljahrshefte für Zeitgeschichte* 17, 4 (1969), 383–413. See also Anton Hoch and Lothar

Gruchmann, *Georg Elser: Der Attentäter aus dem Volk* (Frankfurt, 1980). There is now also a film about Elser's attempt on Hitler's life.

56. Watt, *How War Came*, 624.
57. *Gallup Polls*, 22–27, and the following poll results.
58. *Mass Observation*, Wartime Directive No. 4 (December 1939).
59. Angus Calder and Dorothy Sheridan (eds.), *Speak for Yourself. A Mass Observation Anthology 1937–1949* (London, 1984), 114.
60. *Mass Observation*, Wartime Directive No. 4 (December 1939).
61. Cf. Kettenacker, 'Die Diplomatie der Ohnmacht. Die gescheiterte Friedensstrategie der britischen Regierung vor Ausbruch des Zweiten Weltkrieges', in Wolfgang Benz and Hermann Graml (eds.), *Sommer 1939. Die Großmächte und der Europäische Krieg* (Stuttgart, 1979), 223–279.
62. Calder, *The People's War*. On the sociological effects, see Sonya O. Rose, *Which People's War? National Identity and Citizenship in Wartime Britain 1939–1945* (Oxford, 2003).
63. Watt, *How War Came*, 622.
64. Ibid.; '200 Cheers for the F.O.', *The Times*, 3 May 1982.
65. 'The Four-Power Plan', TNA, FO 371/31525/U472; see also Kettenacker, *Krieg zur Friedenssicherung*, 130–146.

13

Disillusionment, Pragmatism, Indifference

German Society after the 'Catastrophe'

Clemens Vollnhals

> Our slave chains rust slowly. Hitler and all his smaller and bigger *Führers*
> drive each and every one of us to work with downright deadly haste,
> with impetuous wantonness. They all apparently know that their
> unnatural reign of lies, violence and terror will not last for ever.
>
> But the war they have provoked, this war is the greatest accelerator of
> their downfall. Every one of Hitler's defeats, every smashing up of a city,
> resembles a gigantic amputation performed on our Reich and the body of
> the people, an amputation with much loss of blood – in our eyes of course a
> gigantic surgical healing. The worst is only that it shatters so many lives.[1]
>
> —Marianna Bronner, teacher evacuated from Munich, 1 March 1945

In the contemporary consciousness of the German people the Battle of Stalingrad in 1942–43 became the symbol of the turn in the war which had in fact already begun with the failed advance on Moscow. It was not the first crushing defeat of the eastern army, but it was widely recognised to be a senseless sacrifice of an entire army group and led to the first doubts about the military genius of the Führer, a vabanque player whose previous successes had silenced all sceptics. Enormous losses (on the eastern front alone the Wehrmacht suffered a third of its total losses between June and November 1944) undermined the fighting spirit: by autumn 1944, the Wehrmacht censor's office on the eastern front estimated that 'absolute assurance of final victory' was expressed in only 2 per cent of forces' letters.[2] The Western Allies' successful landings in Italy and France reinforced the conviction that, given the enemy's manifold superiority, the war could no longer be won.

The same was increasingly true of the German civilian population, which had been suffering under massive air raids since 1943. The first city to be destroyed was Hamburg in July 1943, the victim of a terrible fire storm which took the lives of nearly forty-five thousand people; but in mid 1944 the worst was yet to come for German civilians. Seventy per cent of the bombs that fell on Germany were dropped after this date. The air war, which was primarily concentrated on the western half of the Reich and its capital, became the most drastic and radical civilian experience of the war. Unlike in the First World War, when the poorer classes had gone hungry and starved towards the end but were not directly affected by the warfare, the 'total war' proclaimed by Goebbels before tumultuous 'national comrades' (*Volksgenossen*) in February 1943 at the Berlin Sportpalast, in response to the defeat at Stalingrad, now became a daily experience. It affected the German home front to an unprecedented degree, and included all social classes.[3]

The rhythm of life in big and medium-sized cities mirrored the howl of the warning sirens and eventually undermined confidence in victory and trust in the Party and its leadership. Despite all its promises (one thinks of Göring's boast that if one enemy bomb fell on Germany, then 'I am a Chinaman'), it had been unable to protect the population effectively. Reading the vast number of surviving private diaries, correspondences and official reports on the public mood, we see that fatalism and general exhaustion determined life in the air-raid shelters of the bombed-out cities. Thus the indiscriminate carpet bombing or 'moral bombing' carried out in nightly attacks by the Royal Air Force was not without its effect on German morale, however dubious its moral justification may have been following the successful invasion of France. Attention at home, far from the fronts, now focussed on the hardships of a daily struggle for survival and anxious fears for the welfare of kin, not only those at the front but also those who had been torn from their families in the course of mass evacuations and removal of children to the countryside. The once highly ideologised *Volksgemeinschaft* or 'national community', with its definitely racist sense of superiority, had largely become an apathetic emergency organisation that had only one goal: to survive the war.

If 'many people [stood] with tears in their eyes as they heard the voice of the Führer', as an internal report by the Ministry of Propaganda described the response to Hitler's New Year's radio appeal in 1945,[4] defeatism and the longing for peace were still increasing everywhere. Anti-government remarks were heard in public and were, as the president of the Provincial High Court of Baden noted with consternation, often no longer denounced to the authorities. On 2 January 1945, he noted that even in a solid middle-class city of civil servants like Karlsruhe, 'the ill-feeling embraces the widest circles, even those that otherwise tend to preserve their calm and reserve. Among civil servants in particular a mood is expressed that would earlier have been inconceivable.'[5]

The looming military defeat, which was becoming clearer week by week, drained the charismatically charged Hitler myth, and made people less willing to believe and to suffer. The change of mood did not go unnoticed, as internal instructions by the Reich Ministry of Propaganda document. In the spring of 1945 we find there the following unvarnished observation:

> The broad mass of the middle class has been seized by a profound lethargy. Business leaders, civil servants and intellectuals argue that the war will be lost in three months and it is therefore futile to set about and rebuild. 'In half a year the English and Americans will be here in any case.' This idea paralyses activity and eats away like a slow poison at hearts and minds. … Other sections of the population seek to exempt themselves from the fate of their people not by indifference but by a deliberate distancing. Under the slogan 'The Party is responsible for the war', they are preparing their escape from the war and abet the agitation of our opponents directed at separating the people from their Führer.[6]

By the spring of 1945 at the latest, the *Volk* had separated themselves from the Führer – not in an act of open rebellion, as in 1918 when the command to continue a war that had become senseless provoked the sailors' revolt in Kiel – but separated themselves nonetheless. 'A population which had once wallowed in nationalist intoxication, but which was now increasingly war-weary, was stricken by disillusionment', concludes Henke's extensive study. 'The greater part of society began its "inner retreat" from the Third Reich after the last glimmer of hope at the start of the Ardennes offensive in December 1944, long before the armies of the anti-Hitler coalition occupied the country and destroyed the National Socialist regime.'[7]

The significance of the shocking knowledge that the Nazi leadership itself showed no consideration for its own people should not be under-estimated in accounting for this ideological disillusionment. In September 1944, when American troops stood before Aachen and the Red Army was on the border of East Prussia, Hitler had already ordered the barbaric 'scorched earth' policy within the territory of the Reich to continue: 'It is now a matter of holding the position or annihilation.'[8] The notorious 'Nero Order' of 19 March 1945[9] confirmed this strategy of self-annihilation, which the population could view only as an absolutely irresponsible threat to what remained of their means of existence.

Hand in hand with this went the increased terror manifested in veritable orgies of murder at the end of the Nazi regime.[10] In addition to the death marches of concentration camp inmates and the mass murder of Soviet prisoners-of-war and forced labourers, in many places the population witnessed a fanatical holding out to the end. Drumhead court martials continued to condemn many soldiers and civilians to death as 'defeatists' in the last weeks and days of the war, while the onlookers longed for nothing more than the peaceful surrender of their home towns. It was the shock of this experience that exposed the Nazis for what were once and for all. The politics of the Nazi regime was now seen to be a 'criminal policy of disaster', as a Berlin woman, horrified by the spectacle of a hanged soldier, wrote tellingly in her diary.[11]

In the West, the invasion of the Americans and British was therefore largely welcomed, even longed for. Although certainly only a minority felt themselves to have been politically liberated, the end of the war was nonetheless experienced with dull relief. A report by the Protestant parish office in Ickelheim, Franconia, gave voice to the prevailing mood: 'Now the enemy has taken over in the country. But we can only thank God that He has given us into the power of an enemy that has at least up to now not made reckless use of its power.'[12] For most, the end was a bitter defeat, but the 'enemy' remained friendly, so that everywhere people made arrangements with the occupying forces to their own advantage and enlisted their help in coping with the hardships of a difficult period of transition.[13]

The end of the war was fundamentally different in the East. Here the Germans fought to the bitter end. From January to May 1945 alone, roughly one million soldiers on both sides were killed.[14] But contrary to the post-war legend, the ruthless strategy of holding out to the last man served to prolong the war, not to protect the civilian population; thus the evacuation of Courland and East Prussia was delayed against all reason. The swift advance of the Red Army in mid January then abruptly triggered a disaster of the greatest dimensions for the civilian population.

By the end of the month, four to five million people were fleeing the East in fear of revenge and retaliation by the victors.[15] The completely disorderly evacuation was, as is apparent from numerous eye-witness reports, rightly blamed on Nazi Party officials. That it was often party functionaries and their families who were the first to abscond also caused a great loss of prestige. The chaotic flight in deepest winter turned into a nightmare that exploded the whole framework of middle-class existence: 'Along the way we saw gruesome scenes. Mothers gone mad threw their children into the sea. People hanged themselves; other fell upon dead horses, cut out pieces of their flesh and roasted them over open fires; women gave birth in wagons. Everyone thought only of himself – no one could help the ill and the weak.'[16]

This first wave of refugees was soon followed by the violent expulsion of the German population remaining in the eastern territories, the Sudetenland and other settlement areas in central and eastern Europe. Hundreds of thousands of civilians, including numerous women, were deported to the Soviet Union as forced labour. Altogether, the ethnic cleansing affected fourteen million German citizens and ethnic Germans, about two million of whom did not survive the compulsory resettlement.[17]

The traumatic experience of the unprecedented violence accompanying the advance of the Red Army, a largely unleashed *Soldateska*, left an equally lasting impression. The end of the war in the east, in central Germany and in Berlin was a blood-curdling finale, an orgy of violence that hit women worst, who were raped in their hundreds of thousands.[18] We should not of course forget how this began: in the German war of extermination inspired by racial ideology. Nonetheless, the invasion of the Red Army remained a traumatic encounter for the German population, one that dug itself deep into the collective memory. In general, the East German experience was much more strongly shaped by extreme violence, flight, expulsion, captivity and deportation than in the West. For this reason alone the SED dictatorship that was soon established, the 'the pro-Russian Party', was never able to gain the confidence of the population at large, whereas by no later than the Berlin blockade of 1948 the Western occupying powers were felt to be 'protectors'.

The total defeat, symbolised by the unconditional surrender and the assumption of complete power by the victorious Allied powers, scotched any stab-in-the-back legend, which substantially eased the psychological burden of the second founding of a democracy in Germany. And unlike the years following 1918, memory of the terrors of a 'total war' stamped the entire society, which never wanted to suffer 'something like that' again.

No less momentous was the social levelling that had already begun with the Nazi regime and was considerably accelerated by the consequences of the war. The loss of property in the air war or through flight from the eastern territories naturally hit the propertied classes harder than others, whereas it hardly affected the social status of the working classes. These consequences were gravest for the junkerdom east of the Elbe, which completely perished as a social class (and so no longer constituted an exacerbating factor in German politics).

The emergency organisation of an uprooted, perforce highly mobile failed society levelled traditional class pride and confessional backgrounds, especially since for many the end of the war was not the end of their distress. Millions of refugees filled the camps – in 1950 there were a total of 12.45 million refugees and displaced persons, 7.9 million of whom lived in the Federal Republic and 4.06 million in the German Democratic Republic.[19] At the same time, 11 million soldiers were prisoners-of-war, the last of whom were finally to return home from the Soviet Union in 1956. Personal catastrophe became the sign of a break in the history of lives and experience that could well be encapsulated in the phrase 'from Stalingrad to the currency reform'.[20]

Whether the Germans were aware of the monstrous crimes of the Nazis and of their political co-responsibility for them was a question that mainly occupied foreign observers. Here it seems sensible to distinguish between various levels. Thus the statements of the new democratic elite established by the occupying powers in the western zones left no doubt of their political and moral condemnation of national socialism, a fundamental consensus that united all parties. The same was true, mutatis mutandis, of the Soviet zone of occupation. The commitment to a radical break with the Nazi past was the fundament of the new political beginning in East and West.[21]

Thus, for example, Konrad Adenauer, during his brief re-instatement as mayor of Cologne, addressed its citizens as follows on 8 August 1945:

> The adversity that overwhelms us, materially, spiritually and ethically, is terrible. If we want to rise up out of the abyss into which we have fallen, we must recognise what plunged us into it. 'For they sow the wind and reap the whirlwind!' And 'He who liveth by the sword shall die by the sword!'. True words. We bear the responsibility for our calamity; we must be clear about that. Some have sinned by commission; others by passively looking on, whether because they were blind or because they did not want to see. Still others, who had the power to do so, did not step in and stop the evil, the madness, when it was still possible.[22]

Adenauer was aware of German society's deep entanglement with national socialism and names here the various shades of guilt and co-responsibility. This was one of the main reasons why he shared with many representatives of the 'other Germany' a distinct scepticism towards his own people.

The predominant mood, however, which differed clearly from that of those persecuted by the Nazis, was described by the long-time Berlin correspondent William L. Shirer after his return in 1945: 'They have no feelings of guilt whatever and regret only that they were beaten and now must take the consequences. They are sorry only for themselves, not, for instance, for all those whom they murdered and tortured and wanted to remove from the face of the earth.'[23] This judgement is harsh and in its pointed emphasis probably somewhat unjust, but it describes the dominant feeling: national self-pity. Most Germans felt themselves to be the victims of a war and a regime which they no longer wanted to have anything to do with. Hitler and a small Nazi clique were soley responsible for the crimes, while most Germans counted themselves among the silent majority of apolitical citizens who had maintained their decency, which surely many could personally claim for themselves. From this point of view, all the cheering and enthusiasm was forgotten; the much-invoked community of *Volk* and Führer, of regime and state, had long been dissolved by the private struggle for survival. With this tacit withdrawal from the *Volksgemeinschaft*, the question of political co-responsibility and liability evaporated.

A latent bad conscience was effectively exonerated when even church leaders indulged in a morally highly dubious balancing of wrongs. Thus in June 1945 Cardinal Faulbaber of Munich wrote indignantly to his clergy:

> For weeks now representatives of American newspapers and American soldiers have been shown Dachau and the scenes of horror there documented in photo-

graphs and films, so as to set the dishonour and shame of the German people before the eyes of the whole world down to the last Hottentot village. There were scenes no less horrible when British and American bombers rained calamity on Munich and other cities; I think the thousands and thousands of corpses buried, incinerated or torn to pieces on cellar steps and streets by those bombs could also have been documented in photographs and films, as those others have been in Dachau. Mankind would not be less indignant at these scenes of horror.[24]

Reference to the suffering of the Germans and the 'guilt of others' not only soothed bad consciences but also revived the soul of a people whose national pride had been undermined. The Hamburg bishop Franz Tügel, himself a member of the Nazi Party, spoke for many when he declared that the German people were by no means solely responsible for the Second World War. That was 'a lie before God and history'. Moreover, the air war was an 'accursed crime', and the 'victors of today' were therefore the last people who should be 'preaching repentance to us'.[25] No less indignant was the reaction of the Protestant parishes to the Stuttgart Declaration of Guilt, which the newly founded council of the German Protestant church had submitted in October 1945 to an ecumenical delegation. Yet even this declaration, which its authors did not originally intend to publish, remains more than vague and contains no reference to the murder of European Jewry.[26]

Just 4 per cent of twelve hundred interviewees in the three western zones agreed with the statement that: 'Every German bears a certain guilt for what Germany did during the Third Reich.' A good fifth of them accepted the proposition that 'Not every German must feel guilty, but he should feel responsible and do what he can towards making amends and reparation.' About two thirds, however, were of the opinion that: 'The Germans as a whole have neither reason to feel guilty nor to feel responsible for making amends and reparation. Only those who actually actively participated are guilty of and responsible for what they did.' Thus the vast majority refused to accept collective guilt for the crimes perpetrated and a duty to make amends; one fifth of those questioned were even of the opinion that the Jews had themselves been responsible for their fate under National Socialism.[27] No such opinion surveys are available for the eastern zone, but it is likely that the same tendency in the public mood also prevailed there.

The results of this and other opinion surveys are noteworthy inasmuch as there was no lack of information and intense debate in the years following the war. The leading example of this is the International Military Tribunal's trial of the top leadership of the Third Reich, which began as early as 20 November 1945 in Nuremberg and concluded on 1 October 1946 with a series of graduated verdicts.[28] The daily press and radio coverage over these months met with considerable interest. Thus between 70 and 80 per cent of those questioned in the American zone stated that they followed the reports. More than 80 per cent stated that they gained new information about the concentration camps and the extermination of the Jews from the trial; only 13 per cent declared that they had previously known nothing of the Nazi crimes. More than half of those questioned held the verdicts to be just, and a further fifth held them to be too mild, while the vast majority felt the Allied conduct of trial had been fair.[29] In later years, however, this positive judgement declined sharply, and the Nazi trials were increasingly rejected as 'victor's justice'.

After the Nuremberg trials the Allied powers[30] authorised the press and radio to provide information about the crimes of the Nazi regime, about which many had known during the war at least in vague outline.[31] Thus between August 1945 and September 1946 the Northwest German Broadcasting Corporation alone broadcast 623 reports on National Socialism with an average length of fifteen minutes, transmitted in the prime time slot. The highpoint of the coverage occurred in 1945–46 during the Nazi trials in Bergen-Belsen, Nuremberg and Copenhagen; later, the subjects of 'de-nazification and re-education', 'responsibility and guilt', were discussed with decreasing frequency.[32]

In addition to these media there were (before the currency reform) high circulation cultural journals such as the *Frankfurter Hefte, Die Wandlung, Anfang und Ende* and *Der Ruf*. Several feature films also explicitly discussed the subject; for example, the first DEFA film *The Murderers Are Among Us* (*Die Mörder sind unter uns*, Wolfgang Staudte, 1946), *In Those Days* (*In jenen Tagen*, Helmut Käutner, 1947) and *Marriage in the Shadows* (*Ehe im Schatten*, Kurt Maetzig, 1947), the last of which alone was seen by 10.1 million viewers.[33] Eugen Kogon's study *The SS State* (*Der SS-Staat*) appeared in 1946; a year later Alexander Mitscherlich documented the criminal human experiments in the concentration camps.[34] As may be gathered from a bibliography, by 1948, 103 books and brochures had been published on National Socialism and its crimes, and a further 33 on the resistance and reparations. The offering declined drastically in 1949 and reached the level of 1945 again only in 1958.[35]

The question as to how Hitler had been possible was also intensely discussed in these years. Examples that could be mentioned are Friedrich Meinecke's credible attempt to explain *The German Catastrophe*, Alexander Abusch's essay *Irrweg einer Nation*, and the reflections on *The German Question* by the economist Wilhelm Röpke.[36] These works had a wide circulation and especially addressed the educated middle class. In 1946 the philosopher Karl Jaspers also took up *The Question of German Guilt*, a short book whose analytical clarity still stands out today.[37]

Discussion of the question of guilt also took up a good deal of space in the features pages of the licensed press and in the newly founded cultural journals. Here, however, the dominant mode of explanation was that of moral-philosophical tracts and philosophical-historical speculations, ranging from intellectual lineages, the alleged national character, mass society and Hitler's demonic powers of seduction to secularisation.[38] Conservative cultural criticism and pathetic invocations of fate shifted the debates from concrete analysis to the general, with the result that pressing questions about the structural aberration of German society and its concrete responsibility and complicity tended to be ignored. At the same time, it must be said that this was a serious and contrite discourse in which the apologetic undertones had nothing in common with the aggressive nationalism of the period after the First World War.

The heroic cult and heroicising of war, which had marked the writings of Ernst Jünger and the generation of young nationalists, was out of the question. The two most successful works in the immediate post-war period were Theodor Plievier's *Stalingrad*, a nightmarish collage of interviews with German prisoners-of-war, forces' letters and military situation reports that by 1949 had gone through a dozen editions, and Wolfgang Borchert's drama about a returned veteran *The Man Outside* (*Draußen vor der Tür*), which was first performed in 1947.[39] Although the war novel experienced a new popularity in the fifties, it was without any glorification of battle; instead, the horror of war and senseless suffering were the focus of attention.[40] The tenor of these works is that the German solider was betrayed and misused by the Nazi leadership; and for all their basic pacifist sentiment, they still cherished the image of a German army that had remained 'decent'.

The fires of the Second World War had burned out all nationalist energies. Among university students, who after 1918 had formed the spearhead of an intransigent revisionism, over 90 per cent in 1950 refused to serve as soldiers (again) if the Federal Republic were ever to have an army. A third of the students questioned had themselves served as soldiers in the Second World War. Out of soldiers and Hitler Youth the war had made pacifistically minded citizens with a pragmatic 'count me out!' attitude, which made the rearmament of West Germany during the Cold War anything but popular and triggered vehement inner-political conflicts. This transformation is at first glance all the more surprising as more than half of the students questioned had also stated that National Socialism was a good idea that had simply been badly carried out.[41]

In 1948, 57 per cent of West Germans (and presumably also East Germans) shared this view; only 28 per cent thought that National Socialism was a fundamentally bad idea. Of those who held it to be a good idea in principle, 65 per cent were former Party members, but 49 per cent were non-members.[42] It would be false, however, to interpret this survey conducted by the Allensbach Institute for Demoscopy, which matches American surveys, as evidence that the malign spirit of National Socialism had endured. Closer questioning showed that even those who held National Socialism to be a good idea 'did not once [express] a fundamental, ideological defence of it'. What they liked about the Nazi regime was the guarantee of the pay packet, the orderliness, the social welfare. Or as Götz Aly has recently pointedly formulated this: the social-political bribing of the *Volksgenossen*.[43] Against the background of the Depression, the peaceful years of the Third Reich were for most Germans a personally very satisfactory time, and the exchange of political freedom for prosperity and security was an attractive bargain. In addition, Hitler's foreign policy successes were balm to aggrieved national pride.

Another opinion survey fits into to this context. In response to the question 'When do you feel that things have gone best for Germany in this century?' 45 per cent of those questioned in 1951 said it had been during the German Empire and 42 per cent said the time under National Socialism from 1933 to 1938. Eighty per cent held the worst time to have been the years from 1945 to 1948; only eight per cent said it had been the war years from 1939 to 1945. The perspective of the population had shifted in retrospect. It was not the war years that dominated their consciousness, but rather the time of need immediately following the war, when the food situation dramatically worsened with the loss of plundered occupied territories and culminated in the winter famine of 1947. With the beginning of the 'economic miracle' (*Wirtschaftswunder*), the perspective shifted again. In 1956 the majority of those questioned regarded the present as the best period for Germany for the first time; by 1959, only 18 per cent saw the pre-war years as the best time.[44]

Between 1947 and 1949, on the other hand, 60 per cent of those questioned in the American zone consistently declared that they would be prepared to forego fundamental freedoms in exchange for a government guarantee of economic security and a good income. In a ranking of the most important civic freedoms in 1947, economic freedom (31 per cent) came first, followed by freedom of religion (22 per cent), the right to vote (19 per cent) and freedom of speech (14 per cent).[45]

In summary, we may therefore draw the conclusion that social security clearly ranked above freedom in the canon of values (whereby the parallel to the situation following the collapse of the SED dictatorship is obvious). In the consciousness of wide sections of the population, National Socialism was by no means tantamount to terror, war and crime. The often lamented political and moral indifference of the German population was the product of solidarity in suffering, a community that subconsciously knew all about the profound corruption of German society and therefore preferred to direct its view forward to a better future rather than backwards to a past that it did not want to remember. How indeed should an entire people have suddenly condemned what it had pinned all its hopes on only a few years before and for which it had accepted so much suffering during the war? There could not have been a more profound rupture in the collective national and political identity, in the consciousness of the average citizen. Confrontation with the full extent of Nazi crimes therefore brought about no satisfactory catharsis, but led rather to a hardening of traditional value orientations and attitudes, and to resistance against an alleged collective guilt out of defiant national pride or self-pity.

During the first post-war years attention was focussed on coping with every-day life. The traumatic experience of threat to life, limb and means of existence, sorrow at the loss of loved ones, the loss of property, profession and home – in short, the breakdown of all middle-class security, social structures and moral norms – brought about a far-reaching atomising of society, the retreat to small communities of solidarity. After the extreme political and ideological mobilisation of the Nazi period, energies were now directed to the private sphere of life, to restoring a certain modicum of middle-class normality.[46]

The founding of a new democracy was left to a minority of the population, while the vast majority vociferously protested its dissatisfaction with Allied occupation policy (in the western zones; this was absolutely banned in the eastern zone),[47] but was otherwise politically apathetic. In the American zone, between 60 and 70 per cent of those questioned in surveys consistently declared themselves not interested in politics. Politics was looked upon as a dirty business; correspondingly, only 10 per cent favoured a political career for their sons.[48] Little was to change in this collective opinion. Although a large majority always declared themselves in favour of democracy in surveys, in 1950 a third were still not prepared to venture a definition of it. At the same time, only 45 per cent thought democracy was the best form of government for the Federal Republic, which by then already existed.[49] Authoritarian attitudes were still widespread; thus in 1953 only half of those questioned favoured a multi-party system; one fifth expressly favoured a one-party system; and the rest had no opinion in the matter.[50]

At the end of the immediate period of occupation, it was by no means clear whether the founding of a second German democracy, strongly integrated in the West, would succeed. This question did not arise in the Soviet zone of occupation and the early GDR. Here a new dictatorship had arisen, which never had the majority of the population behind it, as demonstrated by the events of 17 June 1953. But developments in the West were also judged with open scepticism, especially by American analysts. Doubts were aroused particularly by the unabashed policy of integrating even heavily incriminated National Socialists, which was taken to indicate an alarming continuity of an authoritarian, anti-democratic and nationalist mentality.[51]

The returning flood of released members of the Nazi Party had already begun in 1947–48 and largely re-established continuity in the civil service.[52] With the founding of the Federal Republic, all damns broke and the mentality of 'drawing the line under the past', long popular among the population, triumphed over all misgivings. The implementation law to article 131 GG, which the German Parliament passed unanimously in April 1951, allowed tens of thousands of highly incriminated Nazi Party members, eventually even including the majority of the Gestapo, to have their former rights under civil service law re-instated.[53] The second immunity from prosecution law followed in the summer of 1954, with the result that the bulk of the so-called 'final phase crimes' remained unpunished. At the same time, criminal prosecution of Nazi crimes virtually came to a standstill. In 1954, only 183 preliminary investigations were conducted, whereas in 1950 the number had been about 2,500. Correspondingly, the number of legal convictions for Nazi war crimes sank in the following years: from 809 convictions in 1950 to a record low of 15 in 1959.[54]

The mentality of 'drawing a line under the past' reflected in a peculiar way the regained confidence which manifested itself in a massive campaign for the release of all Nazi criminals sentenced by the Allies. This lobbying for pardons, supported not least by prominent church leaders, went beyond all moral limits. Thus, for example, the Protestant regional bishop of Württemberg, Martin Haug, the FDP executive board member Ernst Mayer, the social-democratic vice-president of the German Parliament, Carlo Schmid, and finally Federal President Theodor Heuss supported an amnesty for the SS leader Martin Sandberger, who as head of the task force Ia had organised the murder of the Jews in Estonia.[55] In the fifties a non-partisan consensus of the government and the opposition worked in favour of even seriously incriminated Nazi culprits. In this climate, in which the release of convicted mass murderers was discussed as if it were a question of national honour, the insight into the fundamentally wrong nature of the Nazi regime and its racist war of extermination could no longer flourish. The massive need for amnesty may well be interpreted as 'an indirect admission, more or less confirmed by its contradiction, of the entire society's involvement in National Socialism'.[56]

The same development may be discerned, incidentally, in the GDR. Behind the façade of an anti-fascist pathos, the SED also did without further criminal prosecution of Nazi crimes and spared the population any coming to terms with the major crime of National Socialism: the murder of European Jewry.[57]

The policy of indiscriminate integration and rehabilitation, by which all the measures taken by the Allies to purge Nazis were reversed within a few years, would, however, be falsely characterised by the polemical term *re-nazification*, even if critical contemporaries increasingly felt their backs pushed against the wall by the 'inexorable return of yesterday'.[58] For the former elite of Third Reich functionaries, who organised German reconstruction at the level just below the political leadership of the Federal Republic, did not become involved in political activities in support of neo-fascist organisations, but led instead lives that were as inconspicuous as possible, completely centred on career and family.[59] This was an unhoped-for second chance which no one wanted to jeopardise after the experience of internment and de-nazification, which for several hundred thousands in 1945–46 had meant detention in prison camps and temporary release, and which had constituted a profound rupture in their social existence.[60] What was wanted now was pragmatic adaptation, willingness to work and technocratic efficiency. The restorative spirit of the 1950s combined with a vehement anti-communism to facilitate the gradual identification of millions of former Nazis, the chastened and the intransigent, with the new state.

The successful, if precarious, transformation of an intensely nazified society into the citizenry of the Federal Republic was due, in addition to the profound disillusionment prevalent by the end of the war, to the institutional order whose normative moorings remained inviolate and which was not afflicted by the slow wasting disease that had befallen the Weimar Republic. The comprehensive integration took place largely on the basis of people's opportunist adaptation to what was in their own best interests, that is, political and ideological moderation. This was especially true after the ban on the neo-Nazi Socialist Reich Party (SRP), which had won 11 per cent of the votes in the Lower Saxony state election in 1951; the ban clearly marked the limits of tolerance.[61] In January 1953 the British sent another signal by invoking their rights as an occupying power and arresting the circle round Werner Naumann, former state secretary in the Reich Propaganda Ministry, thus preventing the infiltration of the North-Rhine-Westphalian FDP.[62] This drastic action emphatically reminded the world that the status of the Federal Republic was only quasi-sovereign.

Even if we have good reason to take the view that the establishment and anchoring of a German democracy could have come about only at the price of a generous policy of integration towards the millions of former Nazi Party members, since a liberal democracy is incompatible with the permanent exclusion of large segments of the population,[63] there was still undoubtedly greater manoeuvring room: not every scandalous personal decision was unavoidable in this form. The moral indifference weighed most heavily in the legal prosecution of Nazi crimes, which came to a standstill in the 1950s. Nor can the often mean-spirited reparations policy, which again discriminated against and excluded whole groups of victims,[64] be interpreted as an inevitable concomitant of an essentially unavoidable policy of integration. Under the conditions of the Allied intervention clause and the sharp block confrontation, which admitted of no alternative to Western integration, a more courageous policy on the part of democratic elites would definitely have been conceivable, even if it ran contrary to the majority mood of comfortable silence.

The acceptance of the new German democracy rested in the first place primarily on the extraordinary economic showing of the young Federal Republic, which began in the fifties; it constituted the strongest justification for a society decidedly oriented to economic success and state welfare. Conversely, National Socialism had disqualified itself by its failure. The return of middle-class normality and the prosperity attained, combined with regained legal safeguards and the division of powers, provided a sharp contrast to the arbitrary party will that marked life under the Nazi and SED dictatorships. After a decade of chaos and profound traumatic wounds, the past now seemed to have been 'come to terms with'.

It may have required, as Klaus Harpprecht wrote in 1959 in an astute essay, 'an arduous restoration of society, of a reliable state order, of a sense of home, however lacking in attraction and perhaps only provisional, and of an historical awareness in which everything had gone to rack and ruin, before the Germans were capable of presenting themselves on the world stage again'.[65] The time of moral indifference came to an end at the beginning of the 1960s.[66] This was a time of re-visiting the Nazi past; only this, along with a conflict-laden change of generations, brought about an inner foundation of the new democracy and its anchoring in a Western civil society on a broad basis. In the GRD until the peaceful revolution of 1989, on the other hand, a decreed anti-fascism dominated, which served legend and myth more than it contributed to enlightenment. Common to both German states in the first post-war years, however, was social stabilisation through dissociation from guilt and the formation of a collective consciousness of victimhood.

Notes

1. Diary entry from 3 January 1945 (Stadtarchiv München), quoted in *Süddeutsche Zeitung*, 3 January 2005.
2. Quoted in Klaus-Dietmar Henke, *Die amerikanische Besetzung Deutschlands* (Munich, 1995), 81; cf. also Klaus Latzel, *Deutsche Soldaten – nationalsozialistischer Krieg? Kriegserlebnis – Kriegserfahrung 1939–1945* (Paderborn, 1998).
3. For a survey, cf. Ralf Blank, 'Kriegsalltag und Luftkrieg an der "Heimatfront"', in Jörg Echternkamp (ed.), *Die deutsche Kriegsgesellschaft 1939 bis 1945*, vol. 1: *Politisierung, Vernichtung, Überleben* (Munich, 2004), 357–461.
4. Response to the Führer's speech of 1 February 1945, quoted in Klaus-Jörg Ruhl (ed.), *Deutschland 1945. Alltag zwischen Krieg und Frieden in Berichten, Dokumenten und Bildern* (Darmstadt, 1984), 16.
5. OLG-President to the Reich Minister of Justice on 1 February 1945, quoted in Ruhl (ed.), *Deutschland 1945*, 18. For case studies, cf. Hans Siemons, *Kriegsalltag in Aachen. Not, Tod und Überleben in der alten Kaiserstadt zwischen 1939 und 1945* (Aachen, 1998); Wilfried Beer, *Kriegsalltag an der Heimatfront. Alliierter Luftkrieg und deutsche Gegenmaßnahmen zur Abwehr und Schadensbegrenzung dargestellt für den Raum Münster* (Bremen, 1990); Ulrich Borsdorf and Mathilde Jamin, *Überleben im Krieg. Kriegserfahrungen in einer Industrieregion 1939–1945* (Reinbek, 1989); Herfried Münkler, *Machtzerfall: Die letzten Tage des Dritten Reiches dargestellt am Beispiel der hessischen Kleinstadt Friedberg* (Berlin, 1985); Rolf-Dieter Müller, Gerd R. Ueberschär and Wolfram Wette, *Wer zurückweicht wird erschossen. Kriegsalltag und Kriegsende in Südwestdeutschland 1944/45* (Freiburg, 1985); Lutz Niethammer (ed.), *'Die Jahre weiß man nicht, wo man die heute hinsetzen soll.' Faschismus-Erfahrungen im Ruhrgebiet* (Berlin, 1983).

6. 'Merkpunkte zur Versammlungsaktion' February–March 1945, quoted in Ruhl (ed.), *Deutschland 1945*, 54 f.

7. Henke, *Besetzung*, 86 f.; cf. also Ian Kershaw, *Der Hitler-Mythos. Volksmeinung und Propaganda im Dritten Reich* (Stuttgart, 1980); Marlis G. Steinert, *Hitlers Krieg und die Deutschen. Stimmung und Haltung der deutschen Bevölkerung im Zweiten Weltkrieg* (Düsseldorf, 1970); Wolfram Wette, Ricarda Bremer and Detlef Vogel (eds.), *Das letzte halbe Jahr. Stimmungsberichte der Wehrmachtspropaganda 1944/45* (Essen, 2001).

8. Quoted in Heinrich Schwendemann, 'Der deutsche Zusammenbruch im Osten 1944/45', in Bernd-A. Rusinek (ed.), *Kriegsende 1945. Verbrechen, Katastrophen, Befreiungen in nationaler und internationaler Perspektive* (Göttingen, 2004), 125–150, at 125. Cf. also Henke, *Besetzung*, 421–435.

9. Printed in Rolf-Dieter Müller and Gerd R. Ueberschär, *Kriegsende 1945. Die Zerstörung des Deutschen Reiches* (Frankfurt, 1994), 164.

10. Cf. Gerhard Paul, '"Diese Erschießungen haben mich innerlich gar nicht mehr berührt". Die Kriegsendphasenverbrechen der Gestapo 1944/45', in Paul and Klaus-Michael Mallmann (eds.), *Die Gestapo im Zweiten Weltkrieg. „Heimatfront" und besetztes Europa* (Darmstadt, 2000), 543–568.

11. Ruth Andreas-Friedrich, entry from 23 April 1945, quoted in Andreas-Friedrich (ed.), *Deutschland 1945*, 124.

12. Report of 6 June 1945, quoted in Clemens Vollnhals, 'Die Evangelische Landeskirche in der Nachkriegspolitik. Die Bewältigung der nationalsozialistischen Vergangenheit', in W. Benz, *Neuanfang in Bayern* (Munich, 1988), 143–162, at 144.

13. This is pointedly shown by Henke's excellent study, *Besetzung*; cf. also Hans Woller, *Gesellschaft und Politik unter der amerikanischen Besatzungszone. Die Region Ansbach und Fürth* (Munich, 1986).

14. Richard Overy, *Russlands Krieg* (Hamburg, 2003), 400; cf. generally Rüdiger Overmans, *Deutsche militärische Verluste im Zweiten Weltkrieg* (Munich, 2000).

15. Schwendemann, 'Zusammenbruch', 134; cf. generally Manfred Zeidler, *Kriegsende im Osten. Die Rote Armee und die Besetzung Deutschlands östlich von Oder und Neiße* (Munich, 1996).

16. Quoted in Ruhl (ed.), *Deutschland 1945*, 40 f.

17. Statistics in Müller and Ueberschär, *Kriegsende 1945*, 123; cf. also *Dokumentation der Vertreibung der Deutschen aus Ost-Mitteleuropa*, ed. by the Bundesministerium für Vertriebene, (5 vols. with 3 appendices, Bonn, 1953–1961); Wolfgang Benz (ed.), *Die Vertreibung der Deutschen aus dem Osten. Ursachen, Ereignisse, Folgen* (Frankfurt, 1985); Stefan Aust and Stephan Burgdorff (eds.), *Die Flucht. Über die Vertreibung der Deutschen aus dem Osten* (Stuttgart, 2002).

18. Norman M. Naimark, *Die Russen in Deutschland. Die sowjetische Besatzungszone 1945 bis 1949* (Berlin, 1997), 91–179; Antony Beevor, *Berlin 1945: Das Ende* (Munich, 2002), 441–456; Christel Panzig and Klaus-Alexander Panzig, '"Die Russen kommen!" Deutsche Erinnerungen mit "Russen" bei Kriegsende 1945 in Dörfern und Kleinstädten Mitteldeutschlands und Mecklenburg-Vorpommerns', in Elke Scherstjanoi (ed.), *Rotarmisten schreiben aus Deutschland. Briefe von der Front (1945) und historische Analysen* (Munich, 2004), 340–368; for a haunting eye-witness report, cf. Anonyma, *Eine Frau in Berlin. Tagebuchaufzeichnungen vom 20. April bis 22. Juni 1945* (Frankfurt, 2003).

19. Gerhard Reichling, *Die deutschen Vertriebenen in Zahlen*, vol. 1: *Umsiedler, Verschleppte, Vertriebene* (Bonn, 1986), 26.

20. Martin Broszat, Klaus-Dietmar Henke and Hans Woller (eds.), *Von Stalingrad zur Währungsreform. Zur Sozialgeschichte des Umbruchs in Deutschland* (Munich, 1988).

21. Cf. Jeffrey Herf, *Zweierlei Erinnerung. Die NS-Vergangenheit im geteilten Deutschland* (Berlin, 1998).

22. Address of 25 August 1945, quoted in Karola Fings, 'Kriegsenden, Kriegslegenden. Bewältigungsstrategien in einer deutschen Großstadt', in Rusinek (ed.), *Kriegsende 1945*, 219–238, at 226.

23. Entry of 2 November 1945, William L. Shirer, *Berliner Tagebuch. Das Ende. 1944–1945* (Leipzig, 1994), 177 f. Translated from the German.

24. 'Pastorale Anweisungen an den Klerus der Erzdiözese München', mid June 1945, quoted in Gabriele Hammermann, 'Das Kriegsende in Dachau', in Rusinek (ed.), *Kriegsende 1945*, 27–53, at 32; cf. also Sybille Steinbacher, '"... daß ich mit der Totenklage auch die Klage um unsere Stadt verbinde". Die Verbrechen von Dachau in der Wahrnehmung der frühen Nachkriegszeit', in Norbert Frei and Sybille Steinbacher (eds.), *Beschweigen und Bekennen. Die deutsche Nachkriegsgesellschaft und der Holocaust* (Göttingen, 2001), 11–33.

25. Tügel to Woermann on 30 June 1945, quoted by Ursula Büttner, 'Orientierungssuche in heilloser Zeit: der Beitrag der evangelischen Kirche', in Büttner and Bernd Nellessen (eds.), *Die zweite Chance. Der Übergang von der Diktatur zur Demokratie in Hamburg 1945–1949* (Hamburg, 1997), 85–107, at 91 f.

26. Cf. Martin Greschat (ed.), *Die Schuld der Kirche. Dokumente und Reflexionen zur Stuttgarter Schulderklärung vom 18./19. Oktober 1945* (Munich, 1982); Gerhard Besier and Gerhard Sautter, *Wie Christen ihre Schuld bekennen. Die Stuttgarter Schulderklärung 1945* (Göttingen, 1985); Clemens Vollnhals, 'Im Schatten der Stuttgarter Schulderklärung. Die Erblast des Nationalprotestantismus', in Manfred Gailus (ed.), *Nationalprotestantische Mentalitäten: Konturen, Entwicklungslinien und Umbrüche eines Weltbildes* (Göttingen, 2005), 379–431. On the discussion among Catholics, cf. Vera Brücker, *Die Schulddiskussion im deutschen Katholizismus nach 1945* (Bochum, 1989); Birgit Weissenbach, *Kirche und Konzentrationslager. Katholische Aufklärungspublizistik in der Zeit von 1945 bis 1950* (Frankfurt, 2005).

27. HICOG-Report, No. 113 of 12 May 1951, quoted in Peter Reichel, *Politische Kultur der Bundesrepublik* (Opladen, 1981), 116 f.; cf. also Anna J. Merritt and Richard L. Merritt (eds.), *Public Opinion in Semisovereign Germany. The HICOG Surveys, 1949–1955* (Urbana, 1980), 146.

28. Cf. Telford Taylor, *Die Nürnberger Prozesse. Hintergründe, Analysen und Erkenntnisse aus heutiger Sicht* (Munich, 1994).

29. Anna J. Merritt and Richard L. Merritt (eds.), *Public Opinion in Occupied Germany. The OMGUS Surveys, 1945–1949* (Urbana, 1970), 34 f.; cf. Ansgar Diller and Wolfgang Mühl-Benninghaus (eds.), *Berichterstattung über den Nürnberger Prozess gegen die Hauptkriegsverbrecher 1945/46. Edition und Dokumentation ausgewählter Rundfunkquellen* (Potsdam, 1998); Anneke de Rudder, '"Warum das ganze Theater?" Der Nürnberger Prozess in den Augen der Zeitgenossen', in Wolfgang Benz (ed.), *Jahrbuch für Antisemitismusforschung*, 6 (1997), 218–242.

30. Cf. Hans Meiser, 'Der Nationalsozialismus und seine Bewältigung im Spiegel der Lizenzpresse der britischen Besatzungszone von 1946–1949', PhD thesis, Osnabrück University (1980).

31. Cf. David Bankier, *Die öffentliche Meinung im Hitler-Staat. Die 'Endlösung' und die Deutschen. Eine Berichtigung* (Berlin, 1995); Norbert Frei, 'Auschwitz und die Deutschen. Geschichte, Geheimnis, Gedächtnis', in Frei, *1945 und wir. Das Dritte Reich im Bewusstsein der Deutschen* (Munich, 2005), 156–183.

32. Cf. Christof Schneider, *Nationalsozialismus als Thema im Programm des Nordwestdeutschen Rundfunks, 1945–1948* (Potsdam, 1999), 193 ff.

33. Cf. Wolfgang Becker and Norbert Schöll, *In jenen Tagen. Wie der deutsche Nachkriegs-film die Vergangenheit bewältigte* (Opladen, 1995); Bettina Greffrath, *Gesellschaftsbil-der der Nachkriegszeit. Deutsche Spielfilme 1945–1949* (Pfaffenweiler, 1995), 141ff.; Heiko R. Blum, *30 Jahre danach. Dokumentation zur Auseinandersetzung mit dem Na-tionalsozialismus im Film 1945–1975* (Cologne, 1975).

34. Alexander Mitscherlich and Fred Mielke (eds.), *Das Diktat der Menschenverachtung. Der Nürnberger Ärzteprozeß und seine Quellen. Eine Dokumentation* (Heidelberg, 1947).

35. Joseph Melzer, *Deutsch-jüdisches Schicksal in dieser Zeit. Wegweiser durch das Schrift-tum der letzten 15 Jahre* (Cologne, 1960).

36. Friedrich Meinecke, *Die deutsche Katastrophe. Betrachtungen und Erinnerungen* (Wies-baden, 1946); Alexander Abusch, *Der Irrweg einer Nation. Ein Beitrag zum Verständnis deutscher Geschichte* (Berlin [Ost], 1946); Wilhlem Röpke, *Die deutsche Frage* (Erlen-bach-Zürich, 1945); cf. also Hans-Erich Volkmann, 'Deutsche Historiker im Umgang mit Drittem Reich und Zweitem Weltkrieg 1939–1949', in Volkmann (ed.), *Ende des Dritten Reiches – Ende des Zweiten Weltkrieges. Eine perspektivische Rückschau* (Mu-nich, 1995), 861–911; Winfried Schulze, *Deutsche Geschichtswissenschaft nach 1945* (Munich, 1989).

37. Karl Jasper, *Die Schuldfrage* (Heidelberg, 1946).

38. Cf. Barbro Eberan, *Luther? Friedrich „der Große"? Wagner? Nietzsche? Wer war an Hit-ler schuld? Die Debatte um die Schuldfrage 1945–1949* (Munich, 1985); Ingrid Laurien, 'Die Verarbeitung von Nationalsozialismus und Krieg in den politisch-kulturellen Zeitschriften der Westzonen 1945–1949', *GWU* 39 (1988), 220–237; Christoph Cobet, *Deutschlands Erneuerung 1945–1950. Bio-Bibliographische Dokumentation mit 443 Texten* (Frankfurt, 1985).

39. Ulrich Baron and Hans-Harald Müller, 'Die Weltkriege im Roman der Nachkriegs-zeiten', in Gottfried Niedhart and Dieter Riesenberger (eds.), *Lernen aus dem Krieg? Deutsche Nachkriegszeiten 1918/1945* (Munich, 1992), 300–318, at 314; Ursula Heu-kenkamp (ed.), *Unerwünschte Erfahrung. Kriegsliteratur und Zensur in der DDR* (Ber-lin, 1990).

40. Cf., e.g. Peter Bamm, *Die unsichtbare Flagge: ein Bericht* (Munich, 1952); Willi Hein-rich, *Das geduldige Fleisch* (Stuttgart, 1955); Gerd Ledig, *Die Stalinorgel* (Hamburg, 1955); Michael Horbach, *Die verratenen Söhne* (Hamburg, 1957); Heinrich Gerlach, *Die verratene Armee* (Munich, 1957); Heinz Konsalik, *Der Arzt von Stalingrad* (Mu-nich, 1956); Fritz Wöss, *Hunde, wollt ihr ewig leben* (Hamburg, 1958), Manfred Gregor, *Die Brücke* (Wien, 1958); Hans Hellmuth Kirst, *08/15. Trilogie* (Munich, 1959).

41. Quoted in Reichel, *Kultur*, 137.

42. *Das Dritte Reich. Eine Studie über Nachwirkungen des Nationalsozialismus* (Allens-bach, 1949).

43. Cf. Götz Aly, *Hitlers Volksstaat. Raub, Rassenkrieg und nationaler Sozialismus* (Frank-furt, 2005).

44. Elisabeth Noelle and Erich Peter Neumann (eds.), *Jahrbuch der öffentlichen Meinung 1947–1955* (Allensbach, 1956), 125; Noelle and Neumann (eds.), *Jahrbuch der öffentli-chen Meinung 1958–1964* (Allensbach, 1965), 231.

45. Merritt and Merritt (eds.), *Public Opinion in Occupied Germany*, 41 f., 294 f.

46. Cf. Lutz Niethammer (ed.), *'Hinterher merkt man, dass es richtig war, dass es schiefge-gangen ist.' Nachkriegserfahrungen im Ruhrgebiet* (Berlin, 1983).

47. Cf. Joseph Foschepoth, 'Zur deutschen Reaktion auf Niederlage und Besatzung' in Ludolf Herbst (ed.), *Westdeutschland 1945–1955. Unterwerfung, Kontrolle, Integration* (Munich, 1986), 151–165.

48. Merritt and Merritt (eds.), *Public Opinion in Occupied Germany*, 44 f.

49. Eid. (eds.), *Public Opinion in Semisovereign Germany*, 64.

50. *Eine Generation später. Bundesrepublik Deutschland 1953–1979*, ed. by Institut für Demoskopie Allensbach (Allensbach, 1981), table 80.

51. Cf. Petra Marquardt-Bigman, *Amerikanische Geheimdienstanalysen über Deutschland 1942–1949* (Munich, 1995), 257 ff; cf. also Franz Neumann, 'Military Government and the Revival of Democracy' (1948), German translation in: Franz Neumann, *Wirtschaft, Staat, Demokratie. Aufsätze 1930–1954* (Frankfurt, 1978), 309–325; Hajo Holborn, 'Bericht zur deutschen Frage. Beobachtungen und Empfehlungen vom Herbst 1947', ed. by Erich J. C. Hahn, *VfZ* 35 (1987), 135–166.

52. For a survey, cf. Clemens Vollnhals, *Entnazifizierung. Politische Säuberung und Rehabilitierung in den vier Besatzungszonen 1945–1949* (Munich, 1991).

53. Cf. Norbert Frei, *Vergangenheitspolitik. Die Anfänge der Bundesrepublik und die NS-Vergangenheit* (Munich, 1999), 79 f.

54. Adalbert Rückerl, *Die Strafverfolgung von NS-Verbrechen 1945–1978. Eine Dokumentation* (Heidelberg, 1979), 125.

55. Cf. Frei, *Vergangenheitspolitik*, 297 ff.; cf. generally Thomas Alan Schwartz, 'Die Begnadigung deutscher Kriegsverbrecher. John Mc Cloy und die Häftlinge von Landsberg', *VfZ* 38 (1990), 375–414; Frank W. Buscher, *The U. S. War Crimes Trial Program in Germany, 1946–1955* (New York, 1989); Ulrich Brochhagen, *Nach Nürnberg. Vergangenheitsbewältigung und Westintegration in der Ära Adenauer* (Hamburg, 1994), 32–173; Clemens Vollnhals, 'Die Hypothek des Nationalprotestantismus. Entnazifizierung und Strafverfolgung von NS-Verbrechen nach 1945', *GG* 18 (1992), 51–69; Marc von Miquel, *Ahnden oder amnestieren? Westdeutsche Justiz und Vergangenheitspolitik in den sechziger Jahren* (Göttingen, 2004).

56. Frei, *Vergangenheitspolitik*, 399.

57. On criminal prosecution, cf. the statistics in Günter Wieland, 'Die Ahndung von NS-Verbrechen in Ostdeutschland 1945–1990', in *DDR-Justiz und NS-Verbrechen. Sammlung ostdeutscher Strafurteile wegen nationalsozialistischer Tötungsverbrechen. Verfahrensregister und Dokumentenband*, prepared in the Seminarium voor Strafrecht en Strafrechtspleging 'Van Hamel' at the University of Amsterdam by C. F. Rüter (Amsterdam, 2002), 11–99, at 97; Herf, *Zweierlei Erinnerung*; Joachim Käppner, *Erstarrte Geschichte. Faschismus und Holocaust im Spiegel der Geschichtswissenschaft und Geschichtspropaganda der DDR* (Hamburg, 1999); Anette Leo and Peter Reif-Spirek (eds.), *Vielstimmiges Schweigen. Neue Studien zum DDR-Antifaschismus* (Berlin, 2001).

58. Eugen Kogon, 'Beinahe mit dem Rücken zur Wand', *Frankfurter Hefte* 9 (1954), 641–645; cf. also Peter Merz, *Und das wurde nicht ihr Staat. Erfahrungen emigrierter Schriftsteller mit Westdeutschland* (Munich, 1985).

59. Cf. Winfried Loth and Bernd-A. Rusinek (eds.), *Verwandlungspolitik. NS-Eliten in der westdeutschen Nachkriegsgesellschaft* (Frankfurt, 1998).

60. In the western zones about 182,000 people were interned, 86,000 of whom were released by 1 January 1947; cf. Vollnhals, *Entnazifizierung*, 251. A further half million party members were temporarily released.

61. Cf. Frei, *Vergangenheitspolitik*, 326–360.

62. Ibid., 360–396; Ulrich Herbert, *Best. Biographische Studien über Radikalismus, Weltanschauung und Vernunft 1903–1989* (Bonn, 1996), 461 ff.

63. Cf. Hermann Lübbe, 'Der Nationalsozialismus im deutschen Nachkriegsbewußtsein', *Historische Zeitschrift*, 236 (1983), 579–599.

64. Cf. Hans Günter Hockerts and Christiane Kuller (eds.), *Nach der Verfolgung. Wiedergutmachung nationalsozialistischen Unrechts in Deutschland?* (Göttingen, 2003); Constantin Goschler, *Wiedergutmachung: Westdeutschland und die Verfolgten des Nationalsozialismus, 1945–1954* (Munich, 1992); Ludolf Herbst and Constantin Goschler (eds.), *Wiedergutmachung in der Bundesrepublik Deutschland* (Munich, 1989).
65. Klaus Harpprecht, 'Im Keller der Gefühle. Gibt es noch einen deutschen Antisemitismus?', *Der Monat* 11, 128 (1959), 13–20, at 17.
66. Cf. amongst others Peter Graf Kielsmannsegg, *Lange Schatten. Vom Umgang der Deutschen mit der nationalsozialistischen Vergangenheit* (Berlin, 1989); Axel Schildt, 'Der Umgang mit der NS-Vergangenheit in der Öffentlichkeit der Nachkriegszeit', in Loth and Rusinek (eds.), *Verwandlungspolitik*, 19–54; Hartmut Berghoff, 'Zwischen Verdrängung und Aufarbeitung. Die bundesdeutsche Gesellschaft und ihre nationalsozialistische Vergangenheit in den Fünfziger Jahren', *GWU* 49 (1998), 96–114; Peter Reichel, *Vergangenheitsbewältigung in Deutschland. Die Auseinandersetzung mit der NS-Diktatur von 1945 bis heute* (Munich, 2001); Clemens Vollnhals, 'Zwischen Verdrängung und Aufklärung. Die Auseinandersetzung mit dem Holocaust in der frühen Bundesrepublik', in Ursula Büttner (ed.), *Die Deutschen und die Judenverfolgung im Dritten Reich* (Frankfurt, 2003), 381–422.

14

The French after 1945
Difficulties and Disappointments of an Immediate Post-War Period

Fabrice Grenard

Today, historians prefer the term 'immediate post-war period' (*sortie de guerre*) to that of 'post-war' (*après guerre*) to characterise the years directly following the two World Wars. In place of the old tallies of casualty numbers and diplomatic resolutions of conflicts studied by traditional historiography, new approaches tend to focus on the processes of demobilising and reintegrating the former combatants, the problems associated with the reconstruction and reconversion of war economies, the question of mourning and the challenges of how to remember and commemorate the past.[1]

In the case of France, the period immediately following the First World War has been more thoroughly researched than that following the Second. The 1920s have been most frequently studied from the perspective of the legacy of the 1914–1918 war,[2] and numerous detailed studies have been devoted to the former soldiers, to collective mourning and to the cultural and social consequences of the war.[3] Yet the phenomenon of the immediate post-war period beginning in 1945 remains a historiographical work in progress.[4] The situation at the end of the Second World War is more complex than that in 1918, a fact which renders its study more difficult and requires a more nuanced view. In 1945 France did not simply celebrate a victory as it had in 1918; it also had to overcome the trauma represented by the defeat of 1940 and the four years of German occupation. Instead of a society united and triumphant in victory, as had been the case in 1918, the French in 1945 experienced terrible fractures and divisions, and the national conscience appeared to be deeply wounded. Another problem relates to the idea that the Liberation represents a rupture much more significant than the victory of 1918,[5] characterised by an affirmed will to reform and modernise while the years between 1940 and 1944 would be quickly repressed.[6] The episode of the war having thus been quickly closed, after 1945 France would enter into a new era: one of economic growth, the welfare state and the integration of Europe. This approach has contributed to some extent to the neglect of the period of transition that constituted the late 1940s.

The aim of this study is not to re-investigate the restoration of republican government or the reform principals adopted by the state at Liberation, but rather to see how French society lived through and subjectively experienced an immediate post-war period that generated important frustrations and disappointments. Once the 'celebration' of the Liberation was over, the consequences and memory of the war remained omnipresent in France until the early 1950s, having important repercussions for the French people's state of mind, behaviour and daily life. While the aftermath of the war weighed heavily upon the country, French society, deeply wounded by the defeat of 1940, had to rebuild a sense of national identity, to mourn its dead and relocate its missing (e.g. prisoners, deportees). The 'legal purge' (*épuration*) is also at the heart of this process. More important than is sometimes acknowledged and cutting across all social strata, it helped to stir up resentment towards all those individuals who had served the German occupiers and benefited or profited from the occupation, fulfilling at once the functions of regeneration and catharsis. For several years the French continued to suffer in their daily lives, especially from the difficulties in accessing food. This led to serious disappointments following the hope that the Liberation would put an end to all those material restrictions with which France had been battling since 1940. The legacy of the war ultimately manifested itself in the will of the French people to regain a power lost through the defeat of 1940, in spite of the new hardships and the numerous challenges confronting the country.

The Shadow of War: The Presence and Memory of the War and the Occupation in Post-Liberation France

The war could not easily be forgotten during the years following the Liberation of France. The traces of the conflict were everywhere and the French were aware, once the conflict was over, of the extent of the damage that had been caused and of the difficulties that beset both the government and the governed.

The battles of 1944 between the Allies and the Germans on French territory were all the more violent as the final outcome of the war was hanging in the balance. In 1945 the material damage was incomparably greater than that wrought by the First World War, which had left its mark only in those regions where the armies had fought: the north and the east. In 1945, on the other hand, nearly all the French *départements* had suffered damage. Aerial bombardments had taken an especially heavy toll on the cities. After the Allied landing of June 1944, twelve hundred municipalities were declared disaster areas. Certain important cities, such as Le Havre, Caen or Dunkerque, had been almost totally flattened. In addition to the 2.5 million buildings destroyed or damaged, it became necessary to rebuild more than 10,000 bridges, 2,000 pieces of infrastructure (tunnels, viaducts, railroad bridges), 20,000 kilometres of railroad track and 115 railway stations. Three million hectares of cultivated land and several million factories were also classified as either destroyed or unusable.[7] The slow pace and the difficulties of reconstruction in an impoverished country, burdened by a serious lack of materials and machines, meant that ruins and rubble would remain a permanent fixture of the daily lives of the French for several years.

Although the fighting ceased on 8 May 1945, there were still weapons of destruction within France. According to official statistics, five hundred thousand hectares in more than fifty *départements* were strewn with more than 10 million mines. Numerous beaches as well as certain neighbourhoods in cities and villages were therefore completely off limits to the local population. As early as May 1945, Michelin published a map of the mined areas. In spite of clear warnings, accidents, often fatal, were not infrequent. In 1945, about four hundred civilians were killed by mines and five hundred were wounded.[8] An extensive de-mining operation was undertaken under the responsibility of an Office of De-mining created in February 1945 within the Ministry for Reconstruction and Urban Planning. Thirty thousand German prisoners-of-war were mobilised for these operations (against the advice of the Red Cross, which saw this as a violation of the Geneva Convention). In addition, there were three thousand French de-miners, all of whom were volunteers. The de-mining operations were not concluded until the end of 1947 after many de-miners had been killed. According to official statistics, a third of the three thousand French de-miners may have been killed or seriously wounded (in principle only the French were allowed to disarm to mines detected by road workers), while one thousand of the thirty thousand German forced labourers were killed.[9]

Even though, with some six hundred thousand victims,[10] the human losses France suffered during World War II were not as great as those it endured during the First World War, the fact remains that expressions of authentic collective mourning began to appear immediately after the Liberation. This mourning was no doubt less extensive than in the post-1918 period, when all the municipalities were covered with war memorials. However, important continuities exist between the two conflicts, notably due the construction throughout France from 1945 onward of thousands of 'commemorative sites' (*lieux du souvenir*), an act that suggests the French desire to create an immediate remembrance of the events that they had just gone through and to celebrate the memory of the dead. The great majority of the steles, plaques and monuments relating to the Second World War in France were erected between 1944 and 1950.[11] Most often, the initiative came first from family or friends (from the autumn of 1944, the prefecture of Paris was inundated by individual requests for certain streets to be named after people killed during the Liberation).[12] Little by little both municipalities and associations encouraged the creation of commemorative sites by organising numerous public subscriptions to finance the building of steles and monuments. Beginning in 1945, certain associations of Resistance members also established cemeteries close to the hide-outs that had been used under the Occupation, including numerous plaques paying homage to Resistance fighters killed by the Germans.[13]

The rapid construction of these commemorative sites during the months that followed the end of the war had a dual function: a funerary one (paying homage to the dead) but also a patriotic one, recalling the important role played by the French in the fight against the Nazi occupier and for the liberation of their country.[14] We again notice this dual role in the manner in which ceremonies of commemoration were organised in the immediate post-war period. Celebrations on both the national (11 November, 8 May) and local levels (the anniversary of the liberation of a particular municipality or *département*) always unfolded as a double ritual: a meditation designed to pay homage to the dead (a minute's silence, a religious sermon) followed by a celebration of the victory and of the resistance of France (the singing of the Marseillaise and the Song of the Partisans, patriotic speeches).[15] Thus the patriotic character of these commemorations seems more prominent in commemorations of the Second World War than of the First. During the inter-war period, the 11 November celebrations had the air of a civic holiday, honouring the dead but also celebrating the peace, with greater emphasis placed on the cessation of hostilities than on the victory itself.[16] In 1945, on the other hand, the focus was undeniably on the rebuilding of a national identity through the patriotic euphoria symbolised by the Resistance and the victory over Germany. The growth of what amounts to a hierarchy of commemorations seems equally revealing.[17] The martyrs of the Resistance, the hostages shot by the Germans, and individuals (civilian or military) killed in combat during the Liberation were given pride of place whereas certain groups, such as the 'racial' deportees, who did not necessarily convey this patriotic image, seemed totally absent. In Paris, the first plaque commemorating the round-up of the Velodrome d'Hiver only dates from 21 July 1946, which is nearly two years after the Liberation. It was not until 1954, with the introduction of a national Deportation Day, that other plaques mentioning the Shoah deportees were erected.[18] The first important monument dedicated to all the victims of the repression and of deportation by the Nazis (including the Jews) was a memorial to those deported and shot, unveiled at Auxerre on 3 April 1949.[19] However, such examples were very rare and generally speaking – in contrast to the First World War, which had unleashed an authentic sense of communion among Frenchmen – the Second World War created within France a 'splintered memory', according to the modalities of individual or collective experience in the war and in suffering.

If France wept for its dead after the Liberation, the war's end also allowed the nation to relocate its missing, those who since 1940 had been prisoners or deportees in Germany. Their return, which took place between the spring and the autumn of 1945, created a powerful shock, reminding the French of all the horrors of Nazi repression at a time when most of the territory had been liberated for almost a year. More than 2 million Frenchmen had been forcibly detained in Germany, of whom the majority had been prisoners of war (1.2 million), 600,000 had been forced labourers, 200,000 (all former residents of Alsace or Moselle) had been forced to serve in the Wehrmacht, and 60,000 had been 'racial' or political deportees. Beginning in the spring of 1945, the rate of return accelerated, with 310,000 returning in April, 900,000 in May and 275,000 in June. Having accomplished its mission, the Ministry for Prisoners, Deportees and Refugees (PRD) was dissolved in December of 1945.

If the arrival of the first contingents was an occasion for genuine celebrations and choreographed events (decorated railway stations, orchestras etc), the welcome rapidly became less and less warm, giving way to a certain indifference. Here again, a veritable hierarchy began to develop, with the political deportees receiving all the honours, as they symbolised a France that was patriotic and *résistante*, while prisoners of war, in contrast, were implicitly blamed for the defeat of 1940 and the forced labourers were denigrated for not having joined the ranks of the many who had dodged the STO (Service du Travail Obligatoire).[20] Finally, the return of the twenty-five hundred surviving Jews was met with a certain degree of indifference in a French society that did not yet understand and appreciate the specific nature of the Shoah.

For the majority of the prisoners and deportees reintegration was difficult and the return was not always infused with the '*bonheur de vivre*' of which many had dreamed in the camps. Absent for nearly five years, the prisoners of war found a country that had moved on without them and which they could hardly recognise. The numerous bureaucratic hurdles with which they were confronted upon their return sometimes caused serious discontentment, especially as the packages that they received, which included necessary effects (clothing, shoes, food) along with a certain sum of money, often fell far short of their expectations. Under these conditions, an important movement developed in the summer of 1945 against the Ministry of PDR, orchestrated mainly by communists.[21] Many prisoners also had to face familial hardships after such a long absence. Beginning in the summer of 1945, the services of the Ministry of PDR began to worry about the rise in the divorce rate: every week about five hundred petitions for divorce or denials of paternity were filed.[22] However, the most difficult situation remained that of the Jewish deportees, many of whom, being the sole survivor of a family, returned to France to find no one. The trauma of the experience in the concentration camps appeared almost insurmountable and many chose to remain silent, due both to the impossibility of describing the indescribable and to the scant attention that French society seems to have paid them. The return of the victims of the Shoah would thus appear to be 'the event that was most quickly repressed' within French society.[23]

The Legal Purge: A Catharsis both Political and Social

The 'legal purge' lies at the heart of the process whereby a society at war effectuates the return to peace. This phenomenon was not unique to France but there is no doubt that the humiliating defeat of 1940 and the years of occupation that followed, along with the many material hardships, had a very particular effect on the way in which the legal purge took place there.

If a certain unanimity existed at Liberation as to the legitimacy of the purge, significant divisions started to emerge as to the importance it ought to assume. Charles de Gaulle, for instance, hoped at once to mobilise and reunite the whole nation around the reconstruction of the country, while at the same time proposing the idea that France had for the most part resisted between 1940 and 1944. In his eyes the legal purge was therefore meant to set an example while remaining limited in scope. De Gaulle explained to the French in a speech broadcast on 31 December 1944 that 'except for an extremely small number of unfortunates who consciously preferred the triumph of the enemy to the victory of France ... the vast majority of the French people never wanted anything other than the good of the country'.[24] However, this vision of a moderate purge was not universally shared. The communists, especially, wanted a more radical purge, allowing for all those who had been accomplices of Vichy to be eliminated, thereby establishing the basis for a new France, founded upon an authentic social justice.

As it transpired, the purge, while hardly the veritable civil war that it is sometimes made out to have been, was nevertheless a quite important phenomenon in France and was not limited to just a few individual cases. Recent studies have slightly raised the estimate of the total number of incidents of legal purges. More than 350,000 individuals in France, or roughly the equivalent of one Frenchman in 115, may have faced or been threatened with charges.[25] The High Court of Justice responsible for passing sentence on those primarily responsible for the collaboration (the head of state, ministers and general secretaries) adjudicated in 108 cases and handed down 55 sentences, of which 18 were death sentences (three were carried out). The courts of justice organised in each *département* in order to punish individuals who had supported the enemy's aims issued 124,613 judgements against individuals. They pronounced about 7,000 death sentences (767 of which were carried out) and 44,000 prison terms. The civil courts, whose purpose it was to strip the guilty of their citizenship rights, sentenced some 50,000 individuals. Between 22,000 and 28,000 civil servants were also found guilty (dismissed or laid off). Finally, even if they were less visible because of their slow pace and because they extended into the 1950s, economic purges also took place: the committees created in each *département* to confiscate ill-gotten gains examined 124,000 cases between 1945 and 1949. The total number of sentences handed down under the heading of illicit profits obtained through economic collaboration or through the black market under the Occupation amounted to around 150 thousand million francs (68.3 thousand million in confiscations and 78.6 thousand million in fines).[26]

In the end, these figures 'displeased everyone',[27] failing to find a satisfactory middle ground between the advocates of a radical purge and those wishing to limit it to a few high-profile cases. Nevertheless, this purge, in all its facets, played a truly cathartic role in French society. The major trials of those responsible for the collaboration served a primarily political function, whereas the more diffuse purge that took place on the local level, and can be characterised as a 'popular purge', served a social function.

The purge of those responsible for the collaboration was at once the most spectacular and the most widely covered by the media at the time of the Liberation. The most newsworthy trials were those of the leaders of the French state, which were heard before the High Court of Justice, as well as those of the intellectual collaborators (Robert Brasillach, Jean Hérold-Paquis etc.), who had always called for a total alliance with Nazi Germany. While it did not involve any of the individuals responsible for the defeat of 1940, this purge still appeared as a means of finding some explanation for this military disaster, emphasising the fact that France had been betrayed by those who had only been waiting for Nazi Germany's victory in order to take power. The purpose, then, was to punish those who had plunged France into collaborating with Germany but also in a certain way to atone for the defeat of 1940. This is the full meaning of the famous conspiracy theory, which was presented in a very crude manner during the trial of Marshal Pétain. By inaccurately painting the French head of state as a former leader of the Cagoule, an extreme right-wing terrorist organisation, in the 1930s, and by insisting on his ties to Franco and Mussolini before the war, the prosecution endeavoured to establish, without providing any substantial proof, that Pétain had ceaselessly plotted against the Republic before the war.[28] It is also this allegation of treason that explains the importance accorded to the purge of those intellectuals whose ideological commitment in favour of fascism often dated back to the pre-war period.

These journalists were accused of having aided Germany on the eve of the war, thus contributing to the disaster of 1940.[29]

If historians long tended to focus on the upper strata of the purge, today we have a better sense of the manner in which the purge was carried out at the grass-roots level, involving 'ordinary Frenchmen' and having an important social dimension. This 'popular purge',[30] sometimes described as a 'neighbourhood' purge, bears witness to the will of the population to participate in the punishment of traitors. By attacking all those who had profited in some way from the Occupation while the majority had been impoverished, this purge was supposed to serve a second, cathartic function: the point was no longer simply to find scapegoats for the defeat of 1940 but to take revenge for four years of oppression, restrictions and misery.

Although it would appear difficult to quantify due to a lack of statistical data for the whole of the country, this 'popular purge' was indeed a mass phenomenon in France, involving large swathes of French society.[31] It assumed various forms. Summary executions (about eight thousand) do not entirely fall into this category because they were most often carried out by the FTP (*Francs-Tireurs et Partisans*) or FFI (*Forces Françaises de l'Intérieure*), which regarded themselves as a legitimate police force at the time of Liberation, whereas the forms of social exclusion practiced at the local level do. Often, Liberation communities stigmatised collaborators by painting a swastika on their houses or by not allowing them to participate in the victory celebrations. The Liberation also witnessed a wave of denunciations: a huge number of letters of denunciation were sent to the Departmental Committees of Liberation (CDL), local authorities with roots in the Resistance, in an effort to insure that individuals notorious for their immoral or anti-French behaviour be punished. Although ordinarily the CDL should have passed the information on to the competent institutions (courts of justice) so that judicial proceedings could be instigated, there are several cases in which the CDL themselves meted out these punishments (in the form of fines, requisitions and confiscations), thereby largely abusing their authority. For example, at Liberation the CDL of the Haute-Savoie published a list of millionaires against whom sanctions were to be put in place immediately because those individuals had participated in economic collaboration or in the black market.[32]

One of the most characteristic examples of this popular purge was the shaving of women's heads. Most often carried out in public on a village or city square, this represented a form of collective punishment. Although the police force at times have participated in the public head-shavings, either by allowing them to take place or by actively taking part in them, this phenomenon appeared most often to have been spontaneous in nature and to have sprung from popular initiative. About twenty thousand women had their heads shaved in France at Liberation.[33] 'Horizontal collaboration' (having sexual relationships with German soldiers) was the most common accusation but it was not the only one: prostitutes, informants, trafiquants or women who had simply led a life regarded as immoral also had their heads shaved, without necessarily having rubbed shoulders with the occupying forces. This phenomenon of shaving women's heads served an important function of collective atonement by reviving an age-old tradition: that of the adulteress, who used to be led half-naked through the streets of a city upon a horse or a donkey.

Another form of popular purge involved individual attacks with explosives or the machine-gunning of the façades of buildings, targeting the houses of collaborators or presumed collaborators. In the Finistère region, twenty-one acts of aggression of this type were recorded in October and November of 1944, and nineteen others in the Morbihan between June and August of 1945.[34] In the Haute-Savoie, in the single month of January 1945, eleven attacks with explosives took place. Such acts of summary violence continued until the summer of 1945, the main incidents taking place in Chamonix and Megève, which were reputed to be major dens of black-marketeers.[35] Incidences in which money was extorted from farmers suspected of having enriched themselves on the black market or through trading with the Germans were also particularly widespread. The prefects of several *départements* (Savoie, Haute-Loire) reported in 1945 on the existence of organised gangs that, under the pretext of repressing black-market activities, were extorting money from farmers.

In these various guises, this 'popular purge' was a persistent phenomenon that came in several different waves, not just limited to the weeks following the Liberation. After an initial peak during the summer of 1944, a second wave took place during the spring and summer of 1945, when the return of prisoners and deportees rekindled certain resentments. This 'popular purge' witnessed a few resurgences in 1946, suggesting the difficulty many French people experienced in closing the chapter of the war. This phenomenon seems to have been provoked by a legal purge that was seen as too lenient (often, an individual attack took place following a judicial sentence that was viewed as too mild). Several incidents of head-shavings are still recorded at the beginning of 1946, the last one having taken place in a village in the Gard on 14 March 1946.[36] A few residual bombings and farm burnings also took place. In the Côtes-du-Nord, the final act of aggression of this type took place on 14 March 1947 in Saint-Brieux against a brasserie that had just been purchased by an ex-collaborator, recently released from prison.[37]

The question of which individuals were targeted by this 'popular purge' is an interesting one. An important social demand developed so that the purge might allow for all of those who in one way or another might have benefited from the Occupation to be punished. The issue, then, was not only that of punishing political collaborators (who were ultimately but a small minority, as is indicated by low rates of membership in the parties of collaboration) but also all those who had worked for the occupiers, had made 'good profits', or quite simply had exhibited selfish or immoral behaviour. There was thus a significant gap between a legal purge aimed above all at political and ideological collaboration and the purge that the greater part of society desired, and that was supposed to have a much wider reach. In Brittany, for example, half of the letters of denunciation sent by local groups to the public authorities at the Liberation dealt with incidents of economic collaboration or of black market-eering, whereas military and political collaborators made up only about 10 per cent of those denounced.[38] The issue of the black market profiteers occupied an especially important place within this phenomenon of local purges. In small communities, those who had reaped significant benefits from the black market were very often known to everyone. The prefects' reports from the final months of the Occupation describe a true 'social hatred' on the part of consumers, directed at the farmers or shopkeepers suspected of dealing on the black market.[39] At Liberation many people felt that the traffickers deserved punishment just as much as the collaborators themselves.[40]

The construction of a national identity in the immediate post-war period did not rest solely on the image of a people who had resisted, but equally on that of a community that had suffered[41] under the Occupation. All those who had benefited from the country's misfortunes or who had behaved selfishly and amassed large fortunes thanks to the Occupation held a special place in the rogues' gallery of bad Frenchmen: Without necessarily having worked for the Germans, they had inevitably contributed to their effort by aggravating the hardships of daily life and by stoking the flames of division among Frenchmen in their struggle for survival. Certain categories of people judged by public opinion to have enriched themselves between 1940 and 1944 (including farmers, business owners, and all of those who were stigmatised under the label of 'BOF' – short for '*beurre, oeufs, fromage*' – because they had speculated in butter, eggs and cheese) continued for many years to suffer from a bad reputation because of their alleged behaviour under Occupation.[42]

Daily Life still Influenced by the Consequences of the War and of the Occupation

The expression 'the thirty glorious years', popularly utilised in France to refer to the exceptional period of growth from 1945 to 1975,[43] is somewhat flawed, in that it glosses over the numerous economic hardships suffered by the country until the beginning of the 1950s. Many Frenchmen thought that Liberation would mark the return to 'happier days'[44] and the end to all the material suffering that had characterised the Occupation. In most municipalities of liberated France, the departure of the occupier and the arrival of the Allies triggered popular enthusiasm and celebrations (block parties, public dances), which demonstrated an intense desire for life within a wounded society. Under the Occupation, a simplistic logic had reigned: penury and material difficulties were the consequence of the Germans' confiscation of half of France's food resources. However, the narrow focus on these predations led many to overlook the factors that were to delay economic recovery and reconstruction by several years: a dislocated national market, a desperate shortage of raw materials and energy resources, a severely damaged communications infrastructure and outdated industrial equipment. In 1945 numerous bottlenecks plagued the French economy, hindering an immediate resumption of activity. From a base of one hundred in 1938, the industrial production index had fallen to forty-five in May of 1945. With respect to agricultural production, it amounted to only 60 per cent of the pre-war level.[45] There was also the need to recoup the enormous financial losses caused by four years of occupation (the Vichy regime had sent 860 thousand million francs to Germany within the framework of an armistices indemnity and clearing agreements).

Despite the hopes that it had raised, the Liberation did not result in a fundamental turning point in the lives of the French on the level of everyday life. The return to republican legitimacy put an end to the authoritarian and exclusionary politics practiced by Vichy, while the departure of the occupier meant an end to four years of looting and terror. However, an important symbol of the Occupation in the eyes of many – namely the restrictions and the material hardships – persisted for several years. Obviously, a certain number of reforms adopted at Liberation seemed to augur happier days. The Charter of the National Council of the Resistance, adopted in March 1944, appeared to herald the emergence of a more just and egalitarian society.[46] The realization article was the adoption in October 1945 of a plan for social security, allowing for all salaried workers to be insured against the primary social risks (illness, work-related accidents, disability, old age and death). However, even though the foundations of the welfare state were laid in 1945,[47] it would take another five years for French society to truly enter into a new era, that of modernity and of 'better living conditions'. Until the early 1950s, the French continued to feel the consequences of the war and of the Occupation in their daily lives.

One of the most urgent problems concerned housing.[48] The destruction of a significant proportion of the housing stock (cf. above) made it necessary to find housing for the five million citizens of France in 1945 who were homeless or who had been bombed out of their homes. Several temporary measures were adopted. In the bombed-out cities, simple barracks were hastily built in order to provide provisional housing for homeless families. In the most affected *départements*, the prefects asked the municipalities to oblige all those whose homes had been spared to take in at least one homeless family. Such forced communal living arrangements, entered into in the name of national solidarity, were often quite difficult, creating rancour and jealousy among those families compelled to live under the same roof.

The government sometimes intervened when houses were illegally occupied, and some holiday homes were requisitioned, but this often met with strong resistance from the owners, who appealed to the courts of law to denounce such decisions as incompatible with respect for private property.

In the end, all such urgent measures failed to deal with the basic problem: the need to build new housing. They also stirred disappointments and social tensions. For several years, many families had to make do with improvised shelters, wooden huts and concrete prefabs. This housing crisis appeared as one of the dark spots in a reconstruction programme that prioritised infrastructure projects and industry over residential buildings. In 1955 in Dunkerque, eleven thousand people were still being housed in temporary barracks. The first plan, launched in 1947, to spur the reconstruction and modernization of France only addressed six basic aspects (coal, electricity, cement, steel, national transportation networks and farm machinery). It was not until the second plan (1954–1957) that the focus shifted to housing.

Another manifestation of the difficulties of daily life in France after Liberation was the issue of the food supply. Every effort on the part of the Provisional Government to explain to the French that restrictions had to be maintained owing to the significant gap between supply and demand failed (this was one of the main topics addressed by P. Mendes-France in his 'radio chats' while he was economy minister).[49] The policy of rationing was not understood by the general public. Introduced in September 1940, rationing was supposed to ensure, in a climate of scarcity, that all the available products would be equitably distributed. However, as it was introduced a few weeks after the start of the Occupation, the French were convinced that it had been forced upon them by the Germans in order to facilitate the policy of exploitation.[50] Many thought that the ration cards would disappear with the occupying powers. In many French cities, people tore up their ration cards at Liberation.

As a gesture of goodwill, the first post-liberation government did try to increase the rations. The bread ration was raised from 300 to 350 grams per day and that of meat from 90 to 250 grams per week. However, these measures were short-lived due to the poor state of the economy: very quickly, the rationing that people had hoped would soon disappear had to be reinforced. With many products, the official rations even seemed lower in 1945 than they had been under the Occupation. The scarcity of leather and fabric also forced the government to continue rationing clothing and footwear. Restrictions on gas and electricity use were extended.[51] As under the Occupation, the French had a very hard time accessing food, clothing and heat, all of which gave victory a bitter taste. And the continuation of restrictions aroused even more resentment because at Liberation a whole segment of the French population was just discovering the comforts of the consumer society thanks to the presence of US soldiers on French territory. The American military bases, nicknamed 'cigarette camps',[52] were chock full of amenities that French households lacked (bathroom fixtures, furniture, ultra modern radio sets) while the products issued by the Quartermaster's Corps (cigarettes, chocolate bars, Coca Cola etc.) aroused the envy of a French population lacking in everything.

According to various contemporary polls, the availability of food was people's primary concern, far surpassing any interest in the events of that period. In January 1945, 60 per cent of the population felt that the availability of food was worse than during the Occupation.[53] Forty per cent of the French blamed the government for the scarcity while 37 per cent blamed circumstances. This obsession with food availability would last for many years. It was not until 1948 that food worries cease to figure among the main preoccupations of the French, according to the polls.[54] Of all government offices, the least popular by far was the one in charge of food distribution. The public could not understand why rations were not more generous than during the Occupation, and they gave Paul Ramadier, whom General de Gaulle had named as minister of food distribution, the nickname 'Ramadan' or 'Ramadiet'.[55]

Faced with this popular impatience and a protest movement triggered by food scarcities, Ramadier was forced to resign on 30 May 1945. In the autumn of 1945 his successor, Christian Pineau, decided to initiate a return to free trade in certain food staples (poultry, potatoes) and to abolish ration cards for bread. This programme, a political move announced just a few weeks before the legislative elections of October 1945, proved to be largely illusory. The shortfalls in farm production precluded any too-rapid return to free trade and risked further aggravating the strong inflationary tendencies of the post-war period.

That policy was a total failure, forcing Pineau to resign on 21 November 1945. Ration cards for bread were reintroduced on 28 December 1945. Due to the poor wheat harvest, the bread ration was lowered still further, to 300 grams, whereas it had been 350 grams before the experiment with free trade. This 'false move' provoked strong protests. Strikes broke out in Laon, Le Creusot, Nantes and Paris. There was soon looting of bakeries in several cities, and in Tours the prefecture building was assaulted by a crowd intent on burning the new ration cards.[56]

The maintenance of the policy of restrictions and rationing resulted in the continuation of the black market and of a certain number of illicit practices that had been commonplace during the Occupation.[57] The reports of the regional directors of the Economic Control Board, the main office responsible for fighting the black market, suggest that in 1945–1946 it was even larger than in the previous years: 'The black market is flourishing more than ever' (Jura region); 'those who traffic on the black market seem to be earning bigger profits than during the Occupation' (Orléans region).[58] The methods and practices remained the same as under the Occupation. In the countryside, farmers still refused to fulfil the quotas for food distribution to the consumers, preferring to sell their products for higher prices on the black market. In all large cities, the traffickers resumed their activities. In Paris the police prefect stated right after the Liberation: 'The black market, which had seemed to decrease at Liberation, is now reappearing: cigarettes, condensed milk, canned foods, meat … are once again being sold at prohibitive prices.'[59] The police action of 11 September 1945 on the Boulevard de Belleville led to the arrest of about one hundred individuals who were selling various products in a clandestine manner.[60] Beyond the black market in food staples, the trafficking in ration cards also continued and in certain cities veritable auctions of ration cards were held. Thus in their quest for provisions the French continued to resort to various forms of trafficking as well as to the 'DIY system' ('do it yourself').

The maintenance of restrictions and the need to suppress black markets led the provisional government to keep in place the administrative offices set up by Vichy in order to apply and respect the economic regulations (general food distribution, economic controls). This decision to keep in place especially unpopular institutions and control organs triggered a significant protest movement orchestrated by the Communist Party and its associations (notably the Union of French Women). The protest marches and the 'bread marches', which gained in frequency during the winters of 1945 and 1946, were often aimed at the abolition of those offices labelled as 'Vichyist'. In Nantes on 29 January 1945 and in Lyon in February, many thousands of people blockaded the buildings of the Food Distribution Office, demanding its closure and the setting up of committees of housewives responsible for supervising prices and controlling the official food distribution. One of the offices most targeted by this popular anger was the Economic Control Board, whose function it was to punish various violations of the economic regulations. Numerous incidents took place during market inspections and controls of retail shops. On 12 May 1945 in Pontivy (Morbihan), four control officers were threatened with lynching by hundreds of individuals. More than fifty such incidents were recorded in 1945.[61] In a note from 11 July 1945 the general manager of the Economic Control Board wrote: 'A climate of insubordination pervades all strata: the producers, the retailers and consumers, but also the local authorities. We can hear everywhere shouts of "Vichy's henchmen" and "nothing new since Vichy"'.[62]

In 1947, two years after the end of the war, France suffered a very deep social and political crisis (the dismissal of communist ministers from the government in May 1947, growing discontent among the people and a significant strike movement at the end of the year). In its political dimension, this crisis fit into the framework of the start of the Cold War and the Communist Party's move to opposition. But in its social aspect it also appeared as the consequence of persistent material difficulties and of the maintenance of restrictions that had become increasingly resented as time had elapsed since the Liberation. The French despaired of ever seeing the light at the end of the tunnel and began to doubt the purpose of all the sacrifices to which they had consented.

The year 1947 began with a very important wave of protests among certain groups (retailers, craftsmen, small business owners etc.) tired of having to continue implementing regulations (notably price controls) which were seen as the consequences of the Occupation. In January, the government, led by Leon Blum, decided to try to regulate the market by means of a policy of lowering prices in order to halt inflation. A first decrease of 5 per cent was approved in January, then a second one, again of 5 per cent in March, by the new government of Paul Ramadier. It was in fact a return to a policy of price controls.[63] The Economic Control Board was asked to implement 'immediate, massive and repeated controls'.[64] Any and all violations of this policy of lowered prices, even the most insignificant, were to be punished quickly and rigorously. By reinforcing the controls and regulations, this policy triggered a strong protest encouraged especially by the general federation of small and mid-level businesses led by Leon Gingembre. Meetings of retailers were held in many cities. The speakers attacked the government violently and encouraged the audience to rebel against the public authorities. Self-defence committees sprang up all over whose members, alerted as soon as a controller had arrived, used force to prevent any verification. Between April and June of 1947 the general administration of the economic Control Board registered fifty-nine collective actions against some of its agents, actions accompanied by insults and acts of violence.[65] In some cities the premises of the Control Board were invaded by a mob, as happened in Dijon on 21 May when seven thousand persons wrecked its regional offices, setting fire to the files and to the furniture.[66]

This protest movement forced the Ramadier administration to abandon the policy of lowering prices after a few months. But in freeing the prices for most foodstuffs during the summer of 1947 in order to ease people's minds, the government created renewed inflation. At the same time, poor harvests caused new lower levels of the official rations. The bread ration was lowered to 250 grams per day on 1 May 1947 then to 200 grams in August. The shock was considerable because it had reached its lowest point since the introduction of rationing in 1940. The general decline in food availability and the worsening of the restrictions provoked growing discontent among the workers, who were tired of seeing their standard of living drop while they had been making considerable sacrifices since the end of the war within the policy of 'the battle for production'. In the late spring of 1947 bread riots erupted in different regions (sixty-one were documented between May and September 1947)[67] as well as many strike initiatives. The discontent grew again in the early autumn and President Vincent Auriol wrote in his journal on 15 September 1947: 'The authority of the State is being challenged everywhere and violated ... there is a divorce between the public authorities and the rural and urban masses. This sorry state of affairs more closely resembles a true crisis of the regime than a temporary crisis of distrust in the government.' Several prefectures were invaded (according to *L'Annee Politique*, violence might have reached about fifty cities) by rioters asking for better access to food. In October 1947 the government's approval rating with respect to its food distribution policy reached an all-time low, with 92 per cent of the public disapproving of it.[68]

In this context, at the end of 1947 the most widespread wave of strikes during the Fourth Republic erupted.[69] The movement began in Marseilles at the beginning of November, following a rise in tramway fees. This triggered a passengers' strike that soon turned into an uprising. The movement quickly spread and reached the Rhone valley. Many railway stations were occupied and communications were halted. On 15 November it was the miners' turn to strike, and the movement spread to different professional segments (railway personnel, metal workers, textile employees). On 28 November the CGT (Confédération Générale du Travail) organised a central committee to coordinate the operations. Faced with such a broad movement, the government decided to use force by mobilizing the army. After a few sometimes violent encounters between the strikers and the soldiers, the strikes abated in December. Although it was manipulated by the Communist Party for ideological ends, this mobilization of workers can broadly be explained as a reaction to persistent social hardships since Liberation: inflation, the difficulty in accessing food, housing problems, the black market and salaries deemed too low compared to rising prices. The French wanted a permanent end to food ration cards, fabric coupons and queues in front of shops.

Once the hardships of 1947 were over, the economic situation gradually improved. American aid in the form of the Marshall Plan began to arrive while the various bottlenecks slowing reconstruction gradually disappeared (transport, energy). In 1948 farm output regained its pre-war level. By that time, industrial growth had surpassed its 1938 level. This surge in supply allowed those restrictions still in place to be removed. On 1 November 1948 the bread ration card disappeared forever. In 1949 only imported staples (sugar, coffee, rice and oil) were still being rationed. But prices continued to rise. Food shopping ceased to be a problem, giving way to inflation as 'the main preoccupation of the French'. This return to a market economy signalled the end of a decade of scarcities, controls and the regulated distribution of goods. 'Farewell, finally, to the Food Supply Ministry ... an office that no Frenchman will miss', wrote the daily *L'Aurore* in December 1949, when that institution was eliminated.

With the renewal of growth, 'the thirty glorious years' truly began for the French people; the years of restrictions were followed by a period of plenty marked by mass consumption and the creation of new distribution channels.

However, for a whole generation, the decade of restrictions long continued to influence some forms of daily behaviour (the need not to waste food, to recycle used objects) and the habit of hoarding for a rainy day remained important every time a crisis was forecast (such behaviour disturbed the supply channels and created temporary shortfalls during the Korean War and the crises of May 1958 and May 1968).

The Illusion of Power

The great French paradox of the post-war period is that perhaps despite all internal difficulties, the persistence of restrictions, the slow pace of reconstruction and the necessary reliance on foreign aid – especially American – the French still considered their nation to be a Great Power and had not truly appreciated its new status on the international stage. In effect, the French were returning to their pre-war certitude, regaining the idea of the grandeur of France and denying any possibility of decline. According to an IFOP poll in December 1944, 64 per cent of the French thought that France had regained its status as a Great Power. Five months later, this figure had reached 80 per cent. Largely forgetting the four years of collaboration and the switch of alliances made by the Vichy regime in 1940, the French subscribed broadly to the ideas of General de Gaulle: that France now stood among the victorious nations after the war and that it had greatly contributed to its own liberation from Nazi rule, fighting alongside its Anglo-Saxon Allies in the war till the final collapse of Nazi Germany. Some episodes were highlighted, such as the liberation of Paris or the successes of the 1st French Army led by General de Lattre de Tassigny in the battle for Germany.

It is true that within a few months, the rehabilitation of the nation had been spectacular and that France, totally discredited in the eyes of the Allies in the spring of 1944, seemed to have regained its position in 1945 and to have rejoined the concert of the Great Powers. The Provisional Government of the French Republic was recognized de jure by the UK, the USA and the USSR in October 1944. Though France did not participate in the Yalta Conference in February 1945 with the three great architects of the Allied victory (Churchill, Stalin and Roosevelt), it was still given an occupation zone in Germany thanks to Churchill's support. Above all, France obtained a seat on the Security Council of the newly formed UNO, created in San Francisco in June 1945. Finally, de Gaulle was trying to re-establish French sovereignty in all the territories that had formed the Empire prior to the conflict. Many Frenchmen held on to the illusion that the Empire would bring to France a great measure of power as it would prove a true asset in allowing France to compete with larger and more populated powers. This feeling was perfectly summarised by the deputy of the Radical Socialist Party of French Guyana, Gaston Monnerville, on 15 May 1945 before the Consulting Assembly: 'Without its Empire, today France would merely be a liberated country. Thanks to its Empire, France is a victorious nation.'[70]

The years after the war thus maintained and even widened the gap that had existed prior to the conflict between the supposed power and the actual decline of France on the international stage. For several years the French had demonstrated a sort of blindness concerning their growing reliance on outside help, notably American assistance, and also concerning the first signs of the colonial empire breaking up, indicating that far from being an asset it was actually more and more of a burden. They would have to wait almost ten years, until the shock inflicted by the defeat at Dien Bien Phu in May 1954, the start of the Algerian War in November 1954, and/or the diplomatic disaster of the Suez Canal invasion of October 1956, in order to fully appreciate their nation's decline in status on the international stage and to shed their final illusions concerning its power.

Stuck between the dark years of the Occupation and the prosperous period of the 50s and 60s, the late 1940s undeniably constitutes a 'forgotten' period in French history.[71] That period still remains essential in order to understand how the French established the basis for a new France while continuing to experience directly the consequences of the war and the Occupation in their daily lives. And paradoxically, it was only in the early 1950s, when domestic conditions were improving, when the restrictions were disappearing and growth was resuming, that the failures of their foreign and colonial policies finally convinced the French that their nation was no longer a Great Power, a belief they had held on to in the immediate post-war period.

Notes

1. Bruno Cabanes and Guillaume Piketty (eds.), 'Sorties de guerre au XXème siècle', *Histoire@Politique* 3.
2. Jean-Jacques Becker and Serge Berstein, *Victoire et frustrations, 1914–1929* (Paris, 1990).
3. For a historiographical assessment of the First World War and its legacy, see Stéphane Audoin-Rouzeau and Annette Becker, *14–18, Retrouver la Guerre* (Paris, 2000).
4. A few recent publications that deal specifically with the immediate post-war period in France are Philippe Buton, *La Joie douloureuse. La libération de la France* (Brussels, 2004); Fred Kupferman, *Les premiers beaux jours, 1944–1946* (Paris, 1985); *Les collections de L'Histoire*, 28 (July 2005): 'Les drames de l'été 1945: les procès, le deuil, l'espoir'.
5. In 1918, the French wished to close the chapter of the war and return to an idealised society, that of the first decade of the twentieth century known as the *Belle Epoque*.
6. Henry Rousso, *Le syndrome de Vichy de 1944 à nos jours* (Paris, 1987), 19.

7. For a tally of the material consequences of the war, see Jean-Pierre Azéma, 'Faire face aux destructions de la guerre de 1940', in *Reconstructions et modernisation, la France après les ruines* (Paris, 1991), 33–42.

8. The figures are provided by Raymond Aubrac (who directed de-mining operations), *Où la mémoire s'attarde* (Paris, 1996), 179.

9. Danièle Voldmann, *Le déminage de la France après 1945* (Paris, 1998), 111.

10. The total includes 170,000 soldiers killed in combat and 37,000 others who died in prisoner-of-war camps; 150,000 civilian casualties of combat and bombardments; and 250,000 victims of the Nazi politics of repression and deportation.

11. Serge Barcellini and Annette Wieviroka, *Passant souviens-toi! Les lieux du souvenir de la Seconde Guerre mondiale* (Paris, 1995), 18.

12. Marianna Sauber, 'Traces fragiles. Les plaques commémoratives dans les rues de Paris', *Annales ESC* (May/June 1993), 715–728.

13. This was the case for the *Amicale des Pionniers et combattants du Vercors* or the *Anciens des Glières*.

14. Numerous commemorative steles or obelisks were embellished with symbols of the Resistance (the Cross of Lorraine, the V for victory).

15. François Marcot, 'Rites et Pratiques', *La Mémoire des Français, Quarante ans de commémorations de la Seconde Guerre mondiale* (Paris, 1986), 31–39, 32.

16. Antoine Prost, *Les anciens combattants et la société française*, vol. 3 (Paris, 1976), 35–75.

17. Henry Rousso, 'Cet obscur objet du souvenir', *La Mémoire des Français*, ii, 47–61, at 49.

18. Sauber, 'Traces fragiles', ii, 722.

19. Barcellini and Wieviorka, *Passant souviens-toi!*, 15–18.

20. One of the demands of the *Fédération nationale des déportés du travail* created in 1945 was to insist on the heavy price paid by forced labourers (sixty thousand dead, of whom fifteen thousand were executed by the Germans).

21. In June 1945 a demonstration of fifty thousand persons in Paris passed beneath the windows of the PDR minister Henry Frenay, chanting 'food, clothing, shoes' and 'dismiss Frenay'.

22. Cited in Christophe Lewin, *Le retour des prisonniers de guerre français* (Paris, 1986), 60.

23. Rousso, *Le syndrome*, ii, 40.

24. Charles de Gaulle, *Discours et Messages*, vol. 1, (Paris, 1970), 394.

25. Henry Rousso, 'L'épuration en France, une histoire inachevée', *Vingtième siècle* 33 (1992), 78–105, at 90.

26. Centre des Archives Economiques et Financières (CAEF), 30 D 1, note to the minister on illicit profits, 31 July 1950.

27. Rousso, *Le syndrome*, ii, 36.

28. This theme of a plot was evoked from the first days of the trial (Archives Nationales, AN, 3 W 31, stenographic record of the Pétain trial).

29. Pierre Assouline, *L'épuration des intellectuels* (Brussels, 1996). See also Alice Kaplan, *Intelligence avec l'ennemi, le procès Brasillach* (Paris, 2001).

30. This concept of a 'popular purge' is preferable to that of a 'savage purge' one sometimes encounters (Philippe Bourdrel, *L'Epuration sauvage* [Paris, 1988]) because it was framed within certain limits and was often carried out with the complicity of the local authorities.

31. It is above all local approaches that permit us to measure the importance of this phenomenon. Luc Capdevila, *Les Bretons au lendemain de l'Occupation: imaginaire et*

comportement d'une sortie de guerre 1944–1945 (Rennes, 1999); Marc Bergère, *Une société en épuration: épuration vécue et perçue en Maine-et-Loire* (Rennes, 2004).

32. Herbert Lottman, *L'épuration* (Paris, 1986), 205.
33. Fabrice Virgili, *La France virile: des femmes tondues à la Libération* (Paris, 2000), 72.
34. Bergère, *Une société en épuration*, ii, 171–194.
35. CAEF, B 49 525, activity of the brigades, Lyon (1945).
36. Virgili, *La France virile*, ii, 169.
37. Capdevila, *Les Bretons*, ii, 175.
38. Ibid., ii, 250.
39. Fabrice Grenard, *La France du marché noir, 1940–1949* (Paris, 2008), 231.
40. Fabrice Grenard and Kenneth Mouré, 'Traitors, trafiquants and the confiscation of illicit profit in France 1944–1950', *Historical Journal* 51, 4 (2008), 969–990.
41. Luc Capdevila, 'La communauté de souffrance. L'identité nationale à travers l'image du bon Français au lendemain de l'Occupation. L'exemple de la Bretagne', in Stefan Martens and Maurice Vaïsse (eds.), *Frankreich und Deutschland im Krieg (1942–1944). Okkupation, Kollaboration, Resistance* (Bonn, 2000), 831–844.
42. In his novel *Au Bon beurre* (Paris, 1952), Jean Dutourd incorporates all of the clichés in his tale of the rise of a family of shopkeepers thanks to the Occupation.
43. Jean Fourastié, *Les Trente Glorieuses ou la Révolution invisible de 1946 à 1975* (Paris, 1979).
44. Fred Kupferman, *Les Premiers Beaux Jours, 1944–1946* (Paris, 1985).
45. INSEE, *Mouvement économique en France de 1938 à 1948*, (Paris, 1950).
46. Claire Andrieu, *Le Programme commun de la Résistance* (Paris, 1984).
47. Antoine Prost, 'Aux origines de l'Etat Providence', *Les collections de L'Histoire*, 'Les drames de l'été 1945' (no. 28, 2005), 80–85.
48. Danièle Voldman, *La Reconstruction des villes françaises de 1940 à 1954* (L'Harmattan, 1997).
49. See his first broadcast of 11 November 1944, Pierre Mendès France, *Œuvres complètes*, vol. 2 (Paris, 1985), 73
50. Fabrice Grenard, 'Le ravitaillement et ses implications politiques en France 1940–1944', *XXème siècle* 94 (2007), 199–215.
51. On the maintenance of the restrictions, see Dominique Veillon, *Vivre et Survivre en France de 1939 à 1947* (Paris, 1995), 289
52. Elizabeth Coquart, *La France des GI's* (Paris, 2003), 137.
53. Christian Bachelier, 'L'opinion à travers les premiers sondages, 1944–1949', in Dominique Veillon and Jean-Marie Flonneau, *Le temps des restrictions en France 1939–1949* (Paris, 1996), 479–500, at 480.
54. In July 1948, anxieties about accessing food thus dropped from second to sixth place among the preoccupations of the French, behind the question of prices or financial worries (IFOP surveys).
55. Charles de Gaulle, *Mémoires de Guerre*, vol. 3 (Paris, 1954), 124.
56. Jean-Pierre Rioux, *La France de la IVème République*, vol. 1: *1944–1952* (Paris, 1980), 46.
57. Grenard, *La France du marché noir*, 255–262.
58. CAEF, 5 A 28, synopsis of the monthly reports, February 1945.
59. Préfecture de Police de Paris (PP), BA 1810, report of 4 September 1944.
60. PP, BA 1810, dossier 4, note of 12 September 1945.
61. CAEF, B 9860, annual report on economic control activities, 1945.
62. CAEF, B 57 660 (*pelurier* = chronological file, 1945).

63. On the modalities of this policy, see Michel-Pierre Chélini, *Inflation, Etat et opinion en France de 1944 à 1952* (Paris, 1998), 393–400.

64. CAEF, B 9860, annual report on the Economic Control Board for the year 1947, 11.

65. Ibid., 12–13.

66. CAEF, 30 D 2, Côte d'Or, demonstration in Dijon against the Economic Control Board, 21 May 1947.

67. Danielle Tartakowsky, 'Manifester pour le pain, novembre 1940–octobre 1947', in Veillon and Flonneau (eds.), *Le temps des restrictions*, 465–478, at 475.

68. IFOP, state of mind of the French people, October 1947.

69. On the strikes of autumn 1947, see Robert Mencherini, *Guerre froide, grèves rouges: les grèves insurrectionnelles de 1947–1948* (Paris, 1998).

70. Cited by Maurice Vaïsse, 'Le rêve de la grandeur', in *L'Histoire, Les drames de l'été 1945*, 86–90, at 90.

71. Thus Steven Kaplan considers the period between 1945 and the early 1950s 'the forgotten years' (S. L. Kaplan, *Le pain maudit, retour sur la France des années oubliées* [Paris, 2008]).

15

Great Britain

Remembering a Just War (1945–1950)[1]

Toby Haggith

It is widely accepted that the British memory of the Second World War is over-whelmingly positive, even that it is a source of great pride for the majority of the people. Historians and commentators have referred to the war, and with-out irony, as 'just' or 'good' and the role of the British Army in liberating occu-pied Europe as 'a noble crusade'.[2] This contention is supported by the evidence of popular culture where nostalgic, heroic representations of the war abound and, according to one cliché, no Sunday afternoon in the family home is com-plete without the ritual viewing of a British war film on the television.[3] At times of crisis the British have often looked nostalgically back on the war and its victorious end as bringing some solace and sense of security.[4]

Frustration with Britain's relative decline since the end of the Second World War has led some historians to argue that victory and positive memories of the war were a disaster for the British, inducing a false pride that encouraged the post-war government to embark on an ambitious and expensive foreign policy to maintain the nation's super-power status alongside the USA and to defend what was seen as a resurgent British Empire.[5] Correlli Barnett, who is the most strident and withering of these critics, sees the victory celebrations as the final massive self-administered dose in a course of seductive opiates, by which the British had continued to ignore the need for reform of the nation's antiquated and uncompetitive social and economic structure.[6] By contrast these detrac-tors have much admiration for the response of Britain's continental neigh-bours to the experience of defeat, occupation and devastation, which served, in the business jargon favoured by Barnett, as a 'bottom line under the past' encouraging political leaders to put into action a sophisticated programme of industrial modernisation at home and economic and political integration with their neighbours via the EEC.[7]

However, most social and political historians examining the period 1945–50 have been less concerned with how the people remembered their experiences of the war, than with their attitudes to the social and political changes being initiated by the Labour Government.[8] As Barry Turner and Tony Renell put it: 'Historical accounts of 1945 leap effortlessly from the Berlin bunker and VE Day jubilations to rejection of Churchill and the Tories at the General Election two months later and on to the meatier problems of Attlee's Labour Government and the birth of the Welfare State.'[9]

Looking beyond 1950, Mark Connelly and Martin Shaw believe that the memory of the war and the 1945 victory has evolved into a powerful cultural and political force in British society. Connelly argues that a 'continuing appetite for major player status' in the international arena, despite the impracticalities of maintaining this role, has been underpinned by a mythologised memory of the war. Shaw notes that Britain's share in the 1945 victory was the culmination of a series of military victories stretching over more than a century, a factor which, combined with the uniquely fortunate experience of being threatened and bombed, but never occupied, has led to a more positive view of war than that held by other nations.[10] Shaw gives two examples of the importance of this syndrome in recent history, firstly, when it was mobilised by Margaret Thatcher to win support for her response to the Argentine invasion of the Falklands Islands, and secondly, its role in shaping the attitudes of ordinary people to Saddam Hussein and the First Gulf War.[11] As is evident from the on-going national debate about the justification of the war in Iraq, the memory of the Second World War continues to be invoked by those who support the war as providing the 'lesson from history' that one must take a strong line against military dictators.

However, as this chapter will argue, the nature of the British memory of the war today should not be assumed to stand for the whole era. Focussing on the years 1945–50 and concentrating on evidence demonstrating the attitudes of ordinary Britons, this chapter will question the degree to which the memory of the war in its immediate aftermath was such a preoccupation; for most people, memories of the war were not that it was 'just' or 'good', just bloody awful, or perhaps just relief that it was over. Secondly, I also argue that far from remembering the war, civilians and ex-service personnel actively sought to forget it. Thirdly, this study contradicts the assumption that Britain's relatively light entanglement with war (when compared with the other countries involved) made the people temperamentally more war-like and willing to support military solutions to intractable problems of foreign affairs.

Celebrating the End of the War

Correlli Barnett asserts that during the victory celebrations the mass of British people looked back with a boastful pride on their achievements.[12] However, closer analysis of the numerous reflective commentaries published at the war's end, shows that, along with pride and self-congratulation, there was nearly always full acknowledgment of how narrow had been Britain's escape from the abyss (and thus how much was owed to its allies) and also a realistic note of caution about the future.

The immediate, private reactions of many ordinary Britons to the end of the war in Europe were altogether more prosaic and non-committal. Among private records it is unusual to find people actively reflecting on the meaning of the war in the summer of 1945. Partly this is because the protracted ending of the Second World War made it difficult to take stock. For servicemen in the Far East or those about to be sent there, VE Day was fairly meaningless. This also explains why civilians frequently expressed feelings of the celebrations on VE Day as being bitter-sweet and tinged with anxiety about the continuing war in the Far East against the Japanese. As one ex-serviceman explained: 'The war against Japan was not yet over: we had to remind ourselves constantly of that. It was the big fly in the ointment, the bitter difference between 1918 and 1945. It was a peace without a peace.'[13] And in contrast to the general perception of VE Day, shaped by newsreel and amateur film, of massed crowds cheering, dancing and partying in the streets of British cities, it seems that exhaustion and hunger often precluded riotous celebrations. Rose Cottrell, a young woman who lived in Bromley, sending an account of VE Day to her sister in Switzerland, poignantly described the street celebrations as 'a gently moving scene, just a ripple', and confessed that: 'We didn't go to town because to be perfectly frank no one seems to have the energy to do anything except to sit around. After all nearly six years on short rations must have their effect and so no one nowadays has much energy. We have enough to get on with the daily grind, and to keep on gently, but we haven't enough to get boisterous or to spare for rushing about.'[14] Food was such a preoccupation that it left little room for reflection on current affairs. Retired electrical engineer Herbert Brush, who spent some of 7 May at the Summer Exhibition at the Royal Academy, made no reference to the excitement and much-leaked ending of the war in Europe, but did, however, record that the three paintings that held his attention for more than five seconds were *Girl Resting* by A. R. Middleton, *Snow in Northumbria* by Henry Moore and *Still Life* by Frederick Elwell, which showed a 'cold ham with a nice wide cut in the middle showing the inside lean part, and a pork pie with a couple of bottles of sprit alongside. It made me feel hungry, and I remembered that I had a sausage roll in my pocket, but I could not eat a sausage roll in the Royal Academy'.[15]

Although the war against the Japanese had been the cause of such worry, when VJ Day eventually came, the celebrations were low-key. Apart from the fact that peace in Europe had removed the direct threat to British civilians and the dismantling of some of the obvious indicators of war, the nation had run out of energy and resources for more partying and excitement. For Leonard

Muddeman VJ Day was a 'complete anti-climax', a mood reinforced by the difficulty he and a fellow soldier had in celebrating. As beer was in short supply in the district where they were stationed, they had gone to catch a bus to a hotel where it was hoped there would be sufficient stocks of booze – but the bus never came and they went back to barracks without having had a single drink to toast the occasion.[16]

Uninhibited rejoicing was further hampered by the Demobilisation Scheme, which meant that most personnel were released on the basis of age and length of service. As a result VE and VJ Day did not mean the end of the war for hundreds of thousands of men and women. Joan Jackson, whose husband was serving in the army in Germany and would not come home until 1946, wrote: 'The war wasn't over for me. VE Day wasn't a fabulous celebration because my man was still in uniform. The peace was very fragile. I was working in Solihull; I would cycle to work to take my mind off it. At night in my room it would hit me. It was a pretty fractious time.'[17] The festivities to mark the end of the war were particularly hollow and painful for those who had lost a lover or relative. For munitions worker Louise White, 7 May 1945 was just another day and another week (as she had dutifully recorded each Monday in her diary for the previous ninety-six weeks) since her husband Jack had been reported missing in an air raid over Krefeld in Germany: 'Every one in suspense. I am not bothered. Worked over. At 9.0 the news was given that it was over in Germany & tomorrow will be V.E.Day. At this moment someone is singing "None but the Weary Heart". How appropriate for me just now. I feel so miserable.'[18] There was also the difficulty of making sense of the war so close to its end. Even as late as October 1945, a reviewer of an exhibition on War Art in the Royal Academy explained: 'It is impossible to be fair and detached in judging a show like this. The war was a ghastly boredom and these pictures very faithfully record ghastliness and boredom on a global scale. In fifty years time it may perhaps be exciting to have these records before one, but it is impossible to be just as critical, far less excited at present.'[19]

A Just War, a Good War

Naturally enough there was great pride in what had been achieved, but this did not lead to complacency or naive confidence about Britain's prospects for the future. Although Rose Cottrell and Mrs Britton did not support the same political parties, they were both realistic about the great problems now facing the world; as Mrs Britton put it, 'It is just possible that the most costly item of the war will be the peace.'[20] While Cottrell, over a month before VE Day, predicted, 'One day it will all be finished thank goodness, Japan as well, but I think people who think they can just sit back into peacefulness will have an unpleasant surprise. There is hard work ahead for generations, to say nothing of the backbiting and quarrelling.'[21]

Moreover, the recent war was not viewed in isolation but in the context of and in comparison with the First World War and its aftermath. Although Mr and Mrs Britton were hopeful that under the new Labour Government a 'Brighter Britain' would emerge, their optimism was tempered by memories of the inter-war years: 'The outcome of the last war was misery and poverty for untold millions. If we can't do better this time with the bitter experience which is the best teacher, then we shall deserve to be wiped off the face of the earth by the atomic power which is now in the hands of mankind.'[22] Similarly, when in March 1946 Rose Cottrell had sketched out for her sister the scenario for the anticipated war with Russia, she had noted with irony: 'Never mind, it will all be over by 1953.'[23] This knowing re-working of the 1914 phrase (repeated by some in 1939): 'It will all be over by Christmas', reveals the cynicism with which many greeted the peace. 'The war to end all wars', being another of the phrases associated with the First World War, which was frequently coined ironically in the summer of 1945 to instil a sense of realism in the revellers.[24]

The British were proud of what their armed forces had achieved, but few overlooked the fact that victory would not have been possible without the considerable assistance of their allies the Americans and especially the Soviets. Many ordinary people, who had no connection to the communist party, made red flags, some with the hammer and sickle emblem, which were much in evidence during the victory celebrations. And a year later spectators watching the Victory Parade in London, were 'hopeful' that the Russians would be represented among the units marching past.[25]

A Noble Crusade

In the spring of 1945, the discovery of the concentration camps, and especially Bergen-Belsen, had a great impact on the British, convincing a previously sceptical public of the existence of the camps and of the atrocities committed against the inmates. For those involved in freeing and helping the beleaguered inmates, there was a realisation that the war had a powerful moral dimension, a message that was amplified in the press and by Allied propagandists.[26] But the impact of the camps on the public conscience was not long-lasting and soon, like other aspects of the memory of the war, it was forgotten. By 1948, the people had become bored of the war crimes trials at Nuremberg and were even beginning to react against what was seen as 'dragging out' the retribution against the German leaders.[27] Sympathy for the Jewish plight in the concentration camps also seemed short-lived. The actions of Jewish terrorists against

British forces in Palestine in 1946 led, as will be seen, to a wave of virulent antisemitism in the UK. Not surprisingly, the story of the camps and of the atrocities committed in occupied Europe – which only indirectly related to the British experience – did not become a key element in the national memory. When in the 1950s British popular culture began to nostalgically explore the Second World War in novels and films, it was the experience of British soldiers, airmen and sailors that provided the source material. The Jewish experience in occupied Europe was barely touched on.[28] And until the late 1970s the subject 'was considered well to the margins' of the Imperial War Museum's terms of reference and it was not until 1989 that the Holocaust was directly covered in the public galleries.[29]

A Just War at Home

Even for those who were not prone to anti-semitism and for whom Britain's contribution to the liberation of the concentration camps remained a source of pride, the most important meaning of the war was whether the British people would be justly rewarded for all their efforts and sacrifices over the previous six years. But as the great problems, predicted by Mrs Britton and Rose Cottrell, began to surface, these just rewards seemed unlikely to be delivered. By the end of 1946 over four million men and women had been demobilised, and had to be accommodated in a decaying national housing stock depleted by the war. To relieve the immediate national crisis it was estimated that 2.5 million homes were required.[30] But a shortage of skilled labour and building materials slowed up the government's efforts and by the autumn of 1946 only 210,000 families had been re-housed.[31] In desperation, many of the homeless were driven to squat in vacant houses or military sites and airfields, with an estimated forty thousand ex-servicemen and their families taking over disused military bases in the summer of 1946.[32] Peace also brought no respite to the strictures of wartime feeding. On the eve of VJ Day, the population was warned that they could expect no easing of food rationing over the forthcoming winter and that the latest issue of coupons for the clothes ration would have to last longer than previously.

By the end of 1945 people were so fed up with the war and all it had imposed upon their lives, that there were clear signs of an effort to forget the past six years. For instance, a trade assessment of book-buying tastes among Christmas shoppers in London and Edinburgh concluded that 'war books were clearly not in demand'.[33] Christina Foyle, of the famous Foyles Bookshop in Charing Cross Road, reported that not only were war books 'virtually unsellable', but that even gardening enthusiasts were 'turning away from austerity and were buying books on flowers rather than on vegetables'.[34] This trend continued until Christmas 1949, with booksellers noticing that, in addition to novels or memoirs about the war, technical books connected with the war and the cheaply produced wartime publications could not be sold.[35]

Victory Day

In this climate, efforts by the State to promote remembrance of the war were treated with indifference and in some cases cynicism. This attitude first became apparent with the lack of celebration with which the population marked the public holiday held to coincide with the first anniversary of VE Day, but became more pronounced on 8 June 1946, the day assigned for the official victory celebrations.[36]

In view of the worsening bread situation, Mass Observer B. Charles thought: 'The idea of having any "Victory" celebration is simply farcical.'[37] Reg Groves, a script-writer for Ministry of Information films, also had practical objections to the idea of imposing another victory celebration on the capital, making travel even more arduous, exhausting the already meagre supply of cigarettes and driving the hapless Londoners from their pubs and cafes.[38] The situation was not helped by the fact that the government had unwisely selected the Saturday of a bank holiday weekend for the celebrations which meant that housewives 'already sufficiently harassed by rationing problems and by the difficulties occasioned at the weekend to secure the essentials to restock the larder' would have to start shopping a day earlier.[39]

An examination of attitudes around the UK to the official Victory Day shows that, as well as concerns about the difficulty of provisioning the junket, there was a feeling that it was wrong to squander resources during such hard times and that the memory of the war was too close and painful for rejoicing. For example, although some towns and villages in the Lancaster area did take part in the festivities on the 8 June, the city itself 'stood aloof', the editor of the *Lancaster Guardian* noting that, 'there was no general rejoicing such as characterised the celebrations of peace after the 1914–18 war.'[40] This pattern was repeated across the nation, with the councils of Birmingham, Brighton, Liverpool and Manchester all deciding against official celebrations. The assessment of *The Times* correspondent covering Lancashire was that many of the people he had spoken to agreed with their own local leaders that 'official celebrations are ill-timed, hollow, unspontaneous', although some also regretted this decision.[41] In the coastal and country districts of north Norfolk, covered by the *Norfolk Chronicle*, there was also a marked level of non-participation, with thirteen out of the twenty-five towns and villages covered deciding that 'the times are too grim for joy-making, and have either declined to hold celebrations, or have postponed them.'[42]

Battle Memories and a Contested Meaning of the War

There is also evidence that the memory of the war was itself being contested, between those who favoured dwelling on the military aspects and an interpretation in which it was the civilians' contribution that was emphasised. As in 1919, the centrepiece of Victory Day was a parade in London with military and auxiliary units of the UK and Empire forces filing past the King and international dignitaries at the 'saluting base' on the Mall. There was also a flypast of military aviation, children's entertainments in the Royal Parks and in the evening a fireworks and light display along the Thames. For some the parade and fly-past conjured up powerful memories of hard-won British military victories, such as the Battle of Britain, the Battle of the Atlantic and the Normandy campaign.[43] Others like the Christian-socialist Reg Groves detested the militarism and imperial pomp of the spectacle:

> Some of us might suggest a better procession – a march of those who have paid or are paying the price of war. The dead we cannot put in line and march past the 'saluting base'. But their widows, orphans and bereaved parents could come in their stead, and next to them those crippled by war – the maimed, the legless, the armless, the witless, the blind; those injured by bullet, shell, bomb. ... Let the generals, admirals, commanders, and political leaders salute the lot and then go off to their speeches and plan their new wars.[44]

While military and nationalistic elements were certainly prominent, the feature that distinguished the 1946 parade from that of 1919 was the space in the procession given over to the many civil defence and non-military units that had served on the home front, with the Home Guard, land girls, factory workers, miners and many others following the Army, much to the delight of the spectators. This reflected the wide acknowledged importance of the home front to the war effort and also the unprecedented danger to which civilians had been put, a factor that had led Churchill to order the striking of a special Defence Medal to be awarded to those who had served in 'non-operational areas subject to air attack or closely threatened'. As *The Times* noticed, there would be few among the spectators of London's Victory Parade who would not feel that they also 'qualified by service' for a place in the parade if there was room: 'That indeed is what separates this from the Victory celebrations of earlier wars. Once the civilian part of the nation saluted the fighting men as the sole victors: now the whole people does honour to the whole.'[45]

However while most did not take such an extreme position as Reg Groves, there were still those who felt that the official celebrations had given insufficient recognition to the role of ordinary civilians in the great victory. The *Daily Mirror* devoted a whole page of its coverage of the parade to a poem called 'Salute to the People' written by Jack Hulbert, which Cicely Courtneidge had read during the BBC Victory Day variety programme. The poem salutes Ada Smith, the cleaning lady and the myriad un-recognised heroes of the home front such as milkmen, teachers, typists, lorry drivers, housewives, telephonists, chorus girls – all of whom had carried on their jobs under great duress and without a grumble. 'They are unimportant people and they're not in the parade. And they didn't wear the badges and they didn't have the braid.'[46]

Political reactionaries such as Evelyn Waugh found this acknowledgment of the 'people's war' most distasteful, as he recorded in his diary:

> Victory Day. At home, having refused an invitation from the *Empire News* to report on a masquerade which Mr Attlee is organising in London. He is driving round in a carriage with Churchill behind the Royal Family at the head of a procession of Brazilians, Mexicans, Egyptians, Naafi waitresses and assorted Negroes claiming that they won the war. It has rained most of the day. I hope it rained hard in London and soaked Attlee.[47]

Nationally, the majority of those who participated in the Victory Day tended towards Jack Hulbert's view, with the militaristic and triumphalist aspects of the victory parades in London and the naval towns of Portsmouth, Southampton and Plymouth, being overshadowed by an inclusive celebration in which the civilians shared and often dominated the proceedings. For example, in Oxford and Ipswich it was decided that while 'pageantry and pomp' along the lines of a military parade was not appropriate, provision should be made for children's entertainments or sports in the parks. This focus on the civilians and on giving the children a really good time was even more marked in the smaller towns and villages. A typical programme was that held in Burnham Thorpe in Norfolk, which began with a united service in the Parish church, followed by a fancy dress parade, sports and tea. Field Dalling and Saxlingham, in common with many other communities, also had a 'social' in the evening with dancing and singing.

Sometimes, as in the villages around Lancaster, direct reference would be made to the armed forces, with the parade, following the church service of thanksgiving, involving units of newly demobilised men and British Legionnaires, or ex-servicemen would be pitted against another team in the tug of war. However, the ex-servicemen shared the 'limelight' with other sections of the community and in general the military and nationalistic aspects of the programme did not dominate. For example, in Low Bentham the fancy dress parade was led by a 'Victory Queen drawn on a gaily decorated vehicle drawn by twelve representatives of the forces and Home Front and led by the band'.[48] These were celebrations of thanksgiving, inward-looking events, in which the community celebrated among itself. In many ways the programmes were much more like a country fair or one of the calendar celebrations associated with spring or harvest.

After Victory Day the Second World War quickly faded from public memory. According to a survey, conducted for this chapter, of four provincial British papers printed during the period 1946–50, anniversaries marking key dates in the Second World War were never observed publicly or commemorated in any formal fashion.[49] The four papers chosen (*Norfolk Chronicle, Lancaster Guardian*, the *Orcadian* and *Saffron Walden Weekly News*) represent vastly different areas of the UK and also included two locations near operational military bases (Debden Airfield – Saffron Walden; Royal Naval harbour at Scapa Flow-Orkney), and where we might expect to find more observance of these anniversaries. Following a decision by the government and endorsed by the British Legion, public or organised activities to remember the Second World War were simply absorbed into the usual Armistice Day commemorations on the 11 November. Local journalists were so preoccupied with the problems of 'austerity Britain' that there was no space for reflection. When a journalist in Saffron Walden did happen to notice the historical significance of 8 May 1947, it merely prompted the writing of a cynical and ironic piece about the dashed hopes of 1945.[50]

By 1948, the lack of public observance of the VE Day anniversary was becoming so marked as to prompt comment from the *Daily Mirror* columnist William Connor, who wrote under the pseudonym *Cassandra*:

> I've been lying in the bushes for some time to see if anybody would spot the third anniversary of VE Day. It tiptoed by, last Saturday, and if anybody saw it they've been keeping it dark for five whole days now. On this tremendous martial anniversary, Bradman was beating up another century at the Oval, Shinwell was steadfastly cussing the Tories at Taunton, a ridge of high pressure was extending south-westwards towards Hereford and 30,000 bees broke loose from a packing case on No.1 platform at East Croydon. VE Day slipped by like the faint shadow of a slim trout darting across a deep pool.[51]

Sustaining the Memory of the War: Ex-Servicemen and Women

Not surprisingly, ex-servicemen were often disillusioned with the situation they found when they returned home; which meant that they were ambivalent about the war and their service. The local press, the *British Legion* journal and private documents are full of protests from ex-servicemen about their poor treatment, especially in terms of housing. A Burma veteran stuck with his in-laws wrote an angry letter to the *Saffron Walden Weekly News* requesting that the points system for allocating council housing be revised, in order that the Labour government might live up to its promise of providing 'homes for heroes'.[52]

Another major grievance was the level of war pensions. Throughout the war, the pensions for those wounded in service was actually much lower than the rates awarded to victims of the 1914–18 war. It was not until 1946–47, and as a result of lobbying by the British Legion, that Second World War veterans achieved parity. For example, the pension for those incapacitated by the war (with 100 per cent disability) was finally increased in 1946 to forty-five shillings, a figure only marginally higher than that available to First World War veterans (forty shillings). Even so, the rates were still low and did not take into consideration rises in the cost of living since the end of the First World War.[53] In fact, it was calculated that whereas the State's obligations to its war pensioners in 1919 had accounted for 3.6 per cent of the national budget, in 1949 it accounted for less than half of this amount.[54] But the deal offered to demobilised Britons was in general inferior to that offered to ex-servicemen of Commonwealth nations, with New Zealanders receiving the most generous recompense for their service.[55]

Here is a poem written by an ex-servicemen commenting on his lot:

If you've got your civvy suit on
And the world looks good to you;
If you're full of rum and butter
And you never have to queue;

If the shops have all you ask for
And there's service with a smile;
If your petrol is unrationed
And you need not walk a mile;

If there's lots of smoke and toffee
And the beer is flowing free;
If you've bought a modern villa
With your war gratuity;

If there's coal inside your cellar
And your married life's begun
In a home that's newly furnished…
You're in the U.S.A. my son!!

M. Brand, London S.W.17.[56]

Many were so disillusioned with Britain and the 'rewards' offered for their services, that they decided to 'jump ship' – often literally.[57] Between 1946 and 1949, 1.5 million young men and women emigrated to Australia, Canada, New Zealand and Rhodesia. They were joined by a further fifty-seven thousand war brides, who mainly headed for North America. Eight thousand servicemen and two hundred servicewomen did not even bother to come home first, preferring to be demobilised overseas.[58] A Gallup survey in 1949 found that 42 per cent of the British population (58 per cent of those under age thirty) said they would emigrate if possible.[59]

Reluctant Heroes

Those veterans who remained at home were not, for a variety of reasons, that good at sustaining the memory of the war. The first problem was that, unlike the First World War, due to the Blitz it was widely felt that civilians had been in as much danger as the men on active service. Moreover, the privations of life on the home front meant that there was often resentment towards the bronzed, well-fed ex-servicemen when they got home. Far from being treated like returning heroes, many men felt a wave of indifference and even hostility when they strode into their local pub.[60] One anonymous veteran of the Manchester Regiment, imparting advice to those about to 'Return to Civvy Street', warned: 'One final word – don't try and tell civilians about your experiences, even if they ask you. The two of you are talking and thinking a different language, metaphorically, and never the twain shall meet. They are as convinced as you are that they had a hard war, and you've got to live with them from now on, so why argue.'[61]

Secondly, there were those servicemen whose wartime experiences had been so traumatic that they would not discuss them when they got home. This was particularly the case for the men who had spent many years as prisoners of the Japanese and had experienced and witnessed diabolical acts of cruelty from their captors. On the journey home after liberation from the prisoner-of-war camps on the island of Java, many men made a pact not to discuss their experiences with family or friends, only with the authorities. This code of silence 'was born out of consideration for the sensibilities of those close to them, as well as the notion that they would not be believed'.[62]

Some men were so traumatised by their wartime experiences that they were unable to return to normal life. In June 1948 it was reported that 143,800 ex-servicemen and women were suffering from psycho-neurosis, more commonly known today as post-traumatic stress disorder. However, government provision to treat these cases was inadequate, with only 41,300 qualifying for pensions and treatment.[63] As these figures suggest, large numbers of ex-servicemen and women were effectively trying to cope with their illness at home. It is not surprising that there are so many recollections by family members of ex-servicemen being taciturn, tense, irascible and also violent. Maureen Curtis's father had been a POW near Munich where he had been brutalised by the guards: 'When my father returned, he couldn't talk about what had happened to him and would spend days staring at the wall, unable to speak. These days he would have had counselling, of course. My mother didn't know how to cope with him and he would fly into violent rages for nothing. At sixteen years old I couldn't understand why he was suffering from the war.'[64] The immensity of their recent experiences or just the difficulty of adjusting to civilian life meant that many men were not just reluctant to share the experiences of the war with family and colleagues, they seemed to have very little to say about anything. In a piece in the *British Legion* journal entitled 'What are they like at Home?', there was a report of a visit to the homes of two recently demobilised ex-servicemen (a sailor, and a soldier who had spent most of the war as a POW). In both cases, the woman of the house noticed an uncharacteristic introspection in the man. 'The trouble is they don't say much', said the mother of the sailor, and she remarked on a new 'reserve' in his personality, and 'that almost stubborn shyness which refused to talk about India and of his adventures at sea.' Husband Ted, 'seemed rather listless, not wanted to do much, and would stand around in the small garden, once his pride, and just look at it or poke around here and there.'[65]

Returning Ex-Servicemen and Family Life

Even for those men who returned home relatively undamaged there was inevitably a difficult period while the family unit adjusted to the introduction of a new parent. This was frequently a confusing time for children who resented the presence of this unfamiliar large male figure who had taken up occupation in mother's bed.[66] Many children had little or no memory of their father and thus, as well as having to share mother's love, they had to get to know a stranger who was expecting affection as well as imposing discipline – neither of which they felt he had a right to demand. For the fathers these times were very distressing, experiencing rejection just at the point when they expected, and most needed, cherishing. Inevitably many of the men made a mess of fathering. Returning ex-servicemen who had spent a long period away from home had forgotten or simply never had the opportunity to learn parenting skills, and so they frequently tried to impose military-style discipline on their families.[67]

Oral history anthologies about this subject are full of accounts from each member of the triangle involved in this painful period of adjustment; sadly many war babies and returning fathers were never able to reconcile these differences.[68] The strife in the family created by the war worked against an environment in which the war was remembered positively. For mothers the dislocation wrought on family life by the extended absence of a husband and father, meant that the memory of the war had negative associations. One woman who was a child during the war, remembered her mother 'burning all my father's photographs of him in uniform. It was as if she didn't want to be reminded of him in the Army. It was not a happy time for us when he returned.'[69] As Turner and Rennell point out, men struggling to rebuild family life and win acceptance from their estranged children and wives realised that the telling of war stories would not help them to 'reintegrate with their families'.[70] Not that these stories were necessarily ones that ex-servicemen wanted to tell the children, as accounts of real warfare could be shocking even for boys who could identify any plane in the sky and had treasure troves of shrapnel. I vividly remember an acquaintance recalling how as a small boy, he had asked an uncle who had just got back from the war, how many Germans he had killed. Expecting him to say two, perhaps three, he was genuinely shocked and frightened when the man nonchalantly replied: 'Oh, about ten.' British Army cameraman Mike Lewis only ever imparted amusing anecdotes of the war to his children; it was not until they were adults that they discovered, independently, that their father had been part of the small team that had recorded the hellish scenes at the liberation of Bergen-Belsen concentration camp.[71]

The problems that the war had created for the parents' relationship, regardless of the children, was also a factor that worked against a positive remembrance of the war. Adulterous affairs were extremely common, for both partners; in half of all divorces in the post-war years, adultery was cited as the grounds for the dissolution of the marriage. Even for those couples who managed to weather the storm of an affair, the war must have remained an uncomfortable topic for discussion, even a taboo, as it would forever be associated with the rival and the indiscretion, by many seen as more inexcusable because the faithlessness had occurred when, in the idealised scenario, true lovers waited.

A high proportion of marriages did not survive these strains. In 1938 the number of petitions for divorce in England and Wales was 9,970; by 1945 this had risen to 24,857 and to 47,041 by 1947.[72] Understandably many looked back on the war as an unwelcome and de-stabilising episode in marriages, the cause of irreconcilable differences in what may have been promising relationships. Children, too, blamed the war for the destructive affect it had on family life and especially on the fractious relationships with their fathers.[73]

All these factors meant that the families of ex-servicemen were often comparatively ignorant on the subject of their fathers' war, and indeed what the war was about. Discussions with the children of men who served in the Second World War and who have come to the Imperial War Museum to research their fathers' military histories, invariably reveal that they rarely if ever talked about their wartime experiences.

Reluctance to join Ex-Servicemen's Associations

Aside from the pressures on men to suppress the memory of the war in the domestic sphere, there was also a great desire among ex-servicemen and women to move on from the war and forge a life in the civilian world. In this mood, veterans quickly turned their back on military experiences and associations. As Joyce Hampson recalled: 'My husband Tom was demobilised in October

1946 and he went back to work for his old employer and settled down to civvy street well, with no hang ups; he kept in touch with a few of his old army mates, but would never even join a Christmas club after that.' Lack of interest in maintaining any association with the war was reflected in the difficulty experienced by the old comrades associations in attracting veterans from the Second World War and the relatively small expansion in the membership of the British Legion in the post-war era. After reaching a peak of 1,234,835 in 1948, Legion membership began to decline, falling to 847,629 by 1954.[74] Even this peak was not an impressive figure, given that it included around 400,000 members who were veterans of the First World War. It was also way below the 5 million plus members that the organisation had optimistically expected at the end of the war.[75] Apart from the fact that the small size of the Legion tended to limit its effectiveness in influencing public opinion and in bringing political pressure to bear to support its causes, such as raising war pensions, the modest size of the Legion had the affect of making the memory of the war more muted.

The decline in membership led to much soul-searching and discussion about the best methods of attracting and retaining younger members who had served in the Second World War. One obvious reason for the drop-off in membership was that as young, recently demobilised men became more settled, got married and started their own families, they had less time and inclination to become involved in the Legion, a pattern that had also been observed in the 1920s; with an upturn in membership after 1929, once the veterans' responsibilities had lessened.[76] As one legionnaire pointed out, 'younger members rather grudge giving their time when there are so many counter-attractions outside the Legion'.[77] Others explained that quite simply, 'Men don't join the Legion primarily for the same reason that they don't join the Territorials, because they are sick of everything connected with the war service'.[78]

The Legion was also not in tune with the outlook of a less deferential generation, dominated as it was by veterans of previous wars and run on hierarchical military lines. One younger member explained that ex-servicemen he knew were put off joining because they believed the Legion to be run by ex-officers.[79] The organisation's conservative and non-party political stance was also frustrating to those younger men who had voted Labour at the end of the war with a commitment to social change. In 1945 a Legion member from the West Country, who was interested in politics, had stood for election to the local parish and trades councils. He was duly elected and consequently received some publicity in the local press. The chairman of his local Legion took objection to these other activities and suggested the member should give them up. Rather than give up politics, the member left the Legion, determined never 'to have anything to do with the Legion now or in the future'.[80]

Rather than going down to the Legion or joining the 'old sweats' in the pub, ex-servicemen took up their pre-war hobbies and leisure pursuits with relish;

attendances at speedway, football matches and greyhound races were never higher than in the years between 1945 and 1950.[81]

Turning their Backs on Military Culture

As some of the comments above reveal, the relatively small membership of the British Legion and the old comrades' associations is partly due to a wholesale rejection of all connections with the war. While a minority of ex-servicemen chose to retain links with their military past, most wanted to turn their backs on the whole culture of military service, saluting, foreign travel, anything that reminded them of the war. Leonard Muddeman only wore his demob suit to work a couple of times, and never without 'a slight sense of shame' as 'both the pattern and the hue made it difficult to hide its patriotic origins'.[82] Jim Lucas, who was employed at the Imperial War Museum, was, along with his old comrades from the 7th Battalion Royal West Kents, so sick of wearing khaki uniforms after six years of war service, that he never wanted to see brown(ish) clothes again and so always chose blue, black or grey suits for the rest of his life.[83] Far from wanting to extend their wartime experiences into civilian life, before the long-awaited demobilisation many servicemen fantasised about home, conjuring up an idealised and untroubled domestic, even hermit-like existence, far from crowds, cities, commitment and military service. One soldier, who had fought in North Africa, Italy and North West Europe, had evidently had enough excitement for one lifetime, writing to his wife: 'For goodness sake find us a little place out in the country. The only thing I long for is a quiet life and time to grow things in a garden. Soon I shall be at home and *must* get away from people for a time.'[84]

'Beach-combing' seems to have been the popular career choice for many a recently demobilised ex-serviceman when quizzed by a civilian about his next step in life. Sadly most returned servicemen could not afford such indolence, but the submariner Commander William King did have the means to escape his painful memories of the war and gradually slough off his warlike carapace, spending two years sailing around the West Indies and ocean-racing before returning to settle down to a life of farming in the west of Ireland.[85]

There is also evidence that to turn one's back on the war and military matters was seen to be the mature and socially approved behaviour for demobilised men and women in the late 1940s with the old military uniform relegated to decorating, gardening and work on the allotment. A journalist in *The Times*, describing the admirable characteristics of those waiting patiently for the Victory Parade, noted approvingly that many were wearing their smart new demob suits, 'in one of the few countries whose inhabitants delight in getting out of uniform rather than getting into it'.[86] Those who failed to adjust to civilian life were seen as a threat to social order, with the ex-commando or other highly trained ex-servicemen who turned to violent crime, becoming one of the folk monsters of the late 1940s, immortalised in British crime films of the era, notably *They Made me a Fugitive* (1947) and *Night Beat* (1948).

War Memoirs and the Literary Legacy of the War

Given the attitudes described above, it is perhaps not surprising that such a relatively small number of memoirs and first-hand accounts of the war were published in its aftermath. The library of the Imperial War Museum, which is the specialist collection for war-related material in the UK, holds only 172 titles published in the years 1945 to 1950; an average of 28 per year. This figure is in stark contrast to the 302 memoirs about the First World War which were published in the years 1918–22 (an average of 60.4 per year), and with the 1,568 Second World War memoirs published in the 1980s and 1990s (at an average of 78.4 per year). It is also striking that, with a few notable exceptions, relatively few established or new professional writers based in Britain recorded their experiences in the years immediately following the Second World War.[87] The majority found other conflicts and subjects more inspiring, typically the First World War, Spain in the era around the Spanish Civil War (Laurie Lee) or, in the case of Norman Lewis, the nationalist unrest in Indo-China and Burma.[88] Roald Dahl did publish an adventurous account of his service as a pilot with the RAF, but he was in the USA when first encouraged to record his experiences.[89] Those stuck in the UK, surrounded by reminders of the war's impact on society were understandably keen to get away, physically and mentally. Laurie Lee bullied his friend Ralph Keene to take him to Cyprus to work on a documentary film, and was glad to escape England where 'the faces of everyone had a jaundiced look, dry and yellow, like bits of old leaves'.[90] Psychological exhaustion forced Norman Lewis to take a rest cure in Pembrokeshire, climbing and bird-watching, followed by three seasons fishing in the small Spanish coastal village of Farol.[91] It was not until the 1970s that Lewis, without much enthusiasm and as an exercise to solve writer's block, decided to try to turn the diary account of his wartime experiences in military intelligence into a publishable form, resulting in *Naples '44,* one of the most vivid and respected accounts of the war.[92]

The popular view is that the Second World War has lacked the poignancy and tragedy of the First World War and the romance and idealism of the Spanish Civil War. A large number of veterans of the International Brigade have penned memoirs full of passion about their experiences in Spain but have rarely bothered to write about their subsequent involvement in the Second World War, which for committed socialists and communists was merely the depressing and predictable continuation of the march of Fascism that they had first observed when Franco's forces began the coup d'état in Morocco. As Bill Alexander remarked in his introduction to a history of the British battalion of the International Brigades:

> I have fought in two wars – the war in Spain (1936–1939) and the Second World War (1939–1945). No one asks me today about my experiences in the world war; but my service in Spain in the International Brigade brings continuing questions and an interest as marked among young people as among older. Much of the interest centres on those who volunteered to fight in the International Brigades of the Spanish Republican Army, putting their ideals and beliefs before comfort security and even life itself.[93]

For Ted Hughes and other writers of his generation who had been too young to serve in the war (Hughes was fifteen in 1945), it was the First World War, their fathers' war, that had been their inspiration:

> In the 1950s when I began to publish my first poems, to me the First World War was my most intimate experience, my mythology. But then I realised all my own generation were writing about the same thing – their father's war. During the 1950s, for several years, that was a dominant theme of writers then in their twenties. They had no interest in the Second World War that they'd lived through. ... In fact rather than shock, there was a general feeling of relief that it had not been like the First World War. ... And from the moment it was over everybody was talking about other things – Cold War, threat of the real (nuclear) war, Russians, Russians, Russians, communists and in England.[94]

The Second World War also did not immediately inspire writers of 'popular fiction', with the first novels about the subject (*The Green Beret, The Wooden Horse* and *The Jungle is Neutral*) not published until 1949, with the majority being released from 1951.[95] Authors of 'literary fiction' took even longer to reflect on the war, not producing their works until the 1960s.[96] There is a consensus among scholars that in Britain the Second World War failed to inspire a body of literature to compare with that produced in the USA or, for that matter, with the great cannon prompted by the experience of the First World War.[97] One explanation for this phenomenon is the 'pervasive sense of déjà vu that stifled creativity'.[98] The poet Keith Douglas, who was killed fighting in Normandy in June 1944, and a writer who did produce a much-admired body of work about the war, still felt that 'there is nothing new from a soldier's point of view, about this war except its mobile character. ... Almost all that a modern poet on active service is inspired to write, would be tautological.'[99] It is also suggested that writers were simply overwhelmed by the scale of the conflict, as the film critic and military historian Milton Shulman put it in 1950, when reviewing the film *A Walk in the Sun* (1950): 'The vast sweep of modern war makes it almost impossible to interpret in artistic terms. No brush or pen or camera can catch more than a fragment of this terrifying colossus.'[100]

Public Remembering of the War up until 1950

The forgetfulness of ex-servicemen and women was not compensated by official efforts to remember the war. Firstly, the rituals by which society publicly remembered and honoured those who had served in the war were hindered by the practical difficulties of austerity in Britain. As a consequence of post-war shortages in metals, skilled craftsmen and even medal ribbons, there were delays in the production and investiture of gallantry and campaign medals.[101] Practicalities also led the government to decide that, unlike the system at the end of the First World War, all campaign medals for ex-servicemen and women would have to be claimed (regular serving personnel would receive them directly through their units), which was done by submitting an application form obtainable from the post office. This policy also included some categories of medals issued for gallantry. More controversially, economy also led the government to decide that medals would not be individually named as they had been after the First World War (although you could pay extra to have this done). These decisions angered the RAF Association and the British Legion, with the Legion requesting that a scheme be set up whereby local silversmiths could carry out the engraving.[102] In the summer of 1949, one MP even made the impractical suggestion that all the medals already issued should be recalled so that they could be engraved with the names of the recipients.[103]

But the question one should ask is how widespread was the opposition to these changes in the medal system? Certainly some ex-servicemen and women felt snubbed, even devalued, particularly by the rather miserly decision not to engrave the recipients' names on each medal. However, searching through the post-war issues of the *British Legion* journal, I found no correspondence on this topic, and would have to concur with Prime Minister Clement Attlee's view was that 'there was no great feeling on the matter', and that to have engraved the names on the medals would have created such a long delay as to create 'a great deal more dissatisfaction than the omission of the name'.[104] Indeed it seems as if it was ex-servicemen's representatives or family members who were the most aggrieved, the returning heroes themselves tended to be far more phlegmatic about the matter. For example, one man who had received his Military Cross by post, was moved by a series of complaining letters to *The Times* from the parents of men who had also received their awards by mail, to counter that he was so delighted to be honoured with his cross that the method of investiture was immaterial and that he was perfectly happy with the letter from the King that had been enclosed expressing his regret at not being able to present it in person.[105] The most striking feature of the 'medal story' is not the opposition to the issuing system, but the apparent disinterest of so many people who were eligible for medals. In February 1950 it was reported that of more than 4 million men who had served in the Army up until June 1945, only 1,538,600 had claimed their medals. Royal Naval veterans had been keener to claim their medals, 238,000 having already received awards, with a further 663,000 applications being processed, however, there were still more than 100,000 ex-sailors who had not applied.[106] And from a total of 1,185,000 ground and aircrew members who had served with the RAF during the war, only 355,071 had applied for medals. One might explain this low take-up by the fact that the campaign medals had only been ready for issue from June 1948 or that they had to be applied for by post. However, applications for medals earned for 1939–45 service remained low throughout the 1950s, 1960s and 1970s. When men did claim their medals belatedly, at the fiftieth and sixtieth anniversaries of the war, they often explained that after the war they had been so preoccupied with getting on with their civilian lives that they had either forgotten about the medals altogether or not bothered to apply.[107] Even those who did claim their medals were often reluctant to wear them. Until my own father died, I had not realised that he possessed a full set of campaign medals sent to him shortly after the war and still sitting unused in the box in which they had been despatched.

Practical difficulties also prevented the bereaved from visiting war graves. Unlike the situation after the First World War, where visits were straightforward because the majority of bodies were concentrated in a small and accessible area of northern France, the bodies of men who had fought in the Second World War were scattered between 330 military cemeteries over nine countries in Europe, not to mention those buried in North Africa and the Far East. In order to get around this problem, the British Legion set up a system whereby wreaths could be laid upon a grave which would then be photographed and the picture sent to the bereaved.[108]

The difficulty of reaching such places was exacerbated by the nation's post-war economic problems, which meant that until 1948, relatives were only allowed to take tiny amounts of British currency abroad. After this, however, in collaboration with the British Legion, the post-war Labour government set up a generous scheme, which ran until 1951, to help relatives visit war graves. However, many bereaved relatives and comrades were never able to visit war graves, particularly if the man had died outside Europe. In the aftermath of the First World War such pilgrimages had become annual events for some groups of First World War veterans, which had helped to keep the memory of the war alive. The proximity of the Western Front had also encouraged the development of 'battlefield tourism' a movement that had helped to sustain the memory of the war in the wider community. By contrast, for many thousands of men who had fought in the 1939–45 war, it was not until the sixtieth anniversary celebrations that special travel grants, made available through the state-funded 'Heroes Return' scheme, enabled them to visit war graves and battlefields for the first time.

Society's Attitude to the Second World War

Aside from these practical constraints on the memorialising process, it is clear that the post-1945 society viewed the recent war in a qualitatively different manner than had the post-1918 generation. One of the most recognisable public responses to the First World War had been the erection of thousands of local monuments and statues to memorialise those who had died in the conflict. Raised voluntarily and funded by public subscription, these remain the most powerful and tangible symbol of the nation's sense of debt to its warriors. After the Second World War however, the people overwhelmingly rejected stone monuments in favour of utilitarian memorials (such as community centres, cottages, scholarships, university grants and training bursaries) that would be of benefit to the survivors of the war or the dependants of those who had died.

There was a common feeling that the ex-servicemen and women of 1945 were not to be tricked with the kind of empty promises that had been made to the men returning home in 1918, and that this time memorials in stone would be seen as fatuous gestures: 'The best war memorial of all will not be any material commemoration, but generous treatment of the servicemen when they come home and of those dependents of those killed in action.'[109] It is striking how far the form of a proposed memorial could be from anything that might be seen as military. In Saffron Walden, local efforts to raise funds through subscription for a joint Anglo-American scheme for a memorial playing field to honour the dead of the USAAF (many of whom had been based at local airfields during the war) foundered because most of the locals objected to the building of a Hall of Remembrance on the sports field, arguing that instead the money should be spent on what the town really needed – a large concert and dance hall.[110] Such a conflict could not have arisen after the First World War, so profound had been the sense of gratitude and even guilt that the civilian population felt to the returning servicemen. The mood was very different in 1945, as it was widely acknowledged that life on the home front had often been just as dangerous and grim as it was for those serving in an offensive role. Therefore many communities felt justified in rewarding their sacrifices by constructing 'memorials' that made no reference to the military.

In addition to the cynicism of what one historian of the memorial movement has described as a 'sceptical generation', there was the fear that the new peace was likely to be short-lived.[111] This mood of gloomy fatalism was well-expressed by the journalist Marguerite Steen in her observation of plans to update the inscription on the Cenotaph in time for the Armistice Day of 1945:

> The proposed addition to the inscription on the cenotaph will sober you. The Glorious Dead 1914–1918 it reads at present: 1939–1945 to be added. No comment is needed on this mute reminder that of a short span of 31 years, ten have been wasted in an orgy of ruin. ... Plans are now going forward for the usual rites at 'Armistice Day' a name which because of its inapplicability to the situation today, strikes a false note for many. Days of memory seems to us better to unite the past with the present, and better to express the occasion it commemorates.[112]

To avoid tempting the fates and so as not to waste money on a dedicated Second World War memorial that would soon need to be superseded, hundreds of other communities around the UK followed the practise employed for the Cenotaph and simply added the names of those who had died in the 1939–45 war to the existing local memorial to the First World War, with a formal re-dedication or unveiling on Remembrance Sunday.

Museums

The Second World War did not excite Britain's historians, curators and collectors, as had the 1914–18 conflict. One reviewer of the first post-war exhibition at the Imperial War Museum (IWM) commented that, while there were plenty of weapons and bombs on display to impress, there was a noticeable lack of relics with any personal history attached to them, especially compared with a similar exhibition the journalist had visited in Washington.[113] The impoverishment of this exhibition can partly be explained by institutional and practical factors. Firstly, until 1945, the museum's terms of reference only covered 1914–19. Secondly, much to the frustration of the trustees, and unlike the situation at the end of the First World War, officers were not appointed by service heads to scour the various theatres of operation and Admiralty bases for items likely to be of interest to the museum. But there is also evidence that the emotional ties that the museum's staff felt to the Great War was, for a time, a hindrance to work to document and memorialise the 1939–45 war. This lack of recognition for the historical significance of the Second World War meant that the Museum's 1939–45 collection was not as comprehensive as the one created after the Great War, forcing its curators to seek out many key, representative objects for decades after. The shortfall in artefacts and documents coming via official military channels was not helped by the fact that the public also did not seem to regard the Second World War as historically noteworthy. For example, by January 1948 the IWM had not yet received any rolls of honour relating to the recent war, forcing the librarian to issue an appeal to redress the situation. This was in contrast to the situation after the First World War when more than two thousand rolls of honour compiled by public schools and colleges had been deposited at the museum for safe-keeping.[114] Public attitudes were also reflected in the pattern of enquiries to the newly re-opened IWM, which received more about the 1914–18 collections than about the new acquisitions from the Second World War.[115] General indifference to the history of the 1939–45 war also created problems for the curators of Britain's smaller military and regional museums. By the summer of 1946 the curators of the Royal Ulster Rifles Regimental Museum at Balymena had received so few war trophies that they were forced to issue an appeal to members of the regiment not to forget the historical value of souvenirs they may have acquired in their war service. The Belfast Museum, which after the First World War had received large numbers of weapons, helmets and other memorabilia captured from the enemy, had not received a single souvenir by August 1946.[116] One explanation offered for this sorry state of affairs was that the modern warrior had gone a bit soft, preferring holiday souvenirs suitable for the family ('a strip of silk or an ashtray or a pipe fashioned by a native craftsman') that had been purchased legitimately during their travels rather than military booty snatched on the field of battle.[117] This may be so, but it is also apparent that official action intervened to prevent much more military booty being smuggled into Britain; some veterans recall that on the troopships returning them home, loudspeaker announcements warning that no souvenir arms could be taken ashore were followed by the comical sight of 'tons of arms' being thrown over the side.[118]

Continuing Warfare

Lack of interest in documenting and remembering the war is understandable in an atmosphere in which peace was not secure. Even before the end of the war men on active service were predicting that another war in Europe, and probably against the USSR, was imminent. These fears were shared by civilians at home in Britain. The day after celebrating VE Day, George Taylor, an accountant living in Sheffield, finished taking down the last of the blackouts from his windows and fanlights, but cautiously 'parcelled them for storage in the loft, ready for the next war. If we do leave this house before then, they will go along with the fixtures.'[119]

The spectre of the atom bomb also added to the sense of dread. Mrs Britton was relieved that the Germans had not had access to such a 'terrible engine of destruction' as it would have 'wiped London and all its inhabitants off the map.'[120] But she also feared the apocalyptic danger it now presented, correcting what she saw as a naïve attitude to the weapon by her daughter: 'Your quotation, "As a matter of fact the atom bomb has made war as we know it obsolete", I think I remember hearing the same remark when gunpowder was invented."[121] The irony that the method by which the war had finally been ended now threatened the peoples of the world with annihilation meant that it was hard to untangle the memory of the war from nightmarish fears for the immediate future. For example, the terrible destructive power of the atom bomb was frequently mentioned by priests at war-memorial unveilings and during sermons delivered at the annual Remembrance-Day services.[122] And journalists who visited the Imperial War Museum found that the new exhibits such as the V1 and V2 rockets and the building's location only served to reinforce anxiety about an impending nuclear war:

> When King George V opened the Museum at its first home in the Crystal Palace he hoped that its contents would help men to 'Look back upon war as belonging to a dead past.
>
> Just Bedlam
>
> The tragic irony of that aspiration is driven home by the fact that the Museum buildings are surrounded by blitz-blasted Lambeth. ... As we left it and saw all around bomb-made open spaces, we reflected that there is plenty of ground available for a third extension to house mementos of a third war. Unless, what is more probable, at the end of that one most of London will be wide and very open spaces.[123]

Although thankfully the third world war did not break out, the onset of the Cold War and the conflicts in Palestine, Malaya and the Korean War meant there was no respite from warfare. One of the obvious indicators of this was the continuation of enforced military service, with call-up under wartime regulations being replaced on 1 January 1947 with conscription through the National Service. Kenneth Morgan argues that the positive memory of the war led the British to accept a continuing emphasis on the military, an aggressive foreign policy and the imposition of National Service.[124] But it is not clear that the people's acceptance of National Service reflected a more independent and war-like mindset. Although opinion polls revealed that a slight majority of the population approved of national service, the historian L. V. Scott argues that this is actually an indication of the way people tend to accept the status quo.[125] This interpretation is borne out by the recollections of ex–national servicemen such as the writer Alan Sillitoe who explained that by the later 1940s, Britons had become resigned to military service and war: 'To begin with I didn't think of it as National Service. It was conscription, a fact of life. Since the age of eleven there had been a war on, which meant that sooner or later I would have to go and get shot at. Such was the state of morale in working-class Nottingham. ... Going to war was expected of everybody, if you were a teenager that is.'[126] While national service was accepted as a necessary obligation, there was no enthusiasm for a career in the military. Optimistic War Office predictions that, after the war, regular recruiting would deliver 275,000 or more men per year soon proved to be very inaccurate, with young men showing reluctance even to sign up to the RAF, the most glamorous of the services. As a result, the forces began to rely on conscription through the national service to maintain operational levels. Regular recruitment had fallen to such a low level by 1951 that national servicemen made up 50 per cent of the Army's total manpower.[127]

Undoubtedly full employment made a career in the armed forces less attractive to young men, especially as the pay and conditions on offer were regarded as a hindrance to recruiting. However, Scott argues that even significant changes to pay and conditions would not have made the military attractive enough to remove the need for national service.[128] Military life, unless enforced, was not an option in the years after the war. People had had enough not just of warfare, but also of the British military. Men who had served in the Second World War were often critical of the undemocratic and old fashioned way in which the services were run and there was particular objection to the poor kit and uniform (especially when compared with that of the Americans) and resentment at the privileged conditions of commissioned officers when compared with those provided for the NCOs and other ranks.[129]

Barnett and Morgan's contention that the general population supported an aggressive foreign policy should also be challenged. War fatigue meant that few would support a profligate use of the nation's youth. The historian Sally Alexander, who was a child in England in the 1940s and 1950s, recalled that her mother wanted the 'third world war that she knew was coming – "world wars come every twenty years" – to happen before my brother grew up. Korea and Suez were met with relief in my family because my brother was too young to go.'[130] As a result there was widespread opposition to the peace-keeping role assigned to seventy thousand British troops in the newly partitioned Palestine.[131] As tensions in the area increased and British soldiers came under attack from Jewish terrorists, public opinion became increasingly antisemitic, as revealed in a sample of reflections on current affairs made by Mass Observers. Edie Rutherford suggested: 'As more and more lads are killed there, I begin to wish we had started the war a bit later, so that Hitler would have exterminated a few more Jews.'[132]

The Mass Observers contradict the belief that the people cared that much about the Empire or maintaining prestige abroad, if such a policy meant more sacrifices by Britain's armed forces. B. Charles offered this commentary on general attitudes to military engagement in the immediate post-war era: 'The mass of people just don't care two hoots whether or not we remain a first class power. In a way I agree with them, as when we were such a power this did not prevent the Boer War and the two world wars from taking place. I think one must just face the fact that our day of "greatness" as a world power is over for good and all. Will it make any difference to us all?'[133] When Herbert Brush thought through the implications of the withdrawal of British troops from Egypt, he concluded that the inevitable diminishing of the Empire would not be a great loss:

> The next thing is that we shall not be allowed to use the Suez canal route to India. However, if we are to lose India, that won't matter very much. The King will be King of England but not Emperor of India, so some of the coins will have to be reminted. No foreigner will look upon the English as people who can be sat upon with impunity. I wonder whether we shall live long enough to see the end of the British Empire, brought about by the Labour Government. The next thing our government will want to do is to give up the rock of Gibraltar to Spain, if she asks for it nicely.[134]

Although Brush's predictions for the 'Rock' were premature, he was spot on about India, which was given independence a year later. His insouciance towards this event was also representative of the wider mood, with the nation accepting what might have been seen as humiliation, with, as Kenneth Morgan points out, none of the trauma and consequent political upheaval experienced in France following the retreat from Indo-China and North Africa.[135] There was certainly no comment on such a momentous event in the provincial papers examined for this chapter.

Conclusion

Mark Connelly and John Ramsden have discerned that 1949–50 was the point at which the British began to revive from their post-war trauma and actively remember their war.[136] They cite a wave of novels such as Eric Williams' *The Wooden Horse* (1949), Nicholas Monsarrat's *The Cruel Sea* (1951) and Paul Brickhill's *The Dambusters* and *The Great Escape* (1951), which re-told the war as romanticised adventure yarns. These novels were immensely popular; for example, by September 1949 the *Wooden Horse* had sold 150,000 copies and was in its ninth edition. They were also circulated in abridged and simplified English forms. These were quickly turned into an equally successful genre of films that later became a staple of British television programming. Further evidence, after 1950, of this 'popular memory' of the war was the development of a wartime culture devised for children, with comics such as the *War Picture Library* (1958–1984) and *Commando* (1961–present) and a whole series of toys based on the war – most notably the *Airfix* plastic kit models, the first of a highly successful line of scale models of Second World War military hardware being the Spitfire, released in 1953.[137]

According to Ramsden and Connelly, the main consumers of this 'pleasure culture of war' were those who had been born around the war or even later.[138] Indeed some of the historians who have explored the popular memory of the Second World War (Connelly, Peter Hennessy) have nostalgically recalled their own engagement as boys with this adventure world of war.[139] But the findings of this chapter suggest that they have wrongly assumed that playing with the memory of the war was something they shared with the 'grown-ups'. For example, closer analysis of the audience for the popular novels and films of the 1950s and 1960s shows that a considerable proportion of the consumers were the 'baby boomers', a group that would have had little or no memory of the war or that would have been protected from its grimmest realities. The Bookseller noted that one feature of the success of The Cruel Sea was its popularity with children and young people – a phenomenon explained by the fact that it was the kind of book children like, 'thrilling and true'.[140] The large cinema audiences of the late 1940s and 1950s were dominated by children and younger men and women; the older generations of men and women who had lived through the war did not, even after 1950, show much interest in remembering the war.[141] Writers and publishers of memoirs avoided the subject until the late 1970s; based on the holdings of the library at the IWM, only around twenty-five first-hand accounts of the war were produced each year between 1951 and 1980. Nor were veterans desirous of spending time with their old comrades – membership of the British Legion settled at around one million in the 1960s and 1970s, 250,000 of whom were women. As well as the British Legion, ex-servicemen could join associations connected with specific campaigns rather than units or regiments. However, these were slow to form, most not being set up until after 1950 and many not for decades after the war had ended.[142]

Those who did retain links with old war associates were seen as slightly eccentric, even arrested and immature. Perhaps this view is most brilliantly expressed in the half-hour television play 'The Reunion Party', which was one episode of the popular, long-running comedy series 'Hancock's Half Hour', written by Ray Galton and Alan Simpson and starring wartime ENSA (Entertainment National Service Association) veteran Tony Hancock. In this episode, broadcast in March 1960, Hancock arranges a party for his closest comrades from the war. The party is a disaster. The legendary warriors, womanisers and drinkers described in Tony's pre-party build-up to his flatmate Sid, prove to be a big disappointment – one has become a vicar, the other a vegetarian with digestive problems, while Ginger Johnson, famed for his shock of red hair and drinking, is now bald, very short-sighted and virtually teetotal. Significantly none of the men are keen to reminisce about the war, partly because this would bring back memories and aspects of their past life which are painful or of which they are now ashamed.

Notes

1. This chapter is dedicated to my friend Suzanna Piesse-Roper, who was present at the conference in Meissen where the first draft was delivered, and whose recollections and general good sense helped to clarify some of my thoughts during its writing.

2. For the 'noble crusade' quote, see A. J. P. Taylor, *England History, 1914–45* (Oxford, 1965), 600.

3. Mark Connelly, *We Can Take It! Britain and the Memory of the Second World War* (Harlow, 2004), 16–17, 301. See also Steven Fielding, 'The Good War: 1939–45', in Nick Tiratsoo (ed.) *From Blitz to Blair: A New History of Britain Since 1939* (London, 1998), 25.

4. Norman Longmate, *When We Won the War: The Story of Victory in Europe 1945* (London, 1977).

5. Kenneth O. Morgan, *The People's Peace: British History, 1945–1989* (Oxford, 2001), 59–60.

6. Correlli Barnett, *The Audit of War: The Illusion and Reality of Britain as a Great Nation* (London, 1986), 8.

7. See Correlli Barnett, *The Lost Victory: British Dreams and British Realities* (London, 1995), 116–120. And David Reynolds, 'Britannia Overruled: The Shrinking of a World Power', in Lesley M. Smith (ed.), *The Making of Britain: Echoes of Greatness* (Basingstoke, 1988), 32–33.

8. See Paul Addison, *Now the War is Over: A Social History of Britain 1945–51* (London, 1985); Peter Hennessey, *Never Again: Britain 1945–1951* (London, 1992); Nick Tiratsoo (ed.) *The Attlee Years* (London, 1991); Steve Fielding, Peter Thompson and Nick Tiratsoo, *England Arise! The Labour Party and Popular Politics in 1940s Britain* (Manchester, 1995).

9. Barry Turner and Tony Renell, *When Daddy Came Home: How Family Life Changed Forever in 1945* (London, 1995), 12–13.

10. Connelly, *We Can Take It*, 268; Martin Shaw, 'Past Wars and Present Conflicts: From the Second World War to the Gulf', in M. Evans and K. Lunn (eds.), *War and Memory in the Twentieth Century* (Oxford, 1997), 192.

11. Shaw, 'Past Wars', 193–201.

12. Barnett, *Lost Victory*, 178.

13. Leonard N. Muddeman (1946), *Decade 1937–1946*, memoirs held in the Department of Documents, Imperial War Museum, 01/4/1, 217.

14. Miss R. G. Cottrell to her sister Patricia, 11 May 1945, Department of Documents, Imperial War Museum, 04/40/1.

15. Herbert Brush in Simon Garfield, *Our Hidden Lives: The Everyday Diaries of a Forgotten Britain, 1945–1948* (London, 2004), 21.

16. Muddeman, *Decade*, 226.

17. Tamasin Day-Lewis (ed.), *Last Letters Home* (London, 1995), 196.

18. From the diary of Mrs L. White, held in the Department of Documents, Imperial War Museum, 86/54/1.

19. *The Scotsman*, 13 October 1945.

20. Mr and Mrs Britton to Florrie, 16 May 1945, Department of Documents, Imperial War Museum, Con Shelf.

21. Rose Cottrell to Patricia, 3 April 1945, Department of Documents, Imperial War Museum, 04/40/1.

22. Mr and Mrs Britton to Florrie, 22 August 1945, Department of Documents, Imperial War Museum, Con Shelf.

23. R. G. Cottrell to Patricia, 1 March 1945, Department of Documents, Imperial War Museum, 04/40/1.

24. As in the *Observer* editorial on VE Day, republished in 2005: 'But it is not a war to end war that we have won. That war begins when peace is declared: we lost it in the 20 years after 1918. Now our second chance is coming; let us learn from looking back how to seize and hold it firm.' The *Observer*, 8 May 2005, 24.

25. In the 'Special Supplement' for the Victory Celebrations, the correspondent reported that as the forty or so allied commanders marched past, 'there were hopeful arguments in the crowd whether the Russians were there or not. They wanted to believe that they were.' *The Times*, 10 June 1946, ib. See also Longmate, *When We Won*, 61, for a description of the flag-bedecked streets during victory celebrations.
26. See the comments by Colonel Hugh Stewart and Paul Wyand in Toby Haggith, 'The filming of the liberation of Bergen-Belsen and its impact on the understanding of the Holocaust', *Holocaust Studies: A Journal of Culture and History* 1–2 (2006), 98.
27. David Cesarani, 'Lacking in Convictions: British War Crimes Policy and National Memory of the Second World War', in Martin Evans and Kenn Lunn (eds.), *War and Memory in the Twentieth Century* (Oxford, 1997), 30.
28. Cesarani, 'Lacking in Convictions', 32–33.
29. Suzanne Bardgett, 'The Depiction of the Holocaust at the Imperial War Museum Since 1961', in *The Journal of Israeli History* 23, no. 1 (2004), 146–156.
30. J. E. D. Hall, *Labour's First Year* (Harmondsworth, 1947), 41.
31. See Michael Sissons and Philip French (eds.), *The Age of Austerity, 1945–1951* (Harmondsworth, 1964), 44.
32. Addison, *Now the War is Over*, 55.
33. 'The First Peacetime Christmas in the Bookshops', *The Bookseller*, 20 December 1945, 869–871.
34. The quote from Christina Foyle is found on page 869 of *The Bookseller*, 20 December 1945.
35. See also the Christmas issues of *The Bookseller* from 1946–49.
36. Sissons and French, *Age of Austerity*, 37.
37. B. Charles, 3 May 1946, in Garfield, *Hidden Lives*, 212.
38. Modern Records Research Centre, University of Warwick: Reg Groves papers, an undated document in a file called 'Own articles', MSS 172/RG/5/16. During the war as a script writer for Strand Films, Groves had written a number of scripts for films commissioned by the Ministry of Information that argued for a radical reconstruction of Britain.
39. The *Lancaster Guardian*, 14 June 1946; *The Times*, 10 June 1946, 4a.
40. The *Lancaster Guardian*, 14 June 1945.
41. *The Times*, 10 June 1946.
42. The *Norfolk Chronicle*, 14 June 1946.
43. *The Times*, 10 June 1946, 4.
44. Modern Records Research Centre, University of Warwick: Reg Groves papers, an undated document in a file called 'Own articles', MSS 172/RG/5/16.
45. *The Times*, 7 June 1946, 7.
46. The *Daily Mirror*, 10 June 1946, 2.
47. Hennessey, *Never Again*, 312.
48. *Lancaster Guardian*, 14 June 1946.
49. For the years 1946–50, I focussed on the anniversaries of the outbreak of the war (September 1939), D-Day (6 June), VE Day (8 May) and VJ Day (15 August).
50. See 'Under the Clock' by *Pendulum*, in the *Saffron Walden Weekly News*, 9 May 1947.
51. Cassandra, 'Temple of Mars', the *Daily Mirror*, 13 May 1948, 4.
52. *Saffron Walden Weekly News*, 4 June 1948.
53. Peter Reese, *Homecoming Heroes: An Account of the Re-Assimilation of British Military Personnel into Civilian Life* (London, 1992), 201.
54. In a report from the British Legion's annual conference, held at Great Yarmouth in June 1949. The *Norfolk Chronicle*, 10 June 1949.
55. Turner and Rennell, *When Daddy Came Home*, 207.

56. *British Legion* journal, January 1946, 2.
57. My own father 'jumped ship' (leaving the ship without permission) when his RN minesweeper docked in Australia, moving around under an assumed name for many years. I have no figures for the number of ex-servicemen and women who emigrated illegally in this fashion.
58. Turner and Rennell, *When Daddy Came Home*, 206.
59. Richard Weight, *Patriots: National Identity in Britain, 1940–2000* (London, 2002), 182.
60. Turner and Rennell, *When Daddy Came Home*, 44.
61. 'The Experiences of One Who Has Just Returned to Civvy Street', *Manchester Regiment Gazette*, Vol. XII (1946–47), 38.
62. From 'A brief history of the Far East Prisoners of War', on the Java FEPOW Club 1942 website; http://thejavafepowclub1942.org./history.html
63. *British Legion* journal, June 1948, 125.
64. Quoted in Ben Wicks, *Welcome Home: True Stories of Soldiers Returning from World War II* (London, 1991), 94.
65. *British Legion* journal, May 1946, 114.
66. Wicks, *Welcome Home*, 71; Turner and Rennell, *When Daddy Came Home*, 73.
67. Turner and Rennell, *When Daddy Came Home*, 96–97, 100; Wicks, *Welcome Home*, 74–75.
68. Turner and Rennell, *When Daddy Came Home*, 72–108; Wicks, *Welcome Home*, 73–116.
69. Turner and Rennell, *When Daddy Came Home*, 137.
70. Ibid., 224.
71. Told to the author by Jeff Lewis (Mike Lewis's son), during a conversation at the Imperial War Museum on 20 October 2006.
72. Addison, *Now the War*, 17.
73. Wicks, *Welcome Home*, 85, 89–91.
74. Graham Wooton, *The Official History of the British Legion* (London, 1956), 305.
75. *British Legion* journal, October 1945, 186.
76. Mr A. E. Hocking, 'Is Our Propaganda on Right Lines?', *British Legion* journal, May 1950, 85.
77. L. A. Musgrove, Wirral, Cheshire, *British Legion* journal, February 1949, 32.
78. 'Old Stager Confesses', from a letter by T. Scott, Legionnaire in Liverpool for twenty-five years, *British Legion* journal, May 1950, 87.
79. Letter from E. Higton (Netherfield, Notts) to *British Legion* journal, August 1950, 143.
80. *British Legion* journal, February 1949, 33.
81. In the peak season of 1948–49, 41 million a week went through the turnstiles at football grounds and in 1946, 45 million 'went to the dogs', see Addisson, *Now the War*, 12, 123.
82. Leonard Muddeman, *Decade 1937–1946* (1946). Memoirs held in the Department of Documents, Imperial War Museum, 01/4/1, p. 362.
83. James Lucas worked first in the Museum's Department of Printed Books and then became Deputy Head of the Photographic Archive. With thanks to Terry Charman for this anecdote.
84. *British Legion* journal, September 1946, 198.
85. King, who was the only submarine captain to have been almost continuously in operational command for the six years of the hostilities, felt at the end of the war 'like an over-wound clockwork mouse', and was haunted by memories of comrades that had been killed, the convoys lost and the enemy warships that had got away. Commander William King, *The Stick and the Stars* (London, 1958), 174–192.

86. *The Times*, 10 June 1946, 9a.
87. Three notable exceptions are Alexander Baron, *From the City, From the Plough* (1948); Dan Billany, *The Trap* (1950); and Colin MacInnes, *To the Victor the Spoils* (London, 1950).
88. Elaine Feinstein, *Ted Hughes: The Life of a Poet* (London, 2001), 18; Laurie Lee, *A Rose for Winter: Travels in Andalucia* (London, 1955), was inspired by Lee's pre-Civil War wanderings in Spain, which he later covered in *As I Walked Out One Midsummer Morning* (London, 1969), and *A Moment of War* (Harmondsworth, 1991), a book chronicling his involvement in the Spanish Civil War. Norman Lewis's trips to South-East Asia are covered in *A Dragon Apparent: Travels in Cambodia, Laos and Vietnam* (London, 1951) and *Golden Earth: Travels in Burma* (London, 1952).
89. Roald Dahl, *Over to You: Ten Stories about Flyers and Flying* (London, 1946).
90. Laurie Lee and Ralph Keene, *We Made a Film in Cyprus* (London, 1947), 1.
91. Norman Lewis, *Jackdaw Cake* (London, 1985), 211–212.
92. Norman Lewis, *Naples '44* (London, 1978).
93. Bill Alexander, *British Volunteers for Liberty: Spain 1936–39* (London, 1982), 11.
94. Ted Hughes in a letter to Nick Gammage, 15 March 1997, in Christian Reid (ed.), *Letters of Ted Hughes: Selected and Edited by Christian Reid* (2007), 592.
95. See Ken Worpole, *Dockers and Detectives* (London, 1980), 50, 72.
96. Alan Munton, *English Fiction of the Second World War* (London, 1989), 74.
97. David Pryce-Jones, 'Towards the Cocktail Party', in Michael Sissons and Philip French (eds.), *The Age of Austerity 1945–1951* (Harmonsdworth, 1963), 218.
98. Gill Plain, 'World War Two Writing', in Faye Hammill, Esme Mismmin and Ashlie Sponenberg (eds.), *Encyclopedia of British Women's Writing, 1900–1950* (Basingstoke, 2006), 297.
99. Written in 1943 and quoted by Desmond Graham (ed.), *Keith Douglas: The Complete Poems* (London, 2000), viii.
100. Shulman in a review of *A Walk in the Sun* in Edgar Anstey et al. (eds.), *Shots in the Dark* (London, 1951), 267.
101. *The Times*, 1 July 1947, 6f. (metal smiths); *The Times*, 28 January 1946, 5d. (medal ribbons).
102. At the annual meeting of the RAFA held in Blackpool, the conference 'expressed its disapproval of the government's decision to issue war medals without the inscription of the person to whom they were awarded', reported in *The Times*, 14 June 1948, 2d. The British Legion's feelings are reported in *The Lancaster Guardian*, 4 June 1948, 4.
103. Mr Lipson, Independent MP for Cheltenham, reported in *The Times*, 29 June 1949, 2b.
104. Report of House of Commons in *The Times*, 29 June 1949.
105. Letter to *The Times*, 17 April 1947, 5g.
106. 'War Medals Unclaimed', *The Times*, 22 February 1950, 8.
107. Liz Bullock (MOD Medal Office, RAF Innstone), in a telephone conversation with Toby Haggith 18 July 2006.
108. Wooton, *History of the Legion*, 293–294.
109. *The Daily Sketch*, 12 February 1945.
110. *Saffron Walden Weekly News*, 19 August 1949, 9.
111. Nick Hewitt, 'A Sceptical Generation? War Memorials and the Collective Memory of the Second World War in Britain, 1945–2000', in Dominik Geppert (ed.) *The Postwar Challenge: Cultural, Social, and Political Change in Western Europe, 1945–58* (Oxford, 2003), 82–83.
112. Marguerite Steen, *Sunday Graphic and Sunday News*, 14 October 1945.

113. *Glasgow Herald*, 19 November 1946.
114. L. P. Yates-Smith (IWM Librarian), in a letter to the editor of *The Daily Telegraph*, 17 January 1948.
115. 'Churchill's Tobruk Map', in the *Evening Standard*, 29 June 1948.
116. 'War Souvenirs' in *Belfast Telegraph*, 30 August 1946.
117. Ibid.
118. D. Bruton, Department of Documents, Imperial War Museum, 10/4/1. Albert Sutton, who had tried to smuggle home a Luger taken from a German commander who had committed suicide, threw the weapon over the side of his troopship after the loudspeaker warned that men smuggling arms would be court-martialed. See Albert Sutton's interview on the DVD *1939–1945: Memories of World War 2 From People Living in Northern Ireland* (Belfast, 2006), published by the Somme Heritage Centre.
119. George Taylor, 9 May 1945, in Garfield, *Hidden Lives*, 22.
120. Mrs Britton to Florrie, 8 August 1945, Department of Documents, Imperial War Museum.
121. Mrs Britton to Florrie, 4 September 1945, Department of Documents, Imperial War Museum.
122. The *Lancaster Guardian*, 12 November 1947; report of a memorial tablet unveiling at Wimbish Parish church, *Saffron Walden Weekly News*, 15 October 1948.
123. *Evening Times*, Glasgow, 5 January 1950; see also Hannen Swaffer's article in *The People*, 30 July 1950.
124. Morgan, *People's Peace*, 59–60.
125. L.V. Scott, *Conscription and the Attlee Government: The Politics and Policy of National Service 1945–51* (Oxford, 1993), 41–42.
126. B. S. Johnson (ed.) *All Bull: The National Servicemen* (London, 1973), 220–221. Sillitoe is probably most famous for *Saturday Night, Sunday Morning* and *The Loneliness of the Long Distance Runner*, both made into films.
127. Trevor Royle, *The Best Years of Our Lives: The National Services Experience, 1945–63* (London, 1986), 22.
128. Scott, *Conscription*, 246.
129. Ibid., 140–143.
130. Sally Alexander & Jim Fyrth (eds.), *Women's Voices from the Spanish Civil War* (London, 1991), 13.
131. 'Bring them Home', *Evening Standard*, 3 December 1947.
132. Edie Rutherford, 3 December 1946, in Garfield, *Hidden Lives*, 321.
133. B. Charles, 12 August 1947, in Garfield, *Hidden Lives*, 346.
134. Herbert Brush, 7 May 1946, in Garfield, *Hidden Lives*, 214.
135. Morgan, *People's Peace*, 47.
136. Connelly, *We Can Take It*, 236; John Ramsden, 'Refocusing "The People's War": British War Films of the 1950s', *Journal of Contemporary History* 1 (1998), 48–49.
137. Connelly, *We Can Take It*, 236, 240.
138. Ibid., 236; Ramsden, *Refocusing the People's War*, 36.
139. Connelly, *We Can Take It*, 236, and with reference to himself, 241; Ramsden, *Refocusing the People's War*, referring to Peter Hennessy, footnote 7, 36–37.
140. *The Bookseller*, 3 September 1949.
141. David Docherty, David Morrison and Michael Tracey, *The Last Picture Show? Britain's Changing Film Audience* (London, 1987), 16–17.
142. Burma Star 1951, Dunkirk Veterans Association 1953, Java Club 1984, Italy Star 1987.

16

Italy after 1945

War and Peace, Defeat and Liberation

Gustavo Corni

During the Second World War, Italy encountered a variety of different diplomatic-military situations which lacerated its social fabric. In an initial phase, Mussolini's regime had taken a stand as a 'non-belligerent' when faced with Hitler's unilateral decision to attack Poland, leaving Mussolini himself in a very uncomfortable position. Such a stand did not match the declarations of a 'masculine and warrior' Italy which had only recently conquered an Empire. On the other hand, he was well aware of the overall lack of military preparation of the armed forces and of the general absence of public enthusiasm which was carefully monitored by the police apparatus and the small, but impassioned, army of informers.[1] It appeared that significant sections of the bourgeoisie would even have preferred to take to the field alongside France and Great Britain, the traditional allies.[2] However, the avalanche of German military victories and, above all, the victorious beginnings of the military campaign against France persuaded Mussolini to make up his mind.[3] A change in public opinion is also perceptible, as many shared (whilst possibly fearing) the duce's expectation of a German victory and therefore hoped for Italian participation in the war to avoid being crushed by Germany's overwhelming strength. In the immediately subsequent period, Mussolini attempted to enact a 'parallel war' which would give the Fascist regime a margin for independent manoeuvre and would allow it to fulfil its territorial ambitions, limited though these were. The parallel war was carried out on two contemporaneous fronts: North Africa, with the aim of invading Egypt and arriving at the much sought-after Suez Canal, and the Balkans.[4] These were both traditional areas of expansion for Italy[5], but, nonetheless, these military campaigns – over and above the grave errors in their preparation and management – emphatically did not arouse feelings of consensus amongst a large proportion of the population. Consequently, they were fought with only a modest degree of support from the internal front – modest, but not wholly absent, as the phenomenon of voluntary participation in the ideologically motivated divisions of the 'black shirts' should not be ignored. The most important Italian military historian has written, in reference to the autumn campaign against Greece: 'The lack of enthusiasm in the attack by the Alpine brigades had two fundamental reasons: lack of training ... and the absence of any motivating drive, the proclamations were not enough.'[6] At the beginning of April 1941, when faced with the threat of a crushing defeat which would have shaken the very foundations of his power, Mussolini asked for Hitler's help in the Balkans. In North Africa, having lost Ethiopia and with the Italian advance in Cyrenaica blocked, the *Afrikakorps* led by Erwin Rommel had entered the field a couple of months earlier. The parallel war was over and the war as a subordinate of the German ally had begun.

It became a subaltern war in which, however, the duce made every attempt to defend and highlight his role as an ally. This is particularly apparent in his decision to accompany Germany in its attack on the Soviet Union. Hitler's decision, although taken many months earlier, was only made known to Mussolini once it was being put into force. This was just one of the many moments of misunderstanding and reciprocal mystification that make the alliance between the two regimes so peculiar when considering their acclaimed ideological affinity.[7] In effect, Mussolini strongly insisted that Italian troops should also participate in the offensive. The duce, with the same conviction as the German military command, was certain that the military campaign would be both brief and victorious. Once he had overcome the objections of the German rulers, who were convinced that the Italians were unreliable as soldiers and not particularly useful in this situation, Mussolini decided to send an army that initially comprised three divisions: the *Corpo di Spedizione Italiano in Russia* (CSIR – Italian Expedition Corps in Russia) led by General Giovanni Messe. Consequently, this was a relatively small military body and to this, between the end of 1941 and the beginning of summer 1942, another six divisions were added gradually with a considerable supply of materials and artillery. This ultimately constituted the VIII Army, more commonly known as ARMIR (*Armata Italiana in Russia* – Italian Army in Russia) which at its zenith counted 230,000 men, 16,700 vehicles, 4,500 motorcycle vehicles, 25,000 horses and mules, 940 cannons and 64 aeroplanes.[8]

At this stage, the ARMIR was a large operational unit equipped with relatively modern weaponry (particularly with regard to artillery) and for which Rome had made strenuous efforts. Nonetheless, it was entirely dependent on Germany, not only with regard to strategic plans but also concerning overall tactics. The ARMIR was used during summer 1942 on the southern wing of the front aiming for Stalingrad and the Caucasus. When, during the late summer months, the offensive push was halted and the terrible battle for control of the industrial city on the Volga began, the Italian and Romanian troops were lined up along the banks of the Don. Here began a debilitating phase of attrition with the Soviet troops who were much more numerous and better equipped, above all in terms of artillery and armoured vehicles. Due to a series of errors of judgement by the Italian command, when the Soviet offensive on Stalingrad and on the southern front began (after 11 December) there was no preparation for a possible withdrawal. The troops at the front were left to their own devices, without sufficient supplies and without any continuous contact with the rear guard.[9]

When faced with the overwhelming strength of the Soviet troops, a precipitous and badly organised retreat was begun. Initially, the units placed in the most northern area of the front directly hit by the Soviet attack retreated ruinously and the Alpine Corps, placed further south and not directly under attack, suddenly found itself exposed in the face of the rapid Soviet advance. By mid January, the Soviet pincer movement, having broken through from both the north and the south, forced the Alpine troops to withdraw. From this moment onwards, the attention of diaries, eye-witness accounts and academic works has concentrated on the tragic retreat from the Don which lasted about fifteen days. It is significant that very little, if almost nothing at all, is known about what happened to the Italian troops in the preceding year and a half when they had advanced for thousands of kilometres, carrying out highly significant military and anti-partisan operations. The entirety of the memory of our presence in Russia is loaded into these two weeks of 'martyrdom' in the snow, without any transport, without contact with the higher commands and in a desperate search for the rear guard where the exhausted march might finally find some rest. This martyrdom came to an end when the Russian pincer movement broke through at Nikolajewka on 27 January. There is no lack of documents concerning the much-longer period of Italian military presence in Russia, but it is completely obscured by its tragic epilogue. Only recently have some studies emerged based on documents ignored by historiography until now,[10] and these reveal the chiaroscuro of a picture which has been overwhelmingly dominated by the image of the good Italian, basically honest and courageous, profoundly linked to deep-seated values of rural life and, therefore, almost in synergy with the Russian peasant population with which they came into contact.[11] However, it appears that, in many instances, Italian units behaved with a severity and violence towards civilians that was completely out of place.

It should not be forgotten that during the war as subordinates of Hitler's Third Reich, the Italian civil and military apparatus was forced to manage huge territories occupied in continental Europe: from the Balkans to southeast France. Once again, memory and collective perception (the dominating elements until recently) must face up to historical facts. It is undeniable that, in many instances, these institutions behaved with considerable benevolence towards civilian populations, as can be seen in the case of the Jews both in Croatia and in France, where the zones occupied by the Italians were seen as areas of refuge, secure from persecution.[12] Nonetheless, from the documents and the most recent studies, it emerges that this 'good Italian' behaviour was less widespread than has been assumed and was frequently more opportunistic than not.[13] What prevailed was violence and profoundly repressive behaviour frequently dictated by open racism. I will give only a few examples, taken from letters written by soldiers which were blocked by the censors. One soldier wrote to his relations from Yugoslavia on 23 February 1942: 'And during the journey on foot in the rain we burnt all the houses, took away all the animals as the Germans had taught us. The peasants resisted but we settled the lot of them. … They're furious at us and call us Italian cowards, beggars and thieves. They say that one Montenegro woman is more than enough for three Italian men.'[14] From the same front, on 4 May 1942, was written: 'By now they're really massacring them, burning villages and killing everyone they find there. If you're kind to them you get nowhere with this sort of folk so you have to behave like this. I'd like to be part of them because when you've got a free hand there's a lot of satisfaction in our vendetta.'[15] What kind of positive memory could the Italians take with them of the Fascist war? To the defeats collected on all fronts, despite the heroism, must be added the weight of the imprisonment suffered by hundreds of thousands of Italians who were first captured by the British and the Americans (and their allies) and, after 8 September 1943, were captured en masse and almost without any resistance by their German ex-allies.[16] In particular, 8 September 1943 was perceived by many as a temporary respite but this was only a momentary sensation which was immediately exchanged for a sense of shame and disarray experienced by the entire nation, beginning with its highest levels of command.[17] A long period of imprisonment in the Reich followed and this was particularly painful due to the anti-Italian prejudices of the gaolers which were augmented by the idea of betrayal (which was not entirely absent for the prisoners held by the British authorities).[18] Whilst the Italian civilians and members of the armed forces present in Germany before the reversal of alliances where attributed a somewhat elevated rank in the rigid racial hierarchy by the National Socialist authorities (with the consequent and very material implications for the way they were treated),[19] after 8 September, the Italians (captured civilian workers and soldiers) ended up on the lowest possible rungs, equal to the Soviets. After the war the protagonists and their families reacted to this painful sequence of events with a protracted and angry silence.[20]

A similar fate awaited those who, for many varied reasons, had supported the *Repubblica Sociale Italiana* (RSI – Italian Social Republic), the puppet regime created at Hitler's behest in mid September 1943. The regime saw the influx of a great many opportunists along with many of the original fascists who believed that the time had finally come for the fulfilment of the movement's ideals, without any further compromises. A large number of young people, both men and women, participated due to a complexity of motives, not easily distinguishable: from patriotism to anti-communism and the fascination that was felt by a significant part of European youth in this period for national socialism. Despite its claims, effectively, the RSI had only very limited autonomy and ended up mainly carrying out acts of repression which accentuated the population's discontent.[21] For at least four decades after the end of the war, the memories of the Social Republic, derogatorily called 'of Salò' after its minuscule capital city, remained on the margins of collective memory.[22] This is due to the prevalent hegemony of anti-fascist memory about which more will be said later.[23] Only recently have the motives of the so-called 'Salò boys' received much attention in historiographical, literary and political circles.[24]

The deep wounds inflicted upon the social body by the war and its immediate aftermath are brought into sharp relief when we contemplate the difficulty the institutions of the new Italian state had in facing the question of grief and its public remembrance. Unlike in 1918,[25] in 1945 the Italian state was not able to promote officially recognized and legitimizing memorials to those who had fallen during the conflict since Italians had fought and died on both sides. It was for this reason that the attempt to remember the victims of the massacre in the Ardeatine caves (24 March 1944) failed. Remembrance of the dead – after a chaotic phase dominated by unofficial initiatives – was ultimately entrusted to the armed forces, which in 1945 (and after) had only a weak claim to represent the nation as a whole. This day of remembrance accordingly assumed a much lower profile than 4 November, which was the day of commemoration for the victory in 1918 and which is still the day for remembering all those who have died during wartime.[26]

The only narrative with any realistic possibility of legitimizing the post-war period of an Italy so divided by the war events of the last five years was that based on the central role of the Resistance. This narrative focused on two main themes: that opposition to the Fascist regime and the occupying Germans was a sentiment shared by almost all the population, and that this sentiment was a morally rather than politically motivated feeling intended to redeem the population from the degradation into which it had fallen during the two decades of fascism. The Resistance was, in short, a war 'of liberation', involving the continuation and completion of the ideas and goals of the Risorgimento. However, on further examination, this heroic image only partially reflects reality. The Italian Resistance had developed along particularly complex lines in which spontaneity existed alongside political awareness.[27] Frequently, the decision to take 'to the mountains' to fight against the occupying forces was motivated by decisions that were dictated either by chance or opportunity. It is sufficient to refer to the many disbanded officers and soldiers who, after 8 September, were determined not to be deported, or to the vast numbers who dodged the draft orders issued by the ineffectual RSI government. There is also an important element of opportunistic motives, sometimes of a criminal nature, since an armed band could easily procure food and valuables from a fearful and helpless civilian population. Political awareness developed by degrees within the partisan formations and not without difficulty, despite the efforts of the political parties re-born (or newly born) after the fall of the Fascist regime in July 1943. In fact, there were partisan groups who proudly defended their own political 'neutrality'. In many cases, the partisans acquired a clear political awareness only by means of a slow process of formation and indoctrination within their groups. This is particularly true of the 'Garibaldi' brigades whose affiliations were to the political ideals of communism as the PCI paid special attention to the indoctrination of partisans.

Consequently, the combination of spontaneity and political awareness is decidedly complex but, nonetheless, it is possible to trace a tendency towards a growing politicising of the Resistance movement in Italy. This was shaped by the main traditional ideologies that existed in the country: from communism and socialism to Catholicism with the addition of original elements such as 'actionism' that harked back to the democratic republicanism of Giuseppe Mazzini, which was strongly libertarian and with traces of socialism (above all with regard to economics). This growing tendency ultimately influenced the partisan war itself, despite the commitment of the main anti-Fascist parties to put aside questions of programmes and politics in their desire to privilege unity in the battle against the occupying German forces and its ally, the Fascists of the Italian Social Republic. There was no lack of attrition and tension between partisan groups of differing political colours, above all in the north-east of Italy. The geographical and ideological proximity to the well-organised Yugoslavian Partisan movement, dominated by the Communists, so greatly influenced a section of the Italian Communist partisans that, in the final phases of the fight for liberation, they preferred agreement with their ideological ally (Tito) to defending 'national' ideals. The massacre of a group of Catholic partisans at Porzûs by Communist partisans from the Friuli area (7 February 1945) was the most bloody apex of the tension between them. This continued in the post-war period whilst the question of the eastern borders was still unresolved. In November 1946 the secretary of the PCI, Palmiro Togliatti, even proposed the exchange of Trieste for Gorizia as he was willing to cede this territory to Tito in order to bring the capital city of the Julian Venetia within the national borders.[28]

Within the partisan movement itself, there were increasingly plans for a profound renewal of Italian institutions, economy and society with a deep-seated expectation that the end of the war would bring about a definitive break in the continuity of Italian history. For many partisans, the Resistance was seen as a war for national liberation from the occupying Germans and the *repubblichini* (from the Italian Social Republic), considered unpatriotic traitors at the command of the occupying authorities. Within this vision of a war of liberation can be found many traces of the Risorgimento movement and many partisans also saw their commitment as a form of class war, since fighting against the occupiers could also mean combating the capitalist economic order and assisting in its overthrow. Nationalist and class considerations could be happily combined and these motivations offered the possibility of considering what they had done as a positive and gratifying commitment.

Such an expectation was ultimately frustrated by both the internal and international conditions. It should not be forgotten that the system of a bipolar division of Europe, consolidated in 1945, and the already dominant Cold War climate, profoundly influenced Italian political life. A move to the left was presented as damaging to national interests and would be basically impossible. It is sufficient to consider the extraordinarily effective political propaganda of the Christian Democrats during the elections of 18 April 1948. They basically blackmailed the electorate into not supporting the left-wing parties by threatening to suspend the American Marshall Plan.[29]

Alongside these international considerations, internal ones also assumed considerable importance. Social stability and institutional continuity were championed by the Christian Democrats[30] who, since the 1946 elections for the Constituent Assembly, had demonstrated their ability to attain wide-ranging consensus in the name of these two elements.[31] As a consequence, the purges principally within the civil service were stopped after an initial convulsive period. The new state needed the bureaucratic and military apparatus although it appeared to have no need at all of the almost fifteen thousand ex-partisans who had initially been enrolled in the ranks of the police after the end of the war. And, with clearly political motives, it freed itself of them within a period of just two years.[32]

At the end of the Second World War, the general internal situation in Italy was extremely difficult. At an economic level, over and above the serious damage suffered, particularly by the infrastructure network (ports and railways but also the steel industry), estimated at an overall cost of 3,200 billions Lire (equal to three times the pre-war annual national income), there was an extremely serious inflation crisis which was linked, amongst other things, to the presence of the occupying Allied forces.[33]

There was also a deterioration in economic morals with the triumph, mainly in the southern regions, of an illegal economy 'intoxicated' by the extraordinary financial capacity of the occupiers. Acquiring the essentials for daily life was still extremely expensive for the average Italian citizen, and, above all for those on fixed salaries (and, therefore, mainly civil servants), the black market was very damaging. This triggered a degree of hostility towards the peasant population, seen by public opinion as cynical exploiters of the difficult post-war situation. This attitude reversed the city-countryside relationship at the end of the First World War when the factory workers were accused of being shirkers and cowards in contrast to the peasants who had sacrificed their lives in the trenches.

Alongside this clear divide between the urban and rural worlds, at the end of the war there was also a marked split between northern Italy and the south and the islands. The latter two had almost no experience of either German occupation or the presence of the bloodthirsty and vindictive fascism of the Social Republic. The war ended here almost a year and a half earlier than in the regions north of the Apennines.[34] At the same time, in northern Italy, the population had both a direct and an indirect experience of the partisan war which was almost entirely lacking in the south[35] where the partisan conflict effectively involved only a very limited part of the population. The most reliable estimates state (although on this subject, there are always margins for discretion in quantification) that in the spring of 1944, the armed partisan combatants in organized groups were only a few thousand. The numbers grew considerably during the summer when, in vast mountain and foothill areas of the north (from the Langhe to Carnia and the Apennines of Modena), they created 'free zones' also called, rather pompously, 'Partisan republics'.[36] On the eve of the final uprising in April 1945, according to Ferruccio Parri (one of the partisan movement's leaders) the *Comitato di Liberazione Alta Italia* (CLNAI – Northern Italy Freedom Committee) had just over seventy thousand men at its disposal. In the days of enthusiasm for the liberation, this partisan army swelled very quickly. Giogio Bocca has written: 'In the days of insurrection, there were 250–300,000 armed and cockaded men wandering around', defining this rapid numerical growth as a 'colourful but not particularly useful rearguard.'[37]

In the north, the civilian population suffered reprisals and horrific massacres at the hands of the Germans and the RSI,[38] whilst in the south, violence was meted out above all by the 'liberators', particularly in the form of bombings, and the abuse of women, mainly by the French North-African troops.[39] It would be reductive to trace the successive evolution of Italian politics back to this difference in experience between the north and the south but it can, nonetheless, partially explain what happened in following years. In large swathes of public opinion, particularly in the south, a desire to forget and put behind them these negative wartime experiences prevailed from the very outset. In this respect, there is significance in the generalised attitude towards military prisoners of war who returned in dribs and drabs – the last ones were freed in the first months of 1947 (the situation in the Soviet Union is different as the last survivors were repatriated a decade after the end of the war).[40] It should be remembered that there were around a million and a half prisoners in all, of whom almost 650,000 were imprisoned by the ex-allied Germany. Their return was accompanied by a resonating silence which created a considerable amount of frustration. On the other hand, they were the defeated and materially represented the defeat of the Fascist regime's dreams (and those of a fair number of Italians) of bringing Italy up to the rank of a great world power. For the *Internati Militari Italiani* (IMI – Italian Military Internees, as the soldiers and officers captured by the German troops after 8 September 1943 were officially called) the sensation of defeat was frequently accompanied by both that of feeling betrayed by their own nation (due to the total disorganisation that characterised the Badoglio government's dealing with the Armistice or, rather, 'not dealing with' it) and the immense frustration of being treated as traitors and cowards by their prison warders.[41] And, despite the fact that, objectively speaking, many of the IMI had made the courageous choice in the concentration camps of refusing to opt for the Social Republic, the perception of others imposed upon them and their own self-perception was decidedly un-heroic. The same can be said for the factory workers coerced into deportation to Germany and for others who were deported – including those for political reasons. This was even more true when compared with the heroic stature (which can, today, be considered as excessive) attributed to the partisans. Post-war Italian society thus attempted, as quickly as possible, to close the 'chapter' of the return of the prisoners of war, surrounding them with a form of oblivion that lasted throughout the following decades.[42]

In the south, attitudes of passive acceptance of the status quo, involving a mixture of nostalgia for the monarchy and political opportunism, quickly took hold. It should not be forgotten that, with regard to the referendum on the constitution of 2 June 1946, the votes in favour of a republic (more than 54 per cent) came mainly from the centre and north whilst in some southern regions the choice in favour of the monarchy's return was clearly predominant. Throughout the southern regions, the percentage of votes in favour of maintaining the Savoy monarchy reached 67.4 per cent and on the two islands 64 per cent. Not even in the partisan north were the votes in favour of the Republic so great (64.8 per cent). Consequently, there was a clear distinction between northern, republican and progressive Italy and the monarchic, moderate-conservative south of the country. It is sufficient to highlight the great success of the *Uomo Qualunque* (Man in the Street) party, above all in the southern constituencies. The party was founded in 1944 by the Neapolitan journalist Guglielmo Giannini and was a protest party that was abrasively anti-establishment and anti-democratic, profoundly hostile to both the Resistance and the Republic. It represented a certain part of the uneasiness and frustrations of the southern middle classes who felt themselves crushed by inflation and by the black market.[43] The *Uomo Qualunque* party took 5.3 per cent of the votes and thirty seats in the elections for the Constituent Assembly of 1946, more than some of the political parties with established traditions – such as the Republican Party – and parties that were effectively the embodiment of the spirit of the Resistance, such as the Action Party. With only 1.4 per cent of the votes this party suffered a notorious collapse and disappeared immediately from the Republican political stage.[44]

In this context it is necessary to highlight the achievement of the Christian Democratic Party in becoming the political party representing the majority of the moderate and conservative forces who were fearful of the political experimentation promoted by the Resistance parties such as the Action Party mentioned above. It was a political grouping that had attracted a large number of votes which, on 2 June 1946, had been cast in support of the monarchy and, in the two preceding years, it had also been capable of absorbing the centrifugal forces of Sicilian separatism which were particularly strong during the period 1943–1945. On studying the evolution of this long period of Italian post-war democracy, it can be seen that the Christian Democrats led by Alcide De Gasperi were able to incorporate and contain the anti-democratic and reactionary urges of a considerable section of Italian society (mainly in the south and, above all, from the middle classes), channelling them towards a complete acceptance of democracy as a system of government. In the eyes of this conservative and moderate Italy, the war should be a distant memory to be put aside as quickly as possible.

On the other hand, the regions of the south were marked in these years by intense and dramatic social upheavals. From 1944 onwards the sensation of liberty created by the end of the Fascist regime, fired a rebellion by the peasants and sharecroppers throughout these regions with the intent of obtaining an agrarian reform that would put an end to the deep-seated social imbalance in the southern countryside. The battles for agrarian reform, led by the Communist Party, initially had some success (under the auspices of the Communist minister Fausto Gullo) but were then brought back – in the second half of the 1940s – into the arms of a stabilising form of reform controlled by the Christian Democrats (under the guidance of the government minister Antonio Segni).[45] Many of the expectations of liberation on the part of the southern peasant masses were disappointed and they had to wait for the start of the economic growth period (almost twenty years later), the so-called 'boom', to see their complete involvement in national life, this time as industrial proletariats who immigrated into the productive regions of the north.

If the 'wind from the south' was predominantly moderate and seeking restoration (although not exclusively so), the 'wind from the north' (as the essence of the demands promoted by the political groups active in the Resistance was called) had a very different content, at least in the very early phases of the post-war period. There was a strong expectation of change, both political and socio-economic. However, the sense of gratification quickly disappeared when faced with the 'betrayal' of the Resistance spirit allegedly committed by the ruling Christian Democrat class and by the conditions imposed by the western allies. The hopes (or illusions) placed in the 'CLN government' to realise the political and institutional plans drawn up during the period 1943–1945 collapsed with the fall of Ferruccio Parri's government at the beginning of December 1945 – a collapse in which the fierce conflicts existing between the anti-fascist parties themselves played their own significant part.[46]

Not all ex-partisans agreed to withdraw or accept a return to a civilian existence within a political and institutional set-up so very different from the ideals for which they had fought. The result, in Italy, was a bloody and increasingly senseless trail of crimes and vendettas which, over and above their political and ideological labels, frequently concealed personal or merely criminal motives. It was mainly in Emilia-Romagna that this trail of vendettas, principally of communist origin (or publicised as such), was the most ferocious; the overall number of victims appears realistically to oscillate between ten and twenty thousand. This is an undoubtedly significant figure but is very far from the three hundred 'martyrs' which neo-fascist literature initially claimed. An international comparison, for example, with France or with the victims of Franco's regime after the end of the Spanish Civil War, demonstrates how Italy's case in 1945–46 can be placed within a much wider context and with numbers that are considerably lower. It has been calculated that the post-war victims of vendettas by Franco's supporters in Spain were around two hundred thousand. Over and above recurring political exploitation, the phenomenon of partisan justice after the war demonstrates the divide between the expectations of many ex-partisans and the political-institutional reality to which they quickly had to adjust.[47]

Without entering into the question of armed vendettas which had clearly become useless as a means of overturning the rigid position of Italy within the context of the Cold War, many ex-partisans and exponents of the political groupings closest to their experience perceived, with a growing sense of frustration, the divide between the official celebrations of the Resistance and the Liberation which centred on the 25 April festivity, and the political reality of the nation in which the left-wing parties were now completely side-lined.[48] These celebrations became increasingly empty and repetitive, and anti-fascist unity, although openly acclaimed, took on an ever more superficial aspect. Beneath the official celebrations of unity under the umbrella of the Resistance myth, there were considerations and motives that differed considerably between each of the various political factions.[49]

However, a strong tradition of rhetoric remained linked to the idea of the war of liberation which vigorously rejected the participation of extreme right-wing parties in the so-called 'constitutional overarch' which represented the basis of the Italian political system until the beginning of the 1990s.[50] On the other hand, party political membership became increasingly entrenched,[51] resulting in the automatic exclusion of any possibility of the Communist Party becoming part of the government. Within the limits of this Resistance rhetoric, the idea that the war for liberation might also have been a form of 'civil war' was for a long period firmly rejected and it took many decades and a persistent commitment on the part of historians and intellectuals to have this categorisation accepted within the republican public discourse.[52]

However, it was conceived as such from the beginning by many of the militants of Mussolini's Social Republic. Only a part of these were young men and women who were naïve idealists wanting to sacrifice their lives for the love of country and moral faith-keeping. Others were 'old guns' of fascism, frustrated during the years of the regime by the compromises that Mussolini had been forced to come to with the traditional ruling classes. Others were merely opportunists who had found themselves at the crucial moment on the wrong side of the front. At the end of the war, the groups of ex-*repubblichini* carefully nurtured the concept of their own war as a sacrifice that public opinion had not understood, but which had been made in the name of the highest patriotic ideals. This was a myth which only in part corresponded to fact whilst, in reality, the RSI had been completely subjugated to the German will, isolated from public opinion which was more concerned with survival and dealing with the serious problems posed by the occupation. The 'puppet-state' installed on the banks of Lake Garda had embraced an unrealistic political goal that was bathed in feelings of rancour and hatred towards its own citizens who were collectively held to be either 'bandits', 'rebels' or 'accomplices'.[53]

Certainly, the neo-fascist and ex-*repubblichini* reading of the recently ended war had very limited circulation, in contrast to the literature of the Resistance which enjoyed the advantage of publication and was widely available. Nonetheless, it is important to note that the extreme right was allowed to re-establish itself immediately after the war. The *Movimento Sociale Italian,* founded by young but important exponents of the Republic who were also 'social', such as Giorgio Almirante and Pino Romualdi, were awarded over half a million votes in the 1948 elections, nearly all from the south which had no experience of the severity of the Nazi-Fascist occupation or the partisan war. From this moment onwards, the party maintained a firm presence on the Italian political scene and, in some circumstances, was even 'flirted' with by the Christian Democrats in its attempts to maintain and consolidate its power (such as, for example, in the 1950s).[54]

The break-up of the governments based on the anti-fascist alliance at the hands of De Gasperi in May 1947 was the prelude to a head-on clash during the elections of 18 April 1948. By using relentless propaganda that raised the spectre of communism, and with strong support from the Church and its organisations, Christian Democracy was able to achieve its best electoral result, gaining 48.5 per cent of the votes and an absolute majority. From then on, the brief period of the large coalition of parties that had been allied in the partisan war was definitively over and it was substituted by a radical confrontation of the two camps: the west, personified by the DC led by De Gasperi and communism. It was an unequal confrontation given that the DC managed, thanks to a careful policy of (internal and international) alliances, to impede any possibility that the other side could arrive at government other than in some limited areas of municipal and regional government. During the electoral encounter of 1948,[55] the political tension culminated in an open confrontation between demonstrators and the police. It was further aggravated by the attempt (unsuccessful) on the life of Palmiro Togliatti, secretary of the Communist Party, on 4 April at the hands of a right-wing student and fears of open civil war re-surfaced. On the other hand, according to official police statistics, between 1945 and 1952 (with a very high upswing in 1948), 171 cannons, 708 mortars, 5,124 machine guns, 35,326 sub-machine guns, 164,978 guns and muskets and 20,877 tons of war explosives were confiscated.[56] Over and above reciprocal political instrumentalization, these statistics provide evidence of the intensity of the political confrontation and the extent to which, at times, it was on the verge of turning into an armed one.

In the 1948 and subsequent electoral campaigns both camps made much use of the positive message of peace, accusing the opposition of wanting to unleash a war. In the prevailing Cold War atmosphere, the memory of the war of liberation became increasingly remote. The celebrations of 25 April became the prerogative of only one political area – the left, mainly the Communists. The state institutions, although formally acknowledging the date which had risen to the ranks of a national holiday, tended gradually to empty it of any significance, turning it into a ceremonial event which was increasingly abstract and detached from current events.

In the decades after 1945 even the discourse about the 'fascist' war or, in other words, the Second World War was widely side-tracked in public consciousness. Or rather, the personal and moralising elements were emphasised along with those focussing on the sacrifices of the soldiers / 'poor souls' uninformed of the reasons why they had been sent to fight in Africa, Egypt or Russia. On the other hand, it was inopportune for any of the political forces, and particularly for the Christian Democrats, to have an in-depth and critical study of our country's recent history. This strongly biased re-reading has contributed to anaesthetising any profound reflection on the blame to be attributed to fascism, the monarchy, the ruling classes and even everyday citizens. What has been allowed free reign is the myth of the 'good Italian'.[57] However, the strong political links with the western bloc, in which the Federal Republic of Germany played a crucial role, have also impeded any critical coming to terms with the position of National Socialist Germany as the occupying force in the terrible two years 1943–1945, and with the crimes committed in that period against the innocent civilian population.[58]

The dramatic experiences of a large number of Italian citizens living on the eastern borders in the immediate post-war period have been widely ignored by national public opinion, although they have been jealously cultivated at a local level and by those directly affected. I refer here to the question of the *foibe*. The *foibe* are natural caves, typical of karst regions such as those in the areas surrounding Trieste and Istria. In these areas, between 1943 and 1945–46, Yugoslavian Communist Partisans carried out round-ups and mass shootings of Italians, Germans, Slovenes and Croatians, from a mixture of political and ethnic motivations. This was a particularly bloody page of history during the final phases of the war. It must be considered, on the one hand, in the light of the extremely tough policies of the occupation and 'ethnic cleansing' carried out by Italians and Germans in the Balkans in the initial stages of the war and, on the other, as fitting in with the strategies of the Yugoslavian Communist Partisan movement to eliminate all its enemies (including those considered as potential enemies). The victims of the *foibe* are presumed to be many thousands. The massacres (in which the victims were thrown, sometimes whilst still alive, into the *foibe*) were followed in subsequent years by the exodus of several hundred thousand Italians from the Istrian and Dalmatian territories in which they had lived for centuries. Even here there was a mixture of coercion and voluntary choice. The exiles numbered between 250,000 and 300,000. It appears that the Italian authorities did very little to help them integrate in a climate of great economic vulnerability of a country that had only recently emerged from the war. To these two phenomena, extremely dramatic for those who lived and suffered them, public opinion and historiography effectively paid very little attention at least until the end of the 1980s.[59]

'In a little under a decade, Italy was downgraded from an "imperial" power to an inferior ranking nation, barely tolerated by its ex-enemies who had become its allies: it was a hugely traumatic experience.'[60] To this were added the traumas of the break-up of the anti-fascist front and the collapse of the hopes for a profound political, cultural and social renewal of the country in accordance with the political outlines traced in the years of armed resistance. All this took place in the context of the Cold War in which Italy held a very delicate position both geographically, and because it had the most powerful communist party in the western world. It is hardly surprising, therefore, that a critical review of the recent and painful wartime experiences had difficulty in coming to the fore.

An in-depth analysis of the war by Italian society and culture only took place during the 1990s when, initially, the war on Iraq (the 'first' war of 1991) and, subsequently, the explosion of civil and ethnic wars in the nearby Balkans refocused attention on the subject of Italy's political and military role after the collapse of the bi-polar system.[61] It should not be forgotten that at the beginning of that decade there was the disintegration, under the weight of corruption and inefficiency, of the party political system that took its lead from the 'constitutional overarch' and the traditions of anti-fascism which had governed republican Italy.[62]

Notes

1. Mimmo Franzinelli, *Delatori. Spie e confidenti anonimi. L'arma segreta del regime fascista* (Milan, 2001). More generally, see S. Colarizi, *L'opinione degli italiani sotto il regime 1929–1943* (Rome, 1991), for an analysis of the evolution of popular consensus towards fascism.
2. See the two large collections of police documents concerning public opinion published by A. Lepre (ed.), *Le illusioni, la paura e la rabbia* (Naples, 1989); and Lepre (ed.), *L'occhio del Duce. Gli italiani e la censura di guerra* (Milan, 1992).
3. See the seminal work by R. De Felice, *Mussolini il Duce. Lo stato totalitario 1936–1940* (Turin, 1981), 626ff.
4. See Giorgio Rochat, *Le guerre italiane 1935–1943. Dall'impero d'Etiopia alla disfatta* (Turin, 2005), 239ff.; and MacGregor Knox, *La guerra di Mussolini* (Rome, 1984) (original edition, *Mussolini Unleashed 1939–1941,* Cambridge, 1982). On the as yet little-studied question of voluntary participation, see Rochat, *Le guerre italiane,* 316ff.
5. Nicola Labanca, *Oltremare. Storia dell'espansione coloniale italiana* (Bologna, 2002); more recently, M. Dominioni, *Lo sfascio dell'impero. Gli italiani in Etiopia 1936–1941* (Rome, 2008).
6. Rochat, *Le guerre italiane,* 273.
7. Jens Petersen, *Hitler e Mussolini. La difficile alleanza* (Rome, 1975); and Erich Kuby, *Il tradimento tedesco* (Milan, 1987).
8. See, amongst others, the well-documented official report of the USE (Ufficio Storico dell'Esercito – Army History Department): *Le operazioni delle unità italiane al fronte russo 1941–1943* (Rome, 1977).
9. The balanced observations of Rochat, *Le guerre italiane 1935–1943,* 378ff., are the most updated.
10. T. Schlemmer, *Die Italiener an der Ostfront 1942/43* (Munich, 2005).
11. Only a few figures serve as evidence of the diffusion and establishment of this literature (mainly in the form of memoirs) which were based on the retreat. The overall literary best-seller about the Italian war is, without any doubt, Giuseppe Bedeschi's book, *Centomila gavette di ghiaccio* (Milan, 1963), which up to 1979 had sold more than one million copies. A good second is the short story by Mario Rigoni Stern, *Il sergente nella neve* (Turin, 1953) which, by the same date, had sold over half a million copies. It is Rigoni Stern's moving book which still stands as almost canonical reading in Italian middle and high schools.
12. J. Steinberg, *All or Nothing. The Axis and the Holocaust 1941–1943* (London, 1990).
13. D. Rodogno, *Il nuovo ordine mediterraneo. Le politiche di occupazione dell'Italia fascista in Europa (1940–1943)* (Turin, 2003); translated as: *Fascism's European Empire: Italian Occupation during the Second World War* (Cambridge, 2006).
14. I. Dalla Costa (a cura di), *L'Italia imbavagliata. Lettere censurate 1940–1943* (Treviso, 1990), 42.

15. Ibid., 64.

16. F. Conti, *I prigionieri di guerra italiani 1940–1945* (Bologna, 1986); G. Schreiber, *I militari italiani internati nei campi di concentramento del Terzo Reich* (Rome, 1992); and G. Hammermann, *Gli internati militari in Germania 1943–1945* (Bologna, 2004). The most recent reconstruction of the most significant moment of armed resistance, leaidng to the massacre of the 'Acqui' division on the Greek island of Cefalonia, is by G. E. Rusconi, *Cefalonia. Quando gli italiani si battono* (Turin, 2004).

17. E. Aga Rossi, *Una nazione allo sbando. L'armistizio italiano del settembre 1943* (Bologna, 1993; revised edition 2003).

18. See B. Moore and K. Fedorowich, *The British Empire and its Italian Prisoners of War, 1940–1947* (Basingstoke, 2002).

19. B. Mantelli, *Camerati del lavoro. I lavoratori emigrati nel Terzo Reich 1938–1943* (Florence, 1992).

20. On the difficulty of constructing memory for the different groups of deported people, see Anna Bravo and Daniele Jalla (eds.), *Una misura onesta. Gli scritti di memoria della deportazione in Italia 1944–1993* (Milan, 1994).

21. L. Ganapini, *La repubblica delle camicie nere. I combattenti, i politici, i socializzatori* (Milan, 1991); D. Gagliani, *Brigate Nere. Mussolini e la militarizzazione del Partito Fascista Repubblicano* (Turin, 1999).

22. With regard to the memory of the war developed by the neo-fascist sub-culture, see F. Germinario, *L'altra memoria. L'Estrema Destra, Salò e la Resistenza* (Turin, 1999).

23. On the political exclusion of the neo-fascist and neo-monarchist parties from the heart of political decisions in the Italian republic, see P. Ignazi, *Il polo escluso. Profilo del Movimento Sociale Italiano* (Bologna, 1989).

24. Mirko Tremaglia, a cabinet minister of the Republic, proudly recalls his past as one of these 'boys'. Interesting examples of self-representation of the RSI militants is the literary memoir by P. Mazzantini, *A cercar la bella morte* (Milan, 1986); and *I balilla andarono a Salò* (Venice, 1995); P. Pisenti, *Una repubblica necessaria* (Rome, 1975); and R. Vivarelli, *La fine di una stagione. Memoria 1943–1945* (Bologna, 2000).

25. See Jay M. Winter, *Il lutto e la memoria. La Grande guerra nella storia culturale europea* (Bologna, 1999; 1st edition, 1994).

26. Guri Schwarz, *Tu mi devi seppelir: Riti funebri e culto nazionale alle origini della repubblicana* (Turin, 2010).

27. S. Peli, *La Resistenza in Italia. Storia e critica* (Turin, 2004).

28. Roberto Gualtieri, *Togliatti e la politica estera italiana dalla resistenza al trattato di pace 1943–1947* (Rome, 1995); E. Aga Rossi and V. Zaslasvki, *Togliatti e Stalin* (Bologna, 2007).

29. Mario Isnenghi and Silvio Lanaro (eds.), *La Democrazia Cristiana dal fascismo al 18 aprile* (Venice, 1978); Edoardo Novelli, *Le elezioni del quarantotto: Storia, strategia e immagini della prima campagna elettorale repubblicana* (Rome, 2008).

30. G. Galli, *Storia della Democrazia Cristiana* (Bari, 1978).

31. C. Pavone, *Alle origini della repubblica. Scritti su fascismo, antifascismo e continuità della Stato* (Turin, 1995); and A. Giovagnoli, *Interpretazioni della repubblica* (Bologna, 1998).

32. Romano Canosa, *Storia dell'epurazione in Italia. Le sanzioni contro il fascismo 1943–1948* (Milan, 1999); Hans Woller, *I conti con il fascismo. L'epurazione in Italia (1943–1948)* (Bologna, 2002).

33. C. Daneo, *La politica economica della ricostruzione 1945–1949* (Turin, 1975).

34. See N. Gallerano (ed.), *L'altro dopoguerra. Roma e il Sud 1943–1945* (Milan, 1985).

35. For a concise reconstruction of events see, G. Corni, 'Italy', in B. Moore (ed.) *Resistance in Western Europe* (Oxford, 2000), 157–188.

36. See the general reconstruction by M. Legnani, *Politica e amministrazione nelle repubbliche partigiane. Studio e documenti* (Milano, 1976).

37. G. Bocca, *Storia dell'Italia partigiana. Settembre 1943 – maggio 1945* (Milan, 1995), 521.

38. For an in-depth overview of the events, see G. Schreiber, *La vendetta tedesca 1943–1945. Le rappresaglie naziste in Italia* (Milan, 2000; 1st edition, 1996).

39. See the recent monographs by G. Gribaudi, *Guerra totale. Tra bombe alleate e violenze naziste. Napoli e il fronte meridionale 1940–1944* (Turin, 2005); T. Baris, *Tra due fuochi. Esperienza e memoria della guerra lungo la linea Gustav* (Rome, 2003) (both partially based on oral testimonies).

40. M. T. Giusti, *I prigionieri italiani in Russia* (Bologna, 2003).

41. Hammermann, *Gli internati militari in Germania.*

42. 'During the past twenty years the situation has changed and a growing number of veterans have published diaries and memoirs and proudly claim the honour of having made a choice and having been imprisoned which, today, are elements fully recognised as aspects of resistance to Nazi-fascism', Rochat, *Le guerre italiane*, 451.

43. See the still-valid monograph by S. Setta, *L'uomo qualunque 1944–1948* (Rome, 1975; quoted from the new edition, 2005).

44. See G. De Luna, *Storia del Partito d'Azione* (Milan, 1982).

45. Of the numerous local studies, I recommend E. Cinanni, *Lotta per la terra e comunisti in Calabria* (Turin, 1977). A summary can be found in P. Ginsborg, *Storia d'Italia dal dopoguerra ad oggi* (Turin, 1989), 160–187.

46. On Parri, see Luca Polese Remaggi, *La nazione perduta. Ferruccio Parri nel Novecento italiano* (Bologna, 2004).

47. G. Pansa, *Il sangue dei vinti. Quello che accadde in Italia dopo il 25 aprile* (Milan, 2003). More balanced is M. Dondi, *La lunga liberazione. Giustizia e violenza nel dopoguerra italiano* (Rome, 1999).

48. On the relationship between government and opposition in the period of 'centralism' based on the central role of Christian Democracy, see G. Caredda, *Governo e opposizione nell'Italia del dopoguerra 1947–1960* (Rome, 1995).

49. See the well-documented book by F. Focardi, *La guerra della memoria. La Reistenza nel dibattito politico italiano dal 1945 ad oggi* (Rome, 2005), 130–168.

50. Pietro Scoppola, *La repubblica dei partiti. Profilo storico della democrazia in Italia (1945–1990)* (Bologna, 1991); Silvio Lanaro, *Storia dell'Italia repubblicana. Dalla fine della guerra agli anni novanta* (Venice, 1992).

51. Angelo Ventrone, *La cittadinanza repubblicana. Forma-partito e identità nazionale alle origini della democrazia in Italia (1943–1948)* (Bologna, 1996).

52. See the seminal work by Claudio Pavone, *Una guerra civile. Saggio storico sulla moralità nella Resistenza* (Turin, 1991).

53. G. Pisanò, *Storia della guerra civile in Italia*, 3 vols. (Milan, 1965–66).

54. Piero Ignazi, *Il polo escluso. Profilo del MSI* (Bologna, 1989).

55. Cf. the analysis by Stefano Cavazza, 'Comunicazione di massa e simbologia politica nelle campagne elettorali del secondo dopoguerra', in P.L.Ballini and M. Ridolfi (eds.), *Storia delle campagne elettorali in Italia* (Milan, 2002), 204ff.

56. Scoppola, *La repubblica dei partiti*, 140.

57. David Bidussa, *Il mito del bravo italiano* (Milan, 1994).

58. This theme has become extremely important over the past few years due to the radical change in the post-war 'anti-fascist' political scene. Of the many studies on the subject,

I suggest Michele Battini, *Peccati di memoria. La mancata Norimberga italiana* (Rome, 2003).

59. From the wealth of literature, which has mostly been produced in very recent years, I suggest: G. Valdevit, *Foibe. Il peso del passato, Venezia Giulia 1943–1945* (Venice, 1997); R. Pupo and R. Spazzali, *Foibe* (Milan, 2003); and G. Crainz, *Il dolore e l'esilio. L'Istria e le memorie divise d'Europa* (Rome, 2005); Gustavo Corni, 'The Exodus of Italians from Istria and Dalmatia, 1946–1956', in J. Reinisch and E. White (eds.), *The Disentanglement of Populations* (London, 2011), 71–90.

60. G. De Luna, 'Partiti e società negli anni della ricostruzione', in AA.VV., *Storia dell'Italia repubblicana*, vol. 1: *La costruzione della democrazia* (Turin, 1994), 722.

61. Alberto Asor Rosa, *La guerra. Sulle forme attuali della convivenza umana* (Turin, 2002).

62. The sudden transformation of the Italian political system, revolving for over forty years around the central role of Christian Democracy, has aroused considerable interest in Anglo-American academics concerned with history and politics. See, amongst others, M. Gilbert, *The Italian Revolution. The End of Democracy, Italian Style?* (Boulder, CO, 1995); P. Ginsborg, *Italy and its Discontent* (Harmondsworth, 2001); and P. McCarthy, *The Crisis of the Italian State* (New York, 1997).

Bibliography

Abusch, Alexander: *Der Irrweg einer Nation. Ein Beitrag zum Verständnis deutscher Geschichte* (Berlin, 1946).

Adamson, Walter L.: 'The Impact of World War I on the Italian Political Culture', in Roshwald, Aviel and Stites, Richard (eds.): *European Culture in the Great War. The Arts, Entertainment, and Propaganda, 1914–1918* (Cambridge, 2002).

Addison, Paul: *Now the War is Over: A Social History of Britain 1945–51* (London, 1985).

Afflerbach, Holger and Stevenson, David (eds.): *An Improbable War? The Outbreak of World War I and European Political Culture before 1914* (New York/Oxford, 2007).

Aga, Rossi E.: *Una nazione allo sbando. L'armistizio italiano del settembre 1943* (Bologna, 1993; revised edition, 2003).

Aga, Rossi E. and Zaslasvki V.: *Togliatti e Stalin* (Bologna, 2007).

Albanese, Giulia: *Alle origini del fascismo. La violenza politica a Venezia 1919–1922*, on behalf of Mario Isnenghi (Padua, 2001).

Alexander, Bill: *British Volunteers for Liberty: Spain 1936–39* (London, 1982).

Alexander, Sally and Fyrth, Jim (eds.): *Women's Voices from the Spanish Civil War* (London, 1991).

Allain, Jean-Claude: *Joseph Caillaux*, vol. 2: *L'oracle (1914–1944)* (Paris, 1981).

Aly, Götz: *Hitlers Volksstaat. Raub, Rassenkrieg und nationaler Sozialismus* (Frankfurt, 2005).

De Ambris, A. and De Felice, Renzo (eds.): *La Carta del Carnaro nei testi di Alceste De Ambris e di Gabriele D'Annunzio* (Bologna, 1973).

Amouroux, Henri: *Le peuple du désastre, 1939–1940, La grande histoire des Français sous l'occupation*, vol. 1 (Paris, 1976).

Andreas-Friedrich, Ruth (ed.): *Tagebuchaufzeichnungen; 1945 – 1948* (Frankfurt, 1986).

Andrieu, Claire: *Le Programme commun de la Résistance* (Paris, 1984).

Anonyma: *Eine Frau in Berlin. Tagebuchaufzeichnungen vom 20. April bis 22. Juni 1945* (Frankfurt, 2003).

Anstey, Edgar; et al. (eds.): *Shots in the Dark* (London, 1951).

Apollinaire, Guillaume: *La petite auto*, in *Calligrammes, Œuvres poétiques* (Paris, 1965), 207, 1085–1086.

Arendt, Hannah: *Elemente und Ursprünge totaler Herrschaft* (Munich, 1986).

Aron, Raymond: *Le spectateur engagé. Entretiens avec Jean-Louis Missika et Dominique Wolton* (Paris, 1981).

———, *Mémoires. 50 ans de réflexion politique*, vol. 1 (Paris, 1983).

———, *Paix et guerre entre les nations* (Paris, 1962).

Asor, Rosa Alberto: *La guerra. Sulle forme attuali della convivenza umana* (Turin, 2002).

Assouline, Pierre: *L'épuration des intellectuels* (Brussels, 1996).

Aubrac, Raymond: *Où la mémoire s'attarde* (Paris, 1996).

Audoin-Rozeau, Stéphane: 'Die Delegation der "gueules cassées" in Versailles am 28. Juni 1919', in Krumeich, Gerd and Fehlemann, Silke (eds.): *Versailles 1919. Ziele – Wirkungen – Wahrnehmungen* (Schriften der Bibliothek für Zeitgeschichte – Neue Folge; 14) (Essen, 2001), 280–287.

Audoin-Rouzeau, Stéphane; et al. (ed.): *La politique et la guerre. Pour comprendre le XXe siècle européen. Hommage à Jean-Jacques Becker* (Paris, 2002).

Audoin-Rouzeau, Stéphane and Becker, Anette: *14–18. Retrouver la Grande Guerre* (Paris, 2003).

——, 'Violence et consentement: la "culture de guerre" du premier conflit mondial', in Rioux, Jean-Pierre and Sirinelli, Jean-François (eds.): *Pour une histoire culturelle* (Paris 1997), 251–271.

Aust, Stefan and Burgdorff, Stephan (eds.): *Die Flucht. Über die Vertreibung der Deutschen aus dem Osten* (Stuttgart, 2002).

Azéma, Jean-Pierre: *De Munich à la Libération, 1938–1944* (Paris, 1979).

——, 'Faire face aux destructions de la guerre de 1940', in Azéma (ed.): *Reconstructions et modernisation, la France après les ruines* (Paris, 1991), 33–42.

Bachelier, Christian: 'L'opinion à travers les premiers sondages, 1944–1949', in Veillon, Dominique and Flonneau, Jean-Marie: *Le temps des restrictions en France 1939-1949* (Paris, 1996), 479–500.

Backes, Uwe; Jesse, Eckhard and Zitelmann, Rainer (eds.): *Die Schatten der Vergangenheit. Impulse zur Historisierung der Vergangenheit* (Frankfurt/Berlin, 1990).

Bahr, Hermann: 'Ideen von 1914', *Hochland* 14 (1917), 431–448.

Balbo, Italo: *Diario 1922* (Milan, 1932).

Bamm, Peter: *Die unsichtbare Flagge: ein Bericht* (Munich, 1952).

Bankier, David: *Die öffentliche Meinung im Hitler-Staat. Die 'Endlösung' und die Deutschen. Eine Berichtigung* (Berlin, 1995).

Barbusse, Henri: *Clarté* (Paris, 1978 ; 1st edition, 1919).

Barcellini, Serge and Wieviroka, Annette: *Passant souviens-toi! Les lieux du souvenir de la Seconde Guerre mondiale* (Paris, 1995).

Barère de Vieuzac, Bertrand: *Mémoires*, 4 vols. (Paris, 1842–1844).

Baris, T.: *Tra due fuochi. Esperienza e memoria della guerra lungo la linea Gustav* (Rome, 2003).

Barnett, Corelli: *The Audit of War: The Illusion and Reality of Britain as a Great Nation* (London, 1986).

——, *The Lost Victory: British Dreams and British Realities* (London, 1995).

Baron, Alexander: *From the City, From the Plough* (London, 1948).

Baron, Ulrich and Müller, Hans-Harald: 'Die Weltkriege im Roman der Nachkriegszeiten', in Niedhart, Gottfried and Riesenberger, Dieter (eds.): *Lernen aus dem Krieg? Deutsche Nachkriegszeiten 1918/1945* (Munich, 1992), 300–318.

Barth, Boris: *Dolchstoßlegenden und politische Desintegration. Das Trauma der deutschen Niederlage im Ersten Weltkrieg 1914–1933* (Düsseldorf, 2003).

Battini, Michele: *Peccati di memoria. La mancata Norimberga italiana* (Rome, 2003).

Baudorre, Philippe: *Barbusse, le pourfendeur de la Grande Guerre* (Paris, 1995).

Baumgarten, Otto; et al. (eds.): *Geistige und sittliche Wirkungen des Krieges in Deutschland* (Stuttgart/Berlin/Leipzig, 1927).

Bavendamm, Gundula: *Spionnage und Verrat. Konspirative Kriegserzählungen und französische Innenpolitik, 1914–1917* (Essen, 2004).

Beaupré, Nicolas: *Écrire en guerre, écrire la guerre. France, Allemagne 1914–1920* (Paris, 2006).

——, 'New Writers, New Literary Genres (1914–1918): The Contribution of Historical Comparatism (France, Germany)', in Purseigle, Pierre (ed.): *Warfare and Belligerence. Perspectives in First World War Studies* (Leyden, 2005), 323–346.

Beaupré, Nicolas; Duménil, Anne and Ingrao, Christian (eds.): *L'ère de la guerre*, vol. 1: *Violence, mobilisations, deuil (1914–1918)* (Paris, 2004).

Becker, Jean Jacques: *1914. Comment les Français sont entrés dans la Guerre. Contribution à l'étude de l'opinion publique, printemps – été 1914* (Paris, 1977).

——, 'Frankreich und der gescheiterte Versuch, das Deutsche Reich zu zerstören', in Krumeich, Gerd and Fehlemann, Silke (eds.): *Versailles 1919. Ziele – Wirkungen – Wahrnehmungen* (Schriften der Bibliothek für Zeitgeschichte – Neue Folge; 14) (Essen, 2001), 65–70.

Becker, Jean-Jacques and Berstein, Serge: *Victoire et Frustrations, 1919–1929* (Nouvelle histoire de la France contemporaine, 12) (Paris, 1990).

Becker, Wolfgang and Schöll, Norbert: *In jenen Tagen. Wie der deutsche Nachkriegsfilm die Vergangenheit bewältigte* (Opladen, 1995).

Bedeschi, Giuseppe: *Centomila gavette di ghiaccio* (Milan, 1963).

Beer, Wilfried: *Kriegsalltag an der Heimatfront. Alliierter Luftkrieg und deutsche Gegenmaßnahmen zur Abwehr und Schadensbegrenzung dargestellt für den Raum Münster* (Bremen, 1990).

Beevor, Antony: *Berlin 1945: Das Ende* (Munich, 2002).

De Begnac, Yvon: *Taccuini mussoliniani* (Bologna, 1990).

Le Beguec, Gilles: 'L'évolution de la politique gouvernementale et les problèmes institutionnels', in Rémond René and Bourdin, Janine (eds.): *Edouard Daladier, chef de gouvernement, avril 1938–septembre 1939* (Paris, 1977).

Begouën, Max: *Quelques poèmes à la gloire de l'armée française* (Toulouse, 1917).

Behrenbeck, Sabine: *Der Kult um die toten Helden. Nationalsozialistische Mythen, Riten und Symbole 1923–1945* (Vierow b. Greifswald, 1996).

Beil, Christine: *Der ausgestellte Krieg: Präsentationen des Ersten Weltkriegs 1914–1939* (Tübingen, 2005).

Bendikat, Elfi: '"Krieg oder Frieden?" Liberale Presse und Kriegsfrage in Berlin und Paris (1911–1914)', *Historische Mitteilungen* 3 (1990), 268–292.

Ben-Ghiat, Ruth: *La cultura fascista* (Bologna, 2001).

Benz, Wolfgang (ed.): *Die Vertreibung der Deutschen aus dem Osten. Ursachen, Ereignisse, Folgen* (Frankfurt, 1985).

Bergère, Marc: *Une société en épuration: épuration vécue et perçue en Maine-et-Loire* (Rennes, 2004).

Berghahn, Volker: *Der Stahlhelm. Bund der Frontsoldaten 1918–1935* (Düsseldorf, 1966).

——, *Europa im Zeitalter der Weltkriege. Die Entfesselung und Entgrenzung der Gewalt* (Frankfurt, 2002).

Berghoff, Hartmut: 'Zwischen Verdrängung und Aufarbeitung. Die bundesdeutsche Gesellschaft und ihre nationalsozialistische Vergangenheit in den Fünfziger Jahren', in *GWU* 49 (1998), 96–114.

Berman, Marshall: *All that is Solid Melts into Air. The Experience of Modernity* (New York, 1982).

Bernhardi, Friedrich von: *Deutschland und der nächste Krieg* (Stuttgart, 1912).

Besier, Gerhard and Sautter, Gerhard: *Wie Christen ihre Schuld bekennen. Die Stuttgarter Schulderklärung 1945* (Göttingen, 1985).

Bessel, Richard: 'Die Heimkehr der Soldaten. Das Bild der Frontsoldaten in der Öffentlichkeit der Weimarer Republik', in Hirschfeld, Gerhard; Krumeich, Gerd and Renz, Irina (eds.): *'Keiner fühlt sich hier mehr als Mensch...'. Erlebnis und Wirkung des Ersten Weltkrieges*, (= Schriften der Bibliothek für Zeitgeschichte; Neue Folge 1), (Essen, 1993), 221–241.

Beßlich, Barbara: *Wege in den 'Kulturkrieg'. Zivilisationskritik in Deutschland, 1890–1914* (Darmstadt, 2000).

Bialer, Uri: *The Shadow of the Bomber. The Fear of Air Attack and British Politics 1932–1939* (London, The Royal Historical Society, 1980).

Bianchi, Roberto: *Bocci-Bocci. I tumulti annonari nella Toscana del 1919* (Florence, 2001).

Bidussa, David: *Il mito del bravo italiano* (Milan, 1994).

Billany, Dan: *The Trap* (1950).

Blank, Ralf: 'Kriegsalltag und Luftkrieg an der "Heimatfront"', in Echternkamp, Jörg (ed.), *Die deutsche Kriegsgesellschaft 1939 bis 1945*, vol.1: *Politisierung, Vernichtung, Überleben* (Munich, 2004), 357–461.

Blasius, Dirk: 'Karl Schmitt und der Heereskonflikt', *Historische Zeitschrift* 281 (2005), 659–682.

———, *Weimars Ende. Bürgerkrieg und Politik 1930–1933* (Göttingen, 2005).

Blatchford, R.: *Germany and England* (London, 1910).

Bloch, Marc: *L'étrange défaite* (Paris, 1946).

———, 'Souvenirs de guerre' in Bloch, Marc, *L'Histoire, la Guerre, la Résistance* (Paris, 2006), 119-120.

Blum, Heiko R.: *30 Jahre danach. Dokumentation zur Auseinandersetzung mit dem Nationalsozialismus im Film 1945–1975* (Cologne, 1975).

Bocca, G.: *Storia dell'Italia partigiana. Settembre 1943 – maggio 1945* (Milan, 1995).

Boden, Matthew: *Richard Strauss* (Vienna, 1999).

Boemeke, Manfred; Chickering, Roger and Förster, Stig (eds.): *Anticipating Total War. The German Experiences 1871–1914* (Cambridge, 1999).

Borne, Dominique and Dubief, Henri: *La crise des années 30, 1929–1938* (Paris, 1989).

Borsdorf, Ulrich and Jamin, Mathilde: *Überleben im Krieg. Kriegserfahrungen in einer Industrieregion 1939–1945* (Reinbek, 1989).

Boudon, Victor: *Avec Charles Péguy. De la Lorraine à la Marne, Août-Septembre 1914* (Paris, 1916).

Bouillon, Jacques and Petzold, Michel: *Mémoire figée, mémoire vivante. Les monuments aux morts* (Paris, 1999).

Bourdin, Janine: 'Les anciens combattants et la célébration du 11 novembre 1938', in Rémond, René and Bourdin, Janine (eds.): *La France et les Français en 1938–1939* (Paris, 1978), 96–97.

Bourdrel, Philippe: *L'Epuration sauvage* (Paris, 1988).

Boyce, David George: *Nationalism in Ireland* (London, 1982).

Bramstedt, E. K.: *Goebbels und die nationalsozialistische Propaganda 1925–1945* (Frankfurt, 1971).

Brandt, Susanne: *Vom Kriegsschauplatz zum Gedächtnisraum. Die Westfront 1914–1939* (Baden-Baden, 2002).

Brasillach, Robert: *Notre Avant-Guerre* (Paris, 1941; 3rd edition, 1981).

Bravo, Anna and Jalla, Daniele (eds.): *Una misura onesta. Gli scritti di memoria della deportazione in Italia 1944–1993* (Milan, 1994).

Brochhagen, Ulrich: *Nach Nürnberg. Vergangenheitsbewältigung und Westintegration in der Ära Adenauer* (Hamburg, 1994).

Broock, Peter: *Pacifism in Europe to 1914* (Princeton, 1972).

Broszat, Martin: 'Plädoyer für eine Historisierung des Nationalsozialismus', in *Merkur*, 1985, 5, 373–385.

Broszat, Martin; Henke, Klaus-Dietmar and Woller, Hans (eds.): *Von Stalingrad zur Währungsreform. Zur Sozialgeschichte des Umbruchs in Deutschland* (Munich, 1988).

Bruch, Rüdiger vom: 'Aufruf der 93', in Hirschfeld, Gerhard; Krumeich, Gerd and Renz, Irina (eds.), *Enzyklopädie Erster Weltkrieg*, 2nd edition (Paderborn, 2004), 356f.

Brücker, Vera: *Die Schulddiskussion im deutschen Katholizismus nach 1945* (Bochum, 1989).

Bruendel, Steffen: *Volksgemeinschaft oder Volksstaat. Die "Ideen von 1914" und die Neuordnung Deutschlands im Ersten Weltkrieg* (Berlin, 2003).

Brunel de Pérard, Jacques: *Carnet de route* (Paris, 1915).

Büttner, Ursula: 'Orientierungssuche in heilloser Zeit: der Beitrag der evangelischen Kirche', in Büttner, Ursula and Nellessen, Bernd (eds.): *Die zweite Chance. Der Übergang von der Diktatur zur Demokratie in Hamburg 1945-1949* (Hamburg, 1997), 85–107.

Buscher, Frank W.: *The U.S. War Crimes Trial Program in Germany, 1946-1955* (New York, 1989).

Buton, Philippe: 'Du parti légal à l'organisation clandestine', in Rioux, Jean-Pierre; Prost, Antoine and Azéma, Jean-Pierre (eds.): *Les communistes français de Munich à Châteaubriant (1938-1941)* (Paris, 1987), 119–133.

——, *La Joie douloureuse. La libération de la France* (Brussels, 2004).

Cabanes, Bruno: *La victoire endeuillée. La sortie de guerre des soldats français (1918-1920)* (Paris, 2004).

Calder, Angus: *The People's War*, paperback edition (London, 1971).

Calder, Angus and Sheridan, Dorothy (eds.): *Speak for Yourself. A Mass Observation Anthology 1937-1949* (London, 1984).

Calì, Vincenzo; Corni, Gustavo and Ferrandi, Giuseppe (eds.): *Gli intellettuali e la Grande guerra* (Bologna, 2000).

Calò, Giovanni: *Doveri del cittadino in tempo di guerra* (Milan, 1915).

Canal, Claudio: 'La retorica della morte. I monumenti ai caduti della Grande guerra', *Rivista di storia contemporanea* 4 (1982), 659–669.

Candeloro, Giorgio: *Storia dell'Italia moderna*, vol. VIII: *La prima guerra mondiale, il dopoguerra, l'avvento del fascismo* (Milan, 1989; 1st edition, 1978).

Canosa, Romano: *Storia dell'epurazione in Italia. Le sanzioni contro il fascismo 1943-1948* (Milan, 1999).

Capdevila, Luc: 'La communauté de souffrance. L'identité nationale à travers l'image du bon Français au lendemain de l'Occupation. L'exemple de la Bretagne', in Martens, Stefan and Vaïsse, Maurice (eds.): *Frankreich und Deutschland im Krieg (1942-1944). Okkupation, Kollaboration, Resistance* (Bonn, 2000), 831–844.

——, *Les Bretons au lendemain de l'Occupation: imaginaire et comportement d'une sortie de guerre 1944-1945* (Rennes, 1999).

Caredda, G.: *Governo e opposizione nell'Italia del dopoguerra 1947-1960* (Rome, 1995).

Carsten, F. L.: *War against War. British and German Radical Movements in the First World War* (London, 1982).

Cavazza, Stefano: 'Comunicazione di massa e simbologia politica nelle campagne elettorali del secondo dopoguerra', in Ballini, P. L. and Ridolfi, M. (eds.): *Storia delle campagne elettorali in Italia* (Milan, 2002), 193–237.

Cendrars, Miriam: *Blaise Cendrars* (Paris, 1984).

Cesarani, David: 'Lacking in Convictions: British War Crimes Policy and National Memory of the Second World War', in Evans, Martin and Lunn, Kenn (eds.): *War and Memory in the Twentieth Century* (Oxford, 1997), 27–42.

Champeaux, Antoine: *Mémoires de la Grande Guerre. Témoins et témoignages* (Nancy, 1989).

Charmley, J.: *Splendid Isolation? Britain, the Balance of Power and the Origins of the First World War* (London, 1999).

Chaumont, Jean-Michel: *La concurrence des victimes: Génocide, identité, reconnaissance* (Paris, 1997).

Chélini, Michel-Pierre: *Inflation, Etat et opinion en France de 1944 à 1952* (Paris, 1998).

Chickering, Roger; Förster, Stig and Greiner, Bernd (eds.): *A World at Total War: Global Conflict and the Politics of Destruction, 1937–1945* (Cambridge, 2005).

Chiurco, Giorgio Alberto: *Storia della Rivoluzione fascista*, vol. 4 (Rome, 1929).

Churchill, Winston S.: *The Second World War*, vol. 1: *The Gathering Storm* (London, 1948).

Cinanni, E.: *Lotta per la terra e comunisti in Calabria* (Turin, 1977).

Clarke, I. F. (ed.): *The Great War with Germany, 1890–1914. Fictions and Fantasies of the War-to-come* (Liverpool, 1997).

——, *The Patterns of Expectation 1644–2001* (London, 1979).

——, *Voices Prophesying War. Future Wars, 1763–3749*, 2nd edition (Oxford, 1992).

von Clausewitz, Carl: *Vom Kriege*, 16th edition (Bonn, 1952).

Cobet, Christoph: *Deutschlands Erneuerung 1945–1950. Bio-Bibliographische Dokumentation mit 443 Texten* (Frankfurt, 1985).

Colarizi, S.: *L'opinione degli italiani sotto il regime 1929–1943* (Rome, 1991).

Colin, Geneviève and Becker, Jean-Jacques: 'Les écrivains, la guerre de 1914 et l'opinion publique', in *Relations internationales* 24 (1980), 482–484.

Connelly, Mark: *We Can Take it! Britain and the Memory of the Second World War* (Harlow, 2004).

Conti, F.: *I prigionieri di guerra italiani 1940–1945* (Bologna, 1986).

Coquart, Elizabeth: *La France des GI's* (Paris, 2003).

Cordova, Ferdinando: *Arditi e legionari dannunziani* (Padua, 1969).

Corner, Paul: *Il fascismo a Ferrara 1915–1925* (Bari, 1975).

Corni, G.: 'Italy', in Moore, B. (ed.) *Resistance in Western Europe* (Oxford, 2000), 157–188.

Corsi, Hubert: *La lotta politica in Maremma 1900–1925* (Rome, 1987).

Dalla, Costa I. (ed.): *L'Italia imbavagliata. Lettere censurate 1940–1943* (Treviso, 1990).

Cowling, Maurice: *The Impact of Hilter. British Politics and British Policy 1933–1940* (Chicago and London, 1977).

Crainz, G.: *Il dolore e l'esilio. L'Istria e le memorie divise d'Europa* (Rome, 2005).

Crémieux-Brilhac, Jean-Louis: *Les Français de l'an 40*, vol. 1: *La guerre oui ou non?*, vol. 2: *Ouvriers et soldats* (Paris, 1990).

Dahl, Roald: *Over to You: Ten Stories about Flyers and Flying* (London, 1946).

Dahlmann, Dittmar: 'Krieg, Bürgerkrieg, Gewalt. Die Wahrnehmung des Ersten Weltkriegs und des Bürgerkrieges in der Sowjetunion in der Zwischenkriegszeit', in Dülffer, Jost and Krumeich, Gerd (eds.), *Der verlorene Frieden* (Essen, 2002), 91–100.

Daneo, C.: *La politica economica della ricostruzione 1945–1949* (Turin, 1975).

Daniel, Ute: *Kompendium Kulturgeschichte*, 3rd edition (Frankfurt, 2002).

Dard, Olivier: *Les années 30. Le choix impossible* (Paris, 1999).

Davis, Calvin D.: *The United States and the First Hague Conference* (Ithaca, 1962).

——, *The United States and the Second Hague Peace Conference* (Durham, NC, 1973).

Day-Lewis, Tamasin (ed.): *Last Letters Home* (London, 1995).

Decleva, Enrico: '*Il Giornale d'Italia*' (*1918–1926*) and the contributions in *La Tribuna, L'Italia e Il Corriere della Sera*, in Brunello, Vigezzi (ed.): *1919–1925. Dopoguerra e fascismo. Politica e stampa in Italia* (Bari, 1965).

Degl'Innocenti, Maurizio: *L'epoca giovane. Generazioni, fascismo e antifascismo* (Manduria-Bari-Rome, 2002).

Deist, Wilhelm: 'Die Aufrüstung der Wehrmacht', in *Das Deutsche Reich und der Zweite Weltkrieg*, ed. by Militärgeschichtliches Forschungsamt, vol. 1 (Stuttgart, 1959), 397f.

Demers, Francis J.: *Le origini del fascismo a Cremona* (Bari, 1979).

Dickuth-Harrach, Gustaf v. (ed.): *Im Felde unbesiegt. Der Weltkrieg in 24 Einzeldarstellungen*, 4 vols. (Munich, 1921).

Digeon, Claude : *La crise allemande de la pensée française 1870–1914* (Paris, 1959).

Dilks, David (ed.): *The Diaries of Sir Alexander Cadogan 1938–1945* (London, 1971).

Diller, Ansgar and Mühl-Benninghaus, Wolfgang (eds.): *Berichterstattung über den Nürnberger Prozeß gegen die Hauptkriegsverbrecher 1945/46. Edition und Dokumentation ausgewählter Rundfunkquellen* (Potsdam, 1998).

Docherty, David; Morrison, David and Tracey, Michael: *The Last Picture Show? Britain's Changing Film Audience* (London, 1987).

Dokumentation der Vertreibung der Deutschen aus Ost-Mitteleuropa, ed. by the Bundesministerium für Vertriebene, 5 vols. with 3 appendices (Bonn, 1953–1961).

Domarus, Max: *Hitler. Reden und Proklamationen*, vol. I, 1 (Munich, 1963).

Dominioni, M.: *Lo sfascio dell'impero. Gli italiani in Etiopia 1936–1941* (Rome, 2008).

Dondi, M.: *La lunga liberazione. Giustizia e violenza nel dopoguerra italiano* (Rome, 1999).

Das Dritte Reich. Eine Studie über Nachwirkungen des Nationalsozialismus (Allensbach, 1949).

Dülffer, Jost (ed.): *100 Jahre Zweite Haager Friedenskonferenz*. Special Issue of *Die Friedenswarte* 4 (2007).

——, 'Die Kreta-Krise und der griechisch-türkische Krieg 1895–1898', in Dülffer, Jost; Mühleisen, Hans-Otto and Torunsky, Vera (eds.): *Inseln als Brennpunkte internationaler Politik. Konfliktbewältigung im Wandel des internationalen Systems, 1890–1984* (Cologne, 1986), 13–60.

——, 'Die zivile Reichsleitung und der Krieg. Erwartungen und Bilder 1890–1914' (1998), in Dülffer, Jost: *Im Zeichen der Gewalt, Frieden und Krieg im 19. und 20. Jahrhundert* (Colgone, 2003), 124–140.

——, 'Dispositionen zum Krieg im wilhelminischen Deutschland', in Dülffer, Jost and Holl, Karl (eds.): *Bereit zum Krieg. Kriegsmentalität im wilhelminischen Deutschland 1890–1914* (Göttingen, 1986), 9–19.

——, 'Internationales System, Friedensgefährdung und Kriegsvermeidung: Das Beispiel der Haager Friedenskonferenzen 1899 und 1907', in Steinweg, Reiner (ed.): *Friedensanalysen*, 23, 95–116.

——, 'Kriegserwartung und Kriegsbild in Deutschland vor 1914' (1994), in Dülffer, Jost: *Im Zeichen der Gewalt, Frieden und Krieg im 19. und 20. Jahrhundert* (Colgone, 2003), 107–123.

——, *Regeln gegen den Krieg? Die Haager Friedenskonferenzen von 1899 und 1907 in der internationalen Politik* (Berlin, 1981).

Dülffer, Jost and Hübner, Hans (in collaboration with Breitenborn, Konrad and Laubner, Jürgen) (eds.): *Bismarck. Person – Politik – Mythos* (Berlin, 1993).

Dülffer, Jost; Kröger Martin and Wippich, Rolf-Harald (eds.): *Vermiedene Kriege. Deeskalation von Konflikten der Großmächte zwischen Krimkrieg und Erstem Weltkrieg, 1856–1914* (Munich, 1997).

Duroselle, Jean-Baptiste: *Politique étrangère de la France: La décadence 1932–1939* (Paris, 1979).

Eberan, Barbro: *Luther? Friedrich „der Große"? Wagner? Nietzsche? Wer war an Hitler schuld? Die Debatte um die Schuldfrage 1945–1949* (Munich, 1985).

Eberle, Matthias: *Der Weltkrieg und die Künstler der Weimarer Republik: Dix, Grosz, Beckmann, Schlemmer* (Stuttgart, 1989).

Egremont, M.: *A Life of Arthur James Balfour* (London, 1980).

Eimermacher, Karl and Volpert, Astrid (eds.): *Stürmische Aufbrüche und enttäuschte Hoff-nungen: Russen und Deutsche in der Zwischenkriegszeit* (Munich, 2006).

—— (eds.), *Verführungen der Gewalt: Russen und Deutsche im Ersten und Zweiten Welt-krieg* (Munich, 2005).

Enciclopedia Italiana (Rome, 1932; 2nd edition, 1949).

Evans, Richard: *The Third Reich in Power* (London, 2005; paperback edition, 2006).

Falasca-Zamponi, Simonetta: *Fascist Spectacle: The Aesthetics of Power in Mussolini's Italy* (Berkeley, 1997).

Falter, Jürgen W.: *Hitlers Wähler* (Munich, 1991).

Fascismo. Inchiesta socialista sulle gesta dei fascisti in Italia (Milan, 1963; 1st edition, 1922).

Feiling, Keith: *The Life of Neville Chamberlain* (London, 1946).

Feinstein, Elaine: *Ted Hughes: The Life of a Poet* (London, 2001).

Feldman, Gerald D.: *Vom Weltkrieg zur Weltwirtschaftskrise. Studien zur deutschen Wirt-schafts- und Sozialgeschichte* (Göttingen, 1984).

De Felice, Renzo (ed.): *Il fascismo. Le interpretazioni dei contemporanei e degli storici* (Bari, 1998).

——, *Mussolini il Duce. Lo stato totalitario 1936–1940* (Turin, 1981).

——, *Mussolini il fascista. La conquista del potere (1921–1925)* (Turin, 1995; 1st edition, 1966).

——, *Mussolini il rivoluzionario. 1883–1920* (Turin, 1995; 1st edition, 1965).

Ferguson, Niall: *The Pity of War* (London, 1998).

Fielding, Steven: 'The Good War: 1939–45', in Nick Tiratsoo (ed.), *From Blitz to Blair: A New History of Britain Since 1939* (London, 1998).

Fielding, Steve; Thompson, Peter and Tiratsoo: Nick, *England Arise! The Labour Party and Popular Politics in 1940s Britain* (Manchester, 1995).

Fings, Karola: 'Kriegsenden, Kriegslegenden. Bewältigungsstrategien in einer deutschen Großstadt', in Rusinek, Bernd-A. (ed.): *Kriegsende 1945. Verbrechen, Katastrophen, Be-freiungen in nationaler und internationaler Perspektive* (Göttingen, 2004), 219–238.

Fischer, Fritz: *Germany's War Aims in the First World War* (New York, 1967).

——, *Griff nach der Weltmacht*, 3rd edition (Düsseldorf, 1964).

——, *Krieg der Illusionen. Die deutsche Politik von 1911–1914* (Düsseldorf, 1969).

Flasch, Kurt: *Die geistige Mobilmachung. Die deutschen Intellektuellen und der Erste Welt-krieg* (Berlin, 2000).

Focardi, F.: *La guerra della memoria. La Reistenza nel dibattito politico italiano dal 1945 ad oggi* (Rome, 2005).

Foreign Relations of the United States, 1939/1 (Washington, 1956).

Förster, Jürgen: 'Geistige Kriegsführung in Deutschland', in *Das Deutsche Reich und der Zweite Weltkrieg*, vol. 9, 1 (Munich, 2004), 570f.

Förster, Stig: *An der Schwelle zum totalen Krieg. Die militärische Debatte über den Krieg der Zukunft, 1919–1939* (Paderborn, 2002).

——, 'Im Reich des Absurden: Die Ursachen des Ersten Weltkrieges', in Wegner, Bernd (ed.): *Wie Kriege entstehen. Zum historischen Inhalt von Staatenkonflikten* (Paderborn, 2002), 211–252.

Foschepoth, Joseph: 'Zur deutschen Reaktion auf Niederlage und Besatzung' in Herbst, Lu-dolf (ed.): *Westdeutschland 1945–1955. Unterwerfung, Kontrolle, Integration* (Munich, 1986), 151–165.

Fourastié, Jean: *Die große Hoffnung des 20. Jahrhunderts* (Munich, 1954).

——, *Les Trente Glorieuses ou la Révolution invisible de 1946 à 1975* (Paris, 1979).

Francescangeli, Eros: *Arditi del popolo* (Rome, 2000).

Franzinelli, Mimmo: *Delatori. Spie e confidenti anonimi. L'arma segreta del regime fascista* (Milan, 2001).

——, *Squadristi. Protagonisti e tecniche della violenza fascista 1919–1922* (Milan, 2004).

Frei, Norbert: 'Auschwitz und die Deutschen. Geschichte, Geheimnis, Gedächtnis', in Norbert Frei: *1945 und wir. Das Dritte Reich im Bewußtsein der Deutschen* (Munich, 2005), 156–183.

——, *Der Führerstaat. Nationalsozialistische Herrschaft 1933–1945*, 6th edition (Munich, 2001).

——, *Vergangenheitspolitik. Die Anfänge der Bundesrepublik und die NS-Vergangenheit* (Munich, 1999).

Fribourg, André: *Croire. Histoire d'un soldat* (Paris, 1917).

Friedrich, Jörg: *Der Brand. Deutschland im Bombenkrieg 1940–1945* (Munich, 2002).

Fussell, Paul: *The Great War and Modern Memory* (Oxford, 2000; 1st edition, 1975).

Gade, C.: *Gleichgewichtspolitik oder Bündnispflege? Maximen britischer Außenpolitik (1909–1914)* (Göttingen, 1997).

Gagliani, D.: *Brigate Nere. Mussolini e la militarizzazione del Partito Fascista Repubblicano* (Turin, 1999).

Gallerano, N. (ed.): *L'altro dopoguerra. Roma e il Sud 1943–1945* (Milan, 1985).

Galli, G.: *Storia della Democrazia Cristiana* (Bari, 1978).

Gallian, Marcelo: *Il Ventennale. Gli uomini delle squadre nella Rivoluzione delle Camicie nere* (Rome, 1941).

Gallup International Public Opinion Polls: Great Britain 1937–1945, vol.1 (New York, 1976).

Galtier-Boissière, Jean: *En rase campagne. 1914. Un hiver à Souchez. 1915–1916* (Paris, 1917).

——, *La fleur au fusil* (Paris, 1928).

Ganapini, L.: *La repubblica delle camicie nere. I combattenti, i politici, i socializzatori* (Milan, 1991).

Gannon, Franklin R.: *The British Press and Germany 1936–1939* (Oxford, 1971).

Garfield, Simon: *Our Hidden Lives: The Everyday Diaries of a Forgotten Britain, 1945–1948* (London, 2004).

Gaulle, Charles de: *Discours et Messages*, vol. 1 (Paris, 1970).

——, *Mémoires de Guerre*, vol. 3 (Paris, 1954).

Geinitz, Christian: *Kriegsfurcht und Kampfbereitschaft. Das Augusterlebnis in Freiburg. Eine Studie zum Kriegsbeginn 1914* (Schriften der Bibliothek für Zeitgeschichte; Neue Folge, 7) (Essen, 1998).

Geiss, Imanuel: *Der lange Weg in die Katastrophe. Die Vorgeschichte des Ersten Weltkrieges 1815–1914* (Munich, 1990).

Gentile, Emilio: *Il culto del littorio. La sacralizzazione della politica nell'Italia fascista* (Bari, 1994).

——, *La grande Italia* (Milan, 1997).

——, *La via italiana al totalitarismo. Il partito e lo Stato nel regime fascista* (Rome, 1995).

——, *Storia del partito fascista, 1919–1922. Movimento e milizia* (Bari, 1989).

Geppert, Dominik: '"The Foul-Visaged Anti-Christ of Journalism"? The Popular Press between Warmongering and International Co-operation', in Geppert, Dominik and Gerwarth, Robert (eds.): *Wilhelmine Germany and Edwardian Britain. Essays in Cultural Affinity* (Oxford, 2008).

——, *Pressekriege: Öffentlichkeit und Diplomatie in den deutsch-britischen Beziehungen (1896–1912)* (Munich, 2007).

Géré, François: *Les volontaires de la mort* (Paris, 2003).

Gerlach, Heinrich: *Die verratene Armee* (Munich, 1957).

Germinario, F.: *L'altra memoria. L'Estrema Destra, Salò e la Resistenza* (Turin, 1999).

Geyer, Michael: *Aufrüstung oder Sicherheit. Die Reichswehr in der Krise der Machtpolitik 1924-1936* (Wiesbaden, 1980).

——, 'Das zweite Rüstungsprogramm 1930-1934', *Militärgeschichtliche Mitteilungen* 17 (1975), 125-172.

——, *Verkehrte Welt. Revolution, Inflation und Moderne: München 1914-1921* (Göttingen, 1998).

Gibelli, Antonio: *Il popolo bambino. Infanzia e nazione dalla Grande guerra a Salò* (Turin, 2005).

——, *La grande guerra degli italiani 1915-1918* (Milan, 1998).

Gilbert, Martin: *The First World War: A Complete History* (New York, 1994).

——, *The Italian Revolution. The End of Democracy, Italian Style?* (Boulder, CO, 1995).

Ginsborg, P.: *Italy and its Discontent* (Harmondsworth, 2001).

——, *Storia d'Italia dal dopoguerra ad oggi* (Turin, 1989).

Giovagnoli, A.: *Interpretazioni della repubblica* (Bologna, 1998).

Giovannini, Paolo: *'Tutto da abbattere, tutto da creare'. Le origini del fascismo nella provincia pesarese: 1919-1922* (Bologna, 1993).

Giraudoux, Jean: *Pleins pouvoirs* (Paris, 1939).

Giro, Helmut Dieter: *Die Remilitarisierung des Rheinlandes 1936* (Essen, 2006).

Giulietti, Serafino: 'Fascio fascisti e antifascisti. Fossombrone 1919-1929', in Giannotti, Paolo (ed.): *La provincia di Pesaro e Urbino nel regime fascista* (Ancona, 1986), 11-77.

Giusti, M. T.: *I prigionieri italiani in Russia* (Bologna, 2003).

Gonzales, Calleja Eduardo: *La violencia en la política. Perspectivas teóricas sobre el empleado deliberado de la fuerza en los conflictos de poder* (Madrid, 2002).

Gorce, P.-M. de La: *La Premiere Guerre mondiale*, vol. 2 (Paris, 1991).

Goschler, Constantin: *Wiedergutmachung: Westdeutschland und die Verfolgten des Nationalsozialismus, 1945-1954* (Munich, 1992).

Gouttenoire de Toury, Fernand: *Poincaré a-t-il voulu la guerre?* (Paris, 1920).

Graham, Desmond (ed.): *Keith Douglas: The Complete Poems* (London, 2000).

Greffrath, Bettina: *Gesellschaftsbilder der Nachkriegszeit. Deutsche Spielfilme 1945-1949* (Pfaffenweiler, 1995).

Gregor, Manfred: *Die Brücke* (Wien, 1958).

Gregory, A.: 'British "War Enthusiasm" in 1914. a Reassesment', in G. Braybon: *Evidence, History and the Great War. Historians and the Impact of 1914-18* (New York/Oxford, 2003), 68-69.

Grenard, Fabrice: *La France du marché noir, 1940-1949* (Paris, 2008).

——, 'Le ravitaillement et ses implications politiques en France 1940-1944', *XXème siècle* 94 (2007), 199-215.

Grenard, Fabrice and Mouré, Kenneth: 'Traitors, trafiquants and the confiscation of illicit profit in France 1944-1950', *Historical Journal* 51, 4 (2008), 969-990.

Greschat, Martin (ed.): *Die Schuld der Kirche. Dokumente und Reflexionen zur Stuttgarter Schulderklärung vom 18./19. Oktober 1945* (Munich, 1982).

Gribaudi, G.: *Guerra totale. Tra bombe alleate e violenze naziste. Napoli e il fronte meridionale 1940-1944* (Turin, 2005).

Griffith, Richard: *Fellow Travellers of the Right. British Enthusiasts for Nazi Germany 1933-1939* (Oxford, 1983).

Gualtieri, Roberto: *Togliatti e la politica estera italiana dalla resistenza al trattato di pace 1943-1947* (Rome, 1995).

Gulick, Edward V.: *Europe's Classical Balance of Power* (Ithaca, 1955).

Gysin, Adolphe: *Jusqu'à la Marne, Bataille de la Marne* (Landerneau, 1916).

Haffner, Sebastian: *Geschichte eines Deutschen* (Stuttgart, 2000).

Hall, J. E. D.: *Labour's First Year* (Harmondsworth, 1947).

Hammermann, Gabriele: 'Das Kriegsende in Dachau', in Rusinek, Bernd-A. (ed.): *Kriegsende 1945. Verbrechen, Katastrophen, Befreiungen in nationaler und internationaler Perspektive* (Göttingen, 2004), 27-53.

Hammermann, G.: *Gli internati militari in Germania 1943–1945* (Bologna, 2004).

Hampe, Karl: *Kriegstagebuch*, ed. by Reichert, Folker and Wolgast, Eike (Munich, 2004).

Hanak, H.: *Great Britain and Austria-Hungary during the First World War: A Study in the Formation of Public Opinion* (Oxford, 1962).

Hanna, Martha: *The Mobilization of Intellect, French Scholars and Writers during the Great War* (Cambridge, MA, 1996).

Hardtwig, Wolfgang (ed.): *Ordnungen in der Krise. Zur politischen Kulturgeschichte Deutschlands 1900–1933* (Munich, 2007)

⸺ (ed.): *Politische Kulturgeschichte der Zwischenkriegszeit* (Göttingen, 2005).

Harpprecht, Klaus: 'Im Keller der Gefühle. Gibt es noch einen deutschen Antisemitismus?', *Der Monat* 11, 128 (1959), 13–20.

Hazlehurst, G. C. L.: *Politicians at War. July 1914–May 1915* (London, 1971).

Heinemann, Ulrich: *Die verdrängte Niederlage. Politische Öffentlichkeit und Kriegsschuldfrage in der Weimarer Republik* (Göttingen, 1983).

Heinrich, Willi: *Das geduldige Fleisch* (Stuttgart, 1955).

Henke, Klaus-Dietmar: *Die amerikanische Besetzung Deutschlands* (Munich, 1995).

Hennessey, Peter: *Never Again: Britain 1945–1951* (London, 1992).

Herbert, Ulrich: *Best. Biographische Studien über Radikalismus, Weltanschauung und Vernunft 1903–1989* (Bonn, 1996).

Herbst, Ludolf and Goschler, Constantin (eds.): *Wiedergutmachung in der Bundesrepublik Deutschland* (Munich, 1989).

Herf, Jeffrey: *Zweierlei Erinnerung. Die NS-Vergangenheit im geteilten Deutschland* (Berlin, 1998).

Herren, Madeleine: *Hintertüren zur Macht. Internationalismus und modernisierungsorientierte Außenpolitik in Belgien, der Schweiz und den USA* (Munich, 2000).

Heukenkamp, Ursula (ed.): *Unerwünschte Erfahrung. Kriegsliteratur und Zensur in der DDR* (Berlin, 1990).

Hewitt, Nick: 'A Sceptical Generation? War Memorials and the Collective Memory of the Second World War in Britain, 1945–2000', in Geppert, Dominik (ed.): *The Postwar Challenge: Cultural, Social, and Political Change in Western Europe, 1945–58* (Oxford, 2003), 81–97.

Hildebrand, Klaus: 'Julikrise 1914: Das europäische Sicherheitsdilemma', *Geschichte in Wissenschaft und Unterricht* 36 (1985), 469–502.

⸺, 'Lord Clarendon, Bismarck und das Problem der europäischen Abrüstung 1870', in *Studien zur Geschichte Englands und der deutsch-britischen Beziehungen*, Festschrift Paul Kluke (Munich, 1981), 130–152.

Hillgruber, Andreas: *La distruzione dell'Europa. La Germania e l'epoca delle guerre mondiali (1914–1945)* (Bologna, 1991).

Hirschfeld, Gerhard; Krumeich, Gerd and Renz, Irina (eds.): *Enzyklopädie Erster Weltkrieg*, 2nd edition (Paderborn, 2004).

⸺, *Keiner fühlt sich hier mehr als Mensch. … Erlebnis und Wirkung des Ersten Weltkriegs* (Frankfurt, 1996).

Hoch, Anton: 'Das Attentat auf Hitler im Münchner Bürgerbräukeller 1939', *Vierteljahrshefte für Zeitgeschichte* 17, 4 (1969), 383–413.

Hoch, Anton and Gruchmann, Lothar: *Georg Elser: Der Attentäter aus dem Volk* (Frankfurt, 1980).

Hockerts, Hans Günter and Kuller, Christiane (eds.): *Nach der Verfolgung. Wiedergutmachung nationalsozialistischen Unrechts in Deutschland?* (Göttingen, 2003).

Hofer, Hans-Georg: *Nervenschwäche und Krieg. Modernitätskritik und Krisenbewältigung in der österreichischen Psychatrie (1880-1920)* (Vienna, 2004).

Hoffmann, Stanley: *Organisations internationales et pouvoirs politiques des etats* (Paris, 1953).

Holborn, Hajo: 'Bericht zur deutschen Frage. Beobachtungen und Empfehlungen vom Herbst 1947', *VfZ* 35 (1987), 135–166.

Holl, Karl: *Pazifismus in Deutschland* (Frankfurt, 1988).

—— (ed.), *Pazifismus in der Weimarer Republik* (Paderborn, 1981).

Hollenberg, G.: *Englisches Interesse am Kaiserreich. Die Attraktivität Preußen-Deutschlands für konservative und liberale Kreise in Großbritannien 1860-1914* (Wiesbaden, 1974).

Horbach, Michael: *Die verratenen Söhne* (Hamburg, 1957).

Horne, John (ed.): *State, Society and Mobilization in Europe during the First World War* (Cambridge, 1997).

Hüppauf, Bernd: 'Kriegsliteratur', in Hirschfeld, Gerhard; Krumeich, Gerd and Renz, Irina (eds.): *Enzyklopädie Erster Weltkrieg*, 2nd edition (Paderborn, 2004), 177–191.

Hynes, S.: *The Edwardian Turn of Mind* (Princeton, 1968).

Hynes, Samuel: *The Soldiers' Tale: Bearing Witness to Modern War* (London, 1998).

Ignazi, P.: *Il polo escluso. Profilo del Movimento Sociale Italiano* (Bologna, 1989).

Imlay, Talbot C.: *Facing the Second World War. Strategy, Politics, and Economics in Britain and France, 1938-1940* (New York, 2003).

INSEE: *Mouvement économique en France de 1938 à 1948* (Paris, 1950).

Isnenghi, Mario: *Il mito della grande guerra* (Bologna, 1989).

Isnenghi, Mario and Silvio, Lanaro (eds.): *La Democrazia Cristiana dal fascismo al 18 aprile* (Venice, 1978).

Isnenghi, Mario and Rochat, Giorgio: *La Grande guerra 1914-1918*, (Florence, 2000).

Gianni, Isola: *Guerra al regno della guerra: storia della Lega proletaria mutilati, invalidi, reduci, orfani e vedove di guerra (1918-1924)* (Florence, 1990).

Jäckel, Eberhard and Kuhn, Axel (eds.): *Hitler. Sämtliche Aufzeichnungen 1905-1924* (Stuttgart, 1980).

Jackson, Julian: *The Fall of France. The Nazi Invasion of 1940* (Oxford, 2003).

Jackson, Peter: *France and the Nazi Menace. Intelligence and Policy Making, 1933-1939* (Oxford, 2000).

Jarausch, Konrad: *Die Umkehr: deutsche Wandlungen 1915-1990* (Munich, 2004).

Jasper, Karl: *Die Schuldfrage* (Heidelberg, 1946).

Johnson, B. S. (ed.): *All Bull: The National Servicemen* (London, 1973).

Jünger, Ernst: *Orages d'acier* (Paris, 1970; 1st edition, Hannover, 1920).

Kallis, Aristotle A.: 'Der Niedergang der Deutungsmacht. Nationalsozialistische Propaganda im Kriegsverlauf', *Das Deutsche Reich und der Zweite Weltkrieg* 9, 2 (Munich, 2005), 222.

Kaplan, Alice: *Intelligence avec l'ennemi, le procès Brasillach* (Paris, 2001).

Kaplan, Steve L.: *Le pain maudit, retour sur la France des années oubliées* (Paris, 2008).

Käppner, Joachim: *Erstarrte Geschichte. Faschismus und Holocaust im Spiegel der Geschichtswissenschaft und Geschichtspropaganda der DDR* (Hamburg, 1999).

Kendall, Tim: *Modern English War Poetry* (Oxford, 2006).

Kershaw, Ian: *Der Hitler-Mythos. Führerkult und Volksmeinung* (Stuttgart, 1999).

——, *Der Hitler-Mythos. Volksmeinung und Propaganda im Dritten Reich* (Stuttgart, 1980).

Kettenacker, Lothar: 'Die Diplomatie der Ohnmacht. Die gescheiterte Friedensstrategie der britischen Regierung vor Ausbruch des Zweiten Weltkrieges', in Benz, Wolfgang and Graml, Hermann (eds.): *Sommer 1939. Die Großmächte und der Europäische Krieg* (Stuttgart, 1979), 223–279.

———, *Krieg zur Friedenssicherung. Die Deutschlandplanung der britischen Regierung während des Zweiten Weltkrieges* (Göttingen, 1989).

Kielsmannsegg, Peter Graf: *Lange Schatten. Vom Umgang der Deutschen mit der nationalsozialistischen Vergangenheit* (Berlin, 1989).

Kienitz, Sabine: 'Beschädigte Helden. Zur Politisierung des kriegsinvaliden Soldatenkörpers in der Weimarer Republik', in Dülffer, Jost and Krumeich, Gerd (eds.): *Der verlorene Frieden* (Essen, 2002), 199–214.

Kießling, Friedrich: *Gegen den "großen Krieg"? Entspannung in den internationalen Beziehungen 1911–1914* (Studien zur Internationalen Geschichte, 12) (Munich, 2002).

———, 'Wege aus der Stringenzfalle. Die Vorgeschichte des Ersten Weltkriegs als "Ära der Entspannung"', *Geschichte in Wissenschaft und Unterricht* 55 (2004), 284–304.

King, Alex: *Memorials of the Great War in Britain* (Oxford, 1998).

King, Commander William: *The Stick and the Stars* (London, 1958).

Kirst, Hans Hellmuth: *08/15. Trilogie* (Munich, 1959).

Kitchen, Martin: *Europe between the Wars: A Political History* (London, 1988).

Kogon, Eugen: 'Beinahe mit dem Rücken zur Wand', *Frankfurter Hefte* 9 (1954), 641–645.

Kolb, Eberhard: *Der Frieden von Versailles* (Munich, 2005).

———, *Die Weimarer Republik,* 6th edition (Munich, 2002).

Konsalik, Heinz: *Der Arzt von Stalingrad* (Munich, 1956).

Krumeich, Gerd: '80 ans de recherche allemande sur la guerre de 14–18', in Maurin, Jules and Jauffret, Jean-Charles (eds.): *La Grande Guerre 1914–18: 80 ans d'historiographie et de représentations* (Montpellier, 2002).

———, *Armaments and Politics in France on the Eve of the First World War* (Leamington, 1985).

———, *Aufrüstung und Innenpolitik in Frankreich vor dem Ersten Weltkrieg* (Wiesbaden, 1980).

———, 'Denkmäler zwischen Mahnmal und Schandmal', in Engelbrecht, Jörg and Looz-Corswarem, Clemens von (eds.): *Krieg und Frieden in Düsseldorf. Sichtbare Zeichen der Vergangenheit* (Düsseldorf, 2004), 219–232.

———, 'Die Dolchstoß-Legende', in Schulze, H. and François, Etienne (eds.): *Deutsche Erinnerungsorte,* 3 vols. (Munic, 2001).

———, "Gott mit uns !' La Grande Guerre fut-elle une guerre de religions ?' in Beaupré, Nicolas; Duménil, Anne and Ingrao, Christian (eds.): *L'ère de la guerre,* vol. 1: *Violence, mobilisations, deuil (1914–1918)* (Paris, 2004), 117–130.

———, 'La place de la guerre de 1914–1918 dans l'histoire culturelle de l'Allemagne', in Becker, Jean-Jacques et al. (eds.): *La très grande guerre* (Paris, 1994), 36–45.

Krumeich, Gerd and Schröder, Joachim (eds.): *Der Schatten des Weltkriegs. Die Ruhrbesetzung 1923* (Essen, 2004).

Krumeich, Gerd and Fehlemann, Silke (eds.): *Versailles 1919. Ziele – Wirkungen – Wahrnehmungen* (Schriften der Bibliothek für Zeitgeschichte – Neue Folge; 14) (Essen, 2001).

Kruse, Wolfgang: 'Die Kriegsbegeisterung im Deutschen Reich. Entstehungszusammenhänge, Grenzen und ideologische Strukturen', in van der Linden, Marcel and Mergner, Gottfried (eds.): *Kriegsbegeisterung und mentale Kriegsvorbereitung* (Berlin, 1991), 73–87.

———, *Krieg und nationale Integration. Eine Neuinterpretation des sozialdemokratischen Burgfriedensschlusses, 1914/15* (Essen, 1993).

———, 'Kriegsbegeisterung? Zur Massenstimmung bei Kriegsbeginn', in Kruse, Wolfgang (ed.): *Eine Welt von Feinden. Der Große Krieg 1914–1918* (Frankfurt, 1997), 159–166.

Kuby, Erich: *Il tradimento tedesco* (Milan, 1987).

Kuehl, Warren F.: *Seeking World Order: The United States and World Order to 1920* (Nashville, TN, 1969).

Kupferman, Fred: *Les premiers beaux jours, 1944–1946* (Paris, 1985).

Labanca, Nicola: *Oltremare. Storia dell'espansione coloniale italiana* (Bologna, 2002).

Laborie, Pierre: *L'opinion française sous Vichy. Les Français et la crise d'identité nationale 1936–1944* (2n edn.; Paris, 2001).

Lacaze, Yvon: *L'opinion publique française et la crise de Munich* (Bern, 1991).

Lachapelle, Georges: *Les élections législatives du 16 novembre 1919. Résultats officiels* (Paris, 1920).

Laity, P.: *The British Peace Movement 1870–1914* (Oxford, 2001).

Lambauer, Barbara: *Otto Abetz et les Français ou l'envers de la Collaboration* (Paris, 2001).

Lamszus, Wilhelm: *Das Menschenschlachthaus. Bilder vom kommenden Krieg* (Hamburg/Berlin, 1912).

Lanaro, Silvio: *Storia dell'Italia repubblicana. Dalla fine della guerra agli anni novanta* (Venice, 1992).

Lankheit, Klaus A.: 'Preußen und die Frage der europäischen Abrüstung 1867–1870', *Einzelschriften zur Militärgeschichte* 37 (Freiburg, 1993).

Latzel, Klaus: *Deutsche Soldaten – nationalsozialistischer Krieg? Kriegserlebnis – Kriegserfahrung 1939–1945* (Paderborn, 1998).

Laurien, Ingrid: 'Die Verarbeitung von Nationalsozialismus und Krieg in den politisch-kulturellen Zeitschriften der Westzonen 1945–1949', *GWU* 39 (1988), 220–237.

Lavisse, Ernest: *Histoire de France* (Colin, 1920).

Ledig, Gerd: *Die Stalinorgel* (Hamburg, 1955).

Lee, Laurie: *A Moment of War* (Harmondsworth, 1991).

———, *A Rose for Winter: Travels in Andalucia* (London, 1955).

———, *As I Walked Out One Midsummer Morning* (London, 1969).

Lee, Laurie and Ralph Keene: *We Made a Film in Cyprus* (London, 1947).

Leed, Eric J.: *No Man's Land. Combat & Identity in World War I* (Cambridge, 1979).

Legnani, M.: *Politica e amminstrazione nelle repubbliche partigiane. Studio e documenti* (Milano, 1976).

Leo, Anette and Reif-Spirek, Peter (eds.): *Vielstimmiges Schweigen. Neue Studien zum DDR-Antifaschismus* (Berlin, 2001).

Leonhard, J.: 'Construction and Perception of National Images: Germany and Britain, 1870–1914', *The Linacre Journal* 4 (2000), 45–67.

Leonhard, Rudolf: *Das Chaos* (Hannover, 1919).

Lepre, A. (ed.): *Le illusioni, la paura e la rabbia* (Naples, 1989).

——— (ed.), *L'occhio del Duce. Gli italiani e la censura di guerra* (Milan, 1992).

Létard, Etienne: *Trois mois au premier corps de cavalerie* (Paris, 1919).

Wette, Wolfram; Bremer, Ricarda and Vogel Detlef (eds.): *Das letzte halbe Jahr. Stimmungsberichte der Wehrmachtspropaganda 1944/45* (Essen, 2001).

Lewin, Christophe: *Le retour des prisonniers de guerre français* (Paris, 1986).

Lewis, Norman: *A Dragon Apparent: Travels in Cambodia, Laos and Vietnam* (London, 1951).

———, *Golden Earth: Travels in Burma* (London, 1952).

———, *Jackdaw Cake* (London, 1985).

———, *Naples '44* (London, 1978).

Lindner-Wirsching, Almut: *Französische Schriftsteller und ihre Nation im Ersten Weltkrieg* (Tübingen, 2004).

Longmate, Norman: *When We Won the War: The Story of Victory in Europe 1945* (London, 1977).

Longworth, Philip: *Unending Vigil: a History of the Commonwealth War Graves Commission, 1917-67* (London, 1967).

Loth, Winfried and Rusinek, Bernd-A. (eds.): *Verwandlungspolitik. NS-Eliten in der westdeutschen Nachkriegsgesellschaft* (Frankfurt, 1998).

Loti, Pierre: *Soldats bleus. Journal intime 1914-1918* (Paris, 1998).

Lottman, Herbert: *L'épuration* (Paris, 1986).

Lübbe, Hermann: 'Der Nationalsozialismus im deutschen Nachkriegsbewußtsein', *Historische Zeitschrift* 236 (1983), 579-599.

Ludendorff, Erich: *Kriegsführung und Politik* (Berlin, 1922).

Ludwig, Emil: *Colloqui con Mussolini* (Milan, 1932).

De Luna, G.: 'Partiti e società negli anni della ricostruzione', in AA.VV., *Storia dell'Italia repubblicana*, vol. 1: *La costruzione della democrazia* (Turin, 1994).

——, *Storia del Partito d'Azione* (Milan, 1982).

Lupo, Salvatore: *Il fascismo. La politica in un regime totalitario* (Rome, 2000).

Lütgemeier-Davin, Reinhold: 'Die Nie-Wieder-Krieg-Bewegung in der Weimarer Republik', in Donat, Helmut (ed.): *Die Friedensbewegung. Organisierter Pazifismus in Deutschland, Österreich und in der Schweiz* (Düsseldorf, 1983).

Luzzatto, Sergio: 'La cultura politica dell'Italia fascista', in: *Storica*, 12 (1998).

Lynn-Jones, S. M.: 'Détente and Deterrence. Anglo-German Relations, 1911-1914', in Miller, S., Lynn-Jones, S. M. and Van Evera, S. (eds.): *Military Strategy and the Origins of the First World War* (Oxford, 1991), 165-194.

Lyttelton, Adrian: *The Seizure of Power. Fascism in Italy 1919-1929* (London, 1973).

MacGregor, Knox: 'Conquest, Foreign and Domestic, in Fascist Italy and Nazi-Germany', *The Journal of Modern History*, 56,1. (1984), 1-57.

——, *La guerra di Mussolini* (Rome, 1984; original edition, *Mussolini Unleashed 1939-1941*, Cambridge, 1982).

MacInnes, Colin: *To the Victor the Spoils* (London, 1950).

Macmillan, Harold: *The Blast of War: 1939-1945* (London, 1967).

——, *Winds of Change* (London, 1966).

Mac Orlan, Pierre: *Les Poissons morts, la Lorraine, l'Artois, Verdun, la Somme* (Paris, 1917).

Maier, Charles S.: *Recasting Bourgeois Europe. Stabilization in France, Germany and Italy in the Decade after World War I* (Princeton, 1975).

Majerus, Benoit: 'La guerre commence – Bruxelles en août 1914 et en mai 1940', in Beaupré, Nicolas; Duménil, Anne and Ingrao, Christian (eds.): *L'ère de la guerre*, vol. 1: *Violence, mobilisations, deuil (1914-1918)* (Paris, 2004), 85-106.

Malaparte, Curzio: *Tecnica del colpo di stato* (Florence, 1994; 1st edition, 1931).

Malatesta, Alberto: *I socialisti italiani durante la guerra* (Milan, 1926).

Mann, Klaus: *Der Wendepunkt. Ein Lebensbericht* (Reinbek bei Hamburg, 1984).

Mantelli, B.: *Camerati del lavoro. I lavoratori emigrati nel Terzo Reich 1938-1943* (Florence, 1992).

Marcot, François: 'Rites et Pratiques', in Marcot, François: *La Mémoire des Français, Quarante ans de commémorations de la Seconde Guerre mondiale* (Paris, 1986), 31-39.

Martel, Gordon (ed.): *The Origins of the Second World War Reconsidered* (London, 1986).

Marquardt-Bigman, Petra: *Amerikanische Geheimdienstanalysen über Deutschland 1942-1949* (Munich, 1995).

Mason, Tim: *Sozialpolitik im Dritten Reich. Arbeiterklasse und Volksgemeinschaft* (Opladen, 1977).

Mawdsley, Ewan: *The Russian Civil War* (Boston/London, 1987).

May Ernest, R.: *Strange Victory. Hitler's Conquest of France* (New York, 2000).

Mazzantini, P.: *A cercar la bella morte* (Milan, 1986).

———, *I balilla andarono a Salò* (Venice, 1995).

McCarthy, P.: *The Crisis of the Italian State* (New York, 1997).

Meinecke, Friedrich: *Die deutsche Katastrophe. Betrachtungen und Erinnerungen* (Wiesbaden, 1946).

———, *Straßburg, Freiburg, Berlin 1901–1919* (Stuttgart, 1945).

Meldungen aus dem Reich. Die geheimen Lageberichte des Sicherheitsdienstes der SS, vol. 9 (Herrsching, 1984).

Melograni, Piero: *Storia politica della Grande guerra* (Milan, 1998; 1st edition, 1969).

Melzer, Joseph: *Deutsch-jüdisches Schicksal in dieser Zeit. Wegweiser durch das Schrifttum der letzten 15 Jahre* (Cologne, 1960).

Mencherini, Robert: *Guerre froide, grèves rouges: les grèves insurrectionnelles de 1947–1948* (Paris, 1998).

Mendès France, Pierre: *Œuvres complètes*, vol. 2 (Paris, 1985).

Merritt, Anna J. and Merritt, Richard L. (eds.): *Public Opinion in Occupied Germany. The OMGUS Surveys, 1945–1949* (Urbana, 1970).

——— (eds.), *Public Opinion in Semisovereign Germany. The HICOG Surveys, 1949–1955* (Urbana, 1980).

Merz, Peter: *Und das wurde nicht ihr Staat. Erfahrungen emigrierter Schriftsteller mit Westdeutschland* (Munich, 1985).

Messerschmidt, Manfred: *Die Wehrmachtsjustiz 1933–1945* (Münster, 2005).

Mew, Charlotte: *Complete Poems* (London, 2000).

Milward, Alan S.: 'The Reichsmark Bloc and the International Economy', in Hirschfeld, Gerhard and Kettenacker, Lothar (eds.): *Der 'Führerstaat': Mythos und Realität. Studien zur Struktur und Politik des Dritten Reiches* (Stuttgart, 1981), 377–413.

Milza, Pierre: *Les Fascismes* (Paris, 1985).

Miquel, Marc von: *Ahnden oder amnestieren? Westdeutsche Justiz und Vergangenheitspolitik in den sechziger Jahren* (Göttingen, 2004).

Mitscherlich, Alexander and Mielke, Fred (eds.): *Das Diktat der Menschenverachtung. Der Nürnberger Ärzteprozeß und seine Quellen. Eine Dokumentation* (Heidelberg, 1947).

Mommsen, Hans: *Aufstieg und Untergang der Republik von Weimar 1918–1933*, 2nd edition (Munich, 2001).

———, 'Militär und zivile Militarisierung in Deutschland 1914–1938', in Frevert, Ute (ed.): *Militär und Gesellschaft im 19. und 20. Jahrhundert* (Stuttgart, 1997), 265–276.

Mommsen, Wolfgang J.: *Bürgerstolz und Weltmachtstreben. Deutschland unter Wilhelm II, 1890–1918* (Propyläen Geschichte Deutschlands 7, 2) (Berlin, 1995).

———, *Der Erste Weltkrieg. Anfang vom Ende des bürgerlichen Zeitalters* (Frankfurt, 2004).

———, 'Der Topos vom unvermeidlichen Krieg. Außenpolitik und öffentliche Meinung in Deutschland in den letzten Jahren vor 1914', in Berghahn, Volker R. and Kitchen, Martin (eds.): *Germany in the Age of Total War* (London, 1981), 23–45.

———, 'Der Topos vom unvermeidlichen Krieg. Außenpolitik und öffentliche Meinung in Deutschland in den letzten Jahren vor 1914', in Dülffer, Jost and Holl, Karl (eds.): *Bereit zum Krieg. Kriegsmentalität im wilhelminischen Deutschland 1890–1914* (Göttingen, 1986), 194–224.

——— (ed.), *Die Organisation des Friedens. Demobilmachung, 1918–1920* (Geschichte und Gesellschaft 9) (Göttingen, 1983).

—— (ed.), *Kultur und Krieg: Die Rolle der Intellektuellen, Künstler und Schriftsteller im Ersten Weltkrieg* (Munich, 1996).

——, *Max Weber und die deutsche Politik*, 2nd edition (Tübingen, 1974).

Monticone, Alberto: 'Il socialismo torinese ed i fatti dell'agosto 1917', in Monticone, *Gli italiani in uniforme 1915/1918: intellettuali, borghesi e disertori* (Bari, 1972).

Moore, B. and Fedorowich, K.: *The British Empire and its Italian Prisoners of War, 1940–1947* (Basingstoke, 2002).

Morgan, Kenneth O.: *The People's Peace: British History, 1945–1989* (Oxford, 2001).

Morris, A. J. A.: *The Scaremongers. The Advocacy of War and Rearmament 1896–1914* (London, 1984).

Morris, Benny: *The Roots of Appeasement. The British Weekly Press and Nazi Germany during the 1930ies* (London, 1991).

Mosse, George: 'The Brutalization of German Politics', in George Mosse: *Fallen Soldiers: Reshaping the Memory of the World Wars* (Oxford, 1990).

——, *Gefallen für das Vaterland. Nationales Heldentum und namenloses Sterben* (Stuttgart, 1993).

——, *The Image of Man: the Creation of Modern Masculinity* (New York, 1996).

——, *Nationalism and Sexuality: Middle-Class Morality and Sexual Norms in Modern Europe* (Madison, 1988).

Müller, Klaus-Jürgen: *Armee und Drittes Reich 1933–1939* (Paderborn, 1987).

——, *Das Heer und Hitler: Armee und nationalsozialistisches Regime 1933–1940* (Stuttgart, 1969).

Müller, Rolf-Dieter and Ueberschär, Gerd R.: *Kriegsende 1945. Die Zerstörung des Deutschen Reiches* (Frankfurt, 1994).

Müller, Rolf-Dieter; Ueberschär, Gerd R. and Wette, Wolfram: *Wer zurückweicht wird erschossen. Kriegsalltag und Kriegsende in Südwestdeutschland 1944/45* (Freiburg, 1985).

Münkler, Herfried: *Machtzerfall: Die letzten Tage des Dritten Reiches dargestellt am Beispiel der hessischen Kleinstadt Friedberg* (Berlin, 1985).

Munton, Alan: *English Fiction of the Second World War* (London, 1989).

Näf, Werner: *Abrüstungsverhandlungen im Jahre 1831* (Bern/Leipzig, 1931).

Natter, Wolfgang G.: *Literature at War. 1914–1940. Representing the 'Time of Greatness' in Germany* (New Haven and London, 1999).

Neitzel, Sönke: *Blut und Eisen. Deutschland im Ersten Weltkrieg* (Zürich, 2003).

Nello, Paolo: *L'avanguardismo giovanile alle origini del fascismo* (Bari, 1978).

Nenni, Pietro: *Storia di quattro anni. 1919–1922* (Milan, 1976; 1st edition, 1946).

Neumann, Franz: *Wirtschaft, Staat, Demokratie. Aufsätze 1930–1954* (Frankfurt, 1978).

Newman, Simon: *March 1939: The British Guarantee to Poland* (Oxford, 1976).

Nicolson, Nigel (ed.): *Harold Nicolson. Diaries and Letters 1930–1939*, vol. 1 (London, 1970).

Niess, Alexandre: 'Monuments aux morts et politique: l'exemple marnais', *Guerres mondiales et conflits contemporains* 212 (2003), 17–32.

Niethammer, Lutz (ed.): *'Die Jahre weiß man nicht, wo man die heute hinsetzen soll.' Faschismus-Erfahrungen im Ruhrgebiet* (Berlin, 1983).

—— (ed.), *'Hinterher merkt man, dass es richtig war, dass es schiefgegangen ist.' Nachkriegserfahrungen im Ruhrgebiet* (Berlin, 1983).

Noelle, Elisabeth and Neumann, Erich Peter (eds.): *Jahrbuch der öffentlichen Meinung 1947–1955* (Allensbach, 1956).

—— (eds.), *Jahrbuch der öffentlichen Meinung 1958–1964* (Allensbach, 1965).

Nora, Pierre: 'Entre mémoire et histoire', in Nora, Pierre (ed.): *Les lieux de mémoire*, vol. 1: *La République* (Paris, 1984), xv–xlii.

Oliviero, Angelo Olivetti: *Dal sindacalismo rivoluzionario al corporativismo*, introduction by Francesco Perfetti (Rome, 1984).

Omissi, David E.: *Air Power and Colonial Control: The Royal Air Force, 1919–1939* (Manchester, 1990).

Oncken, Hermann: 'Die politischen Vorgänge im Juli 1914', in Ernst Jäckh (ed.), *Der Große Krieg als Erlebnis und Erfahrung*, vol.1: *Das Erlebnis* (Gotha, 1916), 1–13.

Onofri, Nazario Sauro: *La strage di Palazzo d'Accursio. Origine e nascita del fascismo bolognese, 1919–1920* (Milan, 1980).

Ory, Pascal: 'La commémoration révolutionnaire en 1939', in Rémond, René and Bourdin, Janine (eds.): *La France et les Français en 1938–1939* (Paris, 1978).

Overmans, Rüdiger: *Deutsche militärische Verluste im Zweiten Weltkrieg* (Munich, 2000).

Overy, Richard: *Rußlands Krieg* (Hamburg, 2003).

Panayi, P.: *The Enemy in our Midst. Germans in Britain during the First World War* (New York, 1991).

Pansa, G.: *Il sangue dei vinti. Quello che accadde in Italia dopo il 25 aprile* (Milan, 2003).

Panunzio, Sergio: *Che cos'è il fascismo* (Milan, 1924).

Panzig, Christel and Panzig, Klaus-Alexander: '"Die Russen kommen!" Deutsche Erinnerungen mit "Russen" bei Kriegsende 1945 in Dörfern und Kleinstädten Mitteldeutschlands und Mecklenburg-Vorpommerns', in Scherstjanoi, Elke (ed.): *Rotarmisten schreiben aus Deutschland. Briefe von der Front (1945) und historische Analysen* (Munich, 2004), 340–368.

Paoloni, Francesco: *I nostri "boches": il giolittismo, partito tedesco in Italia*, with a preface by Benito Mussolini (Milan, 1916).

Parlato, Giuseppe: *La sinistra fascista. Storia di un progetto mancato* (Bologna, 2000).

Paul, Gerhard: *Bilder des Krieges - Krieg der Bilder* (Paderborn, 2004).

———, '"Diese Erschießungen haben mich innerlich gar nicht mehr berührt". Die Kriegsendphasenverbrechen der Gestapo 1944/45', in Paul, Gerhard and Mallmann, Klaus-Michael (eds.): *Die Gestapo im Zweiten Weltkrieg. „Heimatfront" und besetztes Europa* (Darmstadt, 2000), 543–568.

Pavie, André: *Mes troupiers* (Tours, 1917).

Pavone, Claudio: *Alle origini della repubblica. Scritti su fascismo, antifascismo e continuità della Stato* (Turin, 1995).

———, *Una guerra civile. Saggio storico sulla moralità nella Resistenza* (Turin, 1991).

Péan, Pierre: *Une jeunesse française. François Mitterrand, 1934–1947* (Paris, 1994).

Peli, S.: *La Resistenza in Italia. Storia e critica* (Turin, 2004).

Perfetti, Francesco: *Il sindacalismo fascista. Dalle origini alla vigilia dello Stato corporativo (1919–1930)*, (Rome, 1988).

Petersen, Jens: 'Elettorato e base sociale del fascismo italiano degli anni Venti', *Studi storici* 3 (1973), 627–669.

———, *Hitler e Mussolini. La difficile alleanza* (Rome, 1975).

Peukert, Detlev: *Die Weimarer Republik* (Frankfurt, 1987).

Piazzesi, Mario: *Diario di uno squadrista fiorentino* (Rome, 1980).

Pick, Daniel: *War Machine. The Razionalisation of Slaughter in the Modern Age* (New Haven/London, 1993).

Picker, Henry: *Hitlers Tischgespräche im Führerhauptquartier* (Wiesbaden, 1983).

Pierucci, Francesco Alunni: *1921–1922. Violenza e crimini fascisti in Umbria. Diario di un antifascista* (Milan, 2004; 1st edition, 1960).

Pisanò, G.: *Storia della guerra civile in Italia*, 3 vols. (Milan, 1965–1966).

Pisenti, P.: *Una repubblica necessaria* (Rome, 1975).

Plain, Gill: 'World War Two Writing', in Hammill Faye; Mismmin, Esme and Sponenberg Ashlie (eds.): *Encyclopedia of British Women's Writing, 1900–1950* (Basingstoke, 2006), 297.

Plenge, Johann: *Der Krieg und die Volkswirtschaft* (lectures on war at the University of Münster, winter semester 1911–12) (Münster, 1915).

Pogge von Strandmann, Hartmut: 'The Role of British and German Historians in Mobilizing Public Opinion in 1914', in Stuchtey, B. and Wende, P. (eds.): *British and German Historiography 1750–1950. Traditions, Perceptions, and Transfers* (Oxford, 2000), 335–371.

Poincaré, R.: *Messages, discours, allocutions,* vol. 2 (Paris, 1920).

Porché, François: *L'arrêt sur la Marne* (Paris, 1916).

Prazmowska, Anita: *Britain, Poland and the Eastern Front 1939* (Cambridge, 1987).

Premuti, Costanzo: *Come Roma preparò la guerra* (Rome, 1923).

Preti, Luigi: *Le lotte agrarie nella Val Padana* (Turin, 1955).

Procacci, Giovanna: 'La politica interna italiana, la Rivoluzione di febbraio e l'involuzione politica dell'interventismo di sinistra', in Procacci, Giovanna (ed.): *Dalla rassegnazione alla rivolta. Mentalità e comportamenti popolari nella Grande Guerra* (Rome, 1999).

Prochasson, Christophe and Rasmussen, Anne: *Au nom de la Patrie. Les intellectuels et la Première Guerre mondiale (1910–1919)* (Paris, 1996).

Prost, Antoine: 'Le climat social', in Rémond, René and Bourdin, Janine (eds.): *Edouard Daladier, chef de gouvernement, avril 1938–septembre 1939* (Paris, 1977), 100–103.

——, *Les anciens combattants et la société française,* 3 vols. (Paris, 1977).

——, 'Les limites de la brutalisation', *Vingtième Siècle* 81 (2004), 5–20.

Prost, Antoine and Winter, Jay M.: *Penser la Grande Guerre. Un essai historiographique* (Paris, 2004).

Pryce-Jones, David: 'Towards the Cocktail Party', in Sissons, Michael and French, Philip (eds.): *The Age of Austerity 1945–1951* (Harmonsdworth, 1963).

Pullé, Francesco Lorenzo and di Vegliasco, Celesia Giovanni: *Memorie del Fascio Parlamentare di Difesa Nazionale (Senato e Camera)* (Bologna, 1932).

Pupo, R. and Spazzali, R.: *Foibe* (Milan, 2003).

Le Queux, W.: *England's Peril: A Story of the Secret Service* (London, 1899).

——, *The Great War in England in 1897* (London, 1894).

Radkau, Joachim: *Das Zeitalter der Nervosität. Deutschland zwischen Bismarck und Hitler* (Munich, 1998).

Raitel, Thomas: *Das 'Wunder' der inneren Einheit. Studien zur französischen und deutschen Öffentlichkeit bei Beginn des Ersten Weltkrieges* (Bonn, 1996).

Ramsden, John: 'Refocusing "The People's War": British War Films of the 1950s', *Journal of Contemporary History* 1 (1998), 35–61.

Du Réau, Elisabeth: *Edouard Daladier, 1884–1970* (Paris, 1993).

Rédier, Antoine: *Méditations dans la tranchée* (Paris, 1916).

Reese, Peter: *Homecoming Heroes: An Account of the Re-Assimilation of British Military Personnel into Civilian Life* (London, 1992).

Reichel, Peter: *Vergangenheitsbewältigung in Deutschland. Die Auseinandersetzung mit der NS-Diktatur von 1945 bis heute* (Munich, 2001).

Reichling, Gerhard: *Die deutschen Vertriebenen in Zahlen,* vol. 1: *Umsiedler, Verschleppte, Vertriebene* (Bonn, 1986).

Reid, Christian (ed.): *Letters of Ted Hughes: Selected and Edited by Christian Reid* (2007).

Relinger, Jean: *Henri Barbusse écrivain combattant* (Paris, 1994).

Polese, Remaggi Luca: *La nazione perduta. Ferruccio Parri nel Novecento italiano* (Bologna, 2004).

Rémond, René and Bourdin, Janine (eds.): *Edouard Daladier, chef de gouvernement, avril 1938–septembre 1939* (Paris, 1977).

—— (eds.), *La France et les Français en 1938–1939* (Paris, 1978).

Renouvin, Pierre: *Les origines immédiates de la guerre, 26 juin–4 août 1914* (Paris, 1925).

Ridley, Jane: *Edwin Lutyens: his life, his wife, his work* (London, 2003).

Riesenberger, Dieter: 'Zur Geschichte des Pazifismus von 1800 bis 1933. […] 3. Die Friedensbewegung in der Zwischenkriegszeit', in Rajewsky, C. and Riesenberger, D. (eds.): *Wider den Krieg* (Munich, 1987), 220–226.

Rioux, Jean-Pierre: *La France de la IVème République*, vol. 1: *1944–1952* (Paris, 1980).

Robertson, Esmonde M. (ed.): *The Origins of the Second Word War* (London, 1971).

Rochat, Giorgio: *Gli arditi della grande guerra. Origini, battaglie, miti* (Milan, 1981).

——, *Le guerre italiane 1935–1943. Dall'impero d'Etiopia alla disfatta* (Turin, 2005).

Rodogno, D.: *Il nuovo ordine mediterraneo. Le politiche di occupazione dell'Italia fascista in Europa (1940–1943)* (Turin, 2003).

Rohe, Karl: *Das Reichsbanner Schwarz-Rot-Gold* (Düsseldorf, 1966).

Rohkrämer, Thomas: 'August 1914 – Kriegsmentalität und ihre Voraussetzungen', in Michalka, Wolfgang (ed.): *Der Erste Weltkrieg. Wirkung, Wahrnehmung, Analyse* (Munich, 1994), 759–777.

Rolland, Romain : 'Au-dessus de la mêlée' (15 September 1914), in Rolland, Romain (ed.): *Au-dessus de la mêlée* (Paris, 1915).

Röpke, Wilhelm: *Die deutsche Frage* (Erlenbach-Zürich, 1945).

Rose, Sonya O.: *Which People's War? National Identity and Citizenship in Wartime Britain 1939–1945* (Oxford, 2003).

Rosenberger, B.: *Zeitungen als Kriegstreiber? Die Rolle der Presse im Vorfeld des Ersten Weltkrieges* (Köln, 1998).

Rosenhaft, Eve: 'Links gleich rechts? Militante Straßengewalt um 1930', in Lindenberger, Thomas and Lüdtke, Alf (eds.): *Physische Gewalt. Studien zur Geschichte der Neuzeit* (Frankfurt, 1995), 238–275.

Rousso, Henry: 'L'épuration en France, une histoire inachevée', *Vingtième siècle* 33 (1992), 78–105.

——, *Le syndrome de Vichy de 1944 à nos jours* (Paris, 1987).

Roveri, Alessandro: *Le origini del fascismo a Ferrara, 1918–1921* (Milan, 1974).

Royle, Trevor: *The Best Years of Our Lives: The National Services Experience, 1945–63* (London, 1986).

Rückerl, Adalbert: *Die Strafverfolgung von NS-Verbrechen 1945–1978. Eine Dokumentation* (Heidelberg, 1979).

Rudder, Anneke de: '"Warum das ganze Theater?" Der Nürnberger Prozess in den Augen der Zeitgenossen', in Benz, Wolfgang (ed.): *Jahrbuch für Antisemitismusforschung* 6 (1997), 218–242.

Ruhl, Klaus-Jörg (ed.): *Deutschland 1945. Alltag zwischen Krieg und Frieden in Berichten, Dokumenten und Bildern* (Darmstadt, 1984).

Rusconi, G. E.: *Cefalonia. Quando gli italiani si battono* (Turin, 2004).

Sabbatucci, Giovanni: *I combattenti nel primo dopoguerra* (Bari, 1974).

Salaris, Claudia: *Alla festa della rivoluzione. Artisti e libertari con D'Annunzio a Fiume* (Bologna, 2002).

Salewski, Michael: *Der Erste Weltkrieg* (Paderborn, 2003).

——, *Zeitgeist und Zeitmaschine. Science Fiction und Geschichte* (Munich, 1986).

Salvatorelli, Luigi: *Nazionalfascismo* (Turin, 1977; 1st edition, 1923).

Santarelli, Enzo: *Pietro Nenni* (Turin, 1988).

Sauber, Marianna: 'Traces fragiles. Les plaques commémoratives dans les rues de Paris', *Annales ESC* (May/June 1993), 715–728.

Sauvy, Alfred: *Histoire économique de la France entre les deux guerres,* 3 vols. (Paris, 1965–1984).

Schauwecker, Franz: *Im Todesrachen. Die deutsche Seele im Weltkriege* (Halle [Saale], 1919).

Scheer, Friedrich Karl: *Die Deutsche Friedensgesellschaft (1892–1932): Organisation, Ideologie, politische Ziele* (Frankfurt, 1981).

Schildt, Axel: 'Der Umgang mit der NS-Vergangenheit in der Öffentlichkeit der Nachkriegszeit', in Loth, Winfried and Rusinek, Bernd-A. (eds.): *Verwandlungspolitik. NS-Eliten in der westdeutschen Nachkriegsgesellschaft* (Frankfurt, 1998), 19–54.

Schivelbusch, Wolfgang: *Die Kultur der Niederlage. Der amerikanische Süden 1865, Frankreich 1871, Deutschland 1918* (Berlin, 2001).

Schlemmer, T.: *Die Italiener an der Ostfront 1942/43* (Munich, 2005).

Schneede, Uwe M. (ed.): *Max Beckmann. Briefe,* vol. 1: *1899–1925* (Munich, 1993).

Schneider, Christof: *Nationalsozialismus als Thema im Programm des Nordwestdeutschen Rundfunks, 1945–1948* (Potsdam, 1999).

Scholl, L. U.: 'London unter den Hohenzollern. Saki und die Kriegsantizipation vor 1914', in Stamm-Kuhlmann, T.; Elvert, J., Aschmann, B. and Hohensee, J. (eds.): *Geschichtsbilder. Festschrift für M. Salewski zum 65. Geburtstag* (Wiesbaden, 2005), 225.

Schreiber, G.: *I militari italiani internati nei campi di concentramento del Terzo Reich* (Rome, 1992).

———, *La vendetta tedesca 1943–1945. Le rappresaglie naziste in Italia* (Milan, 2000; original edition, 1996).

Schubert, Dietrich: 'Otto Dix zeichnet im Ersten Weltkrieg', in Mommsen, Wolfgang J. (ed.): *Kultur und Krieg: Die Rolle der Intellektuellen, Künstler und Schriftsteller im Ersten Weltkrieg* (Munich, 1996), 179–193.

Schücking, Walther: *Der Staatenverband der Haager Konferenzen. Das Werk vom Haag,* vol. 1 (Munich, 1912).

Schulz, Matthias: *Normen und Praxis: Das Europäische Konzert der Großmächte als Sicherheitsrat* (Munich, 2008).

Schulze, Hagen: *Freikorps und Republik 1918–1920* (Boppard, 1969).

———, *Weimar – Deutschland 1917 – 1933,* 2nd edition (Berlin, 1983).

Schulze, Winfried: *Deutsche Geschichtswissenschaft nach 1945* (Munich, 1989).

Schuster, Kurt G. P.: *Der Rote Frontkämpferbund 1924–1929* (Düsseldorf, 1975).

Schvan, August: *Les bases d'une paix durable* (Paris, 1917).

Schwabe, Klaus (ed.): *Quellen zum Friedensschluß von Versailles* (Darmstadt, 1997).

Schwartz, Thomas Alan: 'Die Begnadigung deutscher Kriegsverbrecher. John Mc Cloy und die Häftlinge von Landsberg', *VfZ* 38 (1990), 375–414.

Schwarz, Guri: 'La morte e la patria. L'Italia e i difficili lutti della Seconda guerra mondiale', *Quaderni storici* 113 (2003), 551–88.

Schwendemann, Heinrich: 'Der deutsche Zusammenbruch im Osten 1944/45', in Rusinek, Bernd-A. (ed.): *Kriegsende 1945. Verbrechen, Katastrophen, Befreiungen in nationaler und internationaler Perspektive* (Göttingen, 2004), 125–150.

Scoppola, Pietro: *La repubblica dei partiti. Profilo storico della democrazia in Italia (1945–1990)* (Bologna, 1991).

Scott, L. V.: *Conscription and the Attlee Government: The Politics and Policy of National Service 1945–51* (Oxford, 1993).

Seeger, Alan: *Alan Seeger, le poète de la Légion étrangère* (Paris, 1918).

Setta, S.: *L'uomo qualunque 1944–1948* (Rome, 1975; new edition, Rome 2005).

Shamir, Haim: 'The *drôle de guerre* and French Public Opinion', *Journal of Contemporary History* 11 (1976), 129–143.

Shaw, Martin: 'Past Wars and Present Conflicts: From the Second World War to the Gulf', in Evans, Martin and Lunn, Ken (eds.): *War and Memory in the Twentieth Century* (Leamington Spa, 1997), 191–205.

Shirer, William L.: *Berliner Tagebuch. Das Ende. 1944–1945* (Leipzig, 1994).

Siemons, Hans: *Kriegsalltag in Aachen. Not, Tod und Überleben in der alten Kaiserstadt zwischen 1939 und 1945* (Aachen, 1998).

Sissons, Michael and French, Philip (eds.): *The Age of Austerity, 1945–1951* (Harmondsworth, 1964).

Snowden, Frank M.: *The Fascist Revolution in Tuscany, 1919–1922* (Cambridge, 1989).

Sontheimer, Kurt: *Antidemokratisches Denken in der Weimarer Republik. Die politischen Ideen des deutschen Nationalismus, 1918–1933* (Munich, 1962).

Spackman, Barbara: *Fascist Virilites: Rhetoric, Ideology, and Social Fantasy in Italy* (Minneapolis/London, 1996).

Spriano, Paolo: *L'occupazione delle fabbriche. Settembre 1920* (Turin, 1964).

Steinbacher, Sybille: '"...daß ich mit der Totenklage auch die Klage um unsere Stadt verbinde". Die Verbrechen von Dachau in der Wahrnehmung der frühen Nachkriegszeit', in Frei, Norbert and Steinbacher, Sybille (eds.): *Beschweigen und Bekennen. Die deutsche Nachkriegsgesellschaft und der Holocaust* (Göttingen, 2001), 11–33.

Steinberg, Jonathan: *All or Nothing. The Axis and the Holocaust 1941–1943* (London, 1990).

Steiner, Zara: *The Lights that Failed. European International History, 1919–1933* (Oxford, 2005).

Steinert, Marlis G.: *Hitlers Krieg und die Deutschen. Stimmung und Haltung der deutschen Bevölkerung im Zweiten Weltkrieg* (Düsseldorf, 1970).

Rigoni, Stern Mario: *Il sergente nella neve* (Turin, 1953).

Sternhell, Zeev; Sznajder, Mario and Asheri, Maia: *Naissance de l'idéologie fasciste* (Paris, 1989).

Stöcker, Michael: *Augusterlebnis 1914 in Darmstadt* (Darmstadt, 1994).

Strachan, Hew: *The First World War,* vol 1: *To Arms!* (Oxford 2001).

Swartz, M.: *The Union of Democratic Control in British Politics during the First World War* (Oxford, 1971).

Sywottek, Jutta: *Mobilmachung für den totalen Krieg. Die propagandistische Vorbereitung der deutschen Bevölkerung auf den Zweiten Weltkrieg* (Opladen, 1976).

Tartakowsky, Danielle: 'Manifester pour le pain, novembre 1940–octobre 1947', in Veillon, Dominique and Flonneau, Jean-Marie (eds.): *Le temps des restrictions en France 1939–1949* (Paris, 1996), 465–478.

Tasca, Angelo: *Nascita e avvento del fascismo* (Bari, 1976; 1st edition, 1938).

Tate, Merze: *The Disarmament Illusion: The Movement for a Limitation of Armaments to 1907* (New York, 1942).

Taylor, A. J. P.: *English History 1914–1945* (Oxford, 1965).

———, *The First World War: an Illustrated History* (London, 1963).

———, *The Origins of the Second Word War* (London, 1961).

Taylor, Telford: *Die Nürnberger Prozesse. Hintergründe, Analysen und Erkenntnisse aus heutiger Sicht* (Munich, 1994).

Thoß, Bruno and Volkmann, Hans-Erich (eds.): *Erster Weltkrieg – Zweiter Weltkrieg: Ein Vergleich. Krieg, Kriegeserlebnis, Kriegserfahrung in Deutschland* (Paderborn, 2002).

Tiratsoo, Nick (ed.): *The Attlee Years* (London, 1991).

Tison, Hubert: 'La mémoire de la guerre 14–18 dans les manuels scolaires français d'histoire (1920–1990)', in *Guerres et cultures 1914–1918* (Paris, 1994), 295–299.

Tison, Stéphane: 'Traumatisme de guerre et commémorations (1870–1940)', *Guerres mondiales et conflits contemporains* 216 (2004), 5–30.

Toller, Ernst: *Eine Jugend in Deutschland. Gesammelte Werke*, vol. 4, (Munich, 1978).

Torsiello, Italo E.: *Il tramonto delle baronie rosse* (Ferrara, 1921).

Treue, Wilhelm: 'Die Hitler Rede vor der deutschen Presse vom 10. November 1938', *VfZ* 6, 1 (1958).

Turati, Filippo: *Socialismo e riformismo nella storia d'Italia. Scritti politici 1878–1932* (Milan, 1979).

Turner, Barry and Renell, Tony: *When Daddy Came Home: How Family Life Changed Forever in 1945* (London, 1995).

Uhlig, Ralph: *Die Interparlamentarische Union 1889–1914* (Wiesbaden, 1988).

Ulrich, Bernd: 'Die Desillusionierung der Kriegsfreiwilligen von 1914', in Wette, Wolfram (ed.), *Der Krieg des kleinen Mannes. Eine Militärgeschichte von unten* (Munich, 1992), 110–126.

Ullrich, Volker: *Kriegsalltag. Hamburg im Ersten Weltkrieg* (Cologne, 1982).

Ungern-Sternberg, Jürgen von: 'Wissenschaftler', in Hirschfeld, Gerhard; Krumeich, Gerd and Renz, Irina (eds.): *Enzyklopädie Erster Weltkrieg*, 2nd edition (Paderborn, 2004), 169–176.

von Ungern-Sternberg, Jürgen and von Ungern-Sternberg, Wolfgang: *Der Aufruf ,An die Kulturwelt'. Das Manifest der 93 und die Anfänge der Kriegspropaganda im Ersten Weltkrieg* (Stuttgart, 1996).

USE (Ufficio Storico dell'Esercito – Army History Department): *Le operazioni delle unità italiane al fronte russo 1941–1943* (Rome, 1977).

Vaïsse, Maurice: 'Le rêve de la grandeur', in *L'Histoire* 28 (2005), 86–90.

Valdevit, G.: *Foibe. Il peso del passato, Venezia Giulia 1943–1945* (Venice, 1997).

Valente, Concetto: *La ribellione antibolscevica di Bologna* (Bologna, 1921).

Valli, Roberta Suzzi: *Le origini del fascismo* (Rome, 2003).

———, 'The Myth of *squadrismo* in the Fascist Regime', *Journal of Contemporary History* (April 2000), 131–150.

Vanzetto, Livio (ed.): *L'anomalia laica. Biografia e autobiografia di Mario e Guido Bergamo* (Verona, 1994).

Vecchi, Ferruccio: *Arditismo civile* (Milan, 1920).

De Vecchi di Val Cismon, Cesare Maria: *Il quadrumviro scomodo* (Milan, 1983).

Veillon, Dominique: *Vivre et Survivre en France de 1939 à 1947* (Paris, 1995).

Verdès-Leroux, Jeannine: *Refus et violences. Politique et littérature à l'extrême droite des années trente aux retombées de la Libération* (Paris, 1996).

Verhey, Jeffrey: 'Augusterlebnis', in Hirschfeld, Gerhard; Krumeich, Gerd and Renz, Irina (eds.), *Enzyklopädie Erster Weltkrieg*, 2nd edition (Paderborn, 2004), 357f.

———, *The Spirit of 1914. Militarism, Myth and Mobilization in Germany* (Cambridge, 2000).

Ventrone, Angelo: *Il nemico interno. Immagini, parole e simboli della lotta politica nell'Italia del '900* (Rome, 2005).

———, *La cittadinanza repubblicana. Forma-partito e identità nazionale alle origini della democrazia in Italia (1943–1948)* (Bologna, 1996).

———, *La seduzione totalitaria. Guerra, modernità, violenza politica (1914–1918)* (Rome, 2003).

Vincent, Charles Paul: *The Politics of Hunger* (Athens/Ohio, 1985).

Virgili, Fabrice: *La France virile: des femmes tondues à la Libération* (Paris, 2000).

Vivarelli, Roberto: *La fine di una stagione. Memoria 1943–1945* (Bologna, 2000).

———, *Storia delle origini del fascismo. L'Italia dalla grande guerra alla marcia su Roma* (Bologna, 1991).

Vogel, Jakob: *Nationen im Gleichschritt. Der Kult der 'Nation in Waffen' in Deutschland und Frankreich (1871–1914)* (Göttingen, 1997).

Voldmann, Danièle: *Le déminage de la France après 1945* (Paris, 1998).

———, *La Reconstruction des villes françaises de 1940 à 1954* (L'Harmattan, 1997).

Volkmann, Hans-Erich: 'Deutsche Historiker im Umgang mit Drittem Reich und Zweiten Weltkrieg 1939–1949', in Volkmann, Hans-Erich (ed.): *Ende des Dritten Reiches - Ende des Zweiten Weltkrieges. Eine perspektivische Rückschau* (Munich, 1995), 861–911.

Vollnhals, Clemens: 'Die Evangelische Landeskirche in der Nachkriegspolitik. Die Bewältigung der nationalsozialistischen Vergangenheit', in Benz, W.: *Neuanfang in Bayern* (Munich, 1988), 143–162.

———, 'Die Hypothek des Nationalprotestantismus. Entnazifizierung und Strafverfolgung von NS-Verbrechen nach 1945', *GG* 18 (1992), 51–69.

———, *Entnazifizierung. Politische Säuberung und Rehabilitierung in den vier Besatzungszonen 1945–1949* (Munich, 1991).

———, 'Im Schatten der Stuttgarter Schulderklärung. Die Erblast des Nationalprotestantismus', in Gailus, Manfred (ed.): *Nationalprotestantische Mentalitäten: Konturen, Entwicklungslinien und Umbrüche eines Weltbildes* (Göttingen, 2005), 379–431.

———, 'Zwischen Verdrängung und Aufklärung. Die Auseinandersetzung mit dem Holocaust in der frühen Bundesrepublik', in Büttner, Ursula (ed.): *Die Deutschen und die Judenverfolgung im Dritten Reich* (Frankfurt, 2003), 381–422.

Volpe, Gioacchino: *Il popolo italiano nella Grande guerra (1915–1916)* (Rome, 1998).

Vondung, Klaus: 'Geschichte als Weltgericht. Genesis und Degradation einer Symbolik', in Vondung, Klaus (ed.): *Kriegserlebnis. Der Erste Weltkrieg in der literarischen Gestaltung und symbolischen Deutung der Nationen* (Göttingen, 1980).

Wallace, S.: *War and the Image of Germany: British Academics 1914–1918* (Edinburgh, 1988).

Walter, Dirk: *Antisemitische Kriminalität und Gewalt. Judenfeindschaft in der Weimarer Republik* (Bonn, 1999).

Watt, Donald Cameron: *How War Came. The Immediate Origins of the Second World War, 1938–1939* (London, 1989).

Weber, Francis J.: 'The Pious Fund of the Californias', *Hispanic American Historical Review* 43 (1963), 78–94.

Weber, Thomas: *Our friend, the Enemy. Elite Education in Britain and Germany before World War I* (Stanford, 2007).

Wegerer, Alfred von: *Wie es zum Großen Kriege kam* (Leipzig, 1930).

Wehler, Hans-Ulrich: *Deutsche Gesellschaftsgeschichte*, vol. 4: *Vom Beginn des Ersten Weltkrieges bis zur Gründung der beiden deutschen Staaten* (Munich, 2002).

Weight, Richard: *Patriots: National Identity in Britain, 1940–2000* (London, 2002).

Weisbrod, Bernd: 'Gewalt in der Politik. Zur politischen Kultur in Deutschland zwischen den beiden Weltkriegen', *Geschichte in Wissenschaft und Unterricht* 43 (1992), 391–404.

Weissenbach, Birgit: *Kirche und Konzentrationslager. Katholische Aufklärungspublizistik in der Zeit von 1945 bis 1950* (Frankfurt, 2005).

Werth, Léon: *Clavel soldat* (Paris, 1919; reprinted 1993).

Wette, Wolfram: 'Ideologien, Propaganda und Innenpolitik als Voraussetzungen der Kriegspolitik des Dritten Reiches', in *Das Deutsche Reich und der Zweite Weltkrieg*, ed. by Militärgeschichtliches Forschungsamt, vol. 1 (Stuttgart, 1959), 115–176.

Wicks, Ben: *Welcome Home: True Stories of Soldiers Returning from World War II* (London, 1991).

Wieland, Günter: 'Die Ahndung von NS-Verbrechen in Ostdeutschland 1945–1990', in *DDR-Justiz und NS-Verbrechen. Sammlung ostdeutscher Strafurteile wegen nationalsozialistischer Tötungsverbrechen. Verfahrensregister und Dokumentenband*, prepared in the Seminarium voor Strafrecht en Strafrechtspleging 'Van Hamel' at the University of Amsterdam by C. F. Rüter (Amsterdam, 2002), 11–99.

Wilson, K., 'Britain', in Wilson, K. (ed.): *Decisions for War 1914* (London, 1995), 179.

Wilson, Trevor: *The Myriad Faces of War. Britain and the Great War, 1914–1918* (Cambridge, 1986).

Winkler, Heinrich August: *Der lange Weg nach Westen* (Bonn, 2002).

——, *Weimar 1918–1933: Die Geschichte der ersten deutschen Demokratie* (Munich, 1998).

Winter, Jay: *Sites of Memory, Sites of Mourning. The Great War in European Cultural History* (Cambridge, 2000).

Winter, Jay M.: *The Great War and the British People* (London, 1985).

Wöss, Fritz: *Hunde, wollt ihr ewig leben* (Hamburg, 1958).

Woller, Hans: *Gesellschaft und Politik unter der amerikanischen Besatzungszone. Die Region Ansbach und Fürth* (Munich, 1986).

——, *I conti con il fascismo. L'epurazione in Italia (1943–1948)* (Bologna, 2002).

Wooton, Graham: *The Official History of the British Legion* (London, 1956).

Worpole, Ken: *Dockers and Detectives* (London, 1980).

Zeidler, Manfred: *Kriegsende im Osten. Die Rote Armee und die Besetzung Deutschlands östlich von Oder und Neiße* (Munich, 1996).

Zibordi, Giovanni: *Critica socialista del fascismo* (Bologna, 1922).

Ziemann, Benjamin: *Front und Heimat. Ländliche Kriegserfahrungen im südlichen Bayern 1914–1923* (Essen, 1997).

——, 'Republikanische Kriegserinnerung in einer polarisierten Öffentlichkeit', *Historische Zeitschrift* 267 (1998), 357–398.

Notes on Contributors

CLAUDE ALLAIN† The late Claude Allain was professor of modern history at the Université de Paris III and one of the leading historians of diplomatic history and international relations. He was director of the research centre *Défense et diplomatie dans le monde contemporain* and editor of two journals on international history. His doctoral thesis on Joseph Calliaux and the Second Maroccow crisis was published in three volumes in 1975. His work has had a great impact on our understanding of twentieth-century history. He died shortly after the submission of this manuscript.

NICOLAS BEAUPRÉ is lecturer at the University Blaise Pascal de Clermont-Ferrand and fellow at the research centre of *La historial de Grand Guerre*, Peronne. His research interests are Franco-German relations, French and German history during the Great War and the inter-war period. His publications include *Le Rhin une géohistoire* (2005) and *Ecrire en guerre: France-Allemagne 1914-1920* (2006). He was awarded the Joseph Saillet and Maurice Baumont price for the latter study of war poetry. He is also co-editor (with Anne Duménil and Christian Ingrao) of *1914–15: L'ère de la guerre* (2004); and (with Caroline Moine) of *L'Europe de Versailles à Maastricht* (2007).

GUSTAVO CORNI is professor of modern history at the University of Trient. His main field of research is twentieth-century European history. He has widely published on Italian and German fascism and its effects on European society. His latest publications include a biography of Hitler (2007) and a study of occupation in Europe during the Second Word War (2005). He is co-editor of *People on the move. Forced population movements in Europe in the Second World War and its aftermath* (2008).

JOST DÜLFFER is emeritus professor of modern history at the University of Cologne and a leading expert in peace and de-escalation studies. Since his seminal study on The Hague Peace conferences (1991) he published and edited eighteen books on twentieth-century history. His latest titles include *Western*

Integration, German Unification and the Cold War (2007) and *Peace, War and Gender from Antiquity to the Present. Cross-Cultural Perspectives* (2008).

TOBY HAGGITH is a historian at the Imperial War Museum, London. He has a PhD in social history from the University of Warwick and has written articles on various aspects of film and history. In the spring of 2007 he was a visiting fellow at the Humanities Research Centre of the Australian National University where he was conducting research into historical re-enactment and military culture in the United Kingdom. He is the joint editor with Joanna Newman of *Holocaust and the Moving Image: Representations in Film and Television Since 1933* (2005).

FRACRICE GRENARD graduated from the *Institut d'Etudes Politiques de Paris* with a doctoral thesis published as *La France du marché noir, 1940–1949* (2008) and is currently working at 'Sciene Po'. He has also published two articles on the economic history of the war and post-war periods entitled 'Traitors, trafiquants, and the confiscation of "illicit profits" in France, 1944–1950', (2008) and 'L'administration du contrôle économique en France, 1940–1950' (2010).

GERHARD HIRSCHFELD is professor of modern history and director of the *Bibliothek für Zeitgeschichte*, Stuttgart, one of the leading European institutions for the study of war and society. During his international career he has worked in Great Britain, Germany and the Netherlands. He has published numerous books and articles and co-edited a groundbreaking encyclopedia of the First World War (2003). He is also editor of two series. Several of his publications have been translated into other languages including his latest title *Scorched Earth. The Germans on the Somme, 1914–1918* (2009).

LOTHAR KETTENACKER was deputy director of the German Historical Institute London (1975–2004) and held a professorship at the Goethe University Frankfurt. He did his PhD on Nazi occupation policy in Alsace and a BLitt thesis in Oxford on Whiggism and historicism. He has published on the history of the Third Reich, on Anglo-German relations and the history of the Federal Republic. His most recent books are *Germany Since 1945* (1997) and *Germany 1989: In the Aftermath of the Cold War* (2009).

GERD KRUMEICH is professor of modern history at the Heinrich Heine University, Düsseldorf, and one of the leading experts on the Great War. His main field of interest is modern French and German history. His PhD thesis on Jeanne d'Arc is one of the few German scholarly publications that have been translated from German into French. His publications incude studies on the

Great War, the inter-war years and the Nazi period. His latest book (co-edited with Jean-Jacques Becker) is entitled *Der Große Krieg. Deutschland und Frankreich im Ersten Weltkrieg 1914–1918.*

BARBARA LAMBAUER is an Austrian historian who lives and works in Paris where she is associated with the research institution IRICE. She is an expert on French and European history during the Second World War. Her doctoral thesis on the German diplomat Otto Abetz – published as *Abetz et les Français ou l'envers de la collaboration* (2001) – won an *Académie française* award. She is co-editor of *Die Heimkehrertafel als Stolperstein: Vom Umgang mit der NS-Vergangenheit* (2007) and also worked on the French translation of the diaries of Joseph Goebbels.

HANS MOMMSEN is emeritus professor at the Ruhr University Bochum. He graduated at Tübingen with a thesis on the Social Democracy in the Habsburg Empire before he started his work on German civil servants during the Third Reich. Mommsen's special research interest is twentieth-century German history with a particular focus on the Weimar Republic and the Nazi period. His publications on German society have been highly influential and include (among the latest) *Alternative zu Hitler. Studien zur Geschichte des deutschen Widerstandes* (2000) and *The Third Reich between Vision and Reality. New Perspectives on German History 1918–1945* (2002).

HARTMUT POGGE VON STRANDMANN is emeritus professor of modern history at the University of Oxford and fellow of University College. He works on German history within a wider European context in the nineteenth and twentieth centuries. He has published widely on German imperialism and colonialism, German domestic politics and German revolutions, German-Russian relations in the inter-war period, the role of industrial interests in modern German society and the causes of the First World War. His latest publication is entitled *Imperialismus vom Grünen Tisch: deutsche Kolonialpolitik zwischen wirtschaftlicher Ausbeutung und 'zivilisatorischen' Bemühungen*

TORSTEN RIOTTE is a lecturer in history at the University of Frankfurt am Main. Educated at Cologne and Cambridge Universities he worked at the German Historical Institute London where he edited the multi-volume edition *British envoys to Germany, 1815–1866.* He is the author of a number of articles on British and European history and co-editor of *The Hanoverian Dimension in British history, 1714–1837* (2007) and *The Diplomats' World. A Cultural History of Diplomacy* (2008).

ANGELO VENTRONE is associate professor of contemporary history at the University of Macerata where he lectures on modern European history. His field of research is European history with a special interest in twentieth-century Italian history. He is author of several books on Italian society and the Second World War including *La seduzione totalitaria. Guerra, modernità, violenza politica* (2003) and his latest title *La cittadinanza repubblicana. Come cattolici e comunisti hanno costruito la democrazia italiana* (2008)

CLEMENS VOLLNHALS is deputy-director of the Hannah-Arend Institute at Dresden and a leading expert on de-Nazification in Germany after 1945. His PhD thesis on the Protestant Church after 1945 was published in 1988. Since then he has published widely on the post-war period including studies on censorship in the GDR and political jurisdiction. He also worked as a scholar for the select committee on the Stasi-archives (*Abteilung Bildung und Forschung beim Bundesbeauftragen für die Unterlagen des Staatssicherheitdienstes der ehemaligen DDR*).

JAY M. WINTER is professor of history at Yale University, where he focuses his research on World War I and its impact on the twentieth century. He obtained his PhD at Cambridge. His special research interests include remembrance of war in the twentieth century, such as memorial and mourning sites, European population decline, the causes and institutions of war, British popular culture in the era of the First World War and the Armenian genocide of 1915. He is completing a biography of René Cassin. He has also co-authored and co-edited books on the First World War, including a survey of the war's historiography, *The Great War in History: Debates and Controversies, 1914 to the Present* (with Antoine Prost, 2006) and *The Great War and the Twentieth Century* (with Geoffrey Parker and Mary Habeck, 2000).

Index